CGI
Developer's Resource

CGI

Developer's Resource

WEB PROGRAMMING IN TCL AND PERL

Prentice Hall PTR
Upper Saddle River, NJ 07458
http://www.prenhall.com

J.M. Ivler
with Kamran Husain

Library of Congress Cataloging-in-Publication Data

Editorial/Production Supervision: Joe Czerwinski
Development Editor: Jim Markham
Acquisitions Editor: Mary Franz
Editorial Assistant: Noreen Regina
Manufacturing Manager: Alexis Heydt
Cover Design: Design Source
Cover Design Direction: Jerry Votta
Art Director: Gail Cocker-Bogusz
Series Design: Meg VanArsdale

 © 1997 Prentice Hall PTR
Prentice-Hall, Inc.
A Simon & Schuster Company
Upper Saddle River, NJ 07458

The publisher offers discounts on this book when ordered in bulk quantities.
For more information, contact

Corporate Sales Department,
Prentice Hall PTR
One Lake Street
Upper Saddle River, NJ 07458
Phone: 800-382-3419; FAX: 201-236-714
E-mail (Internet): corpsales@prenhall.com

Printed in the United States of America

10 9 8 7 6 5 4 3 2 1

ISBN 0-13-727751-2

Prentice-Hall International (UK) Limited, *London*
Prentice-Hall of Australia Pty. Limited, *Sydney*
Prentice-Hall Canada Inc., *Toronto*
Prentice-Hall Hispanoamericana, S.A., *Mexico*
Prentice-Hall of India Private Limited, *New Delhi*
Prentice-Hall of Japan, Inc., *Tokyo*
Simon & Schuster Asia Pte. Ltd., *Singapore*
Editora Prentice-Hall do Brasil, Ltda., *Rio de Janeiro*

In memory of a hero—William M. Ivler.

J.M. Ivler

Trademarks

Macintosh is a registered trademark and Mac and MacOS are trademarks of Apple Computer, Inc.

Digital, AXP, DEC, VAX, and VMS are registered trademarks of Digital Equipment Corporation.

IBM and AIX are registered trademarks of International Business Machines Corporation.

Hewlett-Packard, HP, and HP-UX are registered trademarks of Hewlett-Packard, Inc.

Informix is a registered trademark of Informix Corporation

Microsoft and MS-DOS are registered trademarks and Windows 95, Windows NT and ActiveX are trademarks of Microsoft Corporation

Netscape Navigator is a registered trademark of Netscape Communications Corporation

Motif is a registered trademark of Open Software Foundation

Oracle is a registered trademark of Oracle

SunOS is a registered trademark and Solaris is a trademark of Sun Microsystems

Unix is a registered trademark of Unix Systems Laboratories

CONTENTS

.

Intended Audience

Are you a programmer? Do you understand scripting and shell languages? Do you know Unix? If you can answer yes to these three questions, then the book shouldn't be hard for you.

This text is a bit Unix-centric, but since Tcl and Perl both run on non-Unix platforms most of the code herein is portable. And the book *does* contain code. This book was intended to be used by programmers who have an understanding of systems analysis and design. It would also be good if they have some Tcl or Perl experience.

While Tcl and/or Perl experience isn't required, a programming language is, and if you don't know Tcl or Perl, it is recommended that you look at obtaining one of the texts listed in Appendix B on either or both of the languages.

So, if you want to learn about CGI programming, and you want to learn *why* things are done and not just *how* things are done, then this book will most likely interest you. If you are looking to learn Tcl or Perl from this text, you came to the wrong place.

Reason for Being Here

This book was written after I had a chance to see what was available on the market for people that wanted to really understand how to make the World Wide Web work for them in real-world terms.

I had just completed my first article (what has grown into the code in Chapter 5) on a forms to E-mail CGI for Mecklermedia's *Web Developer Magazine* (initial issue) and I had handed in my second (on firewall selection) when I was asked if I would be interested in writing a book on CGI development. The problem was, I didn't want to write a book that would become another one of those cute things that people buy, but never use. I wanted to do something different.

I was lucky to have been found by the folks at Prentice Hall PTR, who were willing to give a totally untested author a chance to do more than turn out *yet-another-CGI-book*. They allowed me to explain what I wanted and to then follow that vision.

The core reason for this entire book was not to create one you read and tossed away. I wanted it to be more that that. I wanted it to be a teaching tool, a tool that provided a way for you, the reader, to get more out of it than to just solve a problem one way in one language.

A great deal of that has to do with my frustration on how most books are written. Too many times people seem to forget to put the *why* they did something next to the *how* they did it. This leads to the knowledge that a single problem an be solved with a single method. For instance, Chapter 12 takes things taught up to that point and shows you how to use those techniques for another purpose.

In today's parlance you could say this is about code reuse. But it really isn't. A person once told me that there were only seven basic stories in the world, and that all other stories derived from these seven basic as the roots. I wanted to try to show that there are millions of different problems that can be solved with CGIs in the environment of the Web, but that all of these problems have common roots and once you understand that, they can all be solved.

I also wanted to avoid the flame wars that happen when you get language-centric. In Chapter 4 the book goes into greater detail on this, but to get it into it's most simple reason, it's because CGI coding isn't about languages, it's about solving problems.

Let's take Chapter 5 as an example. Why did I create a Tcl-based program to do a forms to E-mail CGI? It all started when I wanted to do more than just dump out the information in a form to E-mail, I wanted to manipulate it. So I took a look at the C program that had been written by Thomas Boutelle and decided that to make some changes. Being a terrible C programmer (my background being VAX Fortran and Macro) I decided to look at other alternatives. At this same time I had just been exposed to Tcl, so I took 20 minutes to generate email.tcl V0.5.

Now, there weren't that many differences between the C program and the Tcl one, but it was working. And it had the added functionality that I had wanted. Then one day someone asked for a program to generate E-mail from a form on the Net, and I gave them mine. They pointed out that I had some serious errors in mine (all having to do with unescaping the passed-in data) and suggested that I look at using uncgi.c (then at version 1.11). I did and rewrote the code. That created version 1.0–the first production version.

The version in this book should be called 3.0 as it has continued to grow over time. Not only did it grow from my needs and those of my employers, but from those who used it from the Net and those that created other forms to E-mail programs that had functionality that I thought would make this program even more useful. Now, why duplicate it in Perl? Why not use Matt Wright's very popular version? Because we wanted to show that the language isn't the issue, the application is. That is what this book is all about–the application.

Who is I?

In 95 percent of all cases, an *I* in this book is J.M. Ivler. The other 5 percent is Kamran Husain. It should be noted that this book wouldn't be as good as it is had I (jmi) not had Kamran here to help. You see I have this problem, my Tcl looks like Fortran, and my Perl looks like bad Tcl. As a Tcl programmer by preference, I knew that I wouldn't be able to do justice to the Perl code if I were to attempt to write both. I really needed someone who could write Perl, and use the features of Perl, not someone who wrote Perl that didn't make use of some of it's key strengths.

I was fortunate enough to find a co-author who was willing to take the requirements for each program in each chapter and generate matching Perl software. The book is designed to allow you to unplug a Tcl routine and plug the Perl one in it's place, and have it work. Kamran was the person who made that happen. So while *I* may be *I* in 95 percent of the book, the book wouldn't have been possible without the *us* that Kamran made it.

Organization

I'm going to start by sharing how I originally envisioned the chapters and then provide a chapter by chapter breakout so you can see what really happened.

Chapter 1: What is CGI Code?

Chapter 2: C, Tcl, Perl, Shell - Language Overview

Chapter 3: UNCGI - Why it is used.

Chapter 4: Basic Form Processing

Chapter 5: Form to E-mail

Chapter 6: Query the files - Building a search processor

Chapter 7: Building a CGI based page counter

Chapter 8: Query a database - Report forms

Chapter 9: Guest books and Comments

Chapter 10: Closing Comments

Well, here is what we actually ended up delivering:

Chapter	Description
1	Introductory information on the technology behind the Internet
2	A more in-depth look at the technology and the methods of the Internet, a sharper focus on Web-based issues like URLs and URIs and the statelessness of transactions
3	A look at CGIs and the HTTP protocols including a look at server side includes and state with cookies.

As you can see, this is much different from what I was going to write originally. Yet, in some strange way, still very much the same.

We (in the following instances is Kamran and me) also had to make some choices. One key choice was how data was to be handled. This was one of those lowest common denominator issues. I really wanted to do a chapter showing how to manipulate a database, but what database was I to use? Oracle? Informix? Sybase?

In order to make sure that this could be used by anyone, we decided to forgo all the above. We went with flat data files instead of a database. We figured that if you could do a join in a flat data file, you should have no problem doing it in an SQL statement on a database.

The tenet of lowest common denominator became a basic principle of this text. The only area where that became a problem was when we got to platforms. In that case we chose to make sure that the code worked on a Unix platform first, and then tried to ensure that it ported to non-Unix platforms. In most cases the software port did work. When it didn't we usually stated so in the chapter by the area that isn't portable.

The CD-ROM

Yes, we have included a compact disk with this book. However, we didn't include all those things that you normally find on a CD. We stuck with the things talked about in the book, the software we created, and some Perl and Tcl distributions.

The CD has been mounted and read on an Apple, PCs under MS Windows 95 and Windows NT 4.0 as well as Linux and BSD. In addition, we mounted and read the CD on an HP's HP-UX, Sun's SunOS and Solaris, IBM's AIX and Digital's AXP. Our guess is that it should be mountable and readable on your system.

Tcl runs under most Unix operating systems, as does Perl. In addition, Tcl distributions are available for PCs and Macs. If you need a C compiler to compile either of the source distributions, we recommend that GNU versions of the ANSII C compiler as acceptable.

As an overview, the CD contains 26 Perl programs, 27 Tcl programs, 3 image libraries (of digits 0-9), some smattering of HTML and some data files (that were used in the chapters). You'll also find a C program for unencoding passed in data, and a number of Tcl and Perl distributions.

In some cases there may be a need to modify a few of the book's programs to run on different platforms. In general we have attempted to keep the code as portable and platform-independent as possible. There are a small number of routines that do have Unix dependencies, but these are pointed out in the comments in the code, and suggestions for work-arounds are provided in the code comments.

A full list of the contents of the disk, as well as some additional information about the CD can be found in Appendix C. In addition, an exclusive Web site for this book (www.prenhall.com/developers_resource_series) will be kept up to date with the latest information on porting issues in the code and pointing to the latest core distributions.

Conventions Used in this Book

To avoid confusion, we have tried to distinguish the different items that appear throughout the book. For example, all in-text names of specific variables, forms, options, commands, file names, etc. appear in helvetica font. *Italics* are used to emphasize key words and terms.

It's also crucial to articulate people's roles precisely in this book. For example, in the heavily coded chapters 5-14, we the authors sometimes take on the role of an application developer or a system designer, while you the reader are sometimes an application engineer who has to deal with various groups within his organization. Hopefully, we haven't muddied the waters.

We also had to make a hard choice on how the book would be read. Fortunately, code written in Tcl and Perl does not require lines to be less than 80 characters long. Unfortunately, the book's production specs do. This created a debate between the authors, who wanted to keep lines intact and make the book landscape, and the editors, who wanted the lines broken up and the book to be portrait. As you can see, the editors won.

In the code we took care of long lines by using standard language continuation marks. In the data files and other locations where the line extended over the character limit for the page, we have indicated that the line is continued by placing a

$\Rightarrow$ at the beginning of the continued line.

Enjoy!

Acknowledgments

I tend to think in lists, and even then I know that I'll leave someone out, I hope I don't.

To those that made this possible, my co-author, Kamran Husain, Acquisitions Editor Mary Franz, Development Editor Jim Markham (even if he is a Pat's fan), and Technical Reviewer Cameron Laird (one of those people who makes me better than I am). I also want to thank David Fiedler of Mecklermedia for agreeing to publish me, way back when.

To Thomas Boutelle, Tom Christiansen, Matt Kruse, Matt Wright and all the rest of the people who make comp.infosystems.www. authoring.cgi the newsgroup that it is. To John Ousterhout for Tcl, and Larry Wall for Perl. To the crew at Sunsoft for keeping Tcl free, and to the folks who populate comp.lang.tcl for making this community ever that much better through their efforts to share *everything*.

To Information Management Associates, Inc. and Daniel Riscalla, Vice President of Research and Development, for their time and patience and for being the alpha test site. To all my co-workers for their constant support and harassment, YES! It is finally completed and no, I couldn't have done it without you. You constantly raised the bar, thanks.

To Mr. Sloan who told me "Just because you're learning disabled doesn't mean you have to prove you're stupid!" And to my brother Robert who said "Find something you like doing and then find someone foolish enough to pay you to do it." I'm not stupid, and I'm getting paid!

To Hattie Little, Lynn Foggle, Myrtle Mallenger, Hannes Callisen, Dan Van Ostrand, Brian McEvoy and Barbara and Hillel Disraelly, you always knew. To Steve, Sunny and Nicholas, thanks for the time (We have no plans for the weekend, come on over).

Lastly, to my three graces. My mother Barbara; was it worth the nine months yet? My wife Thuy, "Honey, I'm home! Now get the heck out of my kitchen." And to my darling angel. one-and-a-half-year-old Brooke, "Now, daddy can play." A more supportive threesome I could never had asked for. Thank you all.

CGI

Developer's Resource

PART ONE

A Solid Foundation

I have made this letter long, only because I lacked the time to make it short.

—Blaise Pascal 1657

In my initial outline I had assumed that in about 30 pages I would be able to cover all the introductory material necessary to get everyone on the same page. After writing those pages it was clear that I would be short changing the readers and possibly not ensuring we were even in the same book.

It is important that there be a common ground early on in order to understand the material that will be presented in Parts 2 and 3 of this book. That common ground has to be placed somewhere, and the beginning is usually a good place to start. Like peeling an onion, Part 1 starts at the outer layer of the model that CGI is part of, and peels it away, getting deeper into the model and the methods, as we move into each chapter. This way there is a common foundation from which we can start to build CGIs in Part 2.

CHAPTER 1

INTERNET OVERVIEW AND HOW IT AFFECTS THE CGI MODEL OF OPERATION

- Basic Client-Server Technologies

- Distributed Computing: DNS and TCP Protocols

- Security Concerns

When you start talking about the Common Gateway Interface (CGI) to the Web, you start talking about things like Client-Server technology. This technology isn't new. It's been around for many years. What is new is how we use the technology.

This chapter will focus on some entry-level concepts that deal with Web technologies, which are really the extension of the Client-Server model to an internetworked distributed computing model.

To discuss CGI development, we have to cover some initial ground on the basic technologies that make up the Internet.

Client-Server Technologies

Both Internets and Intranets have a common model or framework within which they operate. This model is referred to as Client-Server based computing. As the term implies, the activities of the computing process are broken down into two discrete parts: client and server. In the World Wide Web (WWW), client is also referred to as the browser. The browser acts as a client to the server (known as an HTTPd or an HTTP daemon because it runs as a daemon process on the server machine).

In this mode, the basic model looks like that shown in Figure 1.1.

Thick and Thin Clients

Within the Client-Server model there is a concept of thickness. That deals with where the core functionality lies within the model. The model in which a server does little, but a client does a great deal is called thick client-thin server. Conversely, when the server does the most work the model is called thin client-thick server. In general, the browser/server model used on the WWW is thin client-thick server.

Over time, as more functionality has been added to the various commercial and freeware browsers, the WWW process has started to make a shift from a thin client to a thick client. With the expansion of the client from a simple user interface to one that supports vendor application plug-ins via an Advanced Programming Interface (API) to the browsers functionality, the client has been getting thicker.

Figure 1.1: A standard Client-Server model

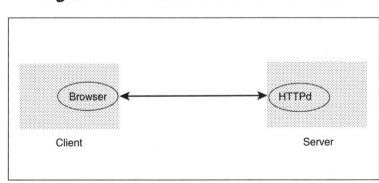

Additionally, we can see the browser taking on even more functionality as Secured Sockets Layer (SSL) and Java Virtual Machine (JVM) are included as part of the functional browser. These additions in functionality create a thick client from the original browser.

The best example of the thin-client browser is the Lynx browser.

Note The most recent release of Lynx is 2.6, which is maintained by Foteos Macrides at the Worcester Foundation for Biological Research. Prior to that, the University of Kansas developed and maintained Lynx through the release of 2.4.2. The university has no plans at this time to continue development or maintenance of Lynx. New or upgrading users are advised to use the 2.6 release of Lynx. Welcome to freeware 101.

The best example of a thick client is the Netscape **Navigator** (or if you prefer, the Microsoft equivalent, **Internet Explorer**). In this case, the program has complex graphics rendering and displays in both graphical mode using X-standards (not Microsoft as of this writing) and Windows and MAC-OS (again, not Microsoft as of this writing). Additionally, there is the SSL module, the JVM module (and in the case of Microsoft, add the features of the ActiveX interface) and the API module (as well as others) that make the client fatter still. (See Figure 1.2.)

Figure 1.2: *Browsers move from thin to thick*

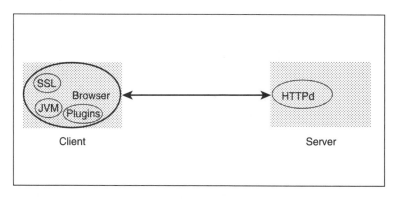

The normalized model usually associates a fat with a thin, but in the case of the Web, this isn't happening. The client is getting fatter, but, at the same time, so is the server. This is happening because the user community is demanding that the protocol for the Web do more, do it faster and do it better.

The development community wants to be able to access databases from the server without entering another client-server process. The general Internet community wants electronic commerce, data validation and security models to be supported as built-in functions of the server. Each of these additional functions, when built into the server, becomes just another wrapper of fat around the server portion of the client-server model. (See Figure 1.3) Today, the fatter model is being followed by many of the database vendors who seek to add their own level of Standard Query Language (SQL) functionality to the HTTP server , permitting them to integrate directly from the HTTP server to the SQL server (generally their product), thereby decreasing the overall response time (using the CGI method) that a request will have from the interaction with the HTTP server and the SQL server.

In the end, we could see a fat client and a fat server; what some would call "the worst of both worlds," as shown in Figure 1.4. In this case, functionality would be processed with both the client and the server. Earlier, we talked about the database companies leveraging the connectivity by making modifications to the server. Think about what will happen when they want to make better use of the distributed model by loading up the client with more and more distributed applications.

Figure 1.3: *The fat server*

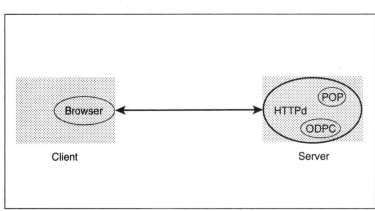

Client

Server

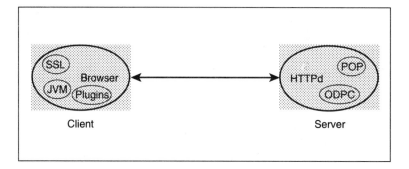

Figure 1.4: *The worst of both worlds, a fat client and a fat server*

All this distribution of the workload to balance the load of data processing between the clients and the servers looks to be a good thing from the user's perspective. While it adds more functionality and seems to provide a myriade of benefits, there are some inherent drawbacks into building large and complex systems. In the distributed models being looked at for Web-based processing, the size of the application space that they are attempting to address increases the possibility for security holes.

Expand Your Horizons

Now would be a good time to relate some issues and concerns that are raised when software projects start to expand. In this case, we will look at what happens when large and complex systems implement bleeding edge technologies.

A good example of that is the initial release of the Java Virtual Machine in the early Netscape client. In this case, a security hole was introduced when a complex system added a layer of additional complexity through the growth of the client/browser. The JVM (as distributed by Sun) and its integration to Javascript (a Netscape product that was originally called

Livescript, but was modified to work with the JVM) was still a bit unstable in its initial release.

The addition of these two products to the browser opened security holes between the client and the server. (Although not nearly as bad as allowing ActiveX applications that write to your local disk to operate across the non-secure environment of the Internet as is provided for in the initial release of the ActiveX component technologies).

It should be noted that the problems that were created by this initial integration in the Netscape client have been taken care of by both partners (at this time the same cannot be said about ActiveX, but there are a large number of people working on making this technology work, and work securely). The problems encountered in the initial release of the JVM and Javascript show the potential problem of attempting to add too much fat to the client. More than that, they also point out one of the key failures of the current Internet development cycles and how the technology is failing to integrate securely in the first release.

These failures have a great deal to do with code complexity. Code complexity is easy to measure, and it has to do with integration issues more than the size of a single program. In the case of the browsers getting fatter and the clients getting fatter as well, there is a higher propensity for errors, and, in some cases, fatal security errors, to be introduced into the system. In the Unix world, there is a saying that the larger the program the greater the possibility that it will violate some security practice.

One of the most widely used Unix programs is called sendmail. It was developed by Eric Allman when he was at UC Berkeley back in 1979. With the exception of a small gap (1982-1990), he has continued to support the product and its growth. Sendmail is considered one of the best Mail Transport Agents (MTA) available, even with its extreme complexity and known security concerns. In fact, it comes pre-loaded on most Unix operating systems. Unfortunately, as stated in the book Eric co-authored, "The sendmail program can be an open door to abuse. Unless the administration is careful, the misuse or misconfiguration of sendmail can lead to an insecure and possibly compromised system."[1]

For those looking at the client-server future of the Web and HTTP protocols, the problems of the client and the server getting fatter are certainly reason for concern.

Distributed Computing Across Internets: DNS and TCP

There is a major difference in developing a distributed computing model when discussing Intranets and Internets. In general, a system administrator has a great deal of control over who has access to what procedures, files and data on a Local Area Network (LAN) or Intranet. A system administrator can limit access to certain functions, programs and protocols when using files like /etc/services and /etc/inetd on a Unix platform. There are additional security systems that can be used to limit access and to add control to the sys-

1. sendmail, Bryan Costales with Eric Allman and Neil Rickert, O'Reilly & Associates, Inc.

tems that are located on a LAN. For example, the data maintained in the /etc/group and /etc/passwd files can be used to limit access to certain programs.

Domain Name Service

A problem arises when you want to use a distributed computing model in a Wide Area Network (WAN) where it is not controlled by a single entity, but by numerous entities across the WAN. The most common name for the largest of these distributed computing environment is The Internet. It should be noted that even a large corporate network fits into the WAN category we are talking about. While a single corporate entity controls the overall network, individual departments have access control over the machines within their department. Although the WAN appears to have central control, it is, in fact, a distributed model of systems control. That means that, just because you control your systems, the person in the next department might not use effective controls on the systems he administers, opening up the entire WAN for attack from the unsecured host.

Since there is no one person or group who has ownership for the Internet, security and control issues are in the domain of each LAN owner. This security and control can be accomplished many ways (from screening routers to complex firewalls). Some of the options available will be discussed later in this chapter.

In the case of the Internet, the WAN is made up of public, semi-public and private resources that use common protocols agreed to by all members of the WAN. Back in the early days of the Internet, when it was called ARPANET, the method was called Network Control Program or NCP. In 1973, this was changed to provide a better level of support of the Open Systems Interconnect (OSI) Reference Model by DARPA.

These protocols are based on the Internet Protocol (IP). This protocol allows information exchange by encapsulating messages using either the Transmission Control Protocol (TCP) or User Datagram Protocol (UDP) as common methods of communication across the WAN. Using these established protocols, an information packet can be routed from one machine to any other known machine on the WAN.

How do diverse machines from numerous vendors communicate? Much the same way that we do/they use addresses. Consider the following address:

John Doe
1122 Main Street
Unit 334
Anytown, NJ 19456-9876

There is a high probability that this address belongs to only one person. There is no way to ensure that, though. And what if the person moves and by happenstance the next resident is also named John Doe? While we may complain about the mail and the US Postal Service, the system does generally work.

To communicate across Internetworks, and to ensure that information is sent and received with total accuracy, the address must be 100 percent correct. You don't want to get accused of attempting to break into someone else's network, do you? To do that, we need an address that is unique, like a fingerprint. In this case, we use a unique 32-bit key to define the address of the location.

These 32-bit addresses range from 0 to over 4.3 billion. The numbers are expressed in a dotted-octet format that references the binary value of the address. This was designed to make it as simple as possible for people to understand and to write out an address. In this case, the binary notation of an address could be:

$$00001010000011111110101000010001$$

This translates into four octets of

$$00001010 \otimes 00001111 \otimes 11101010 \otimes 00010001,$$

which is expressed as the dotted-octet 10.15.234.17 as the Internet Protocol address.

This number and format is derived by translating the binary value of the octet to its decimal value and associating that numeric value, in its original position within a dotted format, where each decimal value is separated by a dot (.).

Consider how much easier the dotted-octet is to read over the binary address. Going back to the postal example, the binary code would be the barstrips that make up the bar code on postal mail. The dotted-octet would be like having the numeric value for the bar code.

It was determined that there might be a need to provide an easier method to allow that address to mean something to the owner and the people who would want to contact the owner of the dotted-octet. As in our postal example, most people don't know the bar code value for their address, they want that to be transparent to them. As postal addresses show, most people can't even remember their ZIP+4, so how can we expect them to remember their IP address?

It was determined that the best way to ensure that people can remember where they live, is to get a special name and address associated to that dotted-octet address. This name is called a Domain Name and is the key piece (along with the dotted-octet, of course) of Domain Name Service (DNS).

So when these addresses are handed out and associated to names, just who does it and how is it done? It is done by an organization called the Internic (the Internet Registry, which has the charter of being a central clearinghouse for the assignment of domain names and IP address space), and single IP addresses aren't the norm. To handle the delivery of address space, the concept of classes as a method of partitioning within the address space has been accepted.

The domain was redefined to be make up of three classes. These three classes (A, B, and C) are defined by the portion of the address that are owned and operated by a particular LAN.

The class differentiation is based on an assigned address space. In the following examples I will be using domain addresses that are referred to as private domains (as defined in RFC 1597). The addresses 10.0.0.0 - 10.255.255.255, 172.16.0.0 - 172.31.255.255 and 192.168.0.0 - 192.168.255.255 should be used on LANs that are not reachable from outside the network.

- Class A—The first address 10.*.*.* allows you to control access by a "Class A" address. A Class A address is one where the

LAN administrator has the ability to define all the last three numbers of the dotted-octet. This is the largest possible class in terms of "space" as it provides a possible 16,777,216 LAN addresses for the network administrator to use within the LAN.

- Class B–A Class B address means that you have been assigned a subgroup of a class A address that contains 16 contiguous numbers in the second octet;in this case, 172.16.*.* through 172.31.*.* are within the control of the LAN administrator. This would provide a total of 1,048,576 possible addresses to be distributed.

- Class C–A Class C address is one that allows you to own one single class B address. In this case, all the addresses under 192.168.*.* are under the LAN administrator's control. In this case, the possible address space for the administrator is 65,536 defined hosts.

> **Tip** A single LAN subnet is limited to a maximum of 256 possible addresses (0-255) on the subnet (192.168.1.*). Just as each machine on the LAN that runs IP will be assigned a unique IP number by the administrator, each sub-net or route on a LAN will share a common first three octets. Routers are used to define the second octet, or subnet, on an internetwork (LAN).

Any enterprise that needs globally unique address space is required to obtain such addresses from an Internet Registry. An enterprise that requests IP addresses for its external connectivity will never be assigned addresses from the blocks defined above.[2]

How does one machine know if it knows another? The key is the routing tables that are maintained by the Internet Registry. When the registry assigns an address to the requester, it also makes that address easier to use by assigning a unique name to that address (a domain name). Generally, the requester will define the desired name while staying within the rules that have been established in the RFCs. There

---

2. RFC 1597 Address Allocation for Private Internets, March 1994, Rekhter, Moskowitz, Karrenberg & de Groot

are a few conventions that are used in the assignment of a name, but almost any available name created using the rules provided, will generally be considered acceptable.

To resolve the name to a dotted-octal address understood by routers, a process called *name resolution* must take place. This, in turn, uses the process called DNS.

A simple explanation of how DNS works is to assume that you want to go from your local machine to a machine at Sun Microsystems. Sun Microsystems' domain name is sun.com. Name resolution of the *sun.com* domain would replace that domain name with the dotted-octet of 192.9.9.1 when translated by DNS.

When a packet of information is crossing a WAN, it knows the final destination of where it is going as the dotted-octet. As the information transverses across the routers, it performs queries to the router tables to determine the best route to travel. This process of routing allows the current machine to figure out the best possible way to send the packet to the next machine on its way to the final destination. It also means that two packets following each other could actually be routed to the serving machine via different routes based on traffic and what is determined by the routers to be the fastest route between the two machines.

There is a Unix-based program called traceroute that allows a person to see the path that the router takes. The following traceroute output was generated to measure the speed and to determine the best route between a machine I use as a personal site and the location *sun.com*. (For my provider's sake, the initial gateway has been omitted in this example. It would have shown up as the 1 value in this list).

```
 2 192.168.4.1 (192.168.4.1) 24.0 ms 8.27 ms 7.53 ms
 3 lngw2.isi.edu (128.9.16.70) 120 ms 9.37 ms 15.8 ms
 4 SWRL-ISI-GW.LN.NET (204.102.78.2) 10.8 ms 26.0 ms
   13.0 ms
 5 border1-hssi1-0.Bloomington.mci.net (204.70.48.5)
   35.0 ms 24.0 ms 26.5 ms
 6 core1-fddi-0.Bloomington.mci.net (204.70.2.129)
   40.7 ms 30.8 ms 29.6 ms
 7 borderx1-hssi-3.SanFrancisco.mci.net (204.70.1.42)
   23.5 ms 23.6 ms 32.4 ms
 8 barrnet.SanFrancisco.mci.net (204.70.158.102)
   44.6 ms * 26.7 ms
 9 paloalto-cr5.bbnplanet.net (131.119.0.205) 26.3 ms
   33.7 ms 27.5 ms
10 sun-1.bbnplanet.net (131.119.28.98) 43.4 ms 26.8
   ms 28.0 ms
11 Sun.COM (192.9.9.1) 31.8 ms 36.2 ms 29.1 ms
```

As can be seen, we went from the service provider to a gateway (192.168 is used for private Intranets), to an educational facility (University of Southern California), to the USC Information Science Institute (Los Nettos) to the backbone supplied by MCI to BBNPlanet's network in Palo Alto, CA, and then finally to Sun computer. The asterisk (*) in line 8 means that we lost packet data for that link via a timeout. The timeout field is a default 3 seconds. (For more information, please see the man pages for the traceroute command.) It should also be noted that it took an average of 32.36 ms for a packet to make a round trip from my machine to sun.com. *That's fast.*

In this distributed computing model, the client builds a message using a known protocol and then places the message in either a TCP packet or UDP datagram. This is required by the service protocol that has been selected. The message is then passed from the client to the server by using the DNS and IP protocols to resolve the server's location and move the packet of information across the Internet.

Once the packet reaches the destination server, a request is made on that machine for the service of the packet. This is done by making a request to a port on the machine. In the case of HTTP (the protocol for Web-based information), the generic port used is 80. (Ports under 1024 are reserved and owned by the *root* account and the programs under those port numbers run with special privileges). That doesn't preclude someone from using another port. Because 8000 and 8080 are not preassigned or privileged, they are used in many cases to perform HTTP.

The ports and associated services are defined in two administrative files on Unix platforms. These aren't listings of program files, but are listings of files that exist on the computer system. The first of these files (/etc/services) is shown here.

Listing 1.1: Sample truncated /etc/services **file**

```
# This file associates official service names and
# aliases with the port number and protocol the
# services use.
#
# The form for each entry is:
# <official service name>   <port number/protocol
# name>   <aliases>
#
# Note: The entries cannot be preceded by a blank space.
```

```
#
echo       7/tcp                                           # Echo
echo       7/udp                                           #
#
# In some cases the protocol of the service allows
# the service to go by either the TCP or UDP method,
# "echo" is a fine example of that.
#
systat     11/tcp  users                    # Active Users
daytime    13/tcp                               # Daytime
daytime    13/udp                                       #
ftp-data   20/tcp            # File Transfer Protocol (Data)
ftp        21/tcp         # File Transfer Protocol (Control)
telnet     23/tcp             # Virtual Terminal Protocol
smtp       25/tcp          # Simple Mail Transfer Protocol
time       37/tcp  timeserver                       # Time
time       37/udp  timeserver                          #
whois      43/tcp  nicname                       # Who Is
domain     53/tcp  nameserver     # Domain Name Service
domain     53/udp  nameserver                         #
hostnames  101/tcp hostname       # NIC Host Name Server
pop        109/tcp postoffice # Post Office Protocol - v.2
uucp-path  117/tcp                      # UUCP Path Service
nntp       119/tcp readnews untp # Network News Transfer
                                               # Protocol
ntp        123/udp            # Network Time Protocol
snmp       161/udp snmpd    # Simple Network Management
                                         # Protocol Agent
snmp-trap  162/udp trapd    # Simple Network Management
                                         # Protocol Traps
#
# UNIX services
#
exec       512/tcp   # remote execution, passwd required
login      513/tcp                           # remote login
who        513/udp whod          # remote who and uptime
shell      514/tcp cmd  # remote command, no passwd used
syslog     514/udp               # remote system logging
printer    515/tcp spooler       # remote print spooling
route      520/udp router routed    # routing information
                                               # protocol
timed      525/udp timeserver              # remote clock
                                         # synchronization
#
# Other HP-UX services
#
lansrm     570/udp                          # SRM/UX Server
DAServer   987/tcp              # SQL distributed access
rlb        1260/tcp       # remote loopback diagnostic
# LISTENER 1521/tcp        # Oracle SQL*Net V2 listener
# infostar 1522/tcp           # Informix-ONLINE server
# infosrv2 1523/tcp           # Informix-ONLINE server
# orasrv   1525/tcp        # Oracle SQL*Net V1 TCP/IP
nft        1536/tcp          # NS network file transfer
```

The second file used is /etc/inetd.conf. This is also referred by many as the super-services configuration file. When inetd is started it will use this configuration file to define what services are recognized and what deamons are to be active on what ports.

In this mode, it is a *superserver* as it controls access to other servers. It knows what programs are to run when requests come to it through different doorways defined in the system. These doorways, or ports, are associated with either active processes (like HTTPd) which are already running and know how to handle the message being received, or the ports are associated with programs that the system will start up when a message is received from that port.

Listing 1.2: Truncated example of a /etc/inetd.conf **file**

```
# Inetd reads its configuration information from this
# file upon execution and at some later time if it is
# reconfigured.
#
# A line in the configuration file has the following fields
# separated by tabs and/or spaces:
#
# service name    as in /etc/services
# socket type     either "stream" or "dgram"
# protocol        as in /etc/protocols
# wait/nowait     only applies to datagram sockets, stream
#                 sockets should specify nowait
# user            name of user as whom the server should run
# server program absolute pathname for the server inetd
#                 will execute
# server program args arguments server program uses as
#                 they normally are starting with
#                 argv[0] which is the name of the
#                 server.
#
# See the inetd.conf(4) manual page for more information.
##
#         ARPA/Berkeley services
##
ftp    stream tcp nowait root   /usr/lbin/ftpd ftpd -l -u 000
telnet  stream tcp nowait root /usr/lbin/telnetd telnetd -u
#
# Before uncommenting the "tftp" entry below, please
# make sure that you have a "tftp" user in /etc/passwd.
# If you don't have one, please consult the tftpd(1M)
# manual entry for information about setting up this
# service.
# tftp dgram  udp wait root   /usr/lbin/tftpd tftpd
bootps dgram   udp wait   root   /usr/lbin/bootpd bootpd
```

```
#fingerstream tcp nowait bin    /usr/lbin/fingerd fingerd
login stream tcp nowait root   /usr/lbin/rlogind rlogind
shell stream tcp nowait root   /usr/lbin/remshd remshd
exec  stream tcp nowait root   /usr/lbin/rexecd rexecd
#uucp stream tcp nowait root   /usr/sbin/uucpd uucpd
#
#        inetd internal services
#
##
daytime           stream tcp nowait root internal
daytime           dgram  udp nowait root internal
time              stream tcp nowait root internal
time              dgram  udp nowait root internal
echo              stream tcp nowait root internal
echo              dgram  udp nowait root internal
```

Tip Because Chapter 1 is a brief overview of name services and TCP/IP, it is suggested that you purchase the texts that were mentioned earlier. Particularly if you plan to manage a site on the Internet. My intent in this chapter is to provide you with some insight into how the process works and what the pieces are. I purposely didn't talk about SOA records, cname records, aliases, MX or PTR records. Nor did I cover named, nslookup, the resolver, the top 8 parent domains or reverse name resolution. To do so would blow my page count sky high. What I want you to get from this section is a feel for how the whole configuration works and plays together on the Internet.

Many people want to know why this has to be done on the server, and why that has to be done on the client. This overview of the entire client-server model, the concepts that make the Internet, or even an Intranet, work, and some of the other issues that we are covering here are designed to provide you with a base for understanding how and why certain things operate as they do.

As stated before, the inetd process, along with the configuration file, now acts as a superserver to the various server processes that are operational on the computer. The inetd processor allows the services to be started when they are requested. This model allows memory to remain free when services are not running. In the fourth field there is a value of nowait or wait. This tells the superserver process whether it should allow multiple copies of the service or if it is required to wait until a currently running service is available for the next request (sequential services verses parallel).

Securing a System from the Internet

How is security related to CGI? Simply put: Anyone who puts a LAN or private WAN on the Internet should consider the security issues related to having an HTTP server and network. Here, I will discuss general security issues and then move on to more specific methods of protecting the trusted systems on your network, such as firewalls.

A firewall is a method of protecting your inner network from external access (and, in some cases, protecting your inner network from people within it). Firewalls come in a number of shapes, sizes and flavors. There are some that have been designed to stop access based upon the IP address or the port the access is being attempted on. There are others that allow and/or disallow access based upon the application being called.

While discussion of these issues may seem like a high level of abstraction for the user, it is included in this book to help in understanding the costs associated with putting up a Web server. It also helps programmers to understand a bit more about the transaction process of going through a firewall and what security considerations should be taken when creating CGI scripts.

I'll wrap up this discussion with some additional options one should consider (all personal opinion mind you, but it's my book, after all).

Let's start by reviewing the /etc/services and the /etc/inetd.conf files mentioned earlier. Clearly, one simple way to add security to the WAN/Internet access is to secure yourself from access by the port numbers. This can be done by two separate methods. In the first, the service you wish to deny is commented out of the /etc/services or /etc/inetd.conf file (as shown in Listings 1.1 and 1.2).

The second method is to use *TCP Wrappers*. These are programs that you run instead of the normal vendor-supplied program. In this case, the active program wraps the operation of the service in such a way as to not permit damage to your machine.

Wrappers allow you to modify the behavior of the system service without making modifications to the source code of the service or the operating system. Consider the following reasons that you might want to wrap a service.

- The service is not validating the information being sent to it
- The service is not logging information that is useful to monitoring the security of the site
- The service needs to be able to be run by specific hosts only

In cases like these, shutting the service off isn't what you want to do. You want to control the service from a higher level. Wrappers offer this capability. Additionally, an administrator doesn't have to be concerned about things like systems upgrades. In this case, the system software is encompassed in its entirety by the wrapper and the security logic resides solely in another program.

Both of these suggestions provide the most simple methods of stopping someone from using your available services against your own computer network. They should be considered key ways to secure an individual machine. Additional wrappers to consider are:

- The sendmail wrapper - Developed by Trusted Information Systems(ftp://ftp.tis.com)
- The tcpwrapper - A general-purpose wrapper for UDP and TCP protocols developed by Wiest Venema. (ftp://ftp.win.te.nl/pub/security/tcp_wrapper_61.tar.gz and ftp://coast.cs.purdue.edu/pub/tools/tcp_wrappers)
- The SOCKS wrapper - Permits outbound TCP connections to tunnel through firewalls, developed by Tom Fitzgerald (http://www.socks.nec.com/ and ftp://ftp.nec.com/pub/security/socks.cstc/)

Here are some excellent security resource locations on the net (that may point to newer and possibly better Unix security tools):

- FTP Archives - http://info.cert.org CERT (Computer Emergency Response Team) and http://coast.cs.perdue.edu/ COAST (Computer Operations, Audit, and Security Technology)

- Advisories - ftp://info.cert.org/pub/cert-advisories CERT and http://ciac.llnl.gov/ciac/ToolsUnixNetSec.html CIAC (U.S. Department of Energy's Computer Incident Advisory Capability)
- Mailing Lists - cert@cert.org CERT andcaic-listproc@llnl.gov CIAC (you must use the form "subscribe CAIC-BULETIN Lastname, Firstname Phone)

Now that we have discussed the securing of the individual services, let's start looking at the role security plays in protecting your network from the evil empire of hackers.net.

My Network is My Castle

The easiest way of looking at the security needs of a LAN is to go back in time, a time before computers and electricity. Consider the castles of England that were circa 1200 AD. In historical study you will find cases where as few as eight men were able to hold the castle safe from an attack of hundreds. How?

Consider your network as a castle that must be protected, as shown in Figure 1.5.

Here we can see that the protected castle has some very basic, but effective, security features, all of which force the enemy to attack the weakest point in the perimeter—the front gate. This process of forcing an

Figure 1.5: *The genesis of today's firewall*

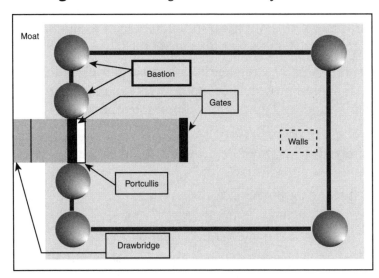

attacker to attack the spot you can control is referred to as minimizing the zone of risk. With limited resources, the castle defenses have pushed the attacker to a spot the defenses can control.

Consider the following attack against someone attempting to storm the castle:

Obstacle	Defense
Drawbridge	Raise/Sink Drawbridge
Moat	Shoot Arrows
Stout Door	Shoot Arrows, Drop Items
Long hall with Stout Door	Drop portcullis and pour boiling pitch or oil on them from above

Note that the defenders are protected at all times. They hide behind 30-foot walls and shoot arrows through slits. In the end, they pour and drop items onto the enemy, still without exposing themselves to risk.

In most cases, this castle protection system worked. Only a prolonged stay by the enemy outside the walls, or subversion from within, would cause this system to fail.

Most security experts will tell you that the greatest threat is not a hacker, but a process called *social engineering*. This occurs when someone on the *inside* provides a hacker on the *outside* with information that can be used to break into a site. The second greatest threat comes from misuse by your own users and system administrators. Improper configuration can ultimately lead to opportunities for someone to leverage the accounts on the system.

A firewall should be designed to allow certain users in. But, more than that, it should provide layers of protection and controlled access for both inbound and outbound communications from your LAN. This model provides four important features:

- Minimized the zone of risk (the front door is the easiest target area, and well protected)
- Built Strong parameters (walls and moat protected by bastions)
- Layered the Failure mode (each failure leads to another control and the default is anything not permitted is denied)
- Controlled the services, access, authorization and authentication on multiple layers of the IP model

Screening Router and Screened Subnet

Figures 1.6 and 1.7 (shown a bit later) are diagrams of technical solutions that you can use on your computer network and are currently used on many others. Figure 1.6, the first model, is referred to as *screening router*, or the screened subnet method. In these methods, a router is used to allow or disallow IP packets based on internal rule sets. In this way, the router is used to provide protection of the inner network.

You must first consider what information to allow (or disallow) when it passes through the router on its way from the WAN (untrusted network) to the LAN (trusted network). If a packet is denied access into the LAN, the packet will be dropped by the router. While this seems like a secure-enough process, it has some drawbacks. The first problem is that anything that is not *specifically* disallowed is permitted to pass through the router (your zone of risk). That means that the router administrator must create rules that deny access via the router's control structure (generally IP, not services based), rather than saying what services are to be allowed. This increases the possibility for human failure and could result in the router and the trusted network being compromised.

Another concern in router-based packet filtering is that you never know when someone is attempting to probe your system for weaknesses. When the packet gets dropped by the router, there is no communication with the LAN. This logging failure means that there is no way to track from where or when an attack is initiated.

Figure 1.6: *Router based filtering*

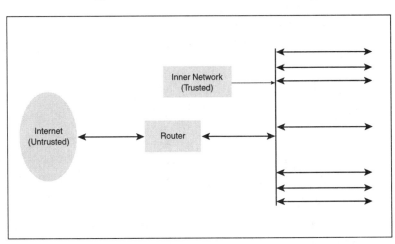

You can establish a more secure router network by using screened subnets. In this case, create a semi-protected subnet (also referred to as the DMZ) on the inside, beyond the first router. Within the DMZ create a large number of servers that provide access to services for both the untrusted and the trusted systems. Beyond the DMZ, there is another router. This second router provides protection and access-control to the trusted LAN from what is allowed to come in from the DMZ. While not as good as having a castle, this type of protection is much better than the screening router alone.

An alternative to this system is to use a router with a proxy server. In this case, the router can only talk to the proxy server and the proxy server can only talk to the router. The router knows that inbound transmissions must go to the proxy server before being passed into the trusted network, and visa-versa. Unfortunately, this too has its cons, as listed here:

- The router allows all packets through unless specifically denied
- It is easy for administrators to misconfigure routers
- Most provide no logging or alarm on detection of attacks
- There is no application protocol configuration
- There is little or no user authentication and authorization

Application Filters

There is one more option to protect yourself from the bad guys on the Internet. It is an applications-based firewall called an *application filter*. In this case, the firewall is designed to filter the IP transmissions based on the applications that are being used.

With an applications filter, the permitted applications are defined and access to those services are turned on by allowing those packets to pass through the filter. In many cases, access to these services can be modified by the systems from which the request for services are coming, the time of day, the day of week, the person who is making the request, and the host to which they are attempting to get with that service. In addition, packets can be controlled, both incoming and outgoing. That allows the same controls that are used to limit inbound access to be placed on what can be sent from the LAN to the WAN.

This model differs from the router-based one in that all services that are not specifically permitted access are denied access to the trusted network from the untrusted systems. It also permits services to be controlled from the reverse direction as well. This enables a firewall administrator to allow outbound HTTP services from all machines on the trusted network, but deny inbound HTTP services to all but the public Internet server.

In some of the better firewall systems, the application gateway software allows the administrator to define users, groups, and addresses that are permitted to access services and when they can access those services (see Figure 1.7). Additionally, basic authentication controls are supported by most application firewalls. These basic access controls can be as simple as a standard multiple use password or as complex as using challenge-response, one time only passwords that require special crypto-key cards.

In most cases, these firewalls use a process of proxy services from within the machine on which they are operating. The data going into the firewall comes across one IP address (the IP gateway to the world), gets validated by the firewall, and then the proxy server passes the data on to the internal server via a different IP address (the internal IP gateway) to get to the internal service machine.

Why are we discussing and spending so much time on this aspect of the communications channel? What does all of this have to do with CGI programming? Even if you are not dealing with firewalls, proxy servers and the like on your network, it is possible that people coming to your site are. While you may think that the address you're

Figure 1.7: Firewall security

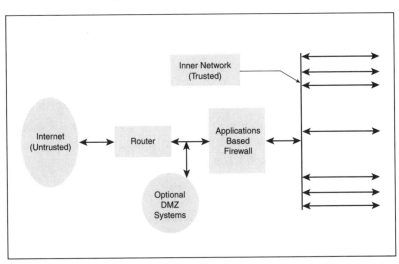

being told in the packet request that arrives on your server from the Web client is the client's machine, it may not be. In many cases, that address being provided is actually the address of the firewall or the proxy server on that visitor's network. In other words, the client system may be intentionally lying to your server.

One of the most popular questions asked in the comp.infosystems.authoring.cgi newsgroup (the usenet newsgroup that many CGI developers ask and answer questions on) deals with validating the requester or visitor to the site. This validation is virtually impossible because a site may be protecting and hiding the identity of its network by:

- Dual-named DNS services
- Proxy filtering
- An applications dual-homed firewall
- Any other security measure that massages the IP and DNS information

Similarly, there is no way, using standard HTTP, to obtain information about the user's visiting the site. In the most simple of terms, there is no way to gain trusted information about a user from the interaction of the HTTP requests.

This overview of firewalls was included because proper security at a site is exceptionally important. Numerous *Internet Service Providers* (ISPs) have denied or limited access to CGI libraries and tools because they were concerned about security issues. Chapter 3 (Server Side Includes (SSI)) discusses security issues on the server in greater detail. For now, it was important to discuss many of the issues dealing with over site security in regards to trusted and untrusted computer systems access.

Consider using the models talked about thus far, where you want to put your services machines. Your choices are somewhat limited. You can place the machine on the DMZ, or within your trusted environment. I have always been a proponent of putting as little as possible on the DMZ. While this puts me in a minority, I would like to take a moment to quote a source and explain why I disagree with the concept that they extol.

If an organization wants to provide full access to a wide variety of services, such as anonymous FTP (File Transfer Protocol), Gopher, and

WWW (World Wide Web) services, it can *provide certain sacrificial hosts* on the outside DMZ.[3]

I added emphasis to this quote to show where I have a major disagreement with most authors of firewall and security books, who are proponents of the Web server being on the DMZ. I believe that no computer resource or system under your control is a sacrificial system.

If you follow something as simple as the checklist provided by Simson Garfinkel and Gene Spafford in their book *Practical Unix & Internet Security*[4] it shows there are any number of procedures and processes one can follow to secure a system on the network (some I've even talked about above). There is no reason to sacrifice a computer system to hackers who just want to prove their bravado by breaking into it, especially a system that you use for interfacing to the world. You can use your firewall and the tips and techniques provided in any number of useful texts to ensure that your services machines are as secure as you can make them.

 Tip In addition to some excellent texts, there are any number of security consultants around who know their stuff and can help you do the right thing. You can also attend conferences. If you're lucky, you will be able to see someone like Rik Farrow provide a full-day workshop on Internet Security (as he has done for many years at the HPWORLD Conferences). I should point out that, while I respect Rik and highly recommend his presentations, he is from the school that feels that you can sacrifice machines. Except for this one small issue, he is one of the best presenters of Unix and Internet security I have had the pleasure to hear speak.

There is one last concern regarding security and access to your Web server. For most of you, this section might be considered a good thing, as it discusses a way to lower the overall traffic impacting your

3. Internet Firewalls and Network Security, Karanjit Siyan, Ph.D., Chris Hare, New Riders Publishing (1995) Page:293 (emphasis by JMI)
4. Practical Unix & Firewall Security 2nd Edition, Simson Garfinkle and Gene Spafford, O'Reilly and Associates (1996) Appendix A

network and server. On the other hand, it also causes information that you get to be inaccurate. The next few paragraphs discuss the issues surrounding the *caching* process used by browsers and, in many cases, proxy servers.

Caching

Caching means that much of the data and information transfer that takes place to and from your server may be stored on a proxy server or the user's own machine. In cases where caching has been done the user may think that they are accessing the data on your site, but in fact, they are not. To ensure that Internet traffic is kept to a minimum, this system loads your information on someone else's platform.

The pages and information served from your site to a user might be served to the viewer from the proxy servers an ISP provides, or their own machine's cache. The best examples of the types of services using proxy servers and caches are the commercial services like Prodigy, America Online and Compuserve. These sites keep gigabytes of Web data on their cache servers to lower the amount of traffic and information that they serve through the WAN/Internet.

This means that many people can access your HTML pages without actually accessing your HTTP server. Potentially, this could lower the load on your servers (a good point and the key reason that this was designed into the HTTP services). But it also creates a false sense of security as the log files maintained by the HTTP server are no longer accurate. Figure 1.8 shows how the proxy services work from a browser's initial request (that obtains the original copy from the requested server) to the noninitial request (that will obtain the item requested from the cache server).

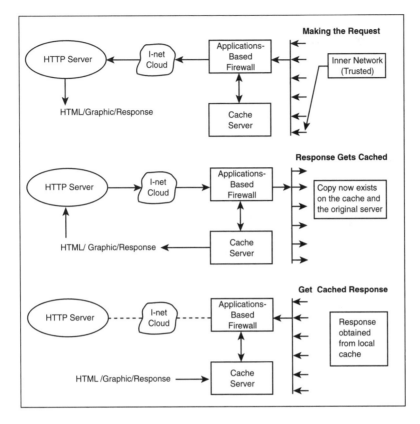

Figure 1.8: *Caching in action*

Summary

In this chapter, we covered some of the basics of the Internet. We started with client-server, moved into TCP, Domain Name Services and security, and closed with caching. In most of the chapter, we were either talking about the underlying protocols of the Internet, or items that have an effect on you and your use of the Internet.

While many of these issues seem as if they have nothing to do with CGI, we have already pointed out how security systems can lie to you (to protect themselves) and how you shouldn't trust all the data that comes across to you. We have looked at some of the issues associated to the transport mechanism (TCP) and the fact that, just because someone says that they are from a domain, doesn't always mean that's where they are from.

As we start to get deeper into the CGI portions of this book, we will be referring back to some of the things that were covered in this chapter. Additionally, we will use this chapter as a reference base when we talk about the issues involved with setting up a server, as well as managing and maintaining one.

In the next chapter, we will focus on some of the key aspects of Web-based systems. We will start with the simple URL and move through it until we get to distributed processing and starting to look at a model for business and data transactions.

Most of all, we want to remind you that we have provided a number of fine additional resources, both in the chapter and in Appendix B. There you'll find references on the Net that focus on the topics that we have covered in this chapter.

CHAPTER 2
COMMUNICATIONS BETWEEN CLIENT AND SERVER

- Understanding Communications

- Distributed Computing and Transaction Processing

- HTML and CGI: Common Grounds

In Chapter 1, we looked at DNS and talked a bit about TCP, IP, and UDP. We also talked about security and the models of trust (and non-trust) between clients and servers. Now we will delve deeper into how the client communicates with the server.

URI, URL, and Other Three-Letter Acronyms

The world of the Internet and the distributed computing model (if not all of computing) is filled with Three Letter Acronyms (TLAs). This may have something to do with the birth of the Internet as part of the

Military Industrial Complex (MIC), but, then again, WRK (Who Really Knows) and IMO (In My Opinion) most of these aren't all that important in the scope of this book. When it comes to Internet and Intranet, TLAs, and the HTTP (a Four Letter Acronym (FLA) for the Hyper Text Transport Protocol) there are two major areas that deal with the intercommunication between the browser and the server. These are the Uniform Resource Locator (URL) and Uniform Resource Identifiers (URI).

URLs

A URL is an instruction that tells two basic pieces of information. First it contains a section that defines the protocol that will be used to communicate. Second it provides the data needed by the protocol. The URL below shows the whole URL followed by the individual pieces:

```
http://www.net-quest.com/~ivler/book/
```

In this example, the protocol is http: and the data is //www.net-quest.com/~ivler/book/

We can see that the request is for the HTTP protocol to be used to access the file //www.net-quest.com/~ivler/book/ . The first thing the client will do is break the data down into what is expected. The HTTP protocol expects data to be //site/filepath/file with the site, filepath, and file all optional arguments (one must always be present at minimum). Table 2.1 defines the actions of the browser, if these option fields are omitted from within a document that has been served to your browser.

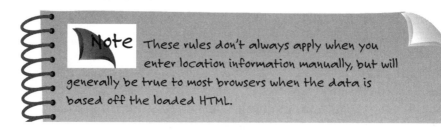

Note These rules don't always apply when you enter location information manually, but will generally be true to most browsers when the data is based off the loaded HTML.

Table 2.1: *Rules used to define missing data from a URL in an HTTP protocol*

Missing items	Action
site	Use last site browser was at, same filepath and file
site and filepath	Use last site and filepath browser was at, look for the file at that location
site and file	Use last site browser was at, use the new filepath, and see the default file for the server (or, if not there and indexing is on, use the index capability)
filepath	Use the last site and look for the file in the root filepath for the site
file	Use the last site and filepath in the browser, look for the server's default file in that filepath (or, if not there and indexing is on, use the index capability)
filepath and file	Use the last site in the browser and look for the server's default file in the root directory for the site (or, if not there and indexing is on, use the index capability)
site filepath and file	Not permitted—one must be supplied

The browser using this protocol will send a request out for a couple of reasons:

- To see if there is a site called www.net-quest.com
- To see if that site resolves from a name to an IP address through DNS and the resolver process within the DNS protocol

(The resolver uses DNS to implement the gethostbyname() and gethostbyaddress() library calls).

If so, a connection will be made using the protocol defined in the URL to that specified (by rule or by input) site. Once the connection is established, the server will expect to see the expected data (the filepath and file). The data will then be supplied per the nonsupplied information in Table 2.1.

In our example the server will see a request to provide a file at ~ivler/book/. It will see if the file at that filepath exists. ~ivler means that the server should look for the default path for the user account ivler on the server as the path (standard Unix translation of the tilde).

If the filepath doesn't exist, an error will be generated and returned to the user. If the path exists then the server will look for the requested file from the data provided.

In this example, there was no data provided for the file field. Therefore, the following rule would take over: it states that first it should look for the default file and, if none was found or no default file is defined in the HTTP configuration, the server will use the indexing method to show all files in the directory.

This is also a feature that is defined in the configuration files for the HTTP server. If there was no default file and indexing is turned off, a 404 error message will be returned. (A 404 error means that the file was not found on the server).

As a side note (covered in detail in Chapters 15 and 16) there is a major potential security hole in having default directory listings. If the default method is to use a file, and that file is not found, the server will drop to the second rule, to display the contents of the directory in a listing. This could open the site to directory tree transversal in and around directories to which you don't want people to have access.

A great example of this common occurrence is when a site is delivering its images on a page from a filepath called /private/images/ . Since this is not an HTML directory, the Webmaster has chosen to not include the default file that he defined in the configuration files for the site. That means that sending the browser to http://site/private/images will generate the default listing for all the files in the directory, if listing is set ON in the configuration of the server.

The easiest way of avoiding this security hole is to create a default file in every directory. On a Unix system, this can be accomplished by creating the file by any name you want in one directory. Then, make symbolic links to that file from all the directories you want to protect and call the symbolic link by the proper default filename.

If the client processor had seen a URL that looked like mailto:book@i-xpress.com, it would have started a different procedure (the E-mail or SMTP processor rather than the HTTP one) to process the data by the requested protocol. In this case, the client would have permitted the user to send an E-mail message to the address supplied in the data.

Table 2.2 lists the types of protocols that most clients and servers recognize according to established standards.

Table 2.2: *Protocols recognized by clients and servers*

http:	Hyper Text Transfer Protocol (the Web)
ftp:	File Transfer Protocol
mailto:	Standard mail protocol
file:	Open a local file
telnet:	Open a telnet session

URIs

What is a URI, and how does it differ from a URL? A URI contains information associated to the current transaction state in addition to the data that is normally passed in a URL. This additional data includes any data that is being sent from the client to the server along with information that is server-specific. The best example of a URI is a query generated by a search engine. In the following example, the Alta Vista search engine, (operated by Digital Equipment Corporation) was used to generate a query on all articles on the Web that contain the phrase Tcl CGI Development.

```
http://www.altavista.digital.com/cgibin/query?pg=q&wh
at=web&fmt=.&q=%22Tcl+CGI+Development%22
```

You can see that the URI consists of a GET request to the server made up of the protocol and data shown in Table 2.3.

Table 2.3: *URI GET request*

Protocol	Data
http	Domain (www.altavist.digital.com) Directory: cgibin Program: query Value-data pairs: pg=q what=web fmt=. q="Tcl CGI Development"

(See Chapter 3 for detailed descriptions on the POST and GET protocols of HTTP.)

Additional information passed by the browser is called *header data*. This provides information,such as the referring page, the browser type, and what formats of response (MIME types) are understood by the browser. And, of course, information that can't be trusted. Refer to Appendix A (or Table 3.4) for a list of browser-supplied header data.

A URL and a URI can be viewed as two items on a package—the URL being the street address and the URI being the packing slip.

In addressing a package with just a street address, the minimal information required is provided to get it to its final destination. If additional information, like a recipient name, isn't given, the package may just end up in a default location—the mailroom. This same process is performed by providing just a URL. If we don't provide any additional data beyond the URL, the server will fill in the blanks we left as best it can.

To ensure that the package is properly handled in its delivery, a packing slip is enclosed. The packing slip contains information about the contents of the package, the person who ordered it, the person to whom it is to be delivered, and in some cases, even a PO number.

Much of the information passed in the example URI was specific to the actual request. However, a large amount of the information required by the server will reside in the header data that is sent with each request to the server.

It is important to note that the header data being sent by a browser is very easy to spoof. It is data that should not be trusted. In fact, this data is not useful in determining authenticity of users or even ensuring that the user is coming from the specified domain or IP.

The header or *packing list* allows the URI to provide a method to transmit value-data pairs in the query_string environment variable in the GET method, or appended to the header data (as part of standard input) in the POST method (both are detailed in Chapter 3).

In addition to the information we described as being contained in the URI or the standard input (by using POST or GET), the browser generally passes information about itself as well. Again, it cannot be stressed enough that this information is passed as clear text from the browser to the server and should not be considered authoritative and accurate data. This data, when received by the server, ends up as environment variables that the server knows about (see Chapter 3).

HTTP: A Model for Distributed Computing

The method or model used in HTTP to allow communication is to use a daemon process at the server end of the connection. This begins in a computer's startup process (on a Unix system, that would be in the .rc files).

The server may start one or many processes in the startup (NCSA HTTPD 1.51 and beyond allows you to define the number of server processes that get started in the configuration files). Each HTTPd process running on the server waits for someone to activate the communication with the process across the port to which it was assigned to listen (again, generally that is port 80, but it could be redefined as any other in the configuration files).

The current model for most of these Unix platform servers is to create multiple instances of themselves on startup. This allows for multiple connections to be performed on the server. If there are more connection requests to the server than the initial startup, the configuration files generally allow for a maximum number of processes to be defined. When there are more *access* requests than there are processes to serve those requests, the process manager (generally the first process started) will not allow additional processes to start if the maximum amount defined in the configuration file have been started.

This multiple connection scheme works well with a number of browsers. In fact, many of these browsers are designed to try to make the best use of the multiple-server processes. When the Netscape browser makes a request to try to download the greatest amount in the shortest time, the browser will create multiple threads (or processes), each sending requests to the servers defined in the URLs that are passed to the browser. To get data for display as fast as possible, Netscape uses a process of multiple calls to servers. If the server has enough idle time, it will run the requests in parallel permitting the page to be loaded faster by the client.

To understand the model a bit better, let's look at a piece of HTML source and see what the browser and the servers will do with it.

```
<title>Test code</title>

<table><tr width=100%><td width=20%><img
src="img.gif"></td><td width=80%><img
src="http://www.othersite.com/imglib/img2.gif" This
is an image on another machine that I like.</td></tr>
</table>
```

This code will create a single page that contains a two-section table. This HTML method is used quite a bit when attempting to create a *paged* look to the screen. For example, a page that has been split up to have a thin column with images in the border and a larger area for text or images within the main page. In this case, let's look at what happens when the client side is told to get the page.

- First the client obtains a copy of the page it was told to get. This is the original request from the client to the server. The client then starts the process of unpacking, parsing and displaying the HTML. As the client parses the page, it follows these steps:
- The first instruction is to put up a title (This is a no-brainer for the client).
- The next instruction is to build a table, and to build the format of the table.
- The browser then scans the line for instructions on what data it will fill within the table. The browser looks inside the <td> fields and sees that there are instructions there to include an image. It sees that the first image has no URL associated to it, so it uses the rules we discussed in the prior section to define where it is to go to obtain the image.
- The client puts a request in to obtain the image.
- The client continues parsing the HTML and sees the request for the second image in the table data tag. In this case, the

client is being told to obtain the second image using the HTTP protocol. It also is being told that the image is located at another location. Rather than waiting for the first image request to complete, a second request using the same HTTP protocol is made from the client.

- This time the client call will be made to the domain specified within the image tag for the requested file.

Once the second request (a different thread) is processed, the client continues to complete the display process. This will continue when the images are transferred down to the client from the respective servers.

Figure 2.1 shows the call process and the browsers functioning in the above example.

During the process of making these calls, the state of the browser is maintained. It knows the sequence in which the calls were requested and the data that each is expected to return. While the model for HTTP is stateless (a connection closes after each request-response sequence), the transmission of the request and the response happen within a single stated environment in the browser.

Figure 2.1. *Browser making two HTTP requests*

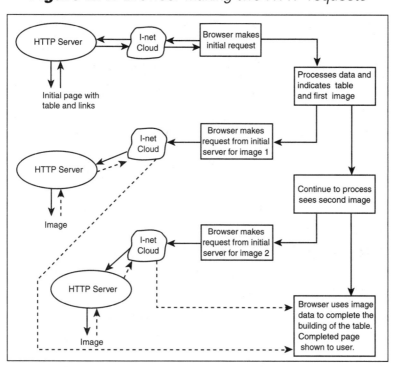

When the data from the request is streamed back to the browser, the process remembers the location associated to the request and starts to fill the data. This is based on header information packaged within the response to within the browser's known location. This process allows a browser to display an entire page of text, while only showing the image locations (with any alt= text) while they are being downloaded from the requested sites.

A good habit to get into, if you want to make the browser run a bit faster for the visitors to your site, is to define the actual space for the browser to reserve on the screen for the image. This is accomplished by providing the height and width in the <img> tag in your HTML. The images in Figures 2.2 and 2.3 do just that (and they load very quickly). The use of this feature allows some of the more advanced browsers to predefine the space on the page and wrap text around it. This allows the readers to see the text first, while the images are loaded into the predefined space as the browser obtains and processes the data.

Figure 2.2: *A browser with unfilled images*

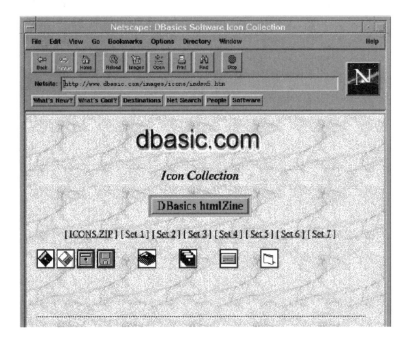

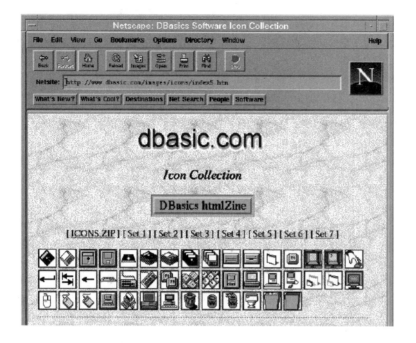

Figure 2.3: *Same page with images loaded*

HTML and Markup Languages

HTML is discussed throughout this book. Appendix B lists a number of resources on the Internet with information about markup languages and the HTML 2.0 and 3.2 standards. While the book will show some examples of HTML, it is expected that you have a basic understanding of the tags and how to use the markup language. In fact, it is a requirement that you understand HTML markup if you will be creating CGI scripts.

While just about anyone can use one of the many available WYSIWYG page builders to create wonderful Web pages, there are many times when you will be creating these pages from within your CGI programs. For instance, a page that creates a table of disk usage and the percentage of used space by disk, based on data obtained from data in the Unix operating system.

The program above, discussed later in Chapter 14, runs a CGI script. The program also builds tables (one per day) and fills in the disk information (in hourly slots in the table). The disk usage is displayed in any one of four colors based on the amount of disk used.

In cases like these, the CGI author must know how to build a table, what the options are for cell padding, cell spacing, table borders, row and data options, just what a <th> is and why you would use it and, of course, how to make the font option work (or maybe we want to change the background color of those table data fields as well as the actual text, so the information will pop out more…).

You should understand why you want to use <head> and <body> within HTML documents. You should also know how to use headers like *location* and define the MIME-type to the client from within the HTML file. These are part of the tools you will use every day in creating CGI scripts that build Web pages on the fly, thus creating a more active and interesting experience for people coming to view your work.

Anyone can output stream data. What's important is to understand the markup to the point where you can leverage the capabilities of the HTML markup language to build your pages on the fly. Remember that the language is a mark-up language, not a coding language. HTML mark-up tags are used to develop a presentation of information, not to do work or perform logic. Java is a good example of a coding language that can be integrated into your markup within a browser's page.

Many Server Side Includes (SSIs), of which we will go into detail in Chapter 3, are CGI programs or actual commands that you will have the user issuing on your server. Yes, this is an area of potential security abuse. The solution is to use a product like cgiwrap that forces all CGI access to be done as the owner of the CGI file. Not, to limit this useful tool and capability of the HTTP server. There are some that use variables known to the server to make life easier for developers. To utilize these, it is generally required that you understand the format and the syntax of the SSI HTML. (It looks a great deal like a comment, but it isn't.) Which brings us to….

How CGI Differs from HTML

A common mistake is to think of CGI and HTML as synonymous when it comes to coding. But they are far from that. CGI is a method of extending the server in the Client-Server relationship. Let's follow the progression of a request from the browser to the server using the model in Figure 2.4. Here the Client-Server is in the box. Then, within the large oval, we can see the relationship that the CGI program has with the server.

The browser user clicks on a highlighted link (in this example, the link will be http://www.server.com/cgi-bin/datetime.tcl) and the protocol is used to determine the service that is being requested by the server (in our example, we will use an HTTP request). The browser then uses the data portion to determine the server to which it will talk (www.server.com).

At this point the client opens a requested link to the server using the defined protocol. For this to happen, the client performs a domain translation of www.server.com to obtain an IP address for the routers. If the request goes through a firewall and/or a proxy server, there is a high possibility that the security features of these facilities will mangle the header information of the data package being sent

In this case, the command portion of this URI was one that told the server that the browser wanted to have a page that included the server's date and time. It states that it wants to go to the cgi-bin area

Figure 2.4: *Relationship of CGI to client-server*

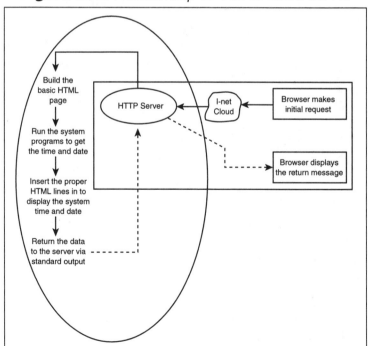

and run a program called datetime.tcl (Listing 2.1). Once the server gets the command request, it reads the stream and sees that the request is to run a command from the cgi-bin directory. At this point, the server opens another process to run the command and establishes a pipe line between the new process and the old as shown in Figure 2.5.

Listing 2.1: datetime.tcl

```
#!/usr/local/bin/tclsh
## datetime.tcl
##
## This is the program that can be used to get the
## date and time from the server
##
## There are no parameters passed into the program so
## no parsing will be done
##
## Format the date and time as two separate fields in
##  a table with labels
##
## Special note: Throughout the text there are a
## number of time functions that are performed using
## a call to unix's date function and parsing the
## returned data. This was done to ensure that the
## code was Tcl 7.4 compliant. It is not necessary to
## use those methods in newer versions of Tcl. In
## those cases you will want to use the clock
## function that we have used in this example.
##
set dv [clock format [clock seconds] -format "%A %D"]
set tv [clock format [clock seconds] -format "%R %Z"]
puts "Content-type: text/html\n\n"
puts "<h1> This is a test of the date time SSI</h1>"
puts "<table border=1 cellpadding=5>"
puts "<tr>"
puts "<td>Date on our machine:</td><td>$dv</td>"
puts "</tr><tr>"
puts "<tr>"
puts "<td>Time on our machine:</td><td>$tv</td>"
puts "</tr></table>"
exit
```

The CGI program is run within the context of the new process, and all the HTML output is returned back to the server from the standard output of the CGI via the pipe that was established for the process. All standard error is piped back to the server and redirected to the error_log. This provides a method to perform debugging of the CGI scripts.

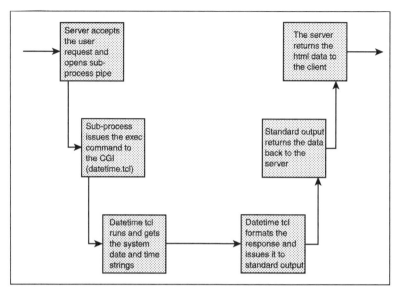

Figure 2.5: The flow control

Finally, the standard output that was generated is returned back to the client that made the request. The standard output shows up as displayed data in the user's browser, like that in Figure 2.6.

Generally, this data would have been proceeded by a header (the code in the Tcl procedure that did this was: puts "Content-type: text/html\n\n"), but servers also allow you to use Non-Parsed Headers (NPH) in your CGI scripts. The use of NPH allows you to return the data without having to include header information within the script. In many cases, this can save your server time (header parsing and validation) and also provide for a cleaner look on the user's browser. The URI data in the GET will not be redisplayed in the location field of the user's browser. NPH will be discussed in greater detail in Chapter 3.

Figure 2.6: Viewing the output through Netscape

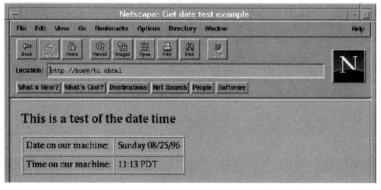

How the Model Works in Distributed Processing

Let's take our example and expand on it. In this case, we want to have information about an order that was placed. The information is maintained in a database located on another company machine, not generally accessible to the outside world.

In this case, we want to have the client send a request to the server which will pass that request to a CGI program. That program will then act as a client to another server and request the data from the foreign host.

Once returned, the data gets processed into an HTML format by the CGI. Or, the server to which the request was made may have already done that and the CGI is just passing the completed information along. (This effects whether the CGI is acting as a thin or a thick client to the distributed server process.) The data is then passed to the first server and returned to the originating client. Figure 2.7 illustrates this process.

Again, we will follow a request through this process.

Figure 2.7: *Distributed processing model*

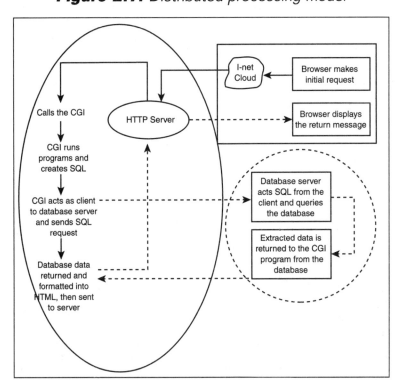

The user submits a request via a browser to obtain the ship date of an order. In this case, the user uses a form and the information is passed in using the *POST* method (discussed in Chapter 3). The POST request tells the server that it should start a process from the CGI area to process the data. The CGI process is started as a piped subprocess of the server. It takes the passed data and determines that it needs to call a process on a second machine to obtain the data.

At this point, the CGI becomes a client to the server processor on the second platform. Using protocols defined for the client-server interaction between the two platforms from within the CGI program, the CGI makes a request for the data.

The CGI is now a client to the database server. It will maintain a stated transaction until the database server completes the process and returns the information back to the CGI process. Once the data is received, the CGI formats the data into HTML. The formatted HTML with the data included is sent back to the HTTP Server. The HTTP Server passes the completed request back to the originating client and closes the transaction.

As for the CGI-server interaction and how that works, the CGI only has to know how to take the data being passed in, and then how to operate as a proper client to the server it needs to communicate with. Every attempt was made to make the process generic in the example. In reality, the CGI could be anything from a program that has been designed to meet a specification or customer need to one that specifically performs certain actions using an open and documented API. A good example of this second type would be a major database manufacture's API standards for SQL.

There are any number of programs that can provide this CGI/Client functionality. Many of these are application-specific programs, like the database ones mentioned carlier or application interfaces designed by companies that make products and are looking to allow their products to integrate to the net-centric based typology of distributed computing.

Many of these product vendors are finding that the generic CGI process creates unacceptable levels of overhead in the Client-Server model as it becomes further distributed. To offset this, some companies are integrating their client processing directly into the HTTP server, removing one layer of distributed processing. This has the potential of creating nonstandard and proprietary servers. Not everything is sugar and spice.

Summary

In this section, we expanded on the basics of the Client-Server model, and how it fits into the distributed computing models of the Internet. In addition, we discussed where CGI programming fits into the Client-Server model, as both an endpoint and as part of the larger distributed computing environment.

In the next chapter, we will continue to build on this client-server model. As we look at how it integrates into the HTTP process, we will review the differences between stated and nonstated transactions, as well as take a look at how stated can be spoofed. Finally, we will look at the methods used by the HTTP processor to parse and to communicate.

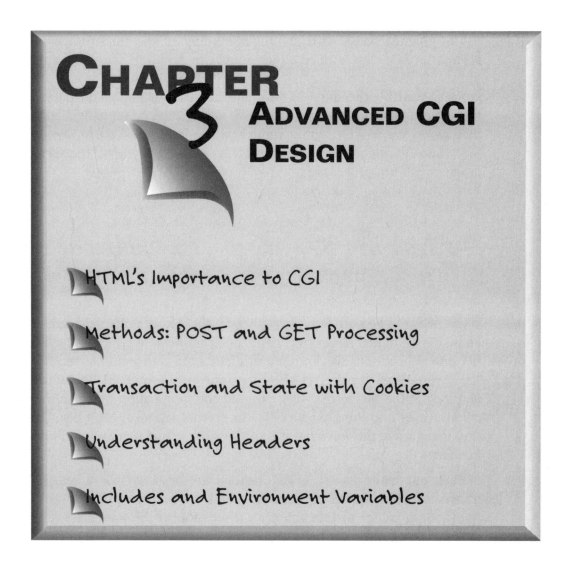

CHAPTER 3

ADVANCED CGI DESIGN

- HTML's Importance to CGI

- Methods: POST and GET Processing

- Transaction and State with Cookies

- Understanding Headers

- Includes and Environment Variables

One of the key problems in defining the CGI process is deciding what languages to use to develop code. Any language is acceptable. If we look hard enough, we can find someone who insists on doing their CGI development in RPG and/or Cobol. Chapter 4 will discuss language decisions, and why this book in particular chose the languages Tcl and Perl.

In this chapter we will be touching on the languages a small amount, but the focus is still on some of the higher level concepts that make up the interaction between the client and the server. In fact, most of the focus in this chapter is on server communications.

The chapter starts with an understanding of the importance of HTML to CGI development, then moves to how the client talks to the server. We will then cover one way to maintain state (or at least appear to) within the stateless environment. That will move us to how the server talks to the browser and we will discuss headers and how they work. We will close the chapter with a look how to use Server Side Includes and at what information is available to you on the server when you are processing.

HTML, HTTP, and the Trouble with Languages

What needs to be addressed here, is how the whole thing fits together. So far we talked about the client-server model and where the CGI fits into it in a non-distributed and distributed transactional model. We covered the way the HTTP process integrates the CGI . Now we will look at the pieces that make up the communication between the client, server and the CGI process. To do this, we must look beyond the languages of the software and see how the actual communications function.

Each command to the HTTP processor (the server) is a unique transaction. The server is stateless and knows of no prior or post transaction. (Refer to this chapter's discussion on Statelessness and Transactions for further details on how this can be overcome).

When the transaction takes place there is information passed in to the server from the client (browser). This information can be passed in using the *POST* or *GET* methods. In the POST method the information is passed in as part of the standard input stream. In the GET method the information is passed in as part of the URI.

Most servers have been developed to meet the standards as defined for HTTP. That doesn't mean that the server can not go beyond the standards and have extensibility that adds value. In fact, there are some servers that do just that.

The Netscape server supports a encryption and security technology called *Secured Sockets Layer* (SSL). This is an example of extensibility from within the server. Additionally, there are other servers that support Secure HTTP (S-HTTP). S-HTTP is another form of providing secured transmission between the clients and the servers.

This extensibility also shows how a server's functionality can be enhanced to perform non-standard HTTP and HTML. In fact, many server vendors have added direct access from the server to the database's that they support. This lowers the overhead of having to call and pipe CGI programs to and from the server allowing connections to be faster, and in some cases even semi-stated.

What of HTML and Standards?

Well once upon a time there were HTML standards. At the time of this writing, there was a standard in the standards approval cycle called *HTML 3.2*. In the early HTML standards there weren't things like tags for tables. For instance, center, and other enhanced items like the width and size values for the <hr> tag were extensions added into the markup language by browser manufacturers. These additions evolved as requests like more functional control over the display came in to the browser developers. The initial <body> command didn't allow for background images or colors. Before the GIF89A format took off there were stated processes called *server pushes* and *server pulls* (using great deals of bandwidth) that kept open the transaction between the server and the client allowing for images to be pushed and pulled across the network to create animations.

As enhanced non-standard HTML developed, it became a race of which vendor could add the greatest value by providing more non-standard markup. Netscape came up with frames, Microsoft went with marquees. Then the standards committees started work on developing HTML 3.0. A standard to replace the unsupported HTML 2.0 that was being overcome with vendor-specific enhancements.

In early May, 1996, it became clear that the 3.0 standard had become antiquated before it even was released. The vendors wanted the standards committee to move faster into developing standards that they could implement. Netscape and Sun fought for Java and CORBA standards and tried to get the Web-based standard to integrate into the ORB (Object Request Broker) standards being used by the Object Management Group (OMG). At the same time, Microsoft wanted to see the proprietary ActiveX methodology accepted as a standard for integrating common desktop interfaces to HTML.

Note As of the writing of this book, the the standards presented in the 3.2 document have not been approved. There are ongoing discussions on how and when certain commercial companies will support portions of the new 3.2 standard, like cascading style sheets (Microsoft claims to support them in Internet Explorer 3.0, and Netscape claims that they will be supporting them, with extensions, in Navigator 4.0). To many developers, this move to a desktop publishing model of HTML is a concern, especially for software that generates HTML on the fly.

Which brings us back to how the entire system works together to provide seamless interactive interfacing between the browser (client) and the server. This is done by using two methods to exchange messages between the client and the server. The first method, that has already been discussed, is the GET method. This method relies on how we interface the client to the server using the URI to act as a transport agent. The second method is the POST method. POST uses standard input to the server and generally requires some level of server processing using CGI scripting to perform actions on data.

In Chapter 4 there will be a discussion of methods that can be used to decode the data that is sent to the server in the GET and POST methods.

POST versus GET

The default manner in which a browser talks to the server is to send a GET request. In it's most simple form a GET request is nothing more than a request to the domain for a document. Let's review the example that we used before in Chapter 2.

In the following request the browser is asked to make a request to a domain using the HTTP protocol:

```
http://www.altavista.digital.com/
```

This request will bring us to the default index page for the Alta Vista search engine on the Internet. If you look at this as a GET request it reads: *Using HTTP go to Digital's Alta Vista site and return to me the default page at that site.*

When you make a request in the form at that page the information is sent to the Alta Vista search processor. In this case it is a program in the cgibin directory called query.

```
http://www.altavista.digital.com/cgibin/query
```

This command would, as presented, fail. The reason is that the query program is expecting to see some value-data pairs. Some of these are set hidden and never appear when you look at the form (but are visible if you use the *view source* capability in the browser). Others are the query or search information that you provided. The line it is expecting would look like:

```
http://www.altavista.digital.com/cgibin/query?pg=q&
⇒ what=web&fmt=.&q=%22Tcl+CGI+Development%22
```

This breaks down to:

Protocol: http

Data:

Domain: www.altavista.digital.com

Directory: cgibin

Program: query

Value-data pairs:

> pg=q
>
> what=web
>
> fmt=.
>
> q="Tcl CGI Development"

Note The process is fairly straight forward when dealing with the GET command. The key problem to using this form is that the information returned to the browser using a GET is displayed in the **location area** of the browser. While this is not fatal, it does tend to look, a bit extreme (the technical term was defined by my nephew as "yuckie!"). In the section of this chapter on **headers**, we will discuss the NPH CGI's and how they can be used to eliminate the "yuckie!" factor.

Now that the default method of HTTP is understood (GET), let's talk about a second method for transferring data from the browser to the server. The POST method.

In this method the data is sent from the browser to the server using the standard input file handle. (Think of it as an open pipe that dumps the browser data to the program). The POST method is called using the following HTML:

```
<form method=post action="path/to/the/program" >
<!— here you would but the form items — >
<!— let's not forget to end the form with a submit
button so they can send the data otherwise the data
won't get posted to the server —>
</form>
```

In both cases the data that is passed from the browser to the server is encoded. This allows the communications process to send special sequences and characters. Why would this matter? Consider the following form and the information being sent to the browser as part of the complete answer to a Web-based self-test in grade school.

```
<title>Test Question 9: Addition</title>
<center><h1>Addition<br>Question 9</h1></center>

This is the Web-based flash-card test. It is not
graded. Please respond with the complete equation.

<p>

<hr>
```

```
<p>
3+?=10

<p>
<form method=get action="/cgi-bin/testcheck">

<input type=hidden name=qnum value=9>

Your answer is:<br>

<dl>
<dd> <input type=text name=ans>

</dl>

<p>

<input type=submit value="click here to see if
you're right">

</form>
```

The student in the self test, if they follow the rules, will enter the full and complete formula:

```
3+7=10
```

If this was processed and not encoded, the request to the server would look like this:

```
http://www.mydomain.edu/cgi-bin/testcheck?qnum=9&ans=3+7=10
```

Which breaks down to:

Protocol: http

Data:

Domain: www.mydomain.edu

Directory: cgi-bin

Program: testcheck

Value-data pairs:

qnum=9

ans=3+7=10

Not quite. Actually, if sent unencoded , the message would look like the following to the server:

Protocol: http

Data:

Domain: www.mydomain.edu

Directory: cgi-bin

Program: testcheck

Value-data pairs:

> qnum=9
>
> ans=3<space>7=10

The server will translate the incoming data using the expected encoding and rules. The rules say that a + sign is to decode to a blank space and that the 7=10 should be a separate data value pair. However the data is missing the &, so the entire request would therefore be suspect as an improper URI by the server. Newer servers would generate an error based on these conditions.

In general, the POST method is preferred because it hides the data from the user (you don't get the "yuckie! effect) and POST provides a larger amount of "data" to be passed in. This second feature comes from the fact that POST uses a stream from standard input and just tells the server how much data it is sending (in the environment variable content_length. GET is limited by the by the fact that the data passed in the GET method will be placed in a environment variable called query_string.

One last note as to why the POST method is preferred. Consider the transaction_log file that is maintained by the HTTP server (discussed in detail in Chapter 6, 15 and 16). This file records each and every access to the HTTP process. Here are some lines that could appear in the file. I would ask you to figure out what's wrong with this picture, but I think my highlighting the differences between a GET and a POST format (in bold face type) clearly shows why POST is preferred.

```
a.corp.com - - [06/Sep/1996:20:19:40 -0700] "GET / HTTP/1.0"
⇒ 200 1211
a.corp.com - - [06/Sep/1996:20:21:46 -0700] "POST
⇒ /cgibin/uncgi/chgpasswd.tcl HTTP/1.0" 200 235
```

```
a.corp.com - - [06/Sep/1996:20:20:18 -0700] "GET
⇒/www/dir1/index.html HTTP/1.0" 200 1567
a.corp.com - - [06/Sep/1996:20:20:52 -0700] "GET
⇒/www/dir2/index.html HTTP/1.0" 200 2537
a.corp.com - - [06/Sep/1996:20:21:46 -0700] "GET
⇒/cgibin/uncgi/chgpasswd.tcl?usern=franklyn&oldpasswd=21to23&old
⇒passwdconf=21to23&newpasswd=btru2me  HTTP/1.0" 200 235
a.corp.com - - [06/Sep/1996:20:21:23 -0700] "GET
⇒/www/dir3/index.html HTTP/1.0" 200 5466
a.corp.com - - [06/Sep/1996:20:21:46 -0700] "GET
⇒/www/dir4/index.html HTTP/1.0" 200 8431
```

I'm sure that the author of chgpasswd.tcl had the best of possible intents, but we now know that franklyn has used the password 21to23 (and possibly others in the corp.com domain) on this system. We also know he has changed his password to btru2me on this system, and possibly others. When the POST method is employed as the first highlighted record shows, that information was not recorded in the log files.

The program we use to make calendars on the fly in Chapter 9 clearly shows how you can create a GET URI from both POST and GET formats. As the comments in the code clearly indicate, this process is not for the weak of heart. It can be done, and is useful to do in many respects. But remember that it will create a "yuckie!" return value in the location field of the client browser.

Statelessness and Transactions: Want a Cookie?

One of the most common problems people have with the HTTP protocol is the need to maintain the state of a transaction. In the simplest of terms, the HTTP protocol doesn't allow for it. In order to get around this weakness in the server there is a concept called a *magic cookie*. This concept attempts to allow the stateless connection to appear to be stated, as if the entire transaction is an *extended conversation*.

Consider the way a client-server database works. In this case the client makes a request to the server and opens up a channel (or path) through which they will communicate. There are then overhead tasks that are performed on the database server. These tasks establish the job at hand

and maintain the transaction state of the communication between the client and the server. This is referred to as *a stated connection*.

This differs greatly from the HTTP protocols. HTTP is a *stateless* environment. That means each connection to the server from the client is unique. Therefore, there is no way to establish a any state between the two transactions.

> **Tip** A good analogy is to look at this as if it was a phone switchboard run by a number of operators. In a **stated** transaction a person calls a switchboard number and gets connected to a party at the other end. This connection is then kept as for long as the conversation between the to parties lasts. Once both parties agree to terminate the connection, the call is ended. This is the model that is used by a database client and database server.
>
> Now consider that switchboard in terms of doing an HTTP transaction. In this instance, you call an operator and request a connection. The operator connects you to the party you want. You ask the party a question and the party answers it. You are then disconnected. You now have to go through the connection process again. Unfortunately, you can't just ask another question. You have to include information from the prior conversation to confirm what said before. That's HTTP. This process is shown in Figure 3.1.

What if we could take the stateless environment and make it stated? How could we do that without making changes to the HTTP protocols? These are just two questions that have been asked by many developers.

The answer is by *magic cookies* or just *cookies*. A cookie is a unique identifier that is provided to the browser and is associated to the site from which it is generated. This magic identifier can be tracked and logged by the site that placed the identifier on the client. Using this identifier a site can see how a user moves around the site, bouncing from link to link. In addition, some people use the cookie identification to tag the users cookie with a time stamp this permits them to determine how much time was spent on a page at the site.

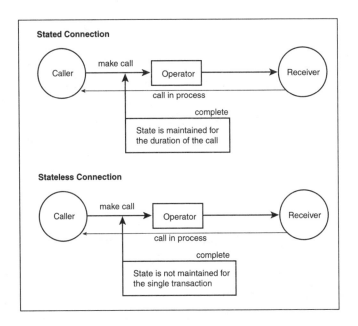

Figure 3.1: *Stated and stateless connections*

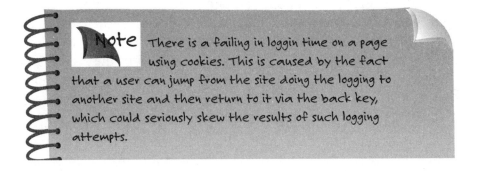

Note There is a failing in loggin time on a page using cookies. This is caused by the fact that a user can jump from the site doing the logging to another site and then return to it via the back key, which could seriously skew the results of such logging attempts.

Cookies Can be Used for Invasive and Non-invasive Purposes

Cookies can be used to maintain user information in ways that some consider to be invasive. Every time the user comes to the server the cookie can be used to update a file of accesses and tracking information. In addition, it might be useful for a site to contain more than the access information on the user or, to associate that access information with personal user information. All of this information could be contained within the cookie, or maintained in special files on the server, and the cookie could contain the name of those files.

In some instances there may be pages at a site where a user can sign up for a chance at a free gift. If the user signs up, the data is added to the cookie-based unique file. After a period of time, site access trends can be seen as we use the cookie information to see where users go within the site. In addition, personal information about the user which we obtained while offering the free gift is also be available. This personal information along with the users habits and usage of the site can be used to do targeted marketing, or to send E-mail to a user to let them know that there is something at the site that might interest them.

This may all sound "big brotherish," but a large number of organizations are using cookies for just those purposes. There are other sites that use cookies to maintain a virtual state, a non-invasive process for which cookies were intended. In this way each connection to the server from the browser appears to be part of a stated transaction. In fact, that is one of the main reasons to use cookies.

Let's revisit the telephone operator analogy. In that example the caller was passed on to an internal location through the operator. Now, let's put some smarts into the phone bank (refer to Figure 3.2). When your call comes in it is assigned a unique identifier that uses your calling number and a date-time stamp. This is similar to a process ID created for you on your initial connection to the server, and the computers time-date stamp. Together they make a great unique cookie identifier.

When the operator transfers your call to the party you want to speak to, an entry is made in a unique log file associated to your unique identifier. You ask the party a question and they answer, also logging the topic/response information in your private log. Then you are disconnected. You dial in again, and the operator sees your unique identifier on the system, and automatically checks your file and passes you back to the party you want to talk with. The party picks up the phone and immediately is told by the system who you are and what was the last query-response.

You ask a another question of the party, and because of the past knowledge the party has, the answer can be built upon the prior response that was given.

If that looks like a stated environment, it is one that exists because the state has been spoofed and appears to be maintained. This is HTTP on cookies.

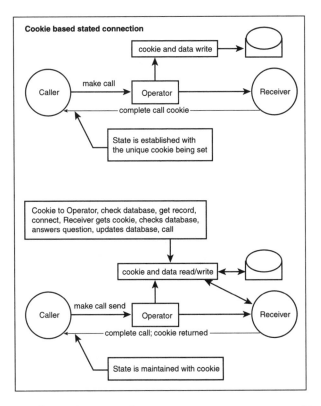

Figure 3.2: *Pseudo-stated connection using passed information*

Using the Netscape preliminary specification, the following line shows how a cookie is supposed to be defined. The values that make up that definition are explained in Table 3.1.

```
Set-Cookie: NAME=VALUE; expires=DATE; path=PATH;
⇒   domain=DOMAINNAME; secure
```

Table 3.1: Cookie format (based on the specifications used by Netscape)

Values	Description
NAME=VALUE	**REQUIRED**: Here you establish your cookie name and it's value. There can be no use of the characters ";" "," or " " unless you use the URL encoding style and force them into hex notation (%[1..f][1..f]).
	Example: MYTRACKER=960825082334-pid13489

Table 3.1 (continued): Cookie format (based on the specifications used by Netscape)

Values	Description
expires=DATE	**OPTIONAL**: You can set an expiry date for the cookie. The date format is defined in RFC's 882, 850, 1036 and 1123 (with the exception of requiring you to use GMT and using the "-" as the date separator) as: Weekday, DD-Mon-YYYY HH:MM:SS GMT If this optional attribute of the cookie is not specified when the cookie is set, then the cookie will have no persistence on the client side, and will expire when the client session is terminated. (Note: Not just the communications with your server, but when they shut down the browser)
	Example: expires=Saturday, 07-Dec-1996 12:00:00 GMT
domain=DOMAIN_NAME	In order for the browser to be able to associate a cookie with a location it creates an association between where it picked up the cookie and the domain it was at when the cookie was assigned. In order to return a cookie the browser will search this list of domains to which it has cookies to see if there is a cookie attached to the URL that it is about to go to.
	The domain searching is done back to front.
	If the URL was www.prenhall.com, the search would start with the fully qualified domain (in this example prenhall.com is the fully qualified domain). If there is no match on the qualified domain name, the search is dropped for that entry and the process moves to the next domain in the list. If a fully qualified domain is found, then the client goes through path matching to see if the cookie should be sent.

Values	Description
	In searching for a qualified domain the client will use a rule set that states that a match is defined by at least two or three periods ("."') within the qualified name. Qualified names in the "top seven" special domains ("EDU", "NET", "COM", "ORG", "MIL", "GOV" and "INT") require the two "."s all others require three periods in the qualified domain name.
	Before you shout that the name prenhall.com only has one period, note that we are saying *qualified domain name*. In order to have a qualified domain name, the system places a period at the end of the name. This makes the prenhall.com domain look like prenhall.com., which is now fully qualified, and has two periods.
	The default value of the domain when the cookie is set is the host that is setting the cookie. This can create problems if you are using a virtual host. For instance, if you have a provider that is setting a cookie on all inbound queries. This could create a problem if you wish to override the cookie, as all queries have a cookie being set by the provider. Below there is an explanation on how you can delete a cookie that has been set from being sent anymore. (The Apache HTTPD server allows the server to set cookies for each person entering the site. These are written to the log file and can be used to track individuals. This could be considered intrusive and is one of the reasons I suggest setting the browser to tell you when someone has assigned a cookie to you).
path=PATH	The path is the location off the root (/) directory that you want to associate with a cookie.

Table 3.1 (continued): Cookie format (based on the specifications used by Netscape)

Values	Description
	This allows you to send numerous cookies back to the client. In the example following this table there is a *shopping cart* method that allows you to store the entire cart in the users client using cookies.
	If a cookie passes domain matching, then the pathname component of the URL is compared with the path attribute. If there is a match, the cookie is considered valid and is transmitted in the header to the server.
	The path "/book" would match "/bookcgi" "/book/cgi/" and "/book/cgi-top.html". The most general path is the root (/). If there is no path specified the default path is the one used in the response from the server as to the path of the document that is being served.
Secure	A secure cookie is one that is only transmitted to a server that is running a secure communications channel. At this time that limits these cookies to only being sent over a channel using HTTPS (HTTP over the SSL security protocol). The default is to not specify a cookie as secure.

As you can see, cookies can provide a great deal of strength to your application. Using this technology allows you to take the non-stated, non-transaction environment of HTTP and spoof a transaction oriented one.

Because cookies are not detailed in Part 2, we have provided some sample Tcl and Perl code here. Listings 3.1 (Tcl) and 3.2 (Perl) show how to create and transmit a cookie from a server to a browser. Listings 3.3 (Tcl) and 3.4 (Perl) show how to create a cookie-file. You could then store information in this file. The filename of the temporary file is now being transmitted back and forth between the browser and the server using the cookie as the transport agent.

Listing 3.1: mkcookie.tcl

```tcl
#!/usr/local/bin/tclsh
## mkcookie.tcl
##
## program to make and set a cookie as part of the
## header return uses the date and the process
## identifier to create a unique identifier the date
## has all spaces replaced with %'s so it can be
## reconstituted if required.
##
## It was decided to use the META tag to ensure that
## any server would be forced to return the cookie as
## part of the header (this even works for old
## versions of NCSA Mosaic).
##
##
## set a temp value using the system date/time
## Note: Requires Tcl7.5 due to "clock"
##
set oval [clock format [clock scan now] -format \
"%d%b%Y%H%M%S"]-[pid]
##
## put the header information, including the cookie
## as a META tag
##
puts "Content-type: text/html\n\n"
puts "<head><META HTTP-EQUIV=\"Set-Cookie\" \
    content=\"newcookie=$oval; expires=09-Nov-99 \
    GMT\">"
##
## title, header and text then exit
##
puts "<title>Cookie set</title></head>"
puts "<h1>Cookie Set</h1>cookie set!"
exit
```

Listing 3.2: mkcookie.pl

```perl
#!/usr/bin/perl
#
# Here's the perl routine to do the same thing
#
$|=1;
$oval = $$ + time;
print << "HTMLHEAD";
```

```
Content-type: text/html
<head><META HTTP-EQUIV="Set-Cookie" content="newcook-
ie=$oval; expires=09-Nov-99 GMT">
<title>Cookie set</title></head><h1>Cookie Set</h1>
cookie set!
HTMLHEAD
```

Listing 3.3: mkcookie2.tcl

```
#!/usr/local/bin/tclsh
## mkcookie2.tcl
##
## program to make and set a cookie as part of the
## header return uses the date and the process
## identifier to create a unique identifier the date
## has all spaces replaced with %'s so it can be
## reconstituted. The date without %s and :s is
## merged with the pid and used to create a temporary
## file. In addition the expiration date is set to
## expire the cookie in two hours
##
## NOTE: Requires Tcl7.5 due to "clock" usage
##
## set a temp value
##
set fval [clock format [clock scan now] -format \
"%d%b%Y%H%M%S"]-[pid]
##
## put the header information, including the cookie
## as a META tag. Note that the expiry is set using
## the system clock on GMT and using the
## expected format.
##
puts "Content-type: text/html\n\n"
puts "<head><META HTTP-EQUIV=\"Set-Cookie\" \
    content=\"newcookie=$fval; \
    expires= [clock format [clock scan "+2 hours"] \
    -format "%d-%b-%Y %H:%M:%S GMT" -gmt T]\">"
##
## create the file
##
[exec touch /tmp/$fval]
##
## title, header and text then exit
##
puts "<title>Cookie set</title></head><h1>Cookie Set</h1>"
puts "cookie set"
exit
```

Listing 3.4: mkcookie2.pl

```perl
#!/usr/bin/perl
#
# Here's the perl routine to do the same thing
#
@monthname = ("Jan","Feb","Mar","Apr","May","Jun",
    "Jul","Aug","Sep","Oct","Nov","Dec");
$|=1;
$oval = $$ + time;
# more portable this way than to use an exec com-
mand.
($sec,$min,$hour,$mday,$mon,$year,$wday,$yday,$isdst)
=    gmtime(time);
$expires = sprintf "%d-%s-%d %d:%d:%d",
    $mday,$monthname[$mon],$year,$hour+2,$min,$sec;
print << "HTMLHEAD";
Content-type: text/html
<head><META HTTP-EQUIV="Set-Cookie" content="newcook-
ie=$oval; expires=$expires GMT">
<title>Cookie set</title></head><h1>Cookie Set</h1>
cookie set!
</head></html>
HTMLHEAD
```

Since not all cookie options are used in these listings, we'll provide some more hints and notes about how cookies work, how they can be used, and a few transaction examples. The specifications for how cookies work are not formalized. Listings 3.1 through 3.4 will work with the specifications that were developed by Netscape and have been presented to the Standards Committee to be included as a formal part of the specification (in HTML 3.2).

Assuming that there is a single cookie in the browser that matches your qualified domain, you would see this returned to the server from the browser:

```
Cookie: NAME=COOKIE_STRING;
```

If there is more than one name value matching the URL of the HTTP request, then the browser will send all the matching cookies over is a single string. That would look like:

```
Cookie: NAME=COOKIE_STRING1; NAME=COOKIE_STRING2;
NAME=COOKIE_STRING3...
```

The NAME value in each of the cookies could be different, or the same. There are pros and cons to using either method of assigning the name to the cookie. For example, a tight loop in Tcl or Perl could find all values associated to a common NAME and store them in a common array by that name. The values then could be looked at as a string of relations to the name that was used.

For example, we could have a NAME of PURITM for purchase items in our shopping cart. In the cookie we store every item selected for purchase into a PURITM cookie. When a user checks out, there are 12 PURITMs in the cookie. The items values were stored as part numbers in a database. Prices and availability are determined from that database. We can take the items and put them into an array that we sort and then use to speed up the database lookup. Listings 3.5 through 3.8 provide the sample code in both Tcl and Perl.

Listing 3.5: getcookie.tcl

```tcl
#!/usr/local/bin/tclsh
## getcookie.tcl
##
## gets the cookie and displays it
##
proc cookie-err {} {
  puts "error with cookie handling"
  exit
}
##
## put the standard header information
##
puts "Content-type: text/html\n\n"
puts "<title>Cookie please</title>"
##
## If the variable that cookies are placed into
## exists then grab the cookie
##
if { [info exists env(HTTP_COOKIE) ] } {
  set icookie $env(HTTP_COOKIE)
} else {
  cookie-err
}
##
## display the cookie
##
puts $icookie
exit
```

Listing 3.6: getcookie.pl

```perl
# ===================================================
#!/usr/local/bin/perl
$| = 1;
print "Content-type: text/html\n\n<title>Cookie
please</title>";

#
$cookie = $contents{'HTTP_COOKIE'};
if ($cookie eq "") { print "<H1> No cookies! </H1>";
} else {
     print $cookie ;
}
```

Listing 3.7: getcookie1.tcl

```tcl
!/usr/local/bin/tclsh
## getcookie1.tcl
##
## gets the cookie and processes multiple cookies
## into an array. The cookie array is then dumped to
## the screen using a reverse sort
##
proc cookie-err {} {
 puts "error with cookie handling"
exit
}
##
## standard header output
##
puts "Content-type: text/html\n\n"
puts "<title>Cookie please</title>
##
## If the cookie exists process it
##
if { [info exists env(HTTP_COOKIE) ] } {
  set icookie $env(HTTP_COOKIE)
} else {
  cookie-err
}
##
## for each cookie in the string, load the cookie
## into an array item and then load all the array
## values into a list for sorting [this wasn't
## required, we could have used the "array names"
## command to get the names of the array values
```

```
## instead. Why use this? It shows another way to do
## it. The "array names" method is use quite a bit in
## later examples ]
##
set caray ""
foreach cooki [split $icookie \;] {
 set aray [string trim \
     [lindex [split $cooki \=] 0] ]
 set val($aray) [lindex [split $cooki \=] 1]
 puts "set val($aray) [lindex [split $cooki \=] 1]"
 set caray "$caray $aray"
 puts $cooki
}
##
## Reverse the order and display
##
foreach aray [lsort -decreasing $caray] {
 puts "$aray == $val($aray)"
}
exit
```

Listing 3.8: getcookie1.pl

```
#!/usr/local/bin/perl

$| = 1;
print "Content-type: text/html\n\n";

$cookie = $contents{'HTTP_COOKIE'};

if ($cookie eq "") { print "<H1> No cookies! </H1>";
exit 0; }

@crumbs = split(';',$cookies); # split on semi-colons
foreach (reverse sort @crumbs) {
($lv,$rv) = split '='; # split x=y, the $_ is
implied
# you can also use: ($lv,$rv) = split('=',$_);
print "$lval $rval<p>";
}
```

Cookie Notes

Here are some quick notes on cookies.

- You can set numerous cookies in a single header

- An expires header doesn't require the client to eliminate the cookie, but states that it should no longer provide that cookie back to the server.

- A cookie can be deleted by the server if it sends a matching cookie (with the same name) and an expires value that has already passed. This will move the cookie to a non-returnable state. At some point, the client will purge it from the clients storage.

- A cookie could be removed from a client prior to a set expiration date if the user has too many cookies in the client.

- If you use the same path and name for a cookie that is returned to the client, that the client already had, then it will overwrite the former instance.

- Cookie names and paths are linked. Using a path of a higher level, but the same cookie name, will not override the more specific instances that existed. It will, on the other hand, add an additional cookie reference to be returned to the server.

- Client Storage Limits for Cookies:

  1. 300 total cookies

  2. The name and the COOKIE_STRING value must be less than 4 kilobytes.

  3. A maximum of 20 cookies per server or domain/host (a fully specified host has a 20 cookie maximum value beyond that of the 20 for the domain).

  4. If the 300-cookie, or the 20-cookie per server, limit is exceeded the client is supposed to delete the least recently used cookie. Cookies exceeding the 4 kilobytes limit will be trimmed to fit.

Cookie Examples

Tables 3.2 and 3.3, and the following text contain transaction examples to show how cookies work within the Web-based client-server environment.

Table 3.2: Sample cookie exchange

Description	Exchange
Server obtains a document request from the Client and responds with:	Set-Cookie: ACTOR=willis; path=/; expires=Wednesday, 16-Nov-99 23:59:59 GMT
Any time the client processor requests a URL in path "/" on this and only this server, it sends:	Cookie: ACTOR=willis
Client requests and selects an item from the form, and receives in the response:	Set-Cookie: WARDROBE=rippedT; path=/
The client requests a URL in path "/" on this server, it sends:	Cookie: ACTOR=willis; WARDROBE=rippedT
The client goes to another page on the site (path /dieharder-rain and fills out the form on special makeup for the scene. Cookie returned:	Set-Cookie: MAKEUP=2ozBlood_3cuts_ 10bruises_blackReye; path=/dieharder-rain
When client requests a URL in path /dieharder-rain on this and only this server, the following cookie is also sent:	Cookie: ACTOR=willis WARDROBE=rippedT MAKEUP=2ozBlood_3cuts_ 10bruises_blackReye;

In this example we are going to another server. This server maintains information on a clients tastes in cigars. Specifically, it uses past purchase information to determine if the page it generates should have recommendations based on past buying patterns.

Information on *types of items* is recorded in 5-character identifiers with a number appended to show the quantity (quantity stock identifier) and an "s" appended to show if the purchase was a special. All final sales are recorded with a cookie with a listing of all identifiers separated by underscores and a six-numeric date field appended to the cookie name (ensuring a unique identifier for each sale).

So the final cookie would look like:

```
PURCHASE_960515=RJCBA2_MAPOR1S_ARIEL3S
```

This shows that the purchase on May 15, 1996 was for 3 items; RJCBA (Romeo and Juliet from Havana 2 boxes), MAPOR1S (Macanudo Portofino 1 box on special) and ARIEL3S (Ariel's 3 boxes on special).

Using this information we can see that the customer has a taste for fine cigars, prefers them on special and tends to order more than one item at a time. If the customer had also ordered a *GCLIP1* (Gold Clipper used to cut the end of the cigar) we would also be able to say that the customer is also willing to purchase high quality items that are used as accessories.

Using this information we can start a search (using a CGI script) that would seek out special offers on high end cigars in box or multi-box lots, or specials on fine accessories. Then we would be able to offer the customer an initial page that was tailored to his tastes and interests. In order to ensure that we keep current with the customer's interests, but don't overuse the space in the customers client, we will, after 10 purchases, assign a new identifier to the customer and write the cookie information into a special log file along with his e-mail address. Then we will expire all the cookie information except for the unique identifier.

When the customer orders now, the system will open his customer record and review his buying patterns, interests and habits and create the page that was generated by using that data. In addition, we can also run special jobs that permit us to see if we have anything in the weekly specials that may interest the customer. We can send the customer an e-mail when we see that there are three items of more that come close to meeting their interests and needs.

In other words, we can be proactive and help the customer. I would suggest creating a screen that allows the customer to choose whether or not to be on an automated mailing list. There is nothing worse than unwanted junk e-mail.

Table 3.3: More sample cookie exchanges

Description	Exchange
Client returns to site for fifth time. Client sends:	Cookie: PURCHASE_960515=RJCBA2_MAPOR1S_ARIEL3S PURCHASE_960615=RJCBA1_MAPOR3_ARIEL1 PURCHASE_960715=MAPOR2S PURCHASE_960815=RJCBA2_HONDR3S CUSTID=2177
Client picks one item to purchase and the system returns the new cookie to go with the old ones	Set-Cookie: PURCHASE_960915=MAPOR3
A different client comes in and has made a number of purchases. Client sends:	Cookie: CUSTID=2177 UNIQKEY=960810 (note: in this case I am using a unique ID that is the date the file was created)
The server returns a page of interesting specials, after reviewing the information in 960810.2177, from which the customer can purchase. The customer selects the items from the screen and transverses the site picking up more items as they do so. Each individual purchase would be placed into a current cookie. Finally the customer completes that sale and the current cookie is sent an expiration command and the data is written out to the customer's datafile. The server returns no new information.	Note: The client could have been receiving a new cookie after each "selection" was completed. This would have allowed the cookie space to be used to record the current purchase.

These examples are very similar to a shopping cart script. These scripts are used to allow you to browse a site and add items to a virtual shopping basket. At the end of the transactions you can total your basket, remove items from it, or check out. Placing orders for all the items in the basket and entering a purchase transaction mode would complete your involvement at the site and empty the shopping basket (remove all the product cookies through forced expiration).

> **Note** In the best of worlds, that is all the process would do. Unfortunately you can't control unscrupulous operators. They could use your purchasing information (along with the packing slip you just completed that has all your personal information in it) to develop and sell directed mailing lists. Or worse yet, use it to make purchases in your name from legitimate operations. So, be very careful when you use the Internet and allow cookies.

To help you control your client, many browsers provide the option of whether or not you accept cookies. In Netscape 3.0 it's through OPTIONS/NETWORK PREFERENCES. There you can select the tab Protocols. This tab selection screen allows you to set the browser cookie function as an *alert required* function. Doing this causes the browser to show an alert button prior to accepting a cookie from a server. Use it. It's amazing to see who thinks that they have the right to set cookies on you (and possibly record information that you don't want tracked).

Figure 3.3 shows the response you get when a site attempts to load cookies in Netscape 3.0.

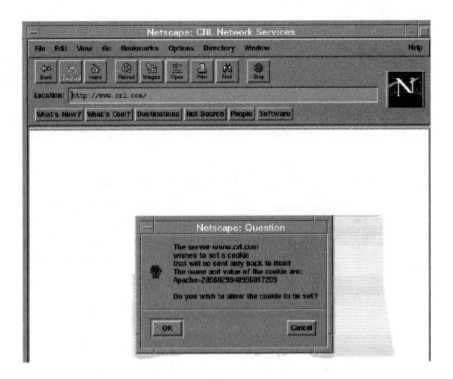

Figure 3.3: *The value of using alert required*

Headers: What They Mean to Your Process (NPH)

When a HTTP server returns information to the client, it uses the *MIME* type to tell the client what it is returning. If you have a client browser open you can bring up the options or preferences section. Once there, you should be able see the area where you can define the options that are available in regards to handling the various MIME types (and what file extensions to which the mime types are associated).

Standard headers that almost every client should be able to understand are shown in Table 3.4.

It is important to remember that the CGI program must return a blank line after any header. This is a common error made by most CGI programmers. In fact, if your CGI doesn't appear to be functioning properly, this is first place check. Make sure that your response looks like:

```
Content-type: text/html \n\n
```

In most languages the carriage return is expressed with the \n character.

Table 3.4: Standard headers returned by CGI programs

Header	Description
Content-type:	The only required header. This header is the mime-type declaration. In the data portion of this header a proper MIME type in the format of type/sub-type must be supplied.
	Example: text/html
Content-length:	This field is used to specify the length of the data being returned in bytes. If it is omitted the server supplies the response. The size must be specified in the number of bytes being returned.
	Example: 1024
Content-encoding:	While not used by everyone (since this information can be supplied by using the clients Mime types defaults) this is a way to specify the encoding method that was used to compress the file. There are two acceptable responses that can be passed to the client. These are: x-gzip (if the file was compressed with the GNU gzip compression method) and x-zip-compress (if the file was compressed with the standard unix compress command).
Expires:	Back when we talking about security and how caching could defeat your logging of information I kept a secret on how the problem of caching could be overcome. The CGI programmer can expire the documents that the clients are served. This allows a date and time (in GMT) to be inserted into the header information. This header information states that a document is no longer considered a

Table 3.4 (continued): Standard headers returned by CGI programs

Header	Description
	valid response from the server. If the document is cached and the client goes for the cached copy and sees the expired header it will go back and get a new copy from the original server.
	Example: Sunday 25-Sep-96 23:00 GMT
Location:	This is used to do a piece of magic called *Redirection*. In Chapter 7 there are examples of how redirection use can enhance a site (click on an advertisement banner. This banner calls a local program to register the click-through, and then redirects your click to a new location).
	Example: http://www.wwinfo.com/fifree/
Status:	Returns the status code for the page. Common status codes are 200 (success), 302 (redirect), 400 (bad request), 500 (server internal error) and the most common 404 (document not found).
	When a redirect is sent the headers used are generally: Status 302 Location: http://site/path/file.

It should also be noted that two of these headers allow the CGI program to talk to the server, not the client. The Status: header is read by the server. Based on the code in the header, the server will return the proper status page to the client for that error response. In a number of HTTP servers this response is a file that is configurable from within the startup configuration files.

Location: is the other header that is processed by the HTTP server instead of the client. In this case the server will redirect the request to the new location rather than return that information to the client and force the client to call the redirected page.

In a number of places this book refers to the "yuckie!" factor of returning all the header information that the document request had in it to the client. This "yuckie!" factor can be over come through the use of non-parsed headers.

A non-parsed header is one that the server knows not to touch. It returns all the data directly to the client as it is specified in the response. In doing this the non-parsed header file must take over many of the automated tasks that the server performs when it returns the data to the client. In simple terms, this means more actual work and responsibility in on the hands of the CGI programmer.

To use a non-parsed header the CGI programmer must first ensure that the CGI program uses a special naming convention. This way the server won't parse the information that it returns. This naming convention states that all non-parsed header programs start with the prefix nph- in the filename.

> **Note** That doesn't mean that a programmer can use a file called Nph-doit.cgi. Nph- is not the same as nph- or nphdoit.cgi (it **must** be nph-) or doit.cgi-nph (it goes in the front, not in the back). If it seems like I'm beating a dead horse here, I am. Using non-parsed headers isn't generally recommended. It may get rid of the "yuckie!" factor, but it is also giving up all the capabilities that the server provides as part of it's processing. For instance, you can't send a Status: or Location: header, because the nph- program isn't parsed by the server and the client won't know what to do with a header that comes back as Location: /newdoc/location/document.html".

Server Side Includes

As we have seen, CGI scripts offer a great deal of power to a Web site. They allow a site to be active and the option to change. Cookies and other tools can also help a site meet the needs of a customer. But what about simple things like accurately displaying a modification date? What if I want to have a counter (discussed in Chapter 6)? Isn't there another way to do this that won't require that I build the page from scratch every time?

The answer to these common questions is *yes*, through a process called Server Side Includes (SSIs). These are commands embedded in the HTML file that look like comments that perform special duties. These command allow you to access special environment variables, access system commands, and even run CGI programs that perform numerous functions and expand that capabilities of the standard HTML page.

There is a drawback with the SSIs model, though. It causes the server to perform more work. The use of SSIs requires that the server parse the lines of the HTML file prior to returning the file. When it does that the load on the server increases, which could have a negative impact on your server performance and your interaction with your customers/users.

Earlier we showed how the datetime.tcl procedure could be used to place the local server date and time on a page returned to the user. The HTML for that SSI procedure is two lines:

```
<title>Test page</title>
<!—#exec cgi="/cgi-bin/datetime.tcl" —>
```

That's it! The whole .shtml file at it's most minimal level. It puts a title and then calls the Tcl CGI to perform the activity. Let's take a closer look at what an SSI can really do.

First the format of an SSI is:

```
<!—#command tag1="value1" tag2="value2" —>
```

This format allows for a server (without SSIs) to view the code as a comment. On the other hand, a parsing server would know that this is an SSI request from the # sign, which indicates that a command is following.

If permitted to, SSIs can run any CGI procedure from a POST or a GET, as long as the procedure doesn't require that any data be passed into it. CGIs are not permitted to use the GET or POST format. The environment variables in Table 3.7 are not supported in SSI execs.

Each SSI command takes different arguments. Some are allowed to have more than one tag (although most don't). Table 3.5 shows the commands, their tags, and a description of how and why the command is used.

Table 3.5: SSI commands and tags

Command	Tag	Description
config	errmsg defines the message returned to the client in the case of an error while parsing. Errors, if they occur are logged in the HTTP Server's error log. Timefmt gives the server a new format to use when providing dates. In Unix it uses the same formatting values used in the strftime library call. Sizefmt is used much like timefmt, but in this case it is used to define the format of sizes of files. File size information can be returned as the number of bytes in the file (the bytes tag value) or using the tag value abbrev the file size will be returned as the number of kilobytes or megabytes.	config is used to define formats for display of both time and file sizes.
include	virtual allows the path given in the tag to be a *virtual* path to a document on the HTTP Server using the Document Root, or a defined Root on the server as the starting point. While the virtual tag allows you to include another .shtml (parsed) file, it will not allow you to access a CGI script in this manner. The file tag allows a path relative to the current	The include SSI command allows the insertion of text or another parsed document into a parsed document.

Table 3.5 (continued): SSI commands and tags

Command	Tag	Description
	directory. The limitations to this are that the uplevel format of "../" is not permitted in this path. Additionally an absolute path can not be used either. This format is best used when you want to include a file that is in the current directory, or one that is under the current directory structure.	
echo	The tag var is used to echo the value of an environment variable (see the table below)	This command allows the value of one of the include variables to be inserted in the output. Dates and filesizes are output in the formats that were defined for them in the config command.
fsize	valid tags are the same as the include command.	This command prints the file size of the specified file. It will use the format as defined in the config command.
flastmod	valid tags are the same as the include command.	This is how you get the *date the file was last modified* in the footer of the displayed HTML (actually, some editors will save it there using macros, but in the case of using and SSI, this is how it's done. Once again, the format is defined using the config command.

exec	The value cmd can be used to pass a shell command to the HTTP Server to be parsed. Yes, this is a dangerous command as a SSI could be written to issue the command "rm -rf /*". The method of protecting yourself from this is discussed in the chapter on system configuration and security in Section 3. The other possible value CGI was shown and discussed in the example that started this portion of the chapter. The path to the CGI is one of the virtual paths defined in the configuration files for the HTTP Server. Be aware that the server performs no error checking, so if you generated a binary dump or a gif file to the standard output it will make a lovely mess of the returned display.	Permits the SSI to issue Unix shell command or run a CGI from a valid CGI virtual path.

The echo command with the var tag listed in Table 3.5 permits you to echo certain environment variables so that they could be inserted into the document. Table 3.6 lists the variable names and their values.

Table 3.6: Accessible Variables in SSIs

Variable	Values
DOCUMENT_NAME	The filename of the document being accessed
DOCUMENT_URI	The virtual path to this document (note that the document URI doesn't include the document root information, so a document at /usr3/wwwspot/docs/thisdoc.shtml would be displayed as /docs/thisdoc.shtml if the document root was set as /usr3/wwwspot

Table 3.6 (continued): Accessible Variables in SSIs

Variable	Values
DATE_LOCAL	The current date and local time zone. (a simple replacement for the datetime.tcl CGI) the format is subject to the format as defined in the config command
DATE_GMT	DATE_LOCAL but in Greenwich mean time
LAST_MODIFIED	The last modification date of the current file in a format as defined by the config command (yes this does appear to duplicate the flastmod command)

The HTML file used in Chapter 9 has the selection of the month and the year on the form set by default. The following two Tcl SSI procedures shown in Listings 3.9 and 3.10 (called with an "<!—#exec cgi="/cgi-bin/[filename].tcl"—>) can be used to generate the current month and year as the selected values.

Listing 3.9: getmon.tcl

```
#!/usr/local/bin/tclsh
puts "Content-type: text/html\n\n"
##
## getmon.tcl
## gets and returns month data for the calendar program
## sets the select statements to default to the current month
## requires that it be called as /cgi-bin/getmon.tcl
##
set molist "<option>Jan <option>Feb <option>Mar <option>Apr \
  <option>May <option>Jun <option>Jul <option>Aug <option>Sep \
  <option>Oct <option>Nov <option>Dec"
set curmo [lindex [exec date] 1]
regsub <option>$curmo $molist "\"<option selected>$curmo\""\
 newmolst
foreach mon $newmolst {
 puts "$mon"
}
```

```
#!/usr/local/bin/tclsh
puts "Content-type: text/html\n\n"
##
## getyr.tcl
##
## gets and returns year data for the calendar program (as an
## ssi) sets the select statements to default to the
## current year
## requires that it be called as /cgi-bin/getyr.tcl
##
set yrlist "<option>1995 <option>1996 <option>1997 \
  <option>1998 <option>1999 <option>2000"
set curyr [lindex [exec date] end]
regsub <option>$curyr $yrlist "\"<option selected>$curyr\"" \
  newyrlst
foreach yr $newyrlst {
 puts "$yr"
}
```

Environment Variables

One of the best features of the HTTP clients-server functionality (for those of us who write CGI programs) is that the system has been designed to tell us all sorts of things about the server and the client. This enables us to perform specialized processing based on client or server information. This information is passed into the environment as environment variables.

Below are a list of environment variables that are passed into the system or expected to be passed into the system in the NCSA server.

The environment variables in Table 3.7 are not request-specific and are set for all requests that are processed by the NCSA HTTPD server (version 1.53).

Based on the type of request that is being performed by the server, any of the variables in Table 3.8 can be passed by the server into the CGI environment (again, these are used in NCSA HTTP 1.53).

Table 3.7: Available Environment Variables to non-SSI on NCSA HTTP 1.5

Variable	Description
SERVER_SOFTWARE	The name and version of the information server software answering the request (and running the gateway). This information shows up in the access_log file and has the format of: name/version (ex: HTTP/1.0)
SERVER_NAME	The server's hostname, DNS alias, or IP address
GATEWAY_INTERFACE	The revision of the CGI specification used on the server. Format: CGI/revision (ex: CGI/1.0)

Table 3.8: Additional Environment Variables

Variable	Description
SERVER_PROTOCOL	The name and revision of the information protocol this request came in with. The format of the environment variable is: protocol/revision
SERVER_PORT	The port number to which the request was sent (generally port 80)
REQUEST_METHOD	The method that the browser used to make the request (ex: "GET", "POST", etc.) This piece of information is also logged in the access_log.
PATH_INFO	The extra path information, as given by the client. To see how this can be used, look at some of the examples that follow.
PATH_TRANSLATED	The server provides a translated version of PATH_INFO. The PATH_INFO data is decoded and any virtual-to-physical mapping required will be done. The resultant output is stored in this variable.

Variable	Description
SCRIPT_NAME	A virtual path to the script being executed. NCSA says that it can be used for self-referencing URLs. I have yet to see a real good use for this, but I could be wrong
QUERY_STRING	The information which follows the ? in the URI that called the CGI. This is part of the GET processor. The query information has been discussed earlier in this chapter. Including why you may not want to use get requests (for security reasons).
REMOTE_HOST	The hostname making the request. If this is unset look to see if the value in REMOTE_ADDR has been set. *THIS IS NOT TO BE TRUSTED INFORMATION*
REMOTE_ADDR	The IP address of the remote host. *THIS IS NOT TO BE TRUSTED INFORMATION*
AUTH_TYPE	If the server supports user authentication, the value in this variable defines which protocol-specific authentication method is to be used to validate the user.
REMOTE_USER	If the server supports user authentication, a protected CGI will use this user name for authentication. *THIS IS NOT TO BE TRUSTED INFORMATION*
REMOTE_IDENT	If the HTTP server supports RFC 931 identification, then this variable will be set to the remote user name retrieved from the server. *THIS IS NOT TO BE TRUSTED INFORMATION (use it for logging only)*
CONTENT_TYPE	This defines the attached information when using the POST method.
CONTENT_LENGTH	The length of the content in stdin as determined by the client.

The NCSA server (and most others) also supports the use of special header information using the special prefix HTTP_ followed by a header name like ACCEPT. If there are dashes "-" in the header name, those dashes will be translated into underbars "_" (CONTENT-TYPE would become CONTENT_TYPE) . The NCSA server also will not reprocess a header that was already processed without the HTTP_ prefixing. So, if the header Authorization is already processed, it would be ignored under the name of HTTP_AUTHORIZA-TION. Finally, if any single HTTP_ environment variable exceeds the servers environment variable limitations (if there are any), the server will not process them into the environment. That makes the HTTP_ variables insecure to use, but worth a try if you really need the information contained therein.

An interesting example of this is the variable HTTP_USER_AGENT. In this case the browser is telling the server about what browser is being used to send the request. This particular variable is very useful if you want to make decisions on what type of information you are going to load to the client based on the User-agent information that they pass. An example of this would be a page that responds with a "best viewed in <browser>" button with an associated link at the bottom of the page, and always using some browser other than the one that is viewing the page. Okay, that's cruel, how about we use it to determine if the browser can handle tables within tables, something Netscape does well, and NCSA Mosaic (at this time) doesn't do very well.

Server Side Includes have a separate list of environment variables available to them when they are used within the HTML file. Go back and re-read the last section if you missed them.

Summary

In this section we focused on client server communication issues and on server side issues that have an effect on what a CGI can and can not do. We also covered some of the more advanced concepts of CGI development including using cookies to maintain state information and the use of Server Side Includes.

This information should provide you a firm base from which to understand the how and the why of utilizing the HTTP Server and the power inherent in the CGI.

Chapter 4 attempts to eliminate two major issues. The first deals with the almost religious-like wars that start when developers claim that their language is the best for developing CGI programs or scripts. The second issue will deal with the concerns people have about decoding the passed data from a GET or POST command. Examples of how to do that in a number of different languages will be discussed. You'll also be treated to some debugging hints and tips.

CHAPTER 4
LANGUAGES, DATA, AND DEBUGGING

- Why Tcl and Perl?

- Unencoding Data

- Debugging Issues

In this chapter, we will cover why Tcl and Perl were chosen for this text, we will mention some of the advantages and the disadvantages of those choices, and we will discuss some strengths related to both languages.

We will then explain the various ways that data can be unencoded when it is sent to a CGI with either a GET or a POST. This discussion will include methods for unencoding in both Tcl and Perl, as well as introduce a program called uncgi that will be used in the book.

Finally, we will wrap up both this chapter and this section of the book with some issues on how to debug your CGIs.

Let the wars begin!

Languages

Ask almost any programmer what is the best language in which to write programs, and he will respond with the language of which he has the most detailed understanding. This is a normal behavior pattern. Get two programmers together who have strengths in different languages and they will most likely agree to disagree, as each will hold that his language is the better one to use. Get three together and it doesn't matter if all three disagree or, if it becomes two against one. THIS IS WAR!

So, we expect that those of you who are Perl programmers will agree to disagree with what is said about Tcl, and the Tcl group will agree to disagree with what is said about Perl. On the other hand, you C programmers are going to want to flame this book for not presenting C as the language in which to write CGI code. And then there are the Scheme programmers. FORTRAN? COBOL? RPG?

Let's cut through the smoke and haze of this issue right now. Every language has its strengths and its weaknesses. Languages are tools we use to enforce the rules of logic on bits of data. Some languages are built to suit certain tasks better than others. We wouldn't use COBOL for an AI application, and we most likely wouldn't choose LISP for a business application. Every language is like a tool within a toolbox and although some can do double duty, you don't sink screws with hammers if it can be avoided.

Tcl and Perl were chosen for varied reasons. Both languages have the following common strengths in CGI development.

- They are highly portable
- They are interpreted
- They are script-based
- They are well supported
- They have a strong community of users
- They have an established tradition of successful commercial applications
- They have well documented texts on usage
- Best of all, they are free

Now, as long as we stay with ANSI C and don't use any advanced features, some of that list is true. We could even say that it is free (the compiler) via the GNU software libraries. In fact, we could point out that there are far more texts on C programming than there are on Perl and on Tcl combined. In fact, In Fact, IN FACT! There are more C programmers than there are Tcl and Perl programmers combined... why I'll even bet there are more Visual Basic (VB) programmers than there are . . . And we can digress from there.

Folks, the bottom line is that this book uses Tcl and Perl, not C, not VB, not Scheme, FORTRAN, COBOL, RPG, LISP (common or uncommon) and not even Java. Now, here is why we choose to use Perl and Tcl, beyond the above-stated reasons.

Tcl

Tcl, or the Tool Command Language, is not generally thought of as a stand-alone tool. That has to do with the fact that Tcl is generally bundled with Tk, a graphical interface toolkit that supports graphical standards (X/Motif). Tk provides a common graphical language that has become platform independent across a number of differing graphical platforms, including Windows-95, MacOS and more flavors of Unix than we would care to count.

The fact that Tcl is so closely coupled with Tk has a great deal to do with how the language and the toolkit came into being. Back in the mid-1980s, Dr. John Ousterhout, a professor at the University of California, Berkeley, ran into a small problem. He wanted a language that could bind together many different other things (or tools) that he had built. Therefore, he created Tcl as a glue language that allowed him to bind his tools together (we haven't done justice to John's work here. We highly recommend his excellent text on the language for further reference). John also created the graphical toolkit: an X-based extension to Tcl which allowed programmers to create graphical interfaces within the language. This would allow Tcl to be used as the communicator between a simple graphical interface and a series of tools. Tcl became the middleware to bind the components of his architecture together.

Well, he got much more than he bargained for. Today the language that he originally thought of as component glue is being used to create real run-time applications that operate power plants and offshore oil rigs. It has grown up quite a bit. It also has proven to be a very strong language for CGI due to its component history.

In Chapters 2 and 3, we talked about client-server models. We even touched on the client-server model where the server also acts as a client for another server. In simple terms, Tcl being used as a CGI language brings it back to its roots as component middleware. Tcl is the glue that holds two different applications together. The key difference is that the Tk portion of Tcl has been replaced with a browser-based client and the communication path is through standard input and standard output to a server. Tcl is back where it started from in this model, the glue that exists between different applications and allows them to work together.

This explains why we believe that Tcl is a good choice to fill the role of a CGI, since that was the task for which it was primarily designed.

Perl

Perl is the language of choice for a lot of system administrators and Web masters. There are many reasons for choosing Perl to do particular tasks. First of all, Perl is portable to many operating systems, including Windows NT, Windows-95 and the Macintosh. Its readily available from the Internet at no cost and is updated every few months. In addition to this, the wonderful parsing features coupled with its use of associative arrays make Perl a very natural choice for processing CGI applications. Perl is easily extensible through the use of Modules that offer a wide array of functionality, such as handling CGI requests, database base access, HTML encoding, and a host of other topics.

 Note One such Module is the CGI.pm module written by Lincoln D. Stein, (lstein@genome.wi.mit.edu). The CGI.pm module makes HTML/CGI encoding in a Perl script look like Perl code. The only real reason for not using the CGI.pm module was that the folks supporting some of the Perl code shown here are not Perl programmers. They know HTML quite well and were able to follow Perl code that generated HTML tags, but the CGI.pm usage confused them. In the interest of maintenance, we chose to use simple Perl code that gave a non-Perl programmer an idea of how HTML tags were being generated.

Also, Perl offers great Object Oriented Programming (OOP) features starting from Perl 5. This book did not target these features, and attempted to use those features that are found in Perl 4. Yes, there are some exceptions to this rule (using the upper case and lower case features was a bit of cheating...but you can write your own Perl 4 functions quite easily). Using the CGI.pm module would have required the explanation of the use of modules and OOP in Perl. That would have proved to be distracting from the purpose of this book.

Its power, portability, strong string manipulation capabilities and extensibility make Perl a very comfortable choice for CGI processing.

Language Conclusions

We have chosen Tcl and Perl because they are easy to use, easy to learn, easy to modify, highly portable, and they have strong user communities and are free of charge. That doesn't mean that your particular language isn't good for your needs; it means that we wanted to make this book useful for a large percentage of the people who will use it.

We also chose two languages for one final key reason: so you would see that the concepts are portable, that you can move from syntax to syntax and that the key isn't what language in which the code is written, but in what we are attempting to accomplish.

We really want you, the reader, to not see this as a language issue, but to see this as a series of problems that need to be solved. And what better way to transition into the first problem that we will have to solve, that of communication between the server and the CGI routines.

Unescaping

We have already talked a bit about URLs and, in Chapter 5, we will be diving into forms and data passing. Before we get there let's look at how we obtain the data that is passed.

Data passed in to the CGI is passed in via standard input, or via environment variables (POST verses GET). This input is in a fashion that is referred to as encoded. That means that the input has been translated in some way. The translation is to ensure that special characters are transportable. These characters are escaped or translated to a format that can be passed without using the special character in the format.

In this case, the HTTPd standard is to process these special characters in a method referred to as hexifying. The characters are translated to their hexadecimal value and that value is inserted in place of the original character. Then, in a few instances, special characters are used to replace other characters that would not transfer well, or have other meanings within the protocol.

For all the gory details on this, see RFC 1738 (available at: http://andrew2.andrew.cmu.edu/rfc/rfc1738.html). We have included the portion specific to encoding (Section 2.2 of the document) in the following sidebar.

RFC 1738: Section 2.2: URL Character Encoding

RFC 1738:
Editors:
Berners-Lee (CERN)
L. Masinter (Xerox Corporation),
M. McCahill (University of Minnesota)
Dated: December 1994
Section 2.2:

2.2. URL Character Encoding Issues

URLs are sequences of characters, i.e., letters, digits, and special characters. A URL may be represented in a variety of ways: e.g., ink on paper, or a sequence of octets in a coded character set. The interpretation of a URL depends only on the identity of the characters used.

In most URL schemes, the sequences of characters in different parts of a URL are used to represent sequences of octets used in Internet protocols. For example, in the ftp scheme, the host name, directory name and file names are such sequences of octets, represented by parts of the URL. Within those parts, an octet may be represented by the character which has that octet as its code within the US-ASCII [20] coded character set.

In addition, octets may be encoded by a character triplet consisting of the character "%" followed by the two hexadecimal digits (from "0123456789ABCDEF") which form the hexadecimal value of the octet. (The characters "abcdef" may also be used in hexadecimal encodings.)

Octets must be encoded if they have no corresponding graphic character within the US-ASCII coded character set, if the use of the corresponding character is unsafe, or if the corresponding character is reserved for some other interpretation within the particular URL scheme.

No corresponding graphic US-ASCII:

URLs are written only with the graphic printable characters of the US-ASCII coded character set. The octets 80-FF hexadecimal are not used in US-ASCII, and the octets 00-1F and 7F hexadecimal represent control characters; these must be encoded.

Unsafe:

Characters can be unsafe for a number of reasons. The space character is unsafe because significant spaces may disappear and insignificant spaces may be introduced when URLs are transcribed or typeset or subjected to the treatment of word-processing programs. The characters "<" and ">" are unsafe because they are used as the delimiters around URLs in free text; the quote mark (""") is used to delimit URLs in some systems. The character "#" is unsafe and should always be encoded because it is used in World Wide Web and in other systems to delimit a URL from a fragment/anchor identifier that might follow it. The character "%" is unsafe because it is used for encodings of other characters. Other characters are unsafe because gateways and other transport agents are known to sometimes modify such characters. These characters are "{", "}", "|", "\", "^", "~", "[", "]", and "`".

All unsafe characters must always be encoded within a URL. For example, the character "#" must be encoded within URLs even in systems that do not normally deal with fragment or anchor identifiers, so that if the URL is copied into another system that does use them, it will not be necessary to change the URL encoding.

Reserved:

Many URL schemes reserve certain characters for a special meaning: their appearance in the scheme-specific part of the URL has designated semantics. If the character corresponding to an octet is reserved in a scheme, the octet must be encoded. The characters ";", "/", "?", ":", "@", "=" and "&" are the characters which may be reserved for special meaning within a scheme. No other characters may be reserved within a scheme.

Usually a URL has the same interpretation when an octet is represented by a character and when it is encoded. However, this is not true for reserved characters: encoding a character reserved for a particular scheme may change the semantics of a URL.

Thus, only alphanumerics, the special characters "$-_.+!*'()," and reserved characters used for their reserved purposes may be used unencoded within a URL.

On the other hand, characters that are not required to be encoded (including alphanumerics) may be encoded within the scheme-specific part of a URL, as long as they are not being used for a reserved purpose.

So based on rules as defined in Section 2.2 of the RFC, we could create a simple way to process a string of data that was sent in.

First, we would break the line at the assignment separator (&), then we would break each half of the assignment into its own variable at the separator for the assignment (=) and then process out all the + signs, replacing them with spaces. Finally, we would replace all the hexified values with their original values.

Sounds simple, doesn't it? Well, we have included some code to show you just how simple this isn't. In fact, we have included the code to unescape it in Tcl, Perl and C.

An Unescape in Tcl

In this book, where we attempt to create all the code for you, we openly admit that some things are already out there that you can use. The code in Listing 4.1 was made available on the NCSA FTP site; it was not written by the authors. Why recreate the wheel?

Listing 4.1: Tcl unencoding routine

```
# arguments are passed on command line. '&' separates
# assignments.
# assignments have the form name=value
# '+'s are spaces and spaces separating words on
# command line are actually part of the word
# In our environment, if argument starts with /,
# then pathname components are assignments
# global variable artype(i) defines what type ar(i)
# should be.
# Currently, list or not.
proc subhex {v} {
    set nv $v
    while {[regexp {%[0-9A-F][0-9A-F]} $v blah]} {
        scan $blah "%%%x" cv
        if {[ctype char $cv]=="&"} {
            regsub -all $blah $v \\& nv
        } else {
            regsub -all $blah $v [ctype char $cv] nv
        }
        set v $nv
    }
    return $v
```

```tcl
}
proc http_proc_args {arg} {
    global ar artype
    upvar $arg argv
    set bigarg ""
    #join words with +'s
    if [llength $argv]==2 {
        set bigarg [split [lindex $argv 1] &]
        set path [lindex $argv 0]
        set args [split [crange $path 1 end] /]
    } else {
        set a0 [lindex $argv 0]
        if {[cindex $a0 0]=="/"} {
            set bigarg {}
            set args [split [crange $a0 1 end] /]
        } else {
            set bigarg [split $a0 &]
            set args {}
        }
    }
    foreach arg [concat $bigarg $args] {
        if [regexp {(.*)=(.*)} $arg foo name value] {
            set name [subhex $name]
            if ![info exists argcount($name)] {
                set argcount($name) 1
            } else {
                incr argcount($name)
            }
        }
    }
    #split assignments on the '&'
    foreach arg [concat $bigarg $args] {
        if [regexp {(.*)=(.*)} $arg foo name value] {
            regsub -all {\+} $value { } newval
            set name [subhex $name]
            set val [subhex $newval]
            if ![info exists ar($name)] {
                if [info exists artype($name)] {
                    if {$artype($name)=="list"} {
                        if {$val!=""} {
                            set ar($name) [list $val]
                        } else {
                            set ar($name) {}
                        }
                    } else {
                        set ar($name) $val
                    }
                } else {
                    set ar($name) $val
                }
            } else {
```

```
                        # multiple selection
                        lappend ar($name) $val
                }
            }
        }
}
# makes URL extended pathname to encode current state
proc pkg_attrs {var attrs} {
    upvar $var ar
    set al ""
    foreach i $attrs {
        if [info exists ar($i)] {
#            regsub { } $ar($i) {+} att
            set al "$al/$i=$att"
        }
    }
    return $al
}

proc http_proc_cgi_args {} {
    global ar artype
    global env
    set bigarg ""
    #join words with +'s
    if [info exists env(PATH_INFO)] {
        set args [split [crange $env(PATH_INFO) 1 end] /]
    } else {
        set args {}
    }
    if [info exists env(QUERY_STRING)] {
        set bigarg [split $env(QUERY_STRING) &]
    } else {
        set bigarg {}
    }
    foreach arg [concat $bigarg $args] {
        if [regexp {(.*)=(.*)} $arg foo name value] {
            set name [subhex $name]
            if ![info exists argcount($name)] {
                set argcount($name) 1
            } else {
                incr argcount($name)
            }
        }
    }

    #split assignments on the '&'
    foreach arg [concat $bigarg $args] {
        if [regexp {(.*)=(.*)} $arg foo name value] {
            regsub -all {\+} $value { } newval
            set name [subhex $name]
            set val [subhex $newval]
```

```
if ![info exists ar($name)] {
    if [info exists artype($name)] {
        if {$artype($name)=="list"} {
            if {$val!=""} {
                set ar($name) [list $val]
            } else {
                set ar($name) {}
            }
        } else {
            set ar($name) $val
        }
    } else {
        set ar($name) $val
    }
} else {
    # multiple selection
    lappend ar($name) $val
}
}
}
}
```

Here are the directions for using this code in a routine:

PROCESSING OF CGI GET SCRIPT ARGUMENTS UNDER TCL

The appropriate way to process arguments is to do http_proc_cgi_args near the beginning of your Tcl script. http_proc_cgi_args splits the PATH_INFO and QUERY_STRING shell environment variables and assigns the values to the global Tcl array ar.

For example, if the script argument assignment foo=bar was passed in, you would access the value bar through $ar(foo). Other CGI-specific variables, such as REMOTE_HOST and REMOTE_USER, are available through the global Tcl array env.

PROCESSING OF OLD GET SCRIPT ARGUMENTS UNDER TCL

The old method of passing arguments to scripts is described here. The appropriate command to parse arguments is to call http_proc_args argv at the beginning of your script. The call assigns the values to the global Tcl array ar, as in CGI. Both methods (old and CGI)(handling of list arguments. If your form contains a SELECT input type that supports multiple selection, called var, the arguments will be passed to the script from the browser this way: var=value1&var=value2. If there is only one selection, only one var=value assignment will be passed to the script. Because of the following reasons: Tcl splits list elements on spaces values can have spaces in them if only one element in a listbox is selected, only one assignment is performed. You need to declare that an argument is supposed to be a list before calling http_proc_cgi_args or http_proc_args. In this example, you would do either: set artype(var) list http_proc_cgi_args or set artype(var) list http_proc_args argv. Then, [lindex $ar(var) 0] will return the right value when values contain spaces.

PASSING ON VALUES VIA THE URL

If you have an array attributes and you wish to pass on each of the values in attributes to a script, you need to encode them in the URL by appending /attr1=val1/attr2=val2/... to the script. The function pkg_attrs does this.

Unescaping in Perl

Several unencoding functions in Perl exist on the Web. Here is one way of doing this in Listing 4.2. This code, in many variations is available at various FTP and Web sites as well, and can be seen in as many different forms. You can probably come up with better ways of doing the same thing. Again, why reinvent the wheel?

After the code shown below is executed, you can access all FORM input variables by their names in the %contents array. For example, if you have a 'name' field in the FORM, you can get its value in the %contents array in the $contents{'name'} variable. We use the code shown in Listing 4.2 to do all CGI processing in the book. You can elect to make it a subroutine and optimize it. We did not make it a subroutine just because we did not see the need.

Listing 4.2: Unencoding in Perl

```
if ($ENV{'REQUEST_METHOD'} eq "POST") {
    read(STDIN,$buffer,$ENV{'CONTENT_LENGTH'});
} else {
    $buffer = $ENV{'QUERY_STRING'};
}
```

```
# ===============================================
# The @contents array will hold all FORM input
# ===============================================
@pairs= split(/&/,$buffer);
foreach $pair (@pairs) {
 ($name,$value) = split(/=/,$pair); # split on equal signs
 $value =~ tr/+/ /; # replace + by a space
 # pack %HH into its ASCII equivalent for all instances.
 $value =~ s/%([a-fA-F0-9][a-fA-F0-9])/pack("C",hex($1))/eg;
 $contents{$name} = $value;
}

# now you can get all the incoming values in the
# %contents associative array!
```

Unescaping in C

uncgi.c is a program that was written by Steven Grimes at Hyperion, where he runs the FTP and WWW services. He has created and made available a wonderful, easy to use tool that allows you to completely forget all about the incoming data's format.

uncgi.c takes the data that is sent from the server to your CGI procedure and places each piece of data into an environment variable that is the name of the variable with which the data was associated. It then prefixes each variable that it creates with a WWW_ in the name. In this way, a variable called addr1 would be turned into WWW_addr1.

This makes the resultant output easy to access and use, as you will see in Chapter 5 where we capture form data that has been processed through uncgi.c.

The source code for uncgi.c is provided in Listing 4.3. Once again, this code was developed by Steven Grimes. Information on the software, its latest releases and a FAQ can be found at: http://www.hyperion.com/~koreth/uncgi.html and copies of the latest version of the software have been included on the CD with this book and will also be available via a link from http://www.prenhall.com/developers_resource_series.

```c
/*
 * @(#)uncgi.c  1.30  12/27/96
 *
 * Unescape all the fields in a form and stick them
 * in the environment so they can be used without
 * awful machinations.
 *
 * Call with an ACTION such as:
 *   http://foo.bar.com/cgi-bin/uncgi/myscript/extra/path/stuff
 *
 * Uncgi will run "myscript" from the cgi-bin
 * directory, and set PATH_INFO to "/extra/path/stuff".
 *
 * Environment variable names are "WWW_" plus the
 * field name.
 *
 * Copyright 1994, Steven Grimm <koreth@hyperion.com>.
 *
 * Permission is granted to redistribute freely and
 * use for any purpose, commercial or private, so
 * long as this copyright notice is retained
 * and the source code is included free of charge
 * with any binary distributions.
 */
#include <stdio.h>
#include <ctype.h>
#include <string.h>
#include <sys/types.h>
#include <sys/stat.h>
#include <stdlib.h>

#define VERSION "1.8"

#ifdef __TURBOC__
#include <process.h>
#pragma warn -pro
#endif

#ifdef __STDC__
#define NOPARAMS void
#else
#define NOPARAMS /**/
#endif

#ifndef __bsdi__
extern char *sys_errlist[];
#endif
extern int errno;
```

```c
#define PREFIX   "WWW_"
#define ishex(x) (((x) >= '0' && (x) <= '9') || ((x) \
    >= 'a' && (x) <= 'f') || ((x) >= 'A' && (x) <= 'F'))
/*
 * Define some directory macros for systems that
 * don't have them.
 */
#ifndef S_IFDIR
# define S_IFDIR 040000
#endif

#ifndef S_ISDIR
# define S_ISDIR(x) ((x & 0170000) == S_IFDIR)
#endif

char *id = "@(#)uncgi.c    1.30 12/27/96";

/*
 * Convert two hex digits to a value.
 */
static int
htoi(s)
    unsigned char    *s;
{
    int value;
    charc;

    c = s[0];
    if (isupper(c))
      c = tolower(c);
    value = (c >= '0' && c <= '9' ? c - '0' : c - 'a' + 10) * 16;

    c = s[1];
    if (isupper(c))
      c = tolower(c);
    value += c >= '0' && c <= '9' ? c - '0' : c - 'a' + 10;

    return (value);
}

/*
 * Get rid of all the URL escaping in a string.
 * Modify it in place, since the result will always
 * be equal in length or smaller.
 */
static void
url_unescape(str)
    unsigned char    *str;
{
    unsigned char    *dest = str;
```

```
    while (str[0])
    {
      if (str[0] == '+')
        dest[0] = ' ';
      else if (str[0] == '%' && ishex(str[1]) && ishex(str[2]))
      {
        dest[0] = (unsigned char) htoi(str + 1);
        str += 2;
      }
      else
        dest[0] = str[0];

      str++;
      dest++;
    }

    dest[0] = '\0';
}

/*
 * Print the start of an error message.
 */
static void
http_head(NOPARAMS)
{
    puts("Content-type: text/html\n");

puts("<html><head><title>Error!</title></head><body>");
    puts("<h1>An error has occurred while processing \
      your request.</h1>");
}

/*
 * Print a standard tagline for Un-CGI error messages.
 */
static void
uncgi_tag(NOPARAMS)
{
    printf("<pre>\n\n\n\n\n\n\n</pre><cite><a href=\"http://www.");
    printf("hyperion.com/~koreth/uncgi.html\">Un-CGI %s", VERSION);
    puts("</a></cite>\n</body></html>");
}

/*
 * Print an HTML error string with the right HTTP
 * header and exit.
 */
static void
html_perror(str)
    char*str;
{
```

```
        http_head();

    puts("<p>The following error was encountered \
      while processing");
    puts("your query.");
    puts("<blockquote>");
    printf("%s: %s\n", str, sys_errlist[errno]);
    puts("</blockquote>");
    puts("<p>Please try again later.");
    uncgi_tag();

    exit(1);
}


/*
 * Stuff a URL-unescaped variable, with the prefix on
 * its name, into the environment.  Uses the "="
 * from the CGI arguments.  Putting an "=" in
 * a field name is probably a bad idea.
 *
 * If the variable is already defined, append a '#'
 * to it along with the new value.
 *
 * If the variable name begins with an underline,
 * strip whitespace from the start and end and
 * normalize end-of-line characters.
 */
static void
stuffenv(var)
    char*var;
{
    char*buf, *c, *s, *t, *oldval, *newval;
    int despace = 0, got_cr = 0;

    url_unescape(var);

    /*
     * Allocate enough memory for the variable name
     * and its value.
     */
    buf = malloc(strlen(var) + sizeof(PREFIX) + 1);
    if (buf == NULL)
      html_perror("stuffenv");

    strcpy(buf, PREFIX);
    if (var[0] == '_')
    {
      strcpy(buf + sizeof(PREFIX) - 1, var + 1);
      despace = 1;
    }
    else
```

```
    strcpy(buf + sizeof(PREFIX) - 1, var);

/*
 * If, for some reason, there wasn't an = in the
 * query string, add one so the environment will
 * be valid.
 *
 * Also, change periods to spaces so folks can
 * get at "image" input fields from the shell,
 * which has trouble with periods in variable names.
 */
for (c = buf; *c != '\0'; c++)
{
  if (*c == '.')
    *c = '_';
  if (*c == '=')
    break;
}
if (*c == '\0')
  c[1] = '\0';

/*
 * Do whitespace stripping, if applicable.
 * Since this can only ever shorten the value,
 * it's safe to do in place.
 */
if (despace && c[1])
{
  for (s = c + 1; *s && isspace(*s); s++)
    ;
  t = c + 1;
  while (*s)
  {
    if (*s == '\r')
    {
      got_cr = 1;
      s++;
      continue;
    }
    if (got_cr)
    {
      if (*s != '\n')
            *t++ = '\n';
      got_cr = 0;
    }
    *t++ = *s++;
  }

  /* Strip trailing whitespace if we copied anything. */
  while (t > c && isspace(*-t))
    ;
```

```c
      t[1] = '\0';
   }

   /*
    * Check for the presence of the variable.
    */
   if ((oldval = getenv(buf)))
   {
     newval = malloc(strlen(oldval) + strlen(buf) + \
       strlen(c+1) + 3);
     if (newval == NULL)
       html_perror("stuffenv: append");

     *c = '=';
     sprintf(newval, "%s#%s", buf, oldval);
     *c = '\0';

     /*
      * Free the entire old environment variable —
      * there really ought to be a library function
      * for this.  It's safe to free here since the
      * only place these variables come from is a
      * previous call to this function; we can
      * never be freeing a system-supplied
      * environment variable.
      */
     oldval -= strlen(buf) + 1; /* skip past VAR= */
     free(oldval);
     free(buf);
   }
   else
   {
     *c = '=';
     newval = buf;
   }

   putenv(newval);
}

/*
 * Scan a query string, stuffing variables into the
 * environment.  This should ideally just use
 * strtok(), but that's not available everywhere.
 */
static void
scanquery(q)
    char*q;
{
    char*next = q;

    do {
```

```
        next = strchr(next, '&');
        if (next)
          *next = '\0';

        stuffenv(q);
        if (next)
          *next++ = '&';
        q = next;
    } while (q != NULL);
}


/*
 * Read a POST query from standard input into a dynamic
 * buffer.  Terminate it with a null character.
 */
static char *
postread(NOPARAMS)
{
    char*buf = NULL;
    int size = 0, sofar = 0, got;

    buf = getenv("CONTENT_TYPE");
    if (buf == NULL || strcmp(buf, \
      "application/x-www-form-urlencoded"))
    {
      http_head();
      puts("<p>No content type was passed to uncgi.");
      uncgi_tag();
      exit(1);
    }

    buf = getenv("CONTENT_LENGTH");
    if (buf == NULL)
    {
      http_head();
      puts("<p>The server did not tell uncgi how \
        long the request");
      puts("was.");
      uncgi_tag();
      exit(1);
    }

    size = atoi(buf);
    buf = malloc(size + 1);
    if (buf == NULL)
      html_perror("postread");
    do
    {
      got = fread(buf + sofar, 1, size - sofar, stdin);
      sofar += got;
    } while (got && sofar < size);
```

```
    buf[sofar] = '\0';

    return (buf);
}

/*
 * Run a shell script.  We use this instead of the
 * OS's "#!" mechanism because that mechanism
 * doesn't work too well on SVR3-based systems.
 */
void
runscript(shell, script)
    char    *shell, *script;
{
    char    *argvec[4], **ppArg = argvec, *pz;

    /*
     *  "shell" really points to the character
     *  following the "#!", not to the name of the
     *  shell program to run.  Skip any leading
     * white space.
     */
    while (isspace( *shell ))
      shell++;

    /*
     *  We only run the shell if there is a full
     *  path name.
     */
    if (*shell != '/')
      return;

    *ppArg++ = shell;

    pz = shell;
    while ((*pz != '\0') && (! isspace( *pz ))) {
      pz++;
    }

#ifdef DEBUG
    printf("Skipped whitespace\n");
    fflush(stdout);
#endif

    /*
     *  We have found the end of the command.
     *  Clip off the trailing white space.
     */
    if (*pz != '\0') {
      *pz++ = '\0';
```

```
        while (isspace( *pz ))
            pz++;

#ifdef DEBUG
        printf("Stripped shell is `%s', args are \
            `%s'\n", shell, pz);
        fflush(stdout);
#endif

        /*
         * If anything follows the command *AND* what
         * follows is not a comment, then insert it
         * into the command argument vect.
         */

        if ((*pz != '\0') && (*pz != '#')) {
            *ppArg++ = pz;

            /*
             *   Trim off anything after the first white
             *   space char.
             */
            while ((*pz != '\0') || (! isspace( *pz ))) {
                pz++;
            }

            *pz = '\0';
        }
    }

    *ppArg++ = script;
    *ppArg   = (char*)NULL;

#ifdef DEBUG
    if (argvec[2] == NULL)
        printf("Executing `%s %s'\n\n", argvec[0], argvec[1]);
    else
        printf("Executing `%s %s %s'\n\n", argvec[0], argvec[1],
            argvec[2]);
    fflush(stdout);
#endif

    execv(shell, argvec);
    /* Fall back to main() on error. */
}

#ifndef LIBRARY
/*
 * Figure out which part of the path information
 * refers to a backend program. This might be more
 * than one path element if the backend is in a
```

```
 * subdirectory of the main script directory.
 */
int
find_program(scriptdir, pathinfo)
    char*scriptdir;
    char*pathinfo;
{
    struct stat st;
    int sdlen = strlen(scriptdir);
    int proglen = 0;
    charpath[1000];

    strncpy(path, scriptdir, sizeof(path));

    while (pathinfo[proglen])
    {
      path[proglen + sdlen] = pathinfo[proglen];
      proglen++;
      if (pathinfo[proglen] == '/' || pathinfo[proglen] == '\0')
      {
        path[proglen + sdlen] = '\0';
        if (stat(path, &st) || !S_ISDIR(st.st_mode))
          return (proglen);
      }
    }

    return (proglen); /* whole path, if it's all directories */
}
#endif

/*
 * Main program, optionally callable as a library function.
 */
void
uncgi(NOPARAMS)
{
    char  *query, *dupquery, *method;

#ifdef DEBUG
    printf("Content-type: text/plain\n\nUn-CGI %s
(%s), debug mode\n",
      VERSION, id);
    fflush(stdout);
#endif

    /*
     * First, get the query string, wherever it is,
     * and stick its component parts into the
     * environment.  Allow combination GET and POST
     * queries, even though that's a bit strange.
     */
```

```c
    query = getenv("QUERY_STRING");
    if (query != NULL && strlen(query))
    {
      /*
       * Ultrix doesn't have strdup(), so we do this
       * the long way.
       */
      dupquery = malloc(strlen(query) + 1);
      if (dupquery)
      {
        strcpy(dupquery, query);
        scanquery(dupquery);
      }
    }

#ifdef DEBUG
    printf("Scanned query string.\n");
    fflush(stdout);
#endif

    method = getenv("REQUEST_METHOD");
    if (method != NULL && ! strcmp(method, "POST"))
    {
      query = postread();
      if (query[0] != '\0')
        scanquery(query);
    }

#ifdef DEBUG
    printf("Read POST query, if any.\n");
    fflush(stdout);
#endif

#ifndef NO_QUERY_OK
    if (query == NULL)
    {
      http_head();
      puts("<p>The 'uncgi' program couldn't find a query to");
      puts("process.\n</body></html>");
      exit(1);
    }
#endif
}

#ifndef LIBRARY /* { */
main(argc, argv)
    int argc;
    char**argv;
{
    char*program, *pathinfo, *newpathinfo;
    char*scriptname, *newscriptname;
```

```
        char*ptrans, *ptend;
        char*argvec[2], shellname[200];
        int proglen;
        FILE*fp;

        uncgi();

#ifndef SCRIPT_BIN
#error SCRIPT_BIN not defined.  Please compile via the Makefile.
#endif

        /*
         * Now figure out which program the caller
         * *really* wants, and adjust PATH_INFO and
         * PATH_TRANSLATED to look right to that program.
         * Also point SCRIPT_NAME to it, so it can figure
         * out what it's called.
         */
        pathinfo = getenv("PATH_INFO");
        if (pathinfo != NULL && pathinfo[0])
        {
          proglen = find_program(SCRIPT_BIN, pathinfo);

#ifdef DEBUG
          printf("Found program, path info is '%s'\n",
pathinfo+proglen);
          fflush(stdout);
#endif

          scriptname = getenv("SCRIPT_NAME");
          if (scriptname == NULL)
            scriptname = "";
          newscriptname = malloc(proglen + strlen(scriptname) + 1 +
                   sizeof("SCRIPT_NAME="));
          if (newscriptname == NULL)
            html_perror("scriptname");
          sprintf(newscriptname, "SCRIPT_NAME=%s", scriptname);
          strncat(newscriptname, pathinfo, proglen);
          putenv(newscriptname);

#ifdef DEBUG
          printf("Script name is '%s'\n", newscriptname);
          fflush(stdout);
#endif

          /*
           * Figure out the path to the backend program.
           */
          program = malloc(proglen + sizeof(SCRIPT_BIN));
          if (program == NULL)
            html_perror("program");
```

```
        strcpy(program, SCRIPT_BIN);
        strncat(program + sizeof(SCRIPT_BIN) - 1, pathinfo, proglen);

#ifdef DEBUG
        printf("Program path is '%s'\n", program);
        fflush(stdout);
#endif

        /*
         * Strip "program" from PATH_TRANSLATED.
         * XXX - this depends on strcpy() copying
         * front to back.
         */
        ptrans = getenv("PATH_TRANSLATED");
        if (ptrans != NULL)
        {
          ptend = ptrans + strlen(ptrans) - strlen(pathinfo);
          strcpy(ptend, ptend + proglen);
          ptend = malloc(strlen(ptrans) +
                  sizeof("PATH_TRANSLATED="));
          if (ptend == NULL)
            html_perror("ptend");
          sprintf(ptend, "PATH_TRANSLATED=%s", ptrans);
          putenv(ptend);
        }

#ifdef DEBUG
        printf("Translated path is '%s'\n", ptend);
        fflush(stdout);
#endif

        pathinfo += proglen;
        newpathinfo = malloc(strlen(pathinfo) + sizeof("PATH_INFO="));
        if (newpathinfo == NULL)
          html_perror("newpathinfo");
        sprintf(newpathinfo, "PATH_INFO=%s", pathinfo);
        putenv(newpathinfo);

#ifdef DEBUG
        printf("New pathinfo is '%s'\n", newpathinfo);
        fflush(stdout);
#endif
      }
      else
      {
        /*
         * No PATH_INFO means no program to run.
         */
        http_head();
        puts("<p>Whoever wrote this form doesn't know
how to use");
```

```
        puts("the 'uncgi' program, because they didn't tell it");
        puts("what to run.");
        puts("<h5>(Bummer.)</h5>");
        uncgi_tag();

        exit(0);
    }


    /*
     * SVR3-based systems seem to have trouble
     * running shell scripts. So if that's what this
     * is, run its shell explicitly.  Don't do
     * it on Linux since some versions have a bug in
     * fgets() that causes them to hang if no
     * newline is encountered.
     */
#ifndef __linux__
    fp = fopen(program, "r");
    if (fp != NULL)
    {
#ifdef DEBUG
        printf("Opened program\n");
        fflush(stdout);
#endif

        if (fgets(shellname, sizeof(shellname), fp) != NULL)
        {
            fclose(fp);
            if (shellname[0] == '#' && shellname[1] == '!')
                runscript(shellname + 2, program);
        }
        fclose(fp);
    }
#endif /* __linux__ */

#ifdef DEBUG
    printf("Executing '%s'\n\n", program);
    fflush(stdout);
#endif

    /*
     * Now execute the program.
     */
    argvec[0] = program;
    argvec[1] = NULL;
    execv(program, argvec);

#ifdef __MSDOS__  /* { */
    /*
     * On DOS systems, try ".exe" and ".com" as well.
     */
```

```
      proglen = strlen(program);
      argvec[0] = malloc(proglen + 5);
      if (argvec[0])
      {
        strcpy(argvec[0], program);
        strcpy(argvec[0] + proglen, ".com");
        execv(argvec[0], argvec);

        strcpy(argvec[0] + proglen, ".exe");
        execv(argvec[0], argvec);
      }
#endif /* } */

      /*
       * If we get here, the exec failed.
       */
      ptend = strrchr(program, '/');
      if (ptend == NULL)
        ptend = program;
      else
        ptend++;
      html_perror(ptend);
}
#endif /* } */
```

Debugging CGI Code

Debugging code is a problem no matter what language or what application you are working with. It gets harder when you move to the client-server environment, as now you have to create a second application that builds the streams of data that are sent to the application, and they have to be able to validate proper activity within the application and get the responses back.

Companies that develop applications that run across client-server environments generally build testing suites and tools that can validate the application and ensure that it works. In most cases, people creating CGI programs just want something that works, and they want to roll it out as soon as possible. This leads, more often than not, to buggy CGI applications being rolled into production environments.

The problem comes in when you have to test these applications. First, we have to create encoded headers that match what you can expect from the browser. Then we have to be able to ensure that the environment that the CGI is being tested in is as restrictive an environment in which the code will be run. We also have to ensure that all the environment variables for the header data are properly set, and that we run the test as the proper user.

If this is starting to look complicated and painful, it can be. One of the more common questions that gets asked in the CGI Usenet newsgroup is "How do I test my CGI?" The key to a successful test is the ability to model the environment as closely as you can. That means that the test environment must run under the same user and group ID that the CGI normally runs under, that the path associated to the account be set to match that of the CGI's environment, that the environment variables be set to model those that are set by the server when it returns a value, and, most importantly, that the information be passed to the program in the same basic way that it is always to be passed.

With all these considerations, there has to be an easier way. There is. One of the best things about uncgi.c is that it makes everything you deal with an environment variable. That means that you don't have to worry about a large number of the issues you considered before.

Once you are dealing with a common input, no matter how the data got to that point, you can start focusing on the other issues of environment. The easiest thing to do, not that you don't need most of the environment, is to set the path of the environment to point to only the most minimal of locations, the /bin area. Beyond that, try to have no other variables except those that you need from the server set (see Appendix A).

Again, we cannot stress enough how useful it is to use uncgi in this environment. Using uncgi and relying on environment variables saves you from having to build the encoded lines. It also saves you from having to worry about how the data is processed. By using uncgi, this process become a matter of starting the CGI from the command line and using the environment variables that are already in place. Then, you can use "puts" or "prints" within the CGI to validate that the input has been correctly processed . As for the output, pipe the output to a file (using a >). The results can be viewed by using an HTML browser to view the output file.

Once you have confirmed that the output is what you want and that all the processing is performing as you expected, prepare to roll out the CGI by creating a live test environment on the server. From within this environment, continue to perform unit testing of the CGI. Remember to use the error log that the server maintains as a resource to validate that you didn't generate any errors in processing (we will touch on that again in Chapter 16).

Summary

We are ready to get into the nitty-gritty of the book (the heart of the matter). By this point, you should have an understanding of the methods being used and how the client-server works, you should understand the concepts of state, or lack thereof, and how URLs and URIs all come together to make this thing called the Web.

I also hope that we have put to rest all the concerns and issues about languages. It is not the intent of this book to teach you how to program in Tcl or in Perl, although this book would make a good companion to a number of other texts that we list in the Appendix in helping you make use of the languages in the CGI environment.

Now on to making it all work in Part 2.

PART TWO

Putting It All Together

A hen is only an egg's way of making another egg.

–Samuel Butler 1902

This section will introduce some actual problems and solutions. Rather than focusing on solving the perceived problem, the chapters will zero in on understanding the problem and solving the root cause of the issue. That means that a portion of each chapter is devoted to analyzing a problem space and focusing on the issues of the software. In doing this the chapter may discuss issues that appear to have nothing to do with CGI; but in exploring the models of the problem space we want to show that the core issues resolve down to simple problems that can be solved in a straight no-nonsense fashion.

The chapters will then provide the design issues that revolve around possible solutions. This may include HTML and data issues as well as software issues. In many cases a number of options are provided and one of them will be recommended.

It should be noted that there are instances where the Tcl code has been written to show the differences between Tcl 7.4 and Tcl 7.5. In these cases the code was originally written to use Tcl 7.4, and was upgraded during the writing of this book to use Tcl 7.5 (the latest stable release at the time this book was published).

It is also important to be aware that although we know about databases, but we don't know about yours. Since some of you will be using Oracle and others will be using Informix . . . we chose to go with the lowest common denominator, data files. If you can do a join with three flat data files you shouldn't have a problem with a relational or object database.

Finally, remember that this text is not attempting to teach Tcl, Perl or HTML, but to show you how you can use the techniques within this text to solve problems.

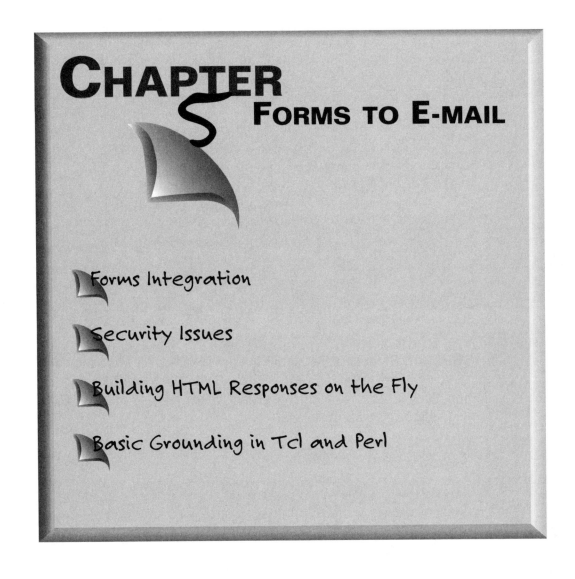

CHAPTER 5
FORMS TO E-MAIL

- Forms Integration

- Security Issues

- Building HTML Responses on the Fly

- Basic Grounding in Tcl and Perl

Everyone wants to process forms. After all, they are the most interactive portion of the World Wide Web and HTML. Forms are what allow feedback. This chapter will introduce the basics of form processing, using an actual case study that focuses on both a proposed system and its suggested requirements. Once the requirements are mapped out, we will move ahead with HTML, Tcl, and Perl design issues.

We will also tackle some security concerns and issues related to calling programs from CGI procedures that send user input executed on the command line, as well as issues involving E-mail and trust.

When discussing HTML design we will talk a bit about form design methods, and why KISS (Keep It So Simple) is important. We will also discuss using tables to align form fields.

> **Note** Remember: It is assumed that you have basic HTML coding skills. In this chapter, HTML examples are provided to show different ways to use key aspects of the design. Generally, this is not done in other chapters. But, because this one deals with how form data will get processed into a text message, it is important to ensure that the process is clear and concise. Most of the process exists in the way the forms are built and how the HTML is used.

Then we will look at the actual dual-purpose code. First, the code allows you to see what data is being sent from the form to the calling script. Second, it will, with the proper fields passed, call the Unix sendmail utility and send E-mail.

Processing Forms

The best way to begin is to present an actual scenario.

Let's say a customer wants a system where a visitor to the site can fill out a form. When the submit button is pressed, the form will send the proper party (based on fields used within the form) E-mail with the data that has been entered on the form. This program will be used on a number of platforms with different requirements, so it should use flags and other methods to permit it to operate across those requirements. This will decrease the odds that the software will have to be modified and, as we all know, software modification can sometimes introduce unexpected enhancements (also known as bugs or defects) into the software.

For instance, one platform that this CGI will operate on will only be accessed by trusted users, so they should be able to fill out a form and send it to any address on the Internet. However, there are also people working on less trustworthy systems. They need to be restricted to sending E-mail only on the system that they are using and there has to be a way of easily setting that capability on and off.

The E-mail message should have support for two different formats. In some cases the message will be the variable name and the data, to know what they answered and how they answered it. A message would contain a group of *paired* variable names and values, like "name = John Doe." Other times, there will be a need for the data, but the field name that the data is associated to will not required. For instance when a person filling out the form is asked for an address, we don't want to see lines like address1 and address2, Only the address data is required.

On the trusted machine, the e-mail from field will be set up so that when people reply the E-mail will be sent to a mailing list, alias or even a users name. In other cases, the default should clearly indicate that the E-mail came from a form and is not replyable. Let's also ensure that anyone who gets form-based E-mail is aware of it and knows that the E-mail is to be considered *untrustworthy* as the default option.

The forms to E-mail program should be able to pass in a *subject* from the form to the E-mail message, as well as the E-mail address *to* which the message is being sent.

The customer also wants to have the default message *sorted* with a simple ASCII ascending sort. Using naming conventions in the form should force certain data to be bundled together in the response. In fact, with the addition of one more control field to the form, some additional functionality can be provided. The sort control field permits the HTML designer to control the return data from the form with even finer granularity. Through this hidden field, the order things are going to be sent back will be declared in a list of variable names. If a variable name is forgotten, there's no need for it to just get dropped in the bit bucket! Any variable name not declared in the user-defined sort list is appended to the list using the same simple sort used as the default sort method.

It is important that the designer is able to test and verify the look of the return data. The designer or the customer shall be able to easily test the form from the browser and see what it would return. This will make it easier and faster to do forms development. It is not expected that the process will pass the "E-mail" header fields, but it is important that all fields returned in the E-mail be done in the same manner when they are echoed to the display for review, test and debugging.

Finally, the user needs to be security aware. Calling sendmail opens a large number of security holes, so make sure that you consider those issues to ensure that the machine remains secure.

Why is Internet E-mail a Concern?

Because of the way the Web works, E-mail sent from a CGI script like this is done so from your http "user" name as established in the httpd.conf configuration file (covered in Chapter 16). Since most sites use the value of "nobody" as the account name, this provides a very nice way to allow anonymous E-mail from within a Web-based environment. In addition, this code allows the form to be used to send any values in the from field, which means that you could spoof any address (assuming that the headers were not checked).

For example, a form could allow the user to specify the E-mail address of the end user. In the code listings that follow, this appears as the hidden field "mailto" in the form, but could also be specified in a list, radio button selection, or even a text area. It doesn't have to be a hidden field, as we are showing. If this form **does** have a textarea entry box, any user would be able to compose a message to any Internet E-mail address and send it out as user nobody@your.site. Or, worse yet, it could be sent out as if the E-mail came from you. Consider someone using that form to E-mail the Commander in Chief at president@whitehouse.gov.

When the Secret Service comes knocking on your door to take away you and your computer equipment, you'll understand the value of disallowing this feature. It can not be stressed enough to consider the consequences of what you are doing in permitting anonymous E-mail on the Internet. To ensure that you have the capability to control this feature, options are provided that permit the Webmaster control over Internet E-mail access using flags provided for within the software. Additionally, a number of options have been preset within the code to keep the default as secure as possible (you can choose to turn them on if you wish). Other options are provided in this article's comments to the code, along with the Tcl code to insert to bring those options to life.

One key question brought up by the requirements is: "Why use associated value pairs and freeform responses?" The answer comes down to how E-mail is processed. Let's say that a user wanted to create E-mail that looked like a letter. It had a header area, a text block, some bulleted items, another text block and then a closing. This CGI would permit that letter to be generated using a form with just those features within it.

Now, if we wanted to process a selection list so we could mail product information back from an auto response script, we would want a slightly different set of input. Here we would want an address and some value pairs so we could ensure that we knew what the user was asking for.

Instead of requiring two scripts, we only need this one CGI script. The first case of generating a letter (I definitely recommend using the sortby option in this case) that is easily human readable is done using freeform mode. The second generates a file that can be processed by a procmail or other pre-processing utility by using the paired value mode.

Requirements

In the most simple terms, the user has asked for two programs in one. One that sends e-mail and another that can be used to dump information to the screen. In addition, the user has asked for the CGI to also support two formats of output, paired lists and freeform.

The idea is to also make a form that is general enough to just be *plug and play* at the CGI level. That way, the user has control over the contents and format of the E-mail from within the form call to the CGI procedure.

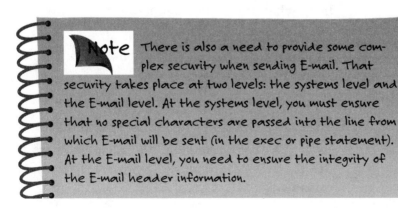

Note There is also a need to provide some complex security when sending E-mail. That security takes place at two levels: the systems level and the E-mail level. At the systems level, you must ensure that no special characters are passed into the line from which E-mail will be sent (in the exec or pipe statement). At the E-mail level, you need to ensure the integrity of the E-mail header information.

The requirements for the customer request are shown in Table 5.1.

Table 5.1: This two-in-one program has four main areas of concern

Requirement	Description
General	Accept data from a form for display or E-mail
E-mail	Systems manager shall be able to allow or disallow Internet E-mail (E-mail going out to the Internet)
	Users shall be able to modify all the following in the E-mail header:
	To: field From: field Subject: field
	The From: field shall allow the users to modify both the E-mail address and the "user name" values
	The From: field shall support some defaults that clearly indicate that the E-mail is not to be trusted
	The Subject: field shall support a default value
	Users shall be able to send message data in either paired values of "variable = data" or data only (associative or freeform)
	There shall be a default standard ascending sort of the variables supported for doing the variable output
	Users shall be able to define what variables should be in what order (user defined sort)
	If user defines variable output, all non-declared variables shall be output post user defined variables in standard sorted order
	keyword variables shall not be sent in the message text
Display	Lack of a mailto reference (the E-mail address for the To: field) will define the process as a display process

Requirement	Description
	No requirements as to look and feel of display
	No requirements on success or failure message on E-mail
Security	The use of the CGI shall not give a user access to any systems commands not declared in the code
	All E-mail shall be clearly defined as unsecure by default

Designing a Form

While not intended to be the book's main focus, the following discussion will provide a style guide for a clean form design, along with some samples. This section is about understanding how the E-mail program will process variables used in the forms and about special variables that you can use to have a finer granularity of control in the design of the form response. To provide the clearest vision, several copies of the form will be described, and the resultant output will be included.

Form Hints

If you're asking for "name/address/E-mail" information, it is best to do that in an area by the submit button. It's also a good idea to use a linebreak (<hr>) to offset this information from the form.

In developing a form, the following style is considered very clean.

```
intro text
<hr>
5-10 questions
<hr>
comment block (text area)
<hr>
Name/address and submit button
<hr>
copyright/authorship
```

HTML Design

In the following forms there are no general questions and no comment block. We have an intro block, a name and address area, and one question with a submit button. Note that the name/address is at the bottom of the form, not at the top to ensure that the user gets to the submit button. In a multiple-page form where the user is required to scroll down the browser, there is the possibility that the user may not get to the scroll down area of the submit button. By putting this information as close as possible to the submit button, there is less of a chance for the user to miss it.

Listing 5.1 provides a sample HTML form.

Listing 5.1: HTML file with a form for user input

```
<title>Register Your Interest</title>
<h2><center>Register Your Interest</h2></center>
This form can be used to register your interest in
Infobahn Xpress and the book <b>Web CGI Programming
using Tcl and Perl</b>. It will send a mail message
to our staff and we will be contacting you in the
near future.

<p>
<hr width=30%>
<FORM METHOD="POST" ACTION="/jmi-
bin/uncgi.cgi/email.tcl">
<input type=hidden name=zmsub value="This is the sub-
ject">
<input type=hidden name=zmailto value="this is the
address">
<table>
<tr><td>Your Name:</td><td> <input name=contact
type=text></td></tr>
<tr><td>Your Company Name: </td><td><input
name=coname type=text>   </td></tr>
<tr><td>Address (line 1): </td><td><input name=coadl1
type=text>   </td></tr>
<tr><td>Address (line 2): </td><td><input name=coadl2
type=text>   </td></tr>
<tr><td>Address (line 3): </td><td><input name=coadl3
type=text>   </td></tr>
<tr><td>City: </td><td><input name=city type=text>
</td></tr>
```

```
<tr><td>State: </td><td><input name=state type=text>
</td></tr>
<tr><td>Zip: </td><td><input name=zip type=text>
</td></tr>
<tr><td>Phone Number:</td><td> <input name=phone
type=text>  </td></tr>
<tr><td>FAX Number:</td><td> <input name=fax
type=text>  </td></tr>
<tr><td>E-mail Address: </td><td><input name=email
type=text> </td></tr>
</table>
<p>
Interests: [Check those that apply]
<p>
<input type=checkbox name=interests value="I-
Xpress">Infobahn Xpress<br>
<input type=checkbox name=interests value="Book">CGI
Programming using Tcl and PERL<br>
<input type=checkbox name=interests
value="Daughters">My greatest love<br>
<p>
To submit, press the <inPUT TYPE="submit" VALUE="sub-
mit"> button.
</form>
<hr>
<address> &#169; Copyright 1996, Infobahn Xpress, Los
Alamitos, CA. All Rights Reserved.</address>
```

The form in Listing 5.1 will produce a paired display shown in Figure 5.2. Note that the mailto and msub have been modified with a *z* prepended to the variable. This will make them display rather than process the message as an E-mail. By adding hidden fields and values to this example, the result will be that shown in Listing 5.2.

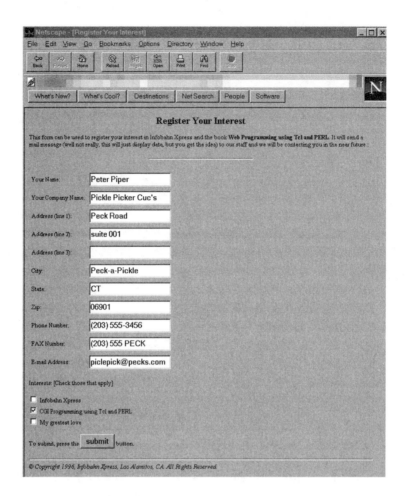

Figure 5.2: *Resultant display*

Listing 5.2: Adding hidden fields and values to a form

```
<title>Register Your Interest</title>
<h2><center>Register Your Interest</h2></center>
This form can be used to register your interest in
Infobahn Xpress and the book <b>Web Programming
using Tcl and PERL</b>. It will send a mail message
(well not really, this will just display data, but
you get the idea) to our staff and we will be con-
tacting you in the near future.:

<p>
<hr width=30%>
<FORM METHOD="POST" ACTION="/jmi-bin/uncgi.cgi/email.tcl">
```

```
<input type=hidden name=zmsub value="This is the subject">
<input type=hidden name=zmailto value="this is the
address">
<input type=hidden name=sendvar value="false">
<table>
<tr><td>Your Name:</td><td> <input name=contact
type=text></td></tr>
<tr><td>Your Company name and address:
</td><td><input name=coname type=text>   </td></tr>
<tr><td>Phone number and/or FAX number:</td><td>
<input name=phone type=text>   </td></tr>
<tr><td>E-mail Address: </td><td><input name=email
type=text> </td></tr>
</table>
<p>
Interests: [Check those that apply]
<p>
<input type=checkbox name=interests value="I am
interested in what I can learn about I-Xpress and
how they can lower my costs and help me build a bet-
ter web-site using CGI programming.">Infobahn
Xpress<br>
<input type=checkbox name=interests value="I am
interested in what I can learn about CGI Programming
using Tcl and Perl.">CGI Programming using Tcl and
Perl<br>
<input type=checkbox name=interests value="I am
interested in what I can learn about the author's
favorite thing, his family.">My greatest love<br>
<p>
To submit, press the <inPUT TYPE="submit" VALUE="sub-
mit"> button.
</form>
<hr>
<address> &#169; Copyright 1996, Infobahn Xpress, Los
Alamitos, CA. All Rights Reserved.</address>
```

Notice the change in the checkbox buttons. These will now load a text string for display. Also notice that sendvar has been set to false. In this case, the long text strings will be sent in the "interests" substitution to the E-mail.

Adding the from and h_fname variables will not show up in the message in display mode, but they will modify the way the message header looks, as shown in Figure 5.3). Changing the sortby would have a dramatic effect as it could be used to change the format of the E-mail. In this case you wouldn't be using the default sort method (a to z), but would be able to define the field sort as you so choose.

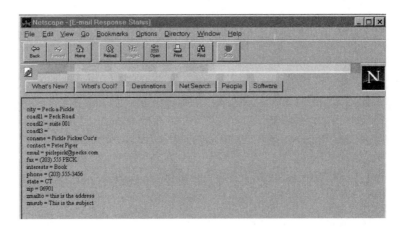

Figure 5.3: Returned display

Tcl Design

In developing this software, there were a number of concerns that were dealt with. First, we had to get the variables generated by the uncgi process. Then we had to evaluate what was sent to us and how that affected what we did to the rest of the data. There is also a need to discuss the use of *regular expressions* and *regular expression substitution*, and how they are invaluable in helping make the process work.

Processing Environment Variables

One of the more powerful commands in Tcl is the foreach command, which allows us to process a list of elements individually. Say we had a list of elements consisting of environment variables. In Tcl, environment variables are stored in an array called env(). Now we will process this Tcl script as if it was launched from uncgi. As stated in Chapter 4, this procedure takes the values passed in the POST and GET data and adds the WWW_ prefix to the variable name. So a series of form values, like mailto, msub, and uname would be transformed into environment variables WWW_mailto WWW_msub and WWW_uname, respectively.

Within Tcl we can list all values of an array (the stuff in the parenthesis after the env) with the command [array names <variable-

name>]. Putting the two concepts together, we could process each variable in the environment with the following line:

```
foreach envvar [lsort [array names env] ] {
```

Now, we are looking to process only those values that start with WWW_. So we can use the regular expression parsing to say that we only want to look at variables that start with WWW_

```
if {[regexp {^WWW_} $envvar]} {
```

The regular expression syntax states that a "^" sign means start-of-string. Another useful syntactical mark in the regular expression is the "$" which means end-of-string.

Once we have a WWW_ variable, we want to store it. There are two ways that these variables can be stored. The variables can be placed into another internal array associated to the actual variable name. In this way the same foreach and [array names <variable-name>] that had been used above can again be used for processing the variable list later in the program. The other option for storage is to put them into values where the form variable name becomes the variable name in the Tcl procedure. Since we are going to want to again process this local list, use the first method and assign the data associated with the environment variable to the internal array name.

```
set varname [join [lrange [split [lindex [split \
$envvar =] 0] _] 1 end ] _]
```

This first line eliminates the WWW_.

```
if {$varname != ""} {
  set var($varname) $env(WWW_$varname)
}
```

The last code example loads the new array with the data from the environment variable if there is data to move.

Regular Expression Substitution

Regular expressions are a powerful method of parsing data to see if it matches your established rules. Regular expressions can get quite complex, and the rules are far from easy to understand. For instance, if we wanted to make sure that a value was numeric, we could do a check that looked like:

```
^[0-9]*$.
```

This translates to:

```
Starts (^) with at least one numeric ([0-9]) and can
have 1-n of them (*) and then ends ($).
```

One tiny typo changes the entire rule. For instance, if we were to have entered the rule as follows [0-9]*$ we would have changed the rule and the expected returns would be very incorrect, if what we had really wanted was the first rule. In this case, the value states that any value that has two or more numeric values before the end of the line is a match. This would match 12345 as the rule we wanted would have, but it also would match 123abc45, not what we wanted at all.

Again, we could have another typo that could generate false data. In this case the rule ^[0-9].$ would allow any value that started with a numeric character, followed by one and only one numeric character and then end-of-line. So the value 12345 would be invalid, but the value 12 would be acceptable.

Note If you are starting to get confused, don't be. People who use regular expressions every day still find new and useful ways to use the toolset and to confuse themselves. One of Perl's key strengths is the power of regular expressions. Unfortunately, the complexity of those same regular expressions are also a key weakness. It is far too easy to create regular expressions that just don't match the way that you think they do. When using regular expressions, always test out the expected and the unexpected against the rules that you create.

Tcl also provides a way to make these regular expressions even more powerful, through the use of the regsub command. This command equates to "regular expression substitution." In this case, you would use the expression to perform a match and then, automatically within the same command, perform substitution upon the match.

Within this code it is at times necessary to eliminate certain values from strings. The best example of this is the desire to avoid passing anything that could possibly execute another command rather than sendmail (discussed earlier in the security sidebar). In this case, we want to eliminate a series of characters from a passed in string. These characters could possibly cause a system to fork another process or command. To eliminate that, yet highlight the possibility that it was done, a substitution will take place that will replace the characters in question with an asterisk (*).

The command:

```
regsub -all {\;|\[|\]|\||\<|\>} $tmsub " * " msub
```

is translated to say:

Take all instances of the individual values ; [ ] | < > and replace them with an instance of " * " in the string $tmsub (the $ causes the string within the variable to be processed rather than the variable itself) and place the resultant string in the variable msub.

This is how the "nasty" characters that could cause a security concern will be substituted. The | between the characters is an "or" and the \ before them says that the character is a literal character. The \ character would allow you to search for all ^H (backspaces). The use of the backslash also acts as an escape character that allows the ";" character to be accepted as a literal character and not processed as an *end of command* value.

Also, as we have stated, a \ by itself is considered a continuation character in Tcl. In order to use a \ in a search it to must be escaped out by a \ —so a proper search for a \ would look like: \\ .

Using Lists and Strings

What is the difference between a string and a list in Tcl? They appear interchangeable in the code. Within Tcl, a list is a string of elements, and a string is an element list. They are basically the same. This makes string parsing very easy to do in Tcl. All it really comes down to is list processing of data items within the string.

A good example of this is the sortby keyword variable. It is permitted to use a string of variable names in the form, each separated by a space. This string is used to set the sort order of the variables being passed into the code. The string is processed within the code as a list of elements.

```
if {[llength sortby] != [expr [llength lst] - $elim]} {
```

Here we are getting a count of the items in the sortby list that was passed in (using the command llength - "list length"). Then we are checking it against the number of variables that were processed by the foreach loop (and we include the variables that were eliminated from that count as well). If they are not equal, we will extract the variables in the sortby from the ones in lst, and then append whatever was left in lst to the ones passed in by sortby. This will guarantee that all variables passed in by uncgi are processed.

```
foreach sval $sortby {
 set loc [lsearch $lst $sval]
 if {$loc != -1} {
 set lst [lreplace $lst $loc $loc ]
 }
}
set slist "$sortby $lst"
```

The "set loc" locates the variable from sortby being processed in the foreach loop within the elements that make up the lst variable. A -1 means that there was no match on a value, and it is ignored. If there is a match, we will do a list replace without replacing the list element at that location with anything, thereby deleting it. In the end, after all the variables in the sortby are finished processing, the output element list is updated to be a list of all the sortby and any other variables that were passed in. The set does a string concatenation between the two element lists creating the new list.

Tcl Arrays

There are some really great commands to help with array processing. One that I feel is most beneficial is the [array names arrayname] command. This command puts the power of associations into the hands of the programmer as we saw in the earlier examples.

A simple example of an associations power can be seen in the following two pieces of code. In these cases, there is a need to sort the "fruit" array. Each fruit is provided with a scalar reference or sort identity. In the first set of examples, we will perform the sort using the scalar reference. Then we will attempt to show the difference between that sort and sorting on the data values (which will result in a different sorted list). In the first case, we will use a paired list to perform the sort on the scalar value, and we will use the [array names] method in the second case.

A paired list, as used here, is a list of elements that are "paired" so that there is an association between the elements in the pair.

```
set a [lsort {2 apple} {1 pear} {4 banana} \
{3 watermelon)]
foreach itm $a {
puts [lindex $itm 1]
}
```

The output of the set would be:

```
{1 pear} {2 apple} {3 watermelon) {4 banana}
```

The output of the puts would be:

```
pear apple watermelon banana
```

Note that this looks very clean and simple. There are only five "functions" called: a set, puts, lindex, foreach and an lsort. When done, the program would have generated the second output above.

In the second case, we build an associative array with the scalar values being used to create the associations between the array contents and the scalar identity. To show how these values are used, the set command for building the array is shown for each element. As the actual code from the program shows, this process is usually performed in a very tight foreach loop.

Using associative arrays, as shown here, provides a faster and more effective way of processing the data. In this case, the first value was used to load an array and the second value was the data. So we loaded each array up with a value:

```
set fruit(2) apple
set fruit(1) pear
```

```
set fruit(4) banana
set fruit(3) watermelon
```

In the foreach loop, we only have to use the puts statement and there is no need to use the lindex function.:

```
foreach val [lsort [array names fruit]] {
 puts fruit($val)
}
```

This method reduces the parsing on the output and when processing large series of paired data values and makes the data processing of the output go much faster.

To modify the first program to perform the sort, we would need to loop through the foreach as just shown and then use the following code within the foreach loop to set and display the sorted output:

```
foreach itm $a {
 set ofruit [lindex $itm 1]
}
puts [lsort $ofruit]
```

The output of the puts would be:

```
apple banana pear watermelon
```

The matching changes could be made to the second program, but there would be no need to use the lindex function each time the data is processed through the foreach loop.

```
foreach val [lsort [array names fruit]] {
 set ofruit fruit($val)
}
puts [lsort $ofruit]
```

In the E-mail program, the associative method is used to accept and to load all the data to be used from the environment variables created by the uncgi processor. Note that we are able to use the foreach to extract all the environment variables. Then we trap those that have a WWW_ prefix (the ones that uncgi is passing to us) and process them by removing the WWW_ so they match the original variable name that was used in the HTML form. Then a variable array called "var" is loaded up with the associative data and the variable name is used as the associative array name value. When the output is processed, a method similar to those described is used. The following code shows how to load the environment variables

```
foreach envvar [lsort [array names env] ] {
  if {[regexp {^WWW_} $envvar]} {
   set varname [join [lrange [split [lindex [split \
$envvar =] 0] _] 1 end ] _]
   if {$varname != ""} {
    set var($varname) $env(WWW_$varname)
   }
  }
}
```

Integrating to System Services

This section could be called *Exec and Why You Should be Concerned*. The exec command is one of the most dangerous commands that you can use in a script. Not by itself, mind you, but when linked to variables that the user has the ability to input.

In the Unix environment, there lies the ability to "string" commands together using the semi-colon (;) to separate the commands. Additionally, some commands allow you to sub-shell commands (`command`) or to use pipes within the command (<,>,|). In all these instances, the server is opening a security hole that *must* be watched. That doesn't mean that the exec command in and of itself is a bad command. In fact, it is a very useful command and one that should be used when required. The key is to limit its use.

The following line is open for abuse:

```
[exec mailx -s "$subject" $towho < $datafile]
```

In this command, we will be executing the mailx command to send a mail message to someone. As long as we, in programming, control the data in the variables, there is no reason for concern. But if we allow the user to control the $towho value, without checking it, the user could issue a value like "root < /dev/null ; cd \; rm -rf *; /dev/null."

That would make the command look like:

```
[exec mailx -s "$subject" root < /dev/null ; cd \; \
   rm -rf *; /dev/null <$datafile]
```

This would send mail to root with a subject but no body. Then it would change to the root directory and attempt to delete every file underneath it (clean the system). Finally, it would send the datafile to the bit bucket.

To avoid this we can use *regular expression substitution* as we showed earlier in the chapter. In this process we try to eliminate those values that can be used to hurt you. They are ";", "<", ">", "|" and possibly """.

Another instance you want to ensure not to use those values is when you are piping. From Tcl, you can pipe to a command by opening a fileid to it. In this program, we will be using this pipe method to process a sendmail call. Like an exec, the pipe is calling directly to the system. Once the fileid is closed, the pipe will execute the command within it, like this:

```
set f1 [open {|/usr/lib/sendmail -t} w]
  puts $f1 "From: $frmname"
  puts $f1 "To: $env(WWW_mailto)"
  puts $f1 "Subject: $msub"
  puts $f1 "[exec cat /tmp/$fname]"
  close $f1
```

In this case, we can see that the sendmail command is sent with a -t modifier when the pipe is opened. Then we process the mail by filling in the header information (From, To and Subject) and then exec'ing a cat of the temp file.

Let's start with the exec. Is it safe? Yes. I am issuing it with a command that I control, and it is hard coded as to what it will be doing. The variable $fname is one that I create and it is not passed in. As for the data in the file, since it is enclosed in a "", it is safe to have it cat to the pipe. If the user were to put in the data *";cd /;rm -rf *"* as a response, that is exactly what would have been sent in the E-mail message, and it wouldn't have affected the pipe.

Next we have the $frmname and $msub values for the From: and Subject: E-mail headers. Earlier in the code we issued the following command against the data in those fields:

```
regsub -all {\;|\[|\]|\||\<|\>} $tfrmname " * " frmname
```

This says that I want to make every instance of ; | > < [and] an instance on " * " . In doing this, I decrease the chance that any user-supplied data could perform commands outside the scope of the subprocess.

The last variable is env(WWW_mailto). It is expected that this variable will not be set by the *user* but by the *form developer*, and that the person developing the form is trustworthy enough to not want to destroy the machine that they are on.. This value bothers some people, so I used a small "trick" to fix that. Early in the program the environment variable is run through the regsub and written it back out to the environment variable, as shown here:

```
if {[info exists env(WWW_mailto)]} {
  set mailto true
  regsub -all {\;|\[|\]|\||\<|\>} $env(WWW_mailto) \
  " * " tmpv
  set env(WWW_mailto) $tmpv
```

This rewrite makes the mailto value as safe as all the others that we are passing on to the sendmail pipe.

Building HTML Responses on the Fly

This is one of the key reasons that I suggest people learn markup rather than rely on WISIWYG editors to do all their HTML code. At some point there will be a need for a person to create a script and have that script generate information back to the user. You can't use a fancy editor to do that, you have to use HTML.

The nice part is that this isn't too complicated. The most important thing to remember is to start your script, if it does produce any output, with the string:

```
"Content-type: text/HTML\n\n"
```

This string tells a browser that the file it is about to get is HTML. The \n's will add two blank lines to ensure the browser knows that this was a command for it, not for display.

The server works by directing anything that you send to standard output back to the user. Since you started by telling the browser that you were sending HTML back, it now will process all data received as HTML data. You could have told the browser that you were sending it any valid mime-type, and the browser would have processed the data based on the rules that it has for that mime-type.

> **Tip** There is one word of caution to be shared when using standard output. Always make sure to escape your quotes. The line "So he said "Hi Honey, I'm home!"" will end up displaying as:
>
> So he said
>
> By escaping the quotes like so: "So he said \"Hi Honey, I'm home!\"" you will get output that looks like you expected:
>
> So he said "Hi Honey, I'm home!"
>
> The same goes for special characters that can be misinterpreted like [ ] or $. When in doubt, escape with the backslash.

Using Temp Files

Why use them? In this sample piece of code, they weren't really necessary. All the message could have been built up in a long string that was then output to the sendmail process as the message. I decided to use them because they don't hurt anything and it is also a good time to point out how file handling works and how to create unique filenames. These skills will come in handy in some of the later chapters.

First, how do we create a unique ID for a filename? There are any number of methods, such as:

- Use the process id (which is done in this example with a [pid])
- Use the user's site (the value stored in env(REMOTE_ADDR))
- Use the time (set value to the time without colons using the command: [regsub -all \: [lindex [exec date] 3] "" value]) or use the clock command

The problem with all of these is that, by themselves, they aren't unique.

For a file that will only exist transiently, like the ones that we are using in this program, we can use the pid. The file is deleted right after it is created, so there is a relatively low chance of having a name collision. The same can be said for using time. The problem is that time is HH:MM:SS and there is always the possibility that two processes could run in the same second. Had the date been able to generate HH:MM:SS.hh, the use of the hundredths of seconds would have made this a much more accurate and unique filename generation possibility. The worst possible choice is the user's remote address.

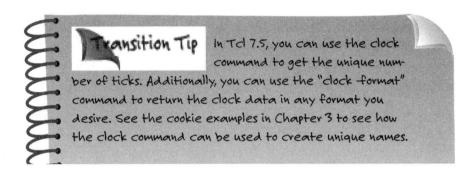

Transition Tip In Tcl 7.5, you can use the clock command to get the unique number of ticks. Additionally, you can use the "clock format" command to return the clock data in any format you desire. See the cookie examples in Chapter 3 to see how the clock command can be used to create unique names.

Why is remote_address a bad choice? Because a site using a proxy firewall will always generate the same address for each user. It's highly possible that you could get a duplicate name using remote_address.

The best way to avoid duplicates is to combine any two of these methods. If I wanted to ensure that a key or filename would be unique, I could use the pid+remote_address. A filename of [pid]_$env(REMOTE_ADDRESS).tmp would create a filename from a user at 122.23.46.191 that looked like:

```
3463_122.23.46.191.tmp
```

If, for some reason, your system can't handle multidot filenames, you could regsub the dots out using the following:

```
regsub -all \. $env(REMOTE_ADDRESS) "" remote
set fname [pid]_$remote.tmp
```

This would create a temporary filename that looked like:

```
3463_1222346191.tmp
```

As you can see, using these two values in combination creates a unique identifier that has a very low possibility of being duplicated on the system.

Writing Your Code in Tcl

The software shown in Listing 5.3 is designed using all the techniques that were discussed in the design section earlier. Throughout the code, there are comments explaining exactly what is happening at that point within the code.

Listing 5.3: email.tcl

```
#!/usr/local/bin/tclsh
##
## email.tcl   - A generic email the form input
## CGI script
##
##
##
## Minimum Tcl Version: 7.4
##
##
##
##
##————————————————————————-
##
## set the localonly option to allow or
##   disallow users to use Internet
## mail specs in the mailto value.
##   Setting to true will allow mail to only
## be sent to valid users at the current host.
##   Setting to false will allow
## any form to be used as an anonymous Internet
##   remailer. While the default
## has been set to false, we ***highly***
##   recommend setting it to true.
##
## localonly - false=allow Internet specs
set localonly false
##
## sendvar defines a default output mode for
##   the mailer. It states that the
## output will either output the varname/value
##   pair, or the value only.
## This has been set up to allow the webmaster
##   to establish a default method
## for a site. The user has the ability to
##   override the default by setting
## the value "sendvar" inside their form to true
```

```
##    or false.
##
## sendvar - true=output "varname=value" pairs
##    -    false=output value only
set sendvar true
##
## start the processing
##
puts "Content-type: text/HTML\n\n"
puts "<title>E-mail Response Status</title>"
set var(h-fname) "Untrusted"
##
## Thanks to Kevin Kenny at GE...
##
foreach envvar [lsort [array names env] ] {
 if {[regexp {^WWW_} $envvar]} {
  set varname [join [lrange [split [lindex [split \
  $envvar =] 0] _] 1 end ] _]
  if {$varname != ""} {
   set var($varname) $env(WWW_$varname)
  }
 }
}
## set some initial flags, and then check
##  for known and expected WWW_ values
## that allow the user to reset some of the flags.
##
## ATTN Webmaster! please modify the frmname
##  as appropriate for your site
##
set elim 0
set msub "Autoprocessed E-mail from form "
set frmname "form-mailbot@site (WWW Mail)"
set mailto false
##
## uses the special value "from" in a form
## frmname - this allows the user to specifically
##   that the mail came from
##            someone... this shouldn't be trusted :-)
##
##
## We have added h-fname so you can out
##  something in rather than "untrusted"
## we put it in a var() array so we
#  wouldn't have to do a test to load it.
## h-fname stands for "hidden from name"
#    - that doesn't mean it has to be hidden
## but in most cases it will be.
##
if {[info exists env(WWW_from)]} {
 set tfrmname "$env(WWW_from) ($var(h-fname))"
```

```
  regsub -all {\;|\[|\]|\||\<|\>} $tfrmname \
    " * " frmname
 incr elim
}
##
## allow the user to change the value of sendvar
## from the Webmasters default to their choice...
##
if {[info exists env(WWW_sendvar)]} {
 set sendvar $env(WWW_sendvar)
 incr elim
}
## User has used their own subject line for
## the mail message
if {[info exists env(WWW_msub)]} {
 set tmsub $env(WWW_msub)
 regsub -all {\;|\[|\]|\||\<|\>} $tmsub " * " msub
 incr elim
}
## User is sending mail, not echoing output to screen
if {[info exists env(WWW_mailto)]} {
 set mailto true
 regsub -all {\;|\[|\]|\||\<|\>} \
      $env(WWW_mailto) " * " tmpv
 set env(WWW_mailto) $tmpv
 set fname [pid].txt
 set f1 [open /tmp/$fname w]
 incr elim
}
##
## Build order of the messages
##
## Minimally, we sort the list and use that.
## if you asked for an order we will use
## that if the number of items you asked for and the
## items passed in were the same. If not, we give you
## your stuff first and then any stuff you didn't
## ask for.
##
set lst [lsort [array names var]]
if {[info exists env(WWW_sortby)]} {
 set sortby "$env(WWW_sortby)"
##
## elim was incremented each time we went
## through an expected variable...
##
 if {[llength sortby] != [expr \
      [llength lst] - $elim]} {
  foreach sval $sortby {
   set loc [lsearch $lst $sval]
   if {$loc != -1} {
```

```
    set lst [lreplace $lst $loc $loc ]
    }
  }
 set slist "$sortby $lst"
} else {
 set slist "$sortby"
 }
} else {
 set slist "$lst"
}
##
## build the mail message or write the
## output to screen
##
## there is a list of "program" variables
## that won't get processed these are the same as
## "keywords" for this program. Don't use them in
## forms if you want to send them or display them.
##
foreach vname $slist {
 if {[lsearch "msub mailto sortby sendvar" \
      "localonly from h-fname" $vname] < 0} {
  if {[info exists var($vname)]} {
   if {$sendvar} {
    set ostring "$vname = $var($vname)"
   } else {
    set ostring $var($vname)
   }
   if {$mailto} {
    puts $f1 "$ostring\n"
   } else {
    puts "$ostring <br>"
   }
  }
 }
}
##
## If mail, then send it
##
if {$mailto} {
 close $f1
##
## Local only processing... this is how we
## stop anonymous E-mailers
##
 if {$localonly} {
  if {[regexp "@|!|%" $env(WWW_mailto)]} {
   puts "<center><h1>An invalid form of E-mail" \
        "notation from this server has been used</h1>"
   puts "Please use the back key to exit.</center>"
   exit
```

```
    }
   }
## If you want to you can use the mailx command
## commented out below, but the preferred way is to
## open a pipe to sendmail and use the Mail
## Transport Agent (MTA) directly.
## exec mailx -s "$msub" $env(WWW_mailto) < \
## /tmp/$fname
##
##
  set f1 [open {|/usr/lib/sendmail -t} w]
  puts $f1 "From: $frmname"
  puts $f1 "To: $env(WWW_mailto)"
  puts $f1 "Subject: $msub"
  puts $f1 "[exec cat /tmp/$fname]"
  close $f1
exec rm /tmp/$fname
puts "<center><h3>Mail sent \
   to $env(WWW_mailto)</h3>"
puts "<h2>Thank you for using the WWW \
   E-mailer.</h2>Please use the back key" \
   to exit.</center> <hr><P> <address> \
   &#169; Copyright 1995-1996, Infobahn \
   Xpress, Los Alamitos, CA. All \
   Rights Reserved.</address>"
}
```

Perl Design and Code

The Perl code here performs the same operations as the previously discussed Tcl code. Basically, it picks up the user input from the form and determines who to send it to. It then uses a variable in the values in the responses to sort the incoming input and appends the rest of the responses to this sorted list. Once done, it uses sendmail to create a mail message and sends it off to the specified user in the responses to the FORM. Using regular expressions the script removes special characters that users could use to damage to the server.

Let's first look at how to do simple search and replace operations in Perl. Perl offers a rich set of features when it comes to parsing regular expressions and in the manipulation of strings. Perl's parsing capability can be a great help when validating contents of strings or doing substitution. For example, if I were to look for room numbers of the form: *Addd*, where d is a digit and A is a letter of the alphabet,

I could use the following expression to check if the format is correct in a string $room:

```
if ($room =~ /^[A-Za-z][0-9][0-9][0-9]$/)
    { print "Correct format \n"; }
else  { print "Incorrect format \n"; }
```

The [A-Za-z] part checks for a letter of the alphabet, and the three [0-9] constructs define an occurrence for each of the digits. The ^ and $ mark the start and the end of line, respectively. If the number of digits following the alphabets is one or more, we can also use the expression:

```
$room =~ /^[A-Za-z][0-9]+$/
```

The + sign indicates "one or more" occurrences of the previous pattern. The pattern above will match strings of the form A1, B34, G3 but will not match patterns of the form G, GG and 33.

The substitution operator uses this match pattern to search for and replace strings given a pattern. The syntax is:

```
s/oldPattern/new/g
```

The g signifies that all occurrences of the oldPattern be replaced with new. You will only substitute the first match of the oldPattern If you leave out the g.

Assignments can also be made and matched on the same line:

```
($left = substr($right,0,9) =~ s/[0-9]/\#/g;
```

The above code takes the first nine characters from the string called $right and assigns them to the $left string. The $right string is not modified in any way. The substr() function simply takes the characters starting from index 0 (the first character) up to the ninth character or the end of string, whichever comes first. (You can get the length of a string by using the length($variable) function.) Then, each digit in the $left string is replaced with the hash character. The # is escaped to avoid Perl from interpreting it as the start of a comment line. The g parameter forces the substitution on all matches of the pattern.

Perl has tremendous power and flexibility in performing string search and replace operations. The examples presented here are only the tip of an iceberg. We can only present enough information as it applies to using Perl for the examples in this book

Listing 5.4. mailme.pl

```perl
#!/usr/local/bin/perl
# ==========================================
#            FORM to email script.
# ==========================================
$| = 1;
print "Content-type: text/html\n\n";
# ==========================================
#  Get input from the Web via the content length
# ==========================================
if ($ENV{'REQUEST_METHOD'} eq "POST") {
read(STDIN,$buffer,$ENV{'CONTENT_LENGTH'});
} else {
$buffer = $ENV{'QUERY_STRING'};
}
@pairs= split(/&/,$buffer);
foreach $pair (@pairs) {
    ($name,$value) = split(/=/,$pair);
    $value =~ tr/+/ /;
    $value =~ s/%([a-fA-F0-9][a-fA-F0-
9])/pack("C",hex($1))/eg;
    $contents{$name} = $value;
    }

# ==========================================
# If you want to limit mail to be sent only
# on local machine use this value for the
# regular expression:
# $regexp = "[\<\>\|\;\@\!\%\,\`]";
# The default shown below allows mail to be
# sent on the internet
# ==========================================
$regexp = "[\<\>\|\;\,\`]";

# ==========================================
# Create an array of responses to use.
# ==========================================
%responses = %contents;
# ==========================================
# Get the mail information here and take
# away all suspect characters
# ==========================================
$mfrom = $contents{'mfrom'};
$mfrom =~ s/$regexp//g;   #  remove suspect chars

# ($mfrom = $contents{'mfrom'}) =~ s/$regexp//g;   #
remove suspect chars

$mailto = $contents{'mailto'};
$mailto =~ s/$regexp//g;   #  remove suspect chars
```

```
$msub = $contents{'msub'};
$msub =~ s/$regexp//g;        #   remove suspect chars



$sendvar = $contents{'sendvar'};

# =========================================
# Remove those fields that you do not need
# from the responses in the FORM. You have
# to edit these fields for yourself.
# =========================================
delete $responses{'mfrom'};
delete $responses{'mailto'};
delete $responses{'msub'};
delete $responses{'sortby'};
delete $responses{'sendvar'};

# =========================================
# Remove items from %contents array into
# the body of the message based on keys in
# the $sortby variable.
# =========================================
$sortby = $contents{'sortby'}; # get keys;
@usekeys = split(' ',$sortby);
@body = ();
$count = 0;
foreach $key (@usekeys) {
    if ($sendvar eq "TRUE") {
    $body[$count++] = $key . " " . $responses{$key};
    } else {
    $body[$count++] = $responses{$key};
    }
    delete $responses{'$key'}; # remove.
}
# =========================================
# Use rest of items in %contents array into
# the body of the message in an alphanumeric
# sort and append to those used via $sortby.
# =========================================
foreach $key (sort keys %responses) {
    if ($sendvar eq "TRUE") {
    $body[$count++] = $key . " " . $responses{$key};
    } else {
    $body[$count++] = $responses{$key};
    }
}

# =========================================
# Now create the message itself and send it
# out with the headers if $mailto is not empty
```

```perl
# otherwise just print a response back.
# ========================================
$message = "";
foreach (@body) {
    $message .= $_ . "\n";
}
$time = time;
$echoback = "";
if ($mailto eq "") {
    $echoback = "<HR>$time: Debug Echo Back<HR>";
    foreach (@body) {
    $echoback .= $_ . "<BR>"
    }
    $echoback .= "<HR>";
}


# ====================================
# Send message via email if $mailto
# ====================================
if ($mailto ne "") {   # A mailto! respond with email
format MAILCOMMENT =
To : @*
$mailto
From: @*
$mfrom
Subject: @*
$msub

This message is sent from our mailbot in response
to the following questions:
==================================================
@*
$message
==================End of Message==================
.

open (MAILCOMMENT,"| /usr/bin/sendmail -t") || die
"Cannot open sendmail $!\n";
write (MAILCOMMENT);
close (MAILCOMMENT);
}


# ====================================
# Always acknowledge to browser....
# ====================================
print <<"HTMLHEAD";
<HTML>
<HEAD>
<TITLE> Ack for Request for Info </TITLE>
```

```
</HEAD>
<BODY>
<HR>
$echoback
<HR>
<P>
<PRE>
To : $mfrom
From: $mailto
Subject: $msub

This message is sent from our mailbot in response
to the following questions:
=====================================================
$message
==================End of Message==================
</PRE>
</BODY>
</HTML>
HTMLHEAD
```

The first line in Listing 5.4 is the standard *bang* line for picking up Perl. Common locations for Perl include the /usr/local/bin and /usr/local/sbin directories. Usually, there is a link from /usr/bin/perl to the actual executable. You can always find out the path to the Perl command interpreter with the which command. For example, the command below returns the path to the Perl interpreter:

```
$ which perl
/usr/bin/perl
$
```

Then, we set the special Perl variable, $|, to a value of 1, like this:

```
$| = 1;
```

This step is required when sending HTML files back to a browser. A non-zero value of $| forces flushing of the input in STDOUT on every write. Forcing the output prevents any delays that may be introduced when internal buffering is used by the underlying system.

We send back a Content-type of HTML to let the browser know what type of input to expect:

```
print "Content-type: text/html\n\n";
```

This output is sent immediately to the browser since we have forced flushing on every write.

Now comes the matter of parsing the incoming input from the browser processing the form. Note that we use the POST type of form processing. This means that the input will be sent to our script via STDIN. Had this form used the GET method of processing, the input would be found in the QUERY_STRING environment variable. The POST form of handling input is the preferred way of sending input to Perl CGI scripts, since it does not limit the length of the input. In the case of GET requests, the input buffer is limited to the length of strings allowed for environment variables. This length could be 256 characters (or less).

In the following line of code, we read in the input from the standard input, STDIN, into the variable $buffer up to the number of byters specified in the environment variable CONTENT_LENGTH.

```
read(STDIN,$buffer,$ENV{'CONTENT_LENGTH'});
```

Transition Tip Keep in mind that Perl functions return values that are either scalar values or arrays. A regular **array** in Perl allows its members to be indexed by numbers. The array itself is represented by a @arrayname. Indices for the array begin from 0 and up. Items in the array are referenced as $arrayname[0], $arrayname[1], ... and so on. Note the use of the $ to indicate the scalar value in the array being referenced. An **associative array** is a special array that allows its members to be referenced as strings. An associative array is shown as %name and the elements of the array are referenced as $name{'index'}. For example, the associative array, %names, could have members such as $names{'kamran'}, $names{'husain'}, etc. So, to recap, an @ symbol in front of a variable name indicates an array, while a % indicates an associative array. Elements within an array are referenced by indexing with a number in between square brackets ([]), and elements within an associative array are referenced with a string using curly braces ({}).

Notice how we get the value of an environment variable for a Perl script. Every Perl program that runs from the command line has a special associative array called %ENV. Each item in the %ENV array is indexed by the name of the environment variable it represents. The values are set by Perl using the environment of the process calling the Perl script. So, in this case, the value for the number of bytes to read is taken using the construct:

```
$ENV{'CONTENT_LENGTH'}.
```

In the case of GET form, we will have to pick the input from the QUERY_STRING variable. In order to accommodate both types of forms, the call to read the function will actually look like this:

```
if ($ENV{'REQUEST_METHOD'} eq "POST") {
read(STDIN,$buffer,$ENV{'CONTENT_LENGTH'});
} else {
$buffer = $ENV{'QUERY_STRING'};
}
```

Based on the type of form submission being used, we can pick the data from either the standard input via a read() command or from the contents of the environment variable QUERY_STRING. Once you have the input in the buffer, your code will process it the same way. To split the contents of the $buffer using the ampersand (&) as the delimiter, we use the following line:

```
@pairs= split(/&/,$buffer);
```

The returned value from the split() function is an array that is stored in the @pairs array. The split command in Perl takes two or three arguments.

```
split(pattern,buffer [,limit]);
```

The *pattern* is specified in between two forward slashes. In this case, we used /&/ to split the contents of the *buffer*. Had the contents of the buffer used a colon (:) to delimit words, such as an entry in the /etc/passwd file, we would have used the call as:

```
split(/:/,$buffer);
```

The *limit* parameter is used to specify the maximum number of items to derive and is ignored if not specified.

```
@pairs= split(/&/,$buffer);
foreach $pair (@pairs) {
```

```
.. loop stuff here ..
}
```

In this instance, the array @pairs contains items, each of which is a string of the form "name=value" that will be assigned to the variable $pair in each iteration of the loop. (if you leave out the $pair in the foreach loop above, the value will be assigned to the special variable $_ .) Now we have to further split each line in the @pairs array to extract the name and value portions. The foreach command allows the script to iterate through the @pairs array. Within each iteration, the value of the variable $pair is assigned a value from an item @pairs array. The loop will stop when all items in the @pairs array have been processed.

We further split each item in the $pair variable by using the equal to (=) sign as the delimiter. The value of $name is set to the name assigned to the HTML FORM variable. $value is assigned to the string with the value of the HTML FORM variable. This is shown as:

```
($name,$value) = split(/=/,$pair);
```

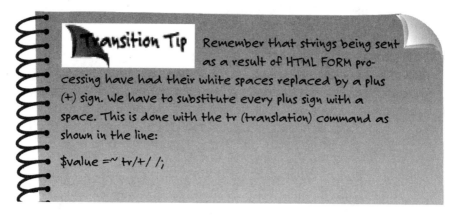

Transition Tip Remember that strings being sent as a result of HTML FORM processing have had their white spaces replaced by a plus (+) sign. We have to substitute every plus sign with a space. This is done with the tr (translation) command as shown in the line:

```
$value =~ tr/+/ /;
```

Also, the %dd syntax may have been used to capture special characters in the HTML FORM input. For example, a space character will be shown as %20 in the text returned by the browser. To use the raw hex value of the character instead of the text representation, we have to pack the hex value as a binary value in the $value string. This extraction of special variables and subsequent packing is done in :

```
$value = ~s/%([a-fA-F0-9][a-fA-F0-9])/pack("C",hex($1))/eg;
```

The regular expression in this line takes a percent sign followed by one or two hex digits and uses the pack() call in Perl to make a hex number. The C signifies one character and the $1 is the number extracted from the string. The g flag indicates that the operation is to be applied to the entire string in $value. The e accepts the replacement string as an expression and forces Perl to evaluate the resulting substitution before inserting it in the contents of $value. The expression to do this extraction is shown as:

```
$value =~ s/%([a-fA-F0-9][a-fA-F0-9])/pack("C",hex($1))/eg;
```

The newly substituted string in $value is then saved away at the entry in the @contents array using the $name as the index.

```
$contents{$name} = $value;
```

After the loop is finished, we have all our input names and variables in the %contents associative array. At this point, it's simply a matter of processing the items in this associative array to construct our mail message.

First, let's create a nice message from the values defined in the check boxes as shown in:

```
$interests = " ";
$interests .= "I-Xpress "  if ($contents{'interests1'});
$interests .= "Perl Tcl "  if ($contents{'interests2'});
$interests .= "daughters"  if ($contents{'interests3'});
```

The values in the $interest variable are concatenated together with the .= operation to construct one string in $interests. Depending on the number of buttons shown in the FORM, you can create a message of any format you see fit.

So, let's see how we handle the incoming variables in the %contents array in the Perl script. First let's copy %contents off into another array %response that we can happily destroy and still maintain a copy in %contents to which we can always refer back.

Now let's eliminate all the characters that pose a security risk for us. This means that we have to eliminate >,<,|,;,[,] and the back tick. The regular expression string to catch these variables is declared in the following variable:

```
$regexp = "[\<\>\|\;\,\`]";
```

If you want to limit mail to be sent only on the local machine use this value for the regular expression so that you can rid of the @, ! and % symbols as well:

```
$regexp = "[\<\>\|\;\@\!\%\,\`]";
```

To remove these extraneous symbols from each of the mfrom, mailto and msub fields you have to apply the replace pattern as follows:

```
$mfrom = $contents{'mfrom'};
$mfrom =~ s/$regexp//g;    # remove suspect chars
$mailto = $contents{'mailto'};
$mailto =~ s/$regexp//g;   # remove suspect chars
$msub = $contents{'msub'};
$msub =~ s/$regexp//g;     # remove suspect chars
```

The g at the end of each replace operation forces the pattern on all occurrences of the matched pattern in the variable. In the pattern shown here, you are eliminating these characters with nothing. If you want to replace them with something else, say an "xyz", you simply use this string:

```
$msub =~ s/$regexp/xyz/g;    # replace with "xyz"
```

Also please note that you can do the following operation:

```
$msub = $contents{'msub'};
$msub =~ s/$regexp//g;     # remove suspect chars
```

in one line like this:

```
($msub = $contents{'msub'}) =~ s/$regexp//g;
```

However, it tends to be a little tough to read for someone not very familiar with Perl. It's really up to you to choose the method you prefer.

Once this is done, we can feel a bit safer that we have eliminated a lot of chances of bogus messages eliminating the hard disk. Now, we have to eliminate those variables that are required to create the mail message (mfrom, mailto, msub) and those variables that are used for sorting and display (sortby and sendvar). So, let's get rid of these entries in the responses in %responses array:

```
delete $responses{'mfrom'};
delete $responses{'mailto'};
delete $responses{'msub'};
```

```
delete $responses{'sortby'};
delete $responses{'sendvar'};
```

Now get the list of variable names to sort by, and make a list of keys for yourself:

```
$sortby = $contents{'sortby'}; # get keys;
@usekeys = split(' ',$sortby);
```

The @body array will be initialized to an empty list. The @body array is used to create the list of responses in the body of the mail message that will be sent later.

```
@body = ();
$count = 0;
```

Now we create the body of the message based on the value of send-var. If it is set to TRUE, we will send keys plus user responses, otherwise we will only send responses. (You can always use a different value than TRUE if you like.)The foreach loop will cycle through the @usekeys array and use each item as an index into the %responses array to get the value of each variable. As each element is added to the @body array, it is deleted from the %responses array. When the loop shown below ends, the @body array will contain all the values for variables listed in the sortby variable:

```
foreach $key (@usekeys) {
    if ($sendvar eq "TRUE") {
    $body[$count++] = $key . " " . $responses{$key};
    } else {
    $body[$count++] = $responses{$key};
    }
    delete $responses{'$key'}; # remove.
}
```

Then whatever is left in the %responses array will be sorted alphanumerically, (based on the values of the keys of the associative array) and appended to the body of the message with this loop:

```
foreach $key (sort keys %responses) {
    if ($sendvar eq "TRUE") {
    $body[$count++] = $key . " " . $responses{$key};
    } else {
    $body[$count++] = $responses{$key};
    }
}
```

Once you have the body of the message as lines in the @body array, you have to glue them together as shown below to get one string to be able print the message out to send mail:

```
$message = "";
foreach (@body) {
    $message .= $_ . "\n";
}
```

The $echoback variable is used to construct a string that will echo back a debug message if the $mailto variable is set to an empty string. You may elect send a message back anyway but I do not advise it since that will betray to person using the Web browser what the format of the returned mail messages looks like. Here's how the echoback variable is constructed:

```
$echoback = "";
if ($mailto eq "") {
    $time = time;
    $echoback = "<HR>$time: Debug Echo Back<HR>";
    foreach (@body) {
    $echoback .= $_ . "<BR>"
    }
    $echoback .= "<HR>";
}
```

Now we are ready to print the body of the message out. Instead of using lots of print statements, we will use indirection. The format for using print indirection is:

```
print <<"HTMLHEAD";
```

Basically, the print command using indirection will print everything it sees verbatim until it sees the word HTMLHEAD on a line by itself with no leading or trailing white spaces. Using this form of indirection makes it easy to write out what's being printed without pesky print statements cluttering up the typing area. Plus, you can block copy, cut or paste into the areas being printed without regard to how Perl print statements will be used. Note how the standard HTML formatting statements are used to print the HTML document out.

Now comes another way of printing out text. This involves using the format statement in Perl. Basically, the output derived from the indirection command does not allow fixed field text output. It does not have to do any typesetting, since the receiving browser will handle most of that chore. It's a different story for a mail message since the text output will be seen by you, untouched.

The syntax for the format command is

```
format FILEHANDLE =
text that will be formatted
.
```

We will cover the details of this formatting in a bit. The period ends the formatting sequence. You will get a syntax error message from Perl if you leave the period out. The FILEHANDLE implies the handle to which this format applies. To print a right justified string, use @>>>> types of formatting. For a centered string, use @|||| types of formatting. For left just strings, use @<<<<<< type of formatting. Perl stops printing when a new line is encountered in the input. To avoid limiting the length of the strings being printed and to allow printing multi-lines, use @* as the formatting type.

Each <, > or | will print one character in the value of the variable. Only those characters shown by a symbol will be printed. If the length of contents being printed is less than the number of characters in the < string, then white spaces are printed out. If the length of the string is greater, then the string is truncated to fit.

Now let's look at the formatting required to get the printout for this mail message.

We use sendmail as before to send our mail message out:

```
open (MAILCOMMENT,"| /usr/bin/sendmail -t ");
write (MAILCOMMENT);
close (MAILCOMMENT);
```

Here, we open a pipe to the sendmail command on the Unix system I happen to be working on. I have deliberately hardcoded the path to the sendmail program. Whatever is written to the MAIL-COMMENT handle will now be sent to the mail command which will send a message to the user specified in the mailto variable, a subject as listed in $msub and a From: field set to the value in $mfrom. The write() command will use the format specified for that handle.

In this case, the name of the format is MAILCOMMENT and is shown below. Note that no mail is sent if the $mailto is set to an empty string. The output (minus some extraneous headers) from the sendmail command is shown in Listing 5.5.

```
if ($mailto ne "") {  # A mailto! respond with email
format MAILCOMMENT =
To : @*
$mailto
From: @*
$mfrom
Subject: @*
$msub
This message is sent from our mailbot in response
to the following questions:
====================================================
@*
$message
==================End of Message==================
.

open (MAILCOMMENT,"| /usr/bin/sendmail -t") || die
"Cannot open sendmail $!\n";
write (MAILCOMMENT);
close (MAILCOMMENT);
}
```

The "HTMLHEAD" format will be used for a response that sent back to the person using the browser. The format uses an extra field called $echoback. By default, you will *not* want the contents of the mail back to the user and therefore it's important to remove the callout when you actually use this code for your scripts.

```
print <<"HTMLHEAD";
<HTML>
<HEAD>
<TITLE> Ack for Request for Info </TITLE>
</HEAD>
<BODY>
<HR>
$echoback
<HR>
<P>
</BODY>
</HTML>
HTMLHEAD
```

Listing 5.5: Sample mail message from the CGI application

```
From nobody@myhost.com  Tue Nov 26 10:13:21 1996
Nov 1996 10:13:20 -0600
Date: Tue, 26 Nov 1996 10:13:20 -0600
...
To: khusain@myhost.com
```

```
From: imranc@myhost.com
Subject: Chapter 5
Status: RO

This message is sent from our mailbot in response
to the following questions:
====================================================
cname mps
lname Husain
fname Kamran
email khusain@ikra.com
fname Kamran
lname Husain
phnum 713 555 1212
tcall cant call
==================End of Message==================
```

One final item when using these Perl scripts: Be sure to check for invalid input. In most cases, your Perl script should be able to live with minimal information. However, to avoid mail messages with empty fields in them, you might want to consider writing a small subroutine such as the one shown here:

```
sub bailOut() {
local ($missing) = shift(@_) # Get the message to
print out.
print << "HTMLHEAD";
<HTML>
<HEAD>
<TITLE>Incomplete Response ..</TITLE>
</HEAD>
  <BODY>
<HR>
<P>Please fill out all the necessary information for
the FORM
<P>We cannot process incomplete forms.
<P> Please provide <B> $missing </B> field information.
<HR>
<P>
<A HREF="http://yourhost.com/index.html">Back to Home
Page</A>
</BODY>
</HTML>
HTMLHEAD;
exit(0);
}
```

Now you can check for empty fields and call the bailOut function for missing critical information. The $missing variable is assigned the first parameter passed into the bailOut function. For example, if the name field is empty, then you can check for it by simply using a statement like:

```
if ($contents{'name'} eq "" ) { &bailout("Error .. no name"); }
```

A series of tests could be made in the script to ensure a full form. For example, the following tests will check if the mfrom, mailto and msub fields are set. You can expand on this list to create your own error checking scenario.For instance:

```
If( ($contents{'mfrom'} eq "" ) || ($contents{'mailto'} eq
"" ) || if ($contents{'msub'} eq "" ))
{ &bailout("Incomplete info: mfrom, mailto and msub Code"); }
```

...could be written as:

```
if ($contents{'mfrom'} eq "" ) { &bailout("No mfrom"); }
if ($contents{'mailto'} eq "" ) { &bailout("No mailto"); }
if ($contents{'msub'} eq "" ) { &bailout("Your subject"); }
```

Only the first error caught will be returned back to the user at the browser. The code to check and bail out on the first error is easy to maintain and read in the future. It's pointless to give a detailed missing fields report to a user who should know which fields to fill out. Obviously, if the user elects to fill one field at a time and press the submit button, your CGI script will be called many times.

Of course, these calls have to be made so that two <HTML> tags are not sent back to the browser. This is why the exit(0) call is necessary in the bailout function. The sooner you catch the error, the less processing your server has to do.

As you can see, it's fairly straightforward to collect user input from an HTML form and create a mail message from it. It's made even easier in Perl by using the split function to extract all the incoming input into one associative array and then use its contents for creating reports. In fact, once you have the input from the form, you can even log it to disk.

Summary

In this chapter we learned about collecting and verifying user input from HTML forms. We also covered how to check the input received in Perl or Tcl scripts and how to handle optional and required fields. The format for the mail message is really up to you. The methods presented in this chapter covered two ways of presenting this information: using Tcl or using Perl.

How many times did someone come to your site? Is there any way to turn a profit from your interactive site? The next section will build on many of the basic skills we covered here. The ability to act and react to user input and the ability to go beyond the static to the active web site. The next chapter will deal with reading from data files, validating display items with string matching and regex, using Server Side Includes (SSI) to allow graphics to be downloaded and data to be updated in real time.

The next chapter will also discuss how to use system log files, and how to build and maintain your own log files. We will be using many of the same commands that were used in this software, so this will start to look familiar to you.

CHAPTER 6

COUNTERS

Using Log Files

Registering Hits

Meaningless Numbers

This chapter is a bit unusual. It starts with a general overview of counters, the pros and cons of using them and other options that are available. From there, the discussion moves on to some code and an explanation on how to place an accurate counter on the Web page in which you are interested.

In this section we will cover some basic topics that involve counters. Some of these include:

- The Common Log File Format
- Basic Logfile counting methods

- Numeric image replacement
- A simple randomizer (which will prepare you for the Chapter 8)

Getting Started With Counters

There are two basic ways to implement a counter. The first and easiest is to leverage the information from the log files kept by the Web Server. Nearly every Web Server today records all services that are executed by the server in a Common Log Format (CLF). The CLF records that are processed and placed in the transaction_log file document who (in a matter of speaking) requested a document, what they requested, the time and date of the request, and the amount of data transferred. The second method used to implement a counter requires that the document being counted create its own record of specific requests to that document with the information that the counter program would need. In this second case, the document would be calling a procedure (a CGI) to create a specialized log file that duplicates most of the information maintained in the CLF transaction_log that was generated by the server.

Sounds simple enough, doesn't it? It's also the most popular topic of conversation in the comp.infosystems.www.authoring.cgi newsgroup. Requests like: "I want a counter that puts the number of visitors on my page"; or "I want to know how many people have visited my page"; or even "I want to know where my visitors come from" are answered in the log files, to a point. Chapter 16 goes into great detail on log file analysis and discusses what gems of wisdom are stored in the log file, and how you can access them.

In the meantime, we will look at a way to make use of this log file data to determine how many people have come to a page. I should state here that I personally have never seen a reason for having a counter script that people visiting your page can see. If you are interested in the numbers, you can obtain them from the log files by using the scripts and programs that we will detail in Chapter 16. On the other hand, why would you care how many people came to a page you were viewing on the Net? Remember, the log files (both the ones created by the server and the ones created by the page) capture all requests, which means that a reload will cause the counter to misinform (we detail this a bit later in this chapter).

But, since so many people ask for them, we will look at what a counter is, how to make one, and what it does.

What actually gets logged each and every time a page is loaded from your server is the IP address (or domain, if DNS is supported by the HTTP server) of the machine that connected and requested the file. Note that you don't get the user's name from this method. In some instances, this could actually end up being an actual person's machine. But, in many cases, it can be a proxy-server or a firewall. With the popularity of Internet Service Providers (ISP) providing SLIP/PPP, it may be a dynamically assigned IP address from the ISP. In other words, it may not be a who that you can identify at all.

This doesn't necessarily mean that the information isn't useful. The domain information can tell you if the visitors are accessing you from Commercial sites, Educational ones, whether the sites are in the United States, or from another country.

Things to Consider Before Using Log Files

Log files, to coin a popular phrase these days, are a good thing. But, as good as they are, it's just as important that the limitations of the transaction log information be understood.

One problem with accurate measurements and counts is the cache. When you look in a browser's directory, you will generally see a subdirectory called cache. This is where pages and images are placed so that you can retrieve them rapidly without returning to the net. This has its advantages (it lowers network traffic) and disadvantages (it invalidates the concept of accurate page counting).

Consider the large commercial providers like America On-line, Prodigy and CompuServe. To improve performance in delivering documents, they create huge disk cache areas for pages and images. If your page is regularly accessed by users of these services, there is a high probability that they won't generate access counts on your server. Instead, these users will be getting cached documents. This creates invalid access counts on your machine as the documents they will be served will come off the cache and will not be loaded by coming to your machine.

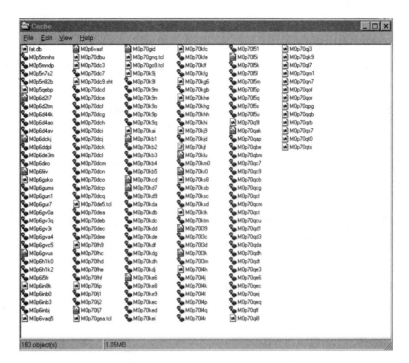

***Figure 6.1: A copy of a directory from
Netscape's Cache using Windows 95***

To the cache there is no server side include process like the one
that processed and placed the count of hits (either text or images) of
the counter on the page being viewed, it was just plain old HTML.
Therefore, the cache and the providers systems are unaware that this
document will update when processed by the server side.

Another way to have bogus counts is by people using the reload
button. Each reload can act as a separate request to the server to generate the document transfer, depending on the browser and its setting.
Each of these transfers gets logged. As much as the other problems
make your page counts seem lower than the actual visitors to them,
this function creates invalid access counts for the same visitor.

One key aspect of how the invalid access counts can cause problems is the way that the service Link Exchange has written their
count policy. In this service, you access a link from your site to a program that will display random advertising images on your site. In
return, the Link Exchange will display your random image on other
sites based on the traffic that generates through your site. This policy
states that if they find you have been "cheating" by front loading the
hits on the site with the reload, they will remove you from the

exchange. Because of caching and reloading, counters have a great amount of inaccuracy to deal with when it comes to presenting a true picture of access to the site.

Generating Counters With Log Files

With that said, it's time to examine just how to generate an access counter using the log files. A user request for this service would look like, "I would like to have people come to my pages and be able to know what number visitor that they are. This information should be displayed for the site, from the home page, or for any page that has a counter. The text should read: "You are visitor: nnnn" or "Hit Count: nnnn." In fact, I want the ability to put the number up as text, or as graphic images strung together, similar to, say, an odometer."

Requirements

For starters, the program needs to be able to do the following:

- Generate on-the-fly page count statistics for a single page
- Report on the page based on the page that you are on
- Display a textual message
- Display the numerical as text or in a series of graphic images

Analysis shows that a directory will have to be created to store the images for numeric image display. Additionally, the transaction log will be used to obtain counts of page hits (a hit is an access to a page that is recorded in the transaction_log file). Each of these counters will be a SSI HTML file and will increase the load that is placed on the server.

The SSI is parsed by the server to determine if there are any commands that the server must execute within the file. This increases the overload as each page passed through the server must be parsed. In order to not have to parse all files being accessed across the server, there is a way to define a certain type of file (as defined in the file extension and in the server's mime.types or in the server's configuration files) as being an SSI based on extension.

> **Tip** For those of you on Unix systems who feel a need to know, I propose use of the following code be issued as a SSI exec instead of a hit counter:
>
> grep page-to-search-for.html /path/to/logfiles/access_log | wc -l
>
> That command will search the access_log for the page you ask for and then count the number of hits the page has. This command works well from the command line if you want to know what you are doing in hit counts, and don't feel the need to share that data with the rest of the world (and the same command works for the refer-er_log file as well, but there you may want to replace the "| wc -l" with a "> tempfile.dat" so you can see just where people are coming from to your pages).

Designing a Counter in HTML

The program will be called from within the page being sent as an SSI. That means that we will have certain pieces of information available to us starting with the DOCUMENT_URI (a value that is passed in as part of the server's variable set when processing SSIs). This will allow us to know the full name of the document (via the URI) for searching the transaction log (also called the access_log in this code).

We want to be able to use the PATH_INFO variable or the QUERY_STRING variable to pass in the keyword for whether or not we will be using text or a graphics library. Unfortunately, SSIs are not permitted to do that. In Chapter 3 we discussed the information in which an SSI has access. Those variables, and only those variables, can be expected in a standard HTTPd server.

The only way to indicate that the selection should be graphical is to do so by allowing the code to make the determination if the display should be done with a graphic or with text. This decision-making process in the code can be accomplished in a number of ways.

The first is to have the code look for a specific subdirectory that contains the graphic images to be used in the display. In this method, we would hard code the actual graphic library into the software. The second method is to support a randomizer that allows use of any 1-n graphic libraries. This will be explored in the small program used to create a random number for a counter, and then randomly choose a method of display. A third way is to support a data file that contains a document URI and the name of an image library to be used with that document. This provides a fine granularity of control over the image library that is supposed to be used for any one document. In the third case the data file might look like that shown in Table 6.1. In this case, the default text wouldn't be in a datafile, but has been include for completeness.

Table 6.1: *Typical datafiles and sample images*

Datafile	Image
/books/index.shtml odom	hit count: ⌛
/tapes/index.shtml bigred	hit count:
/tapes/meatloaf/index.shtml mca001	hit count: *6*
default images - text	hit count: 2

In this sample data file, we have the index page for the /books/ index using a subdirectory in the graphics area called odom (as in odometer-type graphic images of numbers). The /tapes/ index uses a style called bigred and all the Meatloaf tapes use the mca001 graphics (MCA is the company under which Meatloaf releases his records). Image styles can be obtained from numerous places on the Net, and in clip-art libraries. The sample mca001 might be an image style that MCA created for an album that they would make available for people to use as a reference style. .

This is the SSI line that would be included in the HTML page to call up the counter:

```
<!—#exec cgi="/cgi-bin/cntr.tcl" — >
```

> Tip There are any number of graphics libraries
> available on the net. There are also a num-
> ber of excellent counter programs available. One that I
> recommend to people that are interested in having page
> counters is wwcount by Muhammad A. Muquit and Kevin L.
> Walsh. This program is available at
> http://www.semcor.com/~muquit/Count.html. The code is
> quite robust, and there are also numerous graphic
> libraries with great digits. Additional digits can be found
> at: Digit Mania (by Kevin Athey)
> <URL: http://cervantes.learningco.com/kevin/digits/ >

Designing a Counter in Tcl

In designing a Tcl program, remember that the code will take the values and parse them out. Then the code will read and count the log-file entries. This can take some time based on how old the logfile is and how much data it contains. There are two ways that this can be done. The first is to let the system do it for you. In this case, we would Tcl exec command and then execute the system command grep to process the file searching for all instances of the page in which we are interested. After the system command has run, and within the same Tcl exec command, we would also process the Unix command wc, -l which generates the total number of lines that have been produced from the grep command. The end result would be a numeric that could be printed or processed into its component digits and displayed graphically. The other option is to write a very tight loop and process each record in Tcl.

As usual, we will take the latter approach and use Tcl, which is the one that actually involves some coding. It doesn't mean that this process is better, only that the file manipulation method was chosen for the sake of portability.

```
set f1 [file open ../logs/access_log]
set knt 0
while {![eof f1]} {
```

```
gets f1 inline
if {[regexp "$uri" $inline] } {
incr knt
}
}
close f1
```

This code examines every line of the file for the value URI, which is the path passed in the DOCUMENT_URI variable. It then generates a count value (incremented with each positive return from the regular expression checker).

One possible problem arises when a URI is returned that may be an index value. In most cases, this is the file index.html or index.shtml. In those cases, the reference from within the access_log could be one of two references. The first is the full URL for the file, which is returned in the DOCUMENT_URI environment variable. The second is a reference to just the directory path. To get both references, a check is made to validate that the URI returned is an index file. If so, a complex URI is built for checking with the regexp above.

This complex URI is the base directory and the DOCUMENT_URI together, separated with the regexp or value of a pipe "|". The code to perform the validation and build the new URI looks like:

```
set uri $env(DOCUMENTURI)
if {[file rootname [file tail $uri ] ] == "index"} {
    set uri2 "[file dirname $uri]/ "
    set uri "$uri2\|$uri"
}
```

In this case, check to see if the filename is index-ignoring the extension. If it is, build the complex regexp URI value. So a DOCUMENT_URI of /~jones/stuff/index.shtml would turn into the regexp URI of:

```
"/~jones/stuff/ |/~jones/stuff/index.shtml".
```

Note In the URI we build for regexp parsing, there is a space before the pipe that must be there. This is to ensure that the root alone will be picked up. Had the space been omitted, all records that had the directory path "/~jones/stuff/" would have been counted. That would lead to erroneous counts as records like /~jones/stuff/moredirs/morestuff/file.html would have been counted as access hit on the URL /~jones/stuff/index.shtml.

Once the URI value has been generated, the processor closes the log file and then seeks out the image directory location. It will see if there are images in it, or if it contains directories. If there are images, it will do an image replacement. If there are directories, it will make a random directory selection and then perform the image replacement. If there is a file called iref.txt, it will check the file to see if the URI specified has an associated image package it should be using.

First, we will check for a file called iref.txt and, if it exists, search for the URI. If the URI is there, load up that library name into the lib variable. To ensure that this works, we will always use the full URI. That means that the data in the iref.text file will have the format of /~jones/stuff/index.shtml and not just /~jones/stuff/ for the index. This means that all searching in the regexp will be done using the DOCUMENT_URI.

```
set lib "ASCII"
if {[file exists ../data/iref.txt]} {
  set f1 [open ../data/iref.txt]
  while {![eof f1]} {
  gets f1 inline
   if {[regexp {$uri} [lindex $inline 0] ]} {
     set lib [lindex $inline 1]
     break
   }
 }
close f1
}
```

If the value exists in the data file, the count value will be evaluated to a list of single digits and those digits will be replaced by the URL to the image file in the proper library, shown here. It should be noted that a special case exists if the value is in single digits. In that case, we don't want to go through the overhead of the foreach, so we single check to verify that the data is a single digit and then, if it is, process it separately.

```
if {$lib == "ASCII"} {
  puts $knt
 } else {
   if {[string length $knt] > 1} {
     foreach num [split $knt ""] {
       puts "<img src=\"$lib/$num.gif\">"
     }
   } else {
     puts "<img src=\"$lib/$knt.gif\">"
   }
 }
} else {
puts $knt
}
```

In terms of error validation, a check is made at the time the library is defined to ensure that the library exists. If the library doesn't exist, ASCII text will be used.

One fast note on design issues: There are no requirements to capture the date from which we are starting the count. If you wanted to expand the counter's functionality or plan for it, the code could be modified to change the way the transaction log file is read.

In this case, we open the transaction log file, read the first record and capture the first date. Then we enter the while loop, process the record and end with a read. This will also cause Tcl to perform a cleaner exit because it won't run the while loop twice at the end (once with the last record, and once after Tcl confirms that the last record has been read). The code changes for this are included in the code for the procedure below, although there is no print line for the date that was captured. That line might print out something like "visitors since date-value".

Before we move on to the code for this program, I have included a small example in Listing 6.1 for those of you that loathe counters as much as I do. This program (getrancnt.tcl) generates a random count and a random image library to be used, and then displays it as shown in Figure 6.2. I like the 10,000,000 figure, but you can use a lower or higher seed value, based on your needs and desires.

Listing 6.1: getrancnt.tcl

```
#!/usr/local/bin/tclsh
##   getrancnt.tcl
##
```

```tcl
## much like getcnt.tcl - except *much* faster since
## it doesn't produce a real number - it generates a
## random number and puts it into a random
## font/graphic. The code for random number
## generation will be discused in detail within the
## chapter on random number generation and how to
## use random numbers
##
##
puts "Content-type: text/html\n\n"
##
proc random {args} {
  global RNG_seed
  set max 259200
  set argcnt [llength $args]
  if { $argcnt < 1 || $argcnt > 2 } {
    error "wrong # args: random limit | seed ?seedval?"
  }
  if ![string compare [lindex $args 0] seed] {
    if { $argcnt == 2 } {
      set RNG_seed [lindex $args 1]
    } else {
      set RNG_seed [expr ([pid]+[file atime \
          /dev/kmem])%$max]
  }
    return
  }
  if ![info exists RNG_seed] {
    set RNG_seed [expr ([pid]+[file atime \
        /dev/kmem])%$max]
  }
  set RNG_seed [expr ($RNG_seed*7141+54773)%$max]
  return [expr int([lindex $args 0]* \
      ($RNG_seed/double($max)))]
}
##
##
## the code - there are 3 graphic libraries, and the
## random number is set to a seed of 10000000. Why
## three graphic libraries? - no reason, you could
## use 100 if you have the disk space to waste.
##
##
set knt [random 10000000]
set libnum [random 3]
if {$libnum == 0} {
  set libnum 3
}
if {[string length $knt] > 1} {
  foreach num [split $knt ""] {
```

```
##
##
## images are stored in libraries called imagedir1 -
## imagedir3 as <number>.gif   ex: 1.gif, 2.gif,
## 3.gif…
##
##
    puts "<img \
        src=\"/path/giflib/imagedir$libnum/$num.gif\">"
    }
} else {
  puts "<img \
        src=\"/path/giflib/imagedir$libnum/$knt.gif\">"
}
```

Listing 6.1 is my favorite counter, and I like to use it as:

```
You are the
<!—#exec cgi="/jmi-bin/getrancnt.cgi" —>
visitor to this page.
```

You are the 5181567 vistor to this page.

***Figure 6.2: Output generated by
the rancnt.tcl procedure***

A Program to Generate a Counter in Tcl

Listing 6.1 is an attempt to drive home the fact that a counter can produce bogus information. As we discussed, every reload increases a counter's hits. The ability to increase a counter by just doing reloads ensures that the information within the counter is bogus. It doesn't matter if the count information was generated by either a reload, or a multiple visit, if the numbers were pulled from the systems log files or user maintained log files. Bogus counter data is too easy to generate, and placing a counter on a page just increases the likelihood that someone will generate it on purpose.

The code in Listing 6.2 generates a counter that meets the requirements for the system mentioned earlier. As you can most likely tell by now, I'm not enamored with counters or what they provide in information. I have no desire to know how many times a page was seen, unless. of course, I'm an advertiser. In that case, it's nice to know a bit about the click through habits of people visiting a particular site and we will be discussing that over the following two chapters.

Listing 6.2 generates a count of the number of times that a page has been viewed before, based on the entries in the access_log. It will then, using a data file to validate the style of the counter, generate a counter that states how many times this page has been viewed.

Listing 6.2: getcnt.tcl

```
#!/usr/local/bin/tclsh
##    getcnt.tcl
## The counter program.
##
## let's set some paths here
##
set logf /path-to-the-httpd/access_log
set iref /path-to-the-datafile/iref.txt
##
##
puts "Content-type: text/html\n\n"
##
## Always start with setting the URI, that way we
## know who we are in this case we want to make a
## complex search if we were listed as an index
## note: if the system has defaults besides index
## fora "/" (root or index lookup) you will want to
## modify this to support that.
##
## DOCUMENT_URI is the variable name set by the
## server and passed to the SSI that states what
## document is currently being viewed.
##
set uri $env(DOCUMENT_URI)
if {[file rootname [file tail $uri ] ] == "index"} {
  set uri2 "[file dirname $uri]/ "
  set uri "$uri2\|$uri"
}
##
## let's search the log file for all references and
## count them
##
set knt 0
set f1 [open $logf r]
while {![eof $f1]} {
  gets $f1 inline
```

```
    if {[regexp "$uri" $inline]} {
      incr knt
    }
}
close $f1
## This ref. isn't in the log file. Account for it incr knt
##
## reset the uri value as we now want to see if we
## are supposed to use a special library for images
## and number->image replacement
##
set uri $env(DOCUMENT_URI)
set lib "ASCII"
##
## Open a file and determine the replacement
##
if {[file exists $iref]} {
 set f1 [open $iref]
 while {![eof $f1]} {
  gets $f1 inline
  if {[regexp "$uri" [lindex $inline 0] ]} {
      set lib [lindex $inline 1]
      break
  }
 }
 close $f1
##
## we have a replacement or not mattering on if the
## lib was redefined,  if so, replace the numbers
## with images
##
 if {$lib == "ASCII"} {
  puts $knt
 } else {
  if {[string length $knt] > 1} {
##
## this splits the number up and replaces each
## numeric with a library image
##
      foreach num [split $knt ""] {
        puts "<img src=\"$lib/$num.gif\">"
      }
  } else {
## only a single digit
      puts "<img src=\"$lib/$knt.gif\">"
  }
 }
} else {
##
## Boring ASCII
## puts $knt
}
```

Using Perl to Create Counter Values

It's relatively easy to create counters using Perl just as we did in Tcl. The steps we are taking are summarized once more here:

- Read the access_log file to figure out the number of hits for a given URL
- Check if the iref.txt file has this URL listed in it, and if so what type of display is required: plain text or IMG tags
- Generate text if no listing in the iref.txt file.
- Generate IMG tags for each digit if the file's digit library is listed in the iref.txt file.

The first step tests for the existence of the URL being hit in the access_log file. We open the access_log file and count the number of hits for the incoming URL. The code to do this is shown below:

```
open (FH,$access) || die ""; # silent suicide
while(<FH>) { # count the hits on this file
    if ($_ =~ /$url/) {
    $ctr++;  # up the counter
    }
}
close(FH); # you are now done with it.
```

The code shown above reads the access_log file and increments a counter for all the matches on the name of URL in the DOCU-MENT_URI environment variable. The access file is then closed. For URLs that end in "index", we use the special case of also looking at the directory names with the file index.html. You can extend this functionality to look for .shtm,.shtml or other types of extensions.

Once the counter for a URL is derived, we call the function appropriately called showit to display the counts. The guts of this subroutine are defined below. The $usecode variable is set to either ASCII or a location to get images of digits from. The value of the $usecode variable is set to ASCII by default before the file iref.txt is searched for and opened. If the iref.txt file is found, then we look at each line in the file to see if the URL for the current document is listed. If it is listed, then we use the library code listed in the line for the URL as the value for $usecode and stop looking. Multiple listings of the same

URL are not allowed, and in fact are useless, since only the first match of the URL will be used.)

```
while (<MYFH>) {    # check if URL listed
  ($uri,$code) = split(' ',$_);
  if ($uri eq $fname) { # found!
    $usecode = $code;
    last;
    }
  } # while loop ends
close (MYFH);
  }
}
```

Once the value of $usecode is determined, we check if it is set to ASCII or something else. If the value is set to ASCII, a string with the value of the counter is printed. Any other value in $usecode is interpreted as a path name to a directory containing images of digits. We split the digits in the counter value and print a GIF image for each digit in the $counter variable from that directory using IMG tags.

```
if ($usecode eq "ASCII") {
    print "\n Visit $fname = $counter times \n";
}else{ # okay, present GIF images of digits.
    my @str = split('', $counter);
    foreach $i (@str) {
        print "\n <IMG SRC=$usecode/$i.gif>";
    }
}
```

The code shown in Listing 6.3 shows the complete listing for the Perl script. You must modify two variables for it to work: the location of the access log and the iref.txt file. Once you set the paths correctly, you can use the Perl program in the SSI include directive as you did with the Tcl code shown earlier.

Listing 6.3 pcCount.pl

```
#/usr/local/bin/perl

$iref = "/my/path/to/my/file/iref.txt"; #  MODIFY
$access = "/my/path/to/logs/access_log";   #
MODIFY!

my($url,$ctr);
```

```perl
$url = $ENV{'DOCUMENT_URI'};
$ctr = 1;
my $myurl = $url;
if ($url =~ /\/index[\.]*[\w]*$/)   {
   #
   # construct directory name + URL
   #
   my ($dname = $url) =~ s/index[\.]*[\w]*$/;
   $url =   "$url|$dname";
}


open (FH,$access) || die ""; # silent suicide
while(<FH>) { # read the file
   if ($_ =~ /$url/) { # found!
   $ctr++;
   }
}


# =====================================
# Now print the counters out in the
# same way as the tcl code.
# =====================================
&showit($url,$ctr);
exit(0);

sub showit() {
   my $fname = shift @_;   # get URI
   my $counter = shift @_; # get counter
   my ($i,$code,$uri);    #
   my $usecode = 'ASCII';      # no library location
   if ( -e $iref) {          # check codes file.
   open(MYFH,$iref) || die "Cannot open $iref";
   while (<MYFH>) {    # check if URL listed
     ($uri,$code) = split(' ',$_);
     if ($uri eq $fname) { # found!
       $usecode = $code;
       last;
       }
     } # while loop ends
   close (MYFH);
   }
   # =====================================
   # Using default value or no digit GIFs?
   # =====================================
   if ($usecode eq "ASCII") { # show text only
     print $counter;
   }else{ # okay, present GIF images of digits.
     my @str = split('', $counter); # get digits
     foreach $i (@str) {  #print each digit
       print "\n <IMG SRC=$usecode/$i.gif>";
     }
   }
}
```

Summary

This chapter addressed a number of problems with generating a counter, beginning with data validity and ending with the question, "Who really wants to know this information?"

This chapter also allowed you to focus on some of the limitations and abilities of using SSIs to create active pages. This will be expanded in the next chapter when we study how to use the Location header information to make a page transition automatically.

There is a term for those people who go to search sites (like Excite, Alta Vista or Infoseek) and then run a search for their own name. It is called ego-surfing. There is also some of that same ego gratification that one gets when they have a hit counter on their page. It's like brazenly calling out how popular you feel you are. Considering that all it takes to alter the numbers on a hit counter is to load and reload the page, it shows just how little use there is for what remains one of the most asked for capabilities, that of being able to display the number of "visitors" to a site.

For those of you on Unix systems who feel a need to know, I propose the you use following code instead of a hit counter:

```
grep page-to-search-for.html /path/to/logfiles/access_log | wc -l
```

In Chapter 16, we go into greater detail on how you can use standard Unix commands, like the one above, to do some basic site analysis. But before we get involved with management of the site and log file issues, let's turn to Chapter 7. There we'll talk about modifying a header's information that is returned to a browser designed to redirect a user. And how to make a few dollars with banner advertising.

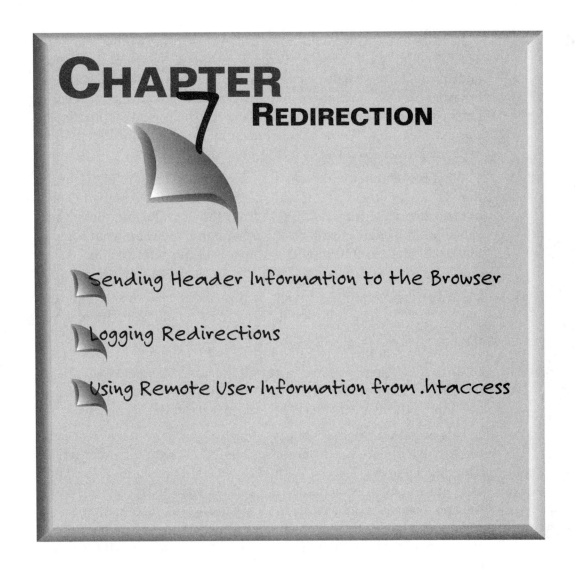

CHAPTER 7 REDIRECTION

- Sending Header Information to the Browser

- Logging Redirections

- Using Remote User Information from .htaccess

Redirection: A Better Way to Count

You've already learned that log files provide a clean way to perform counts. But what if we want to be a bit more accurate? What if we want to know who goes where? The following discussion will look at the concept of Redirection: in this case, having the action from a user to generate a call to an advertiser's home page.

In cases like this we want to be able to perform two basic actions. The first thing we want to do is redirect the user to the new location, and to do that we will discuss the process of passing back header information as the standard output. We also need a higher level of detailed information about what happened than what we find in the standard log files. We need this for many reasons, and these will be explained as we go forward in this chapter.

What this chapter will do is show you how to capture the information. However, it will not provide data reduction tools that you could use to extract the nuggets of gold from this log file, and make them valuable. This chapter will, on the other hand, focus on what some of that useful data is, and how and why it is useful information.

Before we delve into this too far, you may ask, "Why are we dealing with Redirection, and what is this about advertisers and consumers?" Well, let's talk about real life for a moment. In real life, someone has to pick up the costs associated with the operation of the Web site. In real life, someone has to pay for the content to be created. In real life, someone has to pay all the costs associated with being on the net. One of the key models for picking up your expenses in developing these great sites is to "sell space" on the Webpages.

This is not an original concept. Most of you who have surfed the Internet have already, at one time or another, seen a banner advertisement. Figures 7.1 and 7.2 show two sites, Lycos and Yahoo, that use banner advertisements. These banner advertisements provide a site and advertiser the chance to get a message to you, an impression, when you come to the page with the banner on it. A good banner has at least one item to which it will draw your eye so that you will register the company name.

Figure 7.1: *Lycos site using advertising banner*

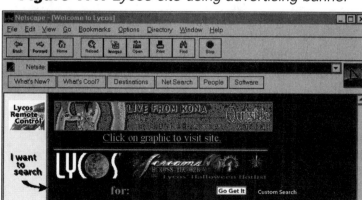

Figure 7.2: *Yahoo site using advertising banner*

In this way banners are much like standard advertising in a newspaper or magazine. With the ability to use animated GIF formatted banners, the banners have a bit more interactivity and could actually have a greater draw than a flat advertisement, even if the footprint on the page is much smaller.

Beyond impressions, there is a concept that the visitor will access the associated banner's site. This is like having the ability to touch the advertisement in the magazine and having a section pop out on that company or its product. In this way, the advertisement on the Web page has a greater sales value than flat and static paper-based display advertisements. Additionally, you can focus advertisements as you can see from the three advertisement banners from Yahoo shown in Figures 7.3. through 7.5. The advertisements seem almost tailored to the possible visitors of the page.

Figure 7.3: *Image from Yahoo apparently tailored to the Computers topic area*

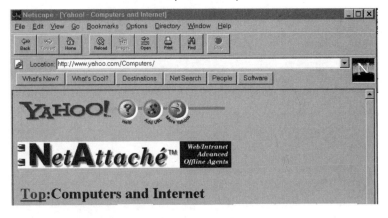

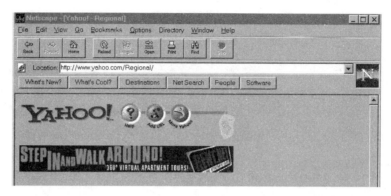

Figure 7.4: *Image from Yahoo apparently tailored to the Regional topic area*

The process of moving the user from your site to the next site is referred to as Redirection. In this case, we wanted to use a real-world example that you see every day, and focus on how you can make use of it in your home pages.

Now, you aren't limited to using this in your site to only advertising banners on the Web pages. With a minor modification, you can use a small SSI script to allow you to force a user on a page to jump to another location. Again, you may have seen this done on the net. If you went to a Web page that has been relocated, you may have seen a notice to the effect that the page has moved. Then, after about five seconds, you find yourself magically transported to the new page. This too is a form of Redirection. It allows a site to redirect users who come back to the site from a bookmarked location in their bookmark files to the new location for what they bookmarked. This means that people coming to the site won't get the dreaded 301 or 404 error message, but they will be taken to the new location.

Figure 7.5: *Image from Yahoo apparently tailored to the Society and Culture topic area*

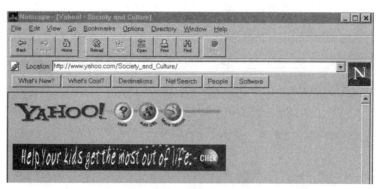

As you can see, the Redirection, or location header, provides a number of useful services. We hope that this chapter will provide you with some ideas on how you can leverage this to your needs.

Note Earlier in the book there was a short discussion on site security and limiting access to information using the .htaccess files. Later in Chapter 15 we will delve deeper in the security aspects of .htaccess and what its full range of uses are. In general, these files limit the ability of people accessing the server to get to data inside the structure of a Web site. The .htaccess file provides finer levels of control that can require a username and a password, or can perform limits based on a combination of factors, like from where the person is coming, or at what page they were last. Within this section, we are going to show how you can obtain the username that a person has used when they went to an area protected by a username/password combination, and place that information into the log file that you are making.

So, let's get back to advertising banners. Why even bother with this? Well, for the most simple of reasons. Money. Stop and think of all the sites you like to go. Don't many of them have advertisements on them? Now, consider the following scenario. You have a customer who owns a site on the Internet. It is a popular site. The cost of maintaining the site keeps on increasing as more information is added and as the site expands in popularity. To offset the costs, the owner decides to ask people if they would like to advertise on the site.

There are any number of models for advertising billing. Some sites charge a flat rate and guarantee a minimum number of impressions (or number of times the advertisement was displayed to a browser). Other sites charge for each impression. And still others use a model that I feel is the most fair to an advertiser, and the model that this program will support. This model is based on the data that it captures in the log files.

In these cases, the site advertising billing rates are broken into two component pieces. There is a base rate for each impression made to a possible customer, and another rate paid for each click-through or referral. To keep track of the referrals, a log of each referral is required. Otherwise, we would only be able to see how many times a graphic was displayed (from the access_log) and could know the impression count but not how many customers were fed to the advertiser's site on the click-through.

So, let's say that we charge 0.5 cents per impression, and 1.5 cents for each click-through (not out of line based on rates as of September 1996) using the two-tiered model. With this advertisement rate, we can see that an impression is worth one-third the value of a click-through. Why? Just because an advertisement is displayed doesn't mean that it is read. Again, let's look at this as a model of a magazine. Just because I bought a magazine doesn't guarantee that I will see your advertisement on page 50. It also doesn't mean that I won't. It also is no guarantee that I will read it or will take down the 800 number, or even remember to call for more information.

In other words, seeing the display advertisement may or may not lead to a sale, or even a impression of the company or product on the consumer. For this reason, the advertiser should pay a lower rate for the impression. The click-through, on the other hand, is substantially more as its use means that a consumer was drawn into your location where they have shown an interest in what you have to offer. In other words, you now have a qualified lead and, in general, a qualified lead has substantially greater value than that of a unqualified one (to validate this, call mail order houses and check to see what the price is for a mailing list of one time buyers and multiple buyers. You shouldn't be surprised that the qualified buyers list (multiple buyers) is substantially more expensive.). That explains why the two-tiered rate actually is much fairer to the advertiser, and also explains why it would be in your greatest interest to focus on market analysis and why those log files are so important, so you can increase the percentages of click-through per impression, thereby increasing the site's income without increasing the site's bandwidth requirements or load average.

The next thing a person using display advertising wants is the ability to add value to the information an advertiser gets from them. Just knowing someone came to the site is nice. But the charge per referral could be increased if we were able to target who was coming (this is pursued further a bit later in Chapter 8). In fact, by targeting the market, performing market analysis and market segmentation, click-throughs could be increased by looking at what is happening, and doing some trends analysis against the log files at the site. To do this accurately, we need to know more about who accesses the sites as well as from where those people access. Again, we can use the log files the current server is keeping to provide some of that information, but by building our own log file filled with personal information, we can expand on that information, adding more value each time.

Additionally, we can ask the users to fill out forms over time that will generate a clearer view of the customer. We can even personalize the forms using CGI scripts to do some limited data analysis from the log files, or to use files that contain the already reduced data. This way, we can ask about the experience they had the time they went to a site, if the site was relevant to them, and what it did or didn't do in terms of meeting their needs. Another plus is to find out if they would be interested in more sites of this type, or how would they have classified the site. Each completed questionnaire will help in analyzing the site, it's usage and the customer that the site interests. All this information is of great value when attracting advertisers and setting rates for impressions and click-throughs.

The more data that we gather from the user, the more valuable the information we have on that user. As the user enters the data, we can obtain a profile of the user, and we can better arrange for advertisers who are interested in the user, and products in which the user may be interested, getting together. In this way we can perform both the user and the advertiser the service of qualifying the advertisements that we display to the user, and qualifying the potential consumers to which we display the advertiser's ad.

The demographic data obtained from following registered users can help us to better manipulate the impressions of the display advertisements to where they will perform the best for the customer (the owner of the display advertisement) and the potential consumers (visitors at the site). In addition, by using the demographic data recorded about the users, we can also see where these users are going and suggest other areas of commonality and overlap for the advertisers at the site. This will end up providing a benefit for both the potential consumer and the potential advertisers by matching the advertisements to the consumer's products and services interests. This is a cleaner form of direct marketing, using banners to meet the directed needs of the site's potential consumers in a way that offers all parties the largest return on their investment.

User Profiling and User Tracking

User profiling was initially discussed in Chapter 3, when we covered cookies. The methods that were used in that chapter were generally hidden and are considered by many who would be forced to have a cookie placed on them as repugnant. There are two other ways that user profiling and user tracking can be accomplished. Neither of these methods is invasive without clearly advising the user that they are allowing the process to invade their personal space.

The first still involves the use of a cookie. In this method, users are told that a cookie or tag will be added to their browser so it will be known when they come to any location in this site in the future. They must then enter a hypertext page where a CGI script will add the cookie to their browser. They will also be informed of any and all limitations associated to the cookie (it can only be accessed by the site that placed the cookie there, etc.).

The second method would require users to register at your site. A simple registration that allows access to your site, with an option form for additional registration information, is considered acceptable by most people. User tracking allows you to associate a user to a page access. This requires that a registered user's name be logged with access to the page. You probably won't want to do that with every page. But once turned on for a directory structure at a site most HTTPd servers will put that information in the access log when anything from within that directory tree structure at the site is accessed by the user. You will want to log this information in your own log file when you forward a user off to the ether of cyberspace using a location directive.

Tracking an Advertising Banner

The log file that will be developed here provides all the data necessary to focus on expanding the vision of marketing. The following information will provide valuable demographic data and will help track each access from the advertising banner to the advertising page. This process is commonly referred to as click-through and is what happens when the potential consumer clicks the advertising banner and passes from the site where the banner was displayed to the site of the owner of the banner (the advertiser). The information we want to capture on this click-through is:

- Are the users registered at the site and, if so, what are their names?
- From what site are they coming?
- What page did they access (jump to) and which one of my pages were they on when doing so (where was the advertisement being displayed)?
- What time did they access the page?

This log file could be e-mailed to the person maintaining the site by a crontab or the same crontab could swap the old log file out and create a new log file at midnight. Then it could perform data analysis on the old log file creating smaller, detailed reports that would be used by the site to provide added value analysis to the advertiser.

Linking the Pages

The links require that the page information is passed as part of the QUERY_STRING of the URI to the CGI. Since this is a selectable item and not an SSI (unlike the counter scripts from the last chapter), this will be possible. The requirements for the logging process are:

- Open a log file (in the code we will call it accesslog.fil) in the log file directory location
- See if the user's name is available and, if it is, make sure we trap it.
- Get the user's IP/Domain
- Get the system time
- Get the URI
- Get the forwarding pagename

• Output the user name (or non-registered), IP/Domain, System-Time, Pagename and URI

Once we have created the entry in the log file and we close it, we have one last responsibilityæto send the user to the new location defined by the link on the banner image. This is done by putting a location header directive to the standard output.

A Simple Page Using HTML

To keep the book short and simple, Figure 7.6 displays the most minimal page we could create. It has a title, a banner (actually two banners to show the difference between a border and a non-border banner), a header, some explanatory text and a closing line. The key piece of this is the banner line. Note that the banner is enclosed within the reference link. That will cause the banner to be highlighted in blue. You could add the border=0 value to the image statement to eliminate the blue highlight. To show how this looks, we have included two banners in the HTML.

One key piece of the banner processing is the information that follows the call to the cgibin in the link. In this case, we are calling uncgi to disassemble the component pieces, and the trackit.cgi program (the Tcl code below). Notice that we are using a complete URI to send the information about where to go next in the loc variable.

Figure 7.6: *If you're a Packer fan, this is the HTML page for you*

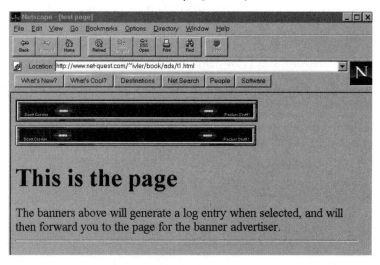

```
<title>test page</title>

<a href="/cgibin/uncgi/trackit.cgi?loc=http://www.advert1.
com/index.html"><img src="/ads/adv1.gif" alt="an ad"></a>

<!- same advertisement without the border showing up
as a blue link -->

<a href="/cgibin/uncgi/trackit.cgi?loc=http://www.advert1.
com/index.html"><img src="/ads/adv1.gif" alt="an ad"
border=0></a>

<h1>This is the page</h1>
```

The banners above will generate a log entry when selected, and will then forward you to the page for the banner advertiser.

Personalizing Your Logging System in Tcl

A click-though should try to capture all the necessary information on the person who is making the click-through. That information, along with other data about the user that may be gathered over time, will permit a detailed report of the user-type who click-through on certain types of advertisements. As usual, data capture could be misused and, instead of helping consumers, it could come back to haunt you.

To avoid this state, I suggest that, after the users coming in have "signed in" for the session by coming to a site that requires user names and passwords, or is using cookies, that they are apprised of the fact that their visits are still being tracked for statistical purposes. Also, let them know that this information is being used to try to ensure that they have a higher propensity of seeing products that you thought would meet their needs based on this statistical information.

As long as the user is constantly being reminded that their privacy is being invaded, there is no room open for complaints of unfairness.

As I said earlier, one key item that you want to do is focus on developing a solid foundation of people that have specific interests. This is done through forms, queries, quizzes and, of course, games of chance. The idea here is to capture data that can be used to focus the overall marketing effort to potential customers, as well as to provide information about those consumers to the advertiser.

The following items are what you would want to log and may be used by the CGI if they are passed in by the server to the CGI process.

- REMOTE_USER (if available)
- REMOTE_HOST (if not available, use REMOTE_ADDR)
- WWW_loc (the parsed information on the next location from QUERY_STRING)
- HTTP_REFERER (stripping off the http://SERVER_NAME)

Time will be taken from the system "time" and the log file will have entries that look like:

```
[date-time-stamp] uri pagename ip/domain user

[Sun Apr  7 08:03:25 PDT 1996] /~me/mypage.html
⇒http://www.net-quest.com/subscriptions/index.shtml
⇒192.1.1.23 frank

[Sun Apr  7 08:05:05 PDT 1996] ~me/yetanother/page.html
⇒http://www.yahoo.com/index.shtml gateway.wwinfo.com
⇒non-registered
```

The following Tcl code will validate that certain fields exist and, if not, will fill them with the proper default values.

The first line will remove the information (strip from the left) about the protocol and the server name. We know what they are so there is no need to track them. The next logic section handles getting the remote host name, or, if it doesn't exist, the remote address.

```
regsub "^http://$env(SERVERNAME)" $env(HTTP_REFERER) "" uri
if {![info exists env(REMOTE_HOST)]} {
  set remote $env(REMOTE_ADDR)
} else {
  set remote $env(REMOTE_HOST)
}
```

Here the code looks to see if the remote user variable is set. This will get set to the users name when the visitor goes through a password system using the .htaccess to capture a username/password combination. If we had chosen to use cookies at the site rather than an .htaccess we would change the logic here to obtain the cookie information

```
if {![info exists env(REMOTE_USER)} {
  set user "non-registered"
} else {
  set user $env(REMOTE_USER)
}
```

The line used to output the completed log entry to the log file will look like:

```
puts "\[[exec date]\] $uri $env(WWW_loc) $remote $user"
```

The next and final issue is to forward the user to the new location. This is done using a 302 command. This command tells the browser that the item requested was not found. It also allows you to redirect the browser to an alternate location using the Location: directive. This isn't that complex. The code is :

```
puts "Location: $env(WWW_loc) \n\n"
```

Do Not put a Content-type. There is none. This is the line that will cause the Redirection to take place. In Listing 7.1, the Redirection is done first, so that the user will be forwarded while the script continues to do the logging.

> **Note** The log file must be world writable as the program will have to write to it. You could make it group or user writable, but that would also mean that you would have to ensure that the protections were such that the file was owned by the proper group and owner as to be writable by the CGI program.
>
> After all my warnings on security, you have to be wondering why am I being so insecure in this case. First of all, you are the only person who knows where it is located. Now I generally don't subscribe to this security through smoke and mirrors, but, in this case, there is something to be said about that.
>
> Consider what it is we are protecting here. It isn't the crown jewels, it isn't a file that, if corrupted, would cause any damage to your computer or its operations. What we are dealing with is accounting information. The log file doesn't even provide information about what it is, or its purpose.
>
> Based on that, the only way someone could make use of the data is to try to see what we are logging and why, or to reverse engineer the logging. Since we have no origi-

nal information within the file, this file is a very low risk item. Protection by lack of information, in these few cases, would be sufficient to ensure that the files are protected enough.

Listing 7.1: trackit.tcl

```
#!/usr/local/bin/tclsh
##
## trackit.tcl
##
## Force the location change in the browser
##
puts "Location: $env(WWW_loc) \n\n"
## omit the server information
##
regsub "^http://$env(SERVER_NAME)" \
    $env(HTTP_REFERER) "" uri
## set the remote host if we know it, if not use
## the remote address
if {![info exists env(REMOTE_HOST)]} {
  set remote $env(REMOTE_ADDR)
} else {
  set remote $env(REMOTE_HOST)
}
## if we don't know who the remote user is,
## set the default
if {![info exists env(REMOTE_USER)]} {
  set user "non-registered"
} else {
  set user $env(REMOTE_USER)
}
##
## open the file and write the line out
## (note that we use an a+ when we open the file
## stating that we want to open it with the append
## option on
##
set f1 [open /the-path-to-the-file/accesslog.fil a+]
puts $f1 "\[[exec date]\] $uri $env(WWW_loc) \
    $remote $user"
close $f1
##
## we are done, close the file and exit
##
exit
```

Perl Design and Code

In the Perl version of the trackit.tcl, we will collect the information as before from the URL. Within the Perl script, the %contents array will contain all the elements of the environment during the execution of this script. Basically, all this script does is jump to a different location after logging the user's information. You can think of the CGI script as the launching pad from which a URL request will be redirected to a completely different location.

The command to force the jump for the browser to the new location is as follows:

```
print "Location:$contents{'loc'}\n\n";
```

Now we can collect information for the entry in the log file. First, get the date by executing the Unix date command using the back quotes. Anything between back quotes is executed as a command in Unix. The chop command will get rid of the trailing end of line character, as shown here.

```
$date = `date`;
    chop($date);
```

Then, get information about the user at the browser by looking at the environment variables. The HTTP_REFERER value will have the http:// in it so we have to remove it with this substitution statement:

```
$referer  =~ s/http:\///;
```

The host and user information is collected with the following statements:

```
$host = $ENV{'REMOTE_HOST'};
$host = $ENV{'REMOTE_ADDR'}if ($host eq "" );
$who = $ENV{'REMOTE_USER'};
$sent = $contents{'loc'};
if ($who eq "") {$who = "unregistered"; }
```

There may be some servers who do not provide you with the REMOTE_HOST or REMOTE_ADDR information. In such cases, you have to determine what actions to take and what information to log. Obviously, some testing with your particular server will let you get a feel for what environment variables you can and cannot use.

If a user name is not available, the value of $who is set to a value of unregistered. (Here we chose the value of unregistered over non-registered, because unregistered is a real word and nonregistered does not show up in my spell checker's default vocabulary.) We will let you, the reader, decide which spelling to use!

Now let's write the entry to the disk file.

```
open (LOGFILE,">>../logs/htaccess") || die ;
 print LOGFILE "[$date] $referer $sent $host $who\n";
  close LOGFILE;
```

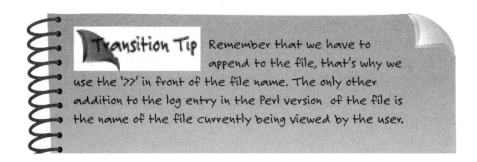

Transition Tip Remember that we have to append to the file, that's why we use the '>>' in front of the file name. The only other addition to the log entry in the Perl version of the file is the name of the file currently being viewed by the user.

Once the file is closed, you can run grep commands on it from the command line and extract all sorts of information about who's been accessing what pages from where and when. Listing 7.2 provides the complete program in Perl.

Listing 7.2: Logging accesses via htaccess.

```
#!/usr/bin/perl
#========================================================
# Generate a log entry before sending the user
# off somewhere
#========================================================
$|=1; # force output back ...
#========================================================
# Grab the URL to jump to
#========================================================
if ($ENV{'REQUEST_METHOD'} eq "POST") {
    read(STDIN,$buffer,$ENV{'CONTENT_LENGTH'});
} else {
```

```
        $buffer = $ENV{'QUERY_STRING'};
}

@pairs= split(/&/,$buffer);
foreach $pair (@pairs) {
    ($name,$value) = split(/=/,$pair);
    $value =~ tr/+/ /;
    $value =~ s/%([a-fA-F0-9][a-fA-F0
9])/pack("C",hex($1))/eg;
    $contents{$name} = $value;
}

#====================================================
# Force their browser off to other location.
#====================================================
print "Location:$contents{'loc'}\n\n";

#====================================================
# Collect information for the entry
#====================================================
$date = `date`;
chop($date);
$referer  = $ENV{'HTTP_REFERER'};
$referer  =~ s/http:\///;
$host = $ENV{'REMOTE_HOST'};
$host = $ENV{'REMOTE_ADDR'}if ($host eq "" );
$who = $ENV{'REMOTE_USER'};
$sent = $contents{'loc'};
if ($who eq "") {$who = "unregistered"; }
#====================================================
# Write the entry to disk.
#====================================================
open (LOGFILE,">>../logs/htaccess") || die ;
      print LOGFILE "[$date] $referer $sent $host
$who\n";
close LOGFILE;
```

Summary

The focus of this chapter was to learn how to perform some Redirection. We also wanted to focus on the reasons you would want to use that Redirection. In particular, emphasis was placed on the use of Redirection for advertisement placement. We also mentioned using these same techniques to auto-forward visitors to a page from one page to another.

The reason we zeroed in on advertisements was to get you better prepared for the next chapter. The chapter we will be going to next focuses on using randomness to generate anything from cute random quotes, to light bulb jokes, to, wouldn't you just be amazed, random advertisement image placement.

The one thing that this section didn't cover was analysis of the log file that is generated by the programs in this chapter. I would love to say that this book is holding that information back so we have something to include in the next updated edition, but that would be untrue. We will get into some aspects of log file analysis when we move on to Chapter 16, but we will be discussing the log files that are maintained by the server. In doing log file analysis on these files you could use a simple Unix command like:

```
grep -i "pagename-forwarded-to" /pathto/logfile | wc -l
```

That command will get a count off all times that an advertisement was displayed that forwarded a user to the advertisers page.

Of course more complex commands and programs can be created to do further and more detailed analysis of the information that is in the log files that were generated by the redirection CGI.

CHAPTER 8
RANDOMIZATION

- Understanding Randomization

- Understanding Weighted Randomization

- Generating Random Information to the User

This chapter will focus on some key concepts. For the more experienced programmers, this may get a bit slow (like talking about the intricacies of the different methods of doing sorts). In addition, I will be introducing a concept that has almost no redeeming value in mathematics, but has any number of extended uses in the real world.

In this section, we will discuss the following concepts:

- Standard randomization
- Weighted randomization
- Internet and intranet usage

When dealing with computers and random numbers, there are some key things that you should remember. The most important one has to do with the generation of a unique seed value to feed into the random number generator. In most cases, this number is either the unique process identifier or an integer value generated from accessing a time-based function. It is also important to remember that no matter how good the random number generation method, there is always the probability that the same seed value could generate a looping sequence of random numbers. In this case, calling the random number generation function from within the software could generate a repeating sequence that will appear nonrandom.

It is important for this chapter to make any sense at all, that there is a clear understanding of *standard* and *weighted* randomization.

Standard Randomization

In standard randomization, we call the random number generator once and use that return value as the random value. We used the standard randomization method when we created the random counter in Chapter 6. With standard randomization, we obtain a single value from the random number generator and use that value as it was returned.

Here is a sample of how a standard random selection could be used.

Within the HTML code you would have a call to the random item generator as part of an SSI directive. In this case, we want to randomly color the font of an item in a list. The line in the HTML file looks like:

```
<li><font color=<!--#exec cgi="/cgi-bin/fcolor.cgi"-->
⇒  >displayed text</font>
```

The fcolor.cgi program could be Tcl, Perl, C, or whatever you choose. A random number is generated in the program and then either the data, already stored within variables in the program or read in from a data file, will be selected from the random number.

So, if there were 10 colors from which to choose (and we were generating a random number within the range of 1-10), we could:

- Associate a color to a number using associative arrays (where color(5) could contain the keyword blue)
- Index a list of colors using a command to index lists (such as lindex in Tcl which would access a list of elements of which the fifth element was the keyword blue)
- Read a record from a datafile (in which the fifth line in the data file would be the keyword blue).

In these cases, the random number generator would generate the random number and replace the associated value for number. This, in turn, would create the actual line of HTML that is returned to the browser, which looks like:

```
<li><font color=blue>displayed text</font>
```

It would then produce the list item displayed text in a blue font. Other examples of randomization would be a Thought for the day-type application. In this case, the application would deal with the data file model (only because it's easier to add and to delete items from the data file model than it is to access and to make modifications within the code all the time). Again, the software used to generate the random hit counter in Chapter 6 is a very nice example of how this type of simple random number generator can work.

Weighted Randomization

As far as I know, I coined this term when I started creating applications that required a bit more direction than that given by a random number. The basic concept is to work with sets instead of with single items. With weighted randomization, we use the randomization to reduce the set of random items from a large superset to a smaller, but random subset of those items. Within this chapter, in most cases, the methods we will be using will focus on weighted randomization. In addition, we will be using the data file model more than any in-line method.

The scope of this chapter will be to focus on a business application, one that you have been partially introduced to already–that of display advertisements. In this instance, we will be using data from a file to modify and to increase the possibility of certain items from within that data file that will have a greater propensity for being selected.

Please Don't Eat the Daisies

A good example of Weighted randomness in building a display advertisement would be the florist at the site buy-flowers.com. In most cases, this advertiser would pay a low cost and expect a low number of impressions and click-throughs (discussed in redirection, Chapter 7) for the advertisement they had placed. But around Mother's Day, the owners of the florist site might want to put up a friendly reminder that it would be best not to forget "mom" and to say it with flowers. So, as a florist, I would arrange for a special advertisement banner to be placed in the week or and a half before Mother's Day. This display advertisement would focus on two issues:

- The florist is On the Net

- A note stating that you can order your flowers while surfing the net

This will remind all the fathers and sons on the Internet that they should be thinking about you know who, and that a gift purchase can be done, nice and easy, from right here. The keyword **mom** would be placed on the advertisement line in the data file, and the pages on which we want to increase the number of hits would also have an added reference to that keyword.

On the day before the holiday, the advertisements might be changed and, to increase the propensity that the florist advertisement is being seen, a one-day increase in purchases (more slots) to the advertising file could be added as well.

The advertising goes from a normal random pattern (with no weighting) to a highly manipulated advertisement, first by adding weighting factors to the pages on which you want the advertisement to display, and then by increasing the number of times that the advertisement is in the data file for it to be picked for display.

This process uses keyword values associated with individual items. It also uses a selection criteria to select the keywords based on the page from which the user is coming. In cases where a page has associated keywords, the number of random numbers to be checked is increased, generating a subset of random elements from the data file. That subset is checked for the keyword value. If there is no keyword found, it acts as any random generator and displays the first random item it retrieved. If an item is found to have an associated keyword, that item is selected from the random subset and is displayed.

In this way, we have added a weighting to the selection of the item, yet we have maintained the randomization factors. We have indicated that there is a preference to display one random value over another, yet we still have a random chance of getting any value returned.

This system of weighted randomization allows the owners of the pages and data files to manipulate the propensity of any single item being selected based on a subjective criteria. While still leaving the core functionality of the randomizer, this process adds the potential to manipulate the randomizer to increase selected target acquisition from a random subset of the data in the file. It should be noted that randomization is still taking place and we are working with more than just certain subsets. Remember, if there is no match between the random selection and the keyword, then the default is to display the first random item selected. In other words, it will act just like a standard randomization.

As discussed in the prior chapter on redirection, the idea behind advertising banners is twofold. First, to generate impressions, and, second, to increase the number of click-throughs to the advertisement. Figure 8.1 shows a site with a banner advertisement. While an impression is nice, a click-through generates a higher level of income using the model we discussed in Chapter 7. In using weighted randomization methods it is easier to increase the propensity of advertisements that work well (generate a larger number of click-throughs) to be displayed at the site. We can utilize the click-though data from the log file and the information from within the standard transaction log to determine where an advertisement works the best at generating click-throughs. This way we can weight the page and the advertisement accordingly thereby increasing overall income to the site, and adding value to the advertiser and the visitor.

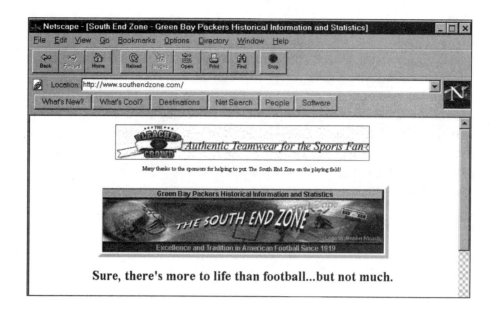

Figure 8.1: *Web site with an advertisement banner at the top*

The transaction log can be used to tune the performance of the site and to increase the income through a finer targeting of the desired customer group. This kind of market analysis provides a way for a commercial site to increase revenues and to provide a finer level of directed marketing.

A good example of this can be found at a sports information site. There, people who go to the "NFL" side get information fed to them about things of interest to football fans. If someone were to go to the "NHL" side of the site they would get information on hockey. But say that there was a city with two teams and that people were also interested in pages that link to the city. We could start both the NHL and the NFL sites out with a sports based advertisement and a city based advertisement. If, after time, we saw that the city advertisement was doing better at the NFL site, in terms of click-throughs, we could increase the propensity of that advertisement getting hit by increasing the weighting of the randomization.

The only problem is that, using raw numbers, this is a self-perpetuating system where we keep on increasing the propensity of the item that gets the largest number of hits. That's why it is necessary to use the transaction log and the click-through log to determine the percentage of click-throughs per impression.

Intranetting Weighted Randomization

For those of you who want to know how this can be used on an Intranet, consider the following two examples.

Example 1: Over 50 percent of all sites have a **What's New** page. Most users will access that page the first time they connect to a particular site. This method will allow for an "advertisement" or a simple text hyperlink.

In designing the What's New page, you could have the company logo at the top left and, on the top right, a **Random Newstuff** banner that links to a random page on the Intranet. This could increase the visibility of certain departments or areas of possible interest that someone may not see if they were to just transverse the locations that they normally access.

This newstuff information could be derived from searching the site for all items that have been added in the last week. After the site has been searched and the items selected, a file could be created that has the path to files and their descriptions (extracted from a meta tag in the head portion of the html, or from the title tag). The random number generator would then pick an instance from that data file of links and descriptions and use that selection to display an internal link.

We can weight this process by increasing the number of entries for certain items, or by using a two file model. In the two file model we would have a file that had keywords in it. These keywords would be words that also show up in the descriptions meta tag or as a comment within the title tag. We could then use this keyword file to allow weighting of the items by increasing the number of specific keywords. The keyword file would be randomly accessed and a keyword selected, and then the description file would be accessed for the random display item.

Using that method we can create a What's New page that has a "link" on it that is generated with weighted randomization.

Example 2: In many places there are **Messages of The Day** that come up. These messages include things like when there will be backups, and items of interest to the Internal community. By replacing the HTML in the "advertiser's file" with internal links to information that could be randomly delivered, it increases the awareness of things available to the users that they may never have found had they just wandered around the site.

Keeping Track of the Numbers

So, let's look at how this works on the Internet, and how we could make this work for a customer who wants a random banner advertisement CGI that uses weighted randomization.

The customer has sold space on 10 of the pages on the Internet site and the pages have been sold in percentage of site portions. Each company which has purchased a percentage of the site for the advertisement display for a page will get an advertising bar placed across the top of the page. There will be 100 advertising slots at the site and each advertiser has an option to purchase a percentage of the site's total hits. Minimum purchase was 5 percent and a maximum of 100 percent, in 5 percent increments. In some cases, advertisers want to be able to have a higher percentage hit rate with pages associated to specific advertiser's interest area. For instance, a page on the Green

Bay Packers should have a higher hit on the Nike advertisement than the one for ladies' undergarments, although a cheese advertisement might give the sports apparel maker a run for their money.

There is also a need to allow the site to make recommendations to clients to increase the click-through rates. The site should be able to track each time an advertiser's page is shown on the site (using the trackit procedure from the prior chapter, there is already a list of people who follow the link). There will also be a need to use the transaction log file and the click-through log to validate activity and to try to increase traffic and volume.

If there is a clear indication that certain advertisements are doing better in one location, there needs to be a way to increase the propensity of hits for that advertiser. Also, there should be a way to self log, in case access to the access log is not available.

To meet the requirements of this customer we will need to follow these steps:

1. Extract the page name and the user name as well as the current date and time

2. Open a file to find out if the page has any associated keywords

3. Select five random numbers if it has keywords

4. Open a file to obtain the advertising line for each random number

5. Check each line for a keyword—if one is found, use that line. If none is found, use the first random number that was generated.

6. Send the HTML to standard output

7. Open and update a log file with the date/time - uri - advertiser - premierflag - user name (if known)

There will be two data files required. The first file will require the HTML to be placed in the pages. In accordance to the needs, this file will have 100 lines of HTML links (the HTML-text in the line below) in it with each advertiser being assigned the number of slots that they purchased (five slots at a time, for each 5 percent purchased). The line will be in the format:

```
keywords-with-dashes   {html-text}
```

The keyword will be one or more words, separated with dashes (this makes the dash a reserved item within this field and you cannot use keywords with dashes in them) that are used to match the keyword value from the second data file that is mentioned in the list.

That second data file will contain the page names (a full URI for the pages, as that information would be shown in the referrer value that the HTTPd creates when sending information to an SSI) and any keywords associated with the pages using the following format:

```
uri {keywords with spaces}
```

Note that the keywords in this file are separated by spaces and are enclosed in {}'s. They are also placed at the end of the file, rather than at the beginning. This was done for clarity of the two data files.

When editing the two data files, if they both looked almost identical, there is a greater possibility (although totally random) that the person making the edits may forget to what file they are making modifications. The easiest way to ensure that errors of this nature do not happen is to ensure that the file's data format tells you exactly what data file you are editing.

Sample Data

As descriptions are never as good as actually having an example, the extraction from the adfile.txt data file is a sample view of how the first file we described would actually look in practice. Note that there are two items per line (anything in {} is considered to be a single item).

ADFIL.TXT

```
* {<a href="/cgi-bin/uncgi/trackit.cgi?loc=http://www.eff.org"><img
⇒   src="/ads/no-cda.gif"></a>}

sports {<a href="/cgi-bin/uncgi/trackit.cgi?loc=http://www.nike.com">
⇒   <img src="/ads/doit.gif"></a>}

ent {<a href="/cgi-bin/uncgi/trackit.cgi?loc=http://www.net-quest.com/
⇒   ~ivler/mc/mc.html"><img src="/ads/mc.gif"></a>}
* {<a href="/cgi-bin/uncgi/trackit.cgi?loc=http://gatekeeper.digital.com">
⇒   <img src="/ads/dec-sw.gif"></a>}

* {<a href="/cgi-bin/uncgi/trackit.cgi?loc=http://www.prenthall.com">
⇒   <img src="/ads/book.gif"></a>}

* {<a href="/cgi-bin/uncgi/trackit.cgi?loc=http://www.eff.org">
⇒   <img src="/ads/no-cda.gif"></a>}
```

The * in the first field says the advertisement is valid on any page. The Blue Ribbon Campaign against the CDA gets a free slot or two in this example, but that is because in the author's opinion, it is a good thing to donate 5 to 10 percent of any advertising space to good causes (it also makes a great donation on the tax form as we can see exactly how much the advertising would have cost (your advertising revenue loss and donation)).

PGFIL.TXT

This data file also contains two items on each line as was described. The first is the URI that is associated to one or more keywords, and the second is the keyword(s) to which the URI is associated. Again note that we are using the braces {} to treat the keywords as a single item, even if there is more than one keyword associated to the URI.

```
/fball/southendzone.shtml {sports fball}
/la/placestogo.shtml {ent}
/la/romanticnites.shtml {ent la hot}
```

Adding an advertisement to a page

As the pgfil.txt page names indicate, these files are SSI-based and no data will be passed in with the line. The SSI line in the HTML file would look like:

```
<!-#exec cgi="/cgi-bin/plopad.tcl" - >
```

Tcl Design

The code we developed is a bit more flexible than actually required. This was done so people could see how to set up the code to be used as an Intranet service with a variable length file. Not everyone will want to have a file containing exactly 100 entries. For this reason, the code will quickly read the file once to obtain the number of unique records in the file. The code will use that number to define the scope for the random number to fall within in the random procedure described below.

First, read the pgfil.txt file. This will create the value urlkey if a record exists. Then take the urlkey and create a unique key that is a regexp, if that is required. That means that we want to add a pipe (|) between the values if there is more than one keyword.

So, a group of keywords in the urlkey (the second field to be read in from the url file (pgfil.txt) will be regsub'd if there is more than one element. This line will replace all the spaces with a pipe:

```
if {[llength urlkey] > 1} {
regsub -all " " $urlkey "|" urlkey
}
```

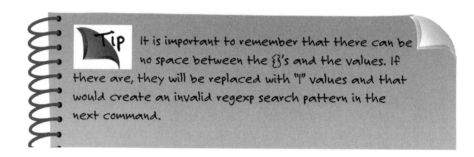

Tip It is important to remember that there can be no space between the {}'s and the values. If there are, they will be replaced with "|" values and that would create an invalid regexp search pattern in the next command.

You have already seen the randomizer used in Chapter 6 during the discussion on counters.

The ultimate counter (random number displayer) provided a nice randomizer based on the one in the Tcl FAQ, but there are any number of ways to generate a random number. The following procedure will also generate random numbers:

```
global _ran
set _ran [pid]
proc rand {range} {
  global _ran
  set _ran [expr ($_ran * 9301 + 49297) % 233280]
  return [expr int($range * ($_ran / double(233280)))]
}
```

A procedure is treated like a new instance of a program. It sees all variables as local to the instance of the procedure that is currently running. In most ways, this is a good thing as it allows recursive calls from a procedure to itself and all the variables are treated as local in each call. The global variable allows for programmers to work around this limitation.

If you have already investigated the procedure, you will notice that the actual random number generation takes place on the return line (as the random number is the value that is returned). In some cases there is the potential that a computer will generate pseudo-random numbers. That means that the seed value to the random number generator creates random numbers that are repetitive sequences (using the same seed you can generate the same sequence of random numbers). To overcome this potential problem, each seed is unique and is used only one time, and the seed value from the main program is changed each time it is used (by making that item global). This allows us to call the procedure a number of times from with the program, yet ensure that there will be a low possibility that a pseudo-random sequence will be obtained.

We need to get five of these random numbers if we have a uri that contains a urikey. We could use a loop and add them to the list:

```
for {set x 4} {$x >= 0} {incr x -1} {
  lappend rannum [random 100]
}
```

or we can just set a value to five separate instances of the procedure call:

```
set rannum \
  " [rand 100] [rand 100] [rand 100] [rand 100] [rand 100] "
```

While the first form has a programming style (or look and feel), it is not necessary and will actually add overhead to the processing without adding value. I recommend and use the second style. Again, this code uses the value of the initial read of the first data file that was done to determine the if this will be a Weighted Randomization.

When reading the data from the adfile.txt file, we can see if the value of the counter, which is incremented with each read, is in the list of random numbers we obtained and put into the rannum variable as a list of number. We can use the Tcl regexp command syntax to search that list of random numbers for the counter number of the record we have just read. If a match exists between the counter and the variable then we will process the random number.

A few items to note. First, regexp (which is preferred in most cases) is used again to match the count number with the random number from the list in rannum. Secondly, we include the spaces in the match using the backslash to escape the space. This forces an exact match of the numeric values.

If the values that had been returned and inserted into rannum were 76 32 48 7 30 and we had used the search of 2 when we were on the second record (the value of $cnt being 2 at that time), we would have hit on the second item in the list, 32. That would have placed a record in the array and incremented the variable *caught* (a counter) in the following code snippit. In this case, we would most likely never get above record 10 before the first five allotted array values are filled with incorrect data.

So, the if statement to load the five items and then break the loop once loaded is:

```
if {[regexp "\ $cnt\ " $rannum]} {
    set dispval($caught) $inline
    incr caught
    if {caught == 6} {
    break
    }
}
```

At this point, we can create a second loop to process the array items. The code coming up uses a single loop construct, which is a tad more complex but runs a bit faster. In the case of the single loop, we will perform a load if we have a match, or if the $cnt is the first value in $rannum and there is no match yet.

Remember that the earlier if statement is bound inside a read loop of the file adfile.txt. That means that the Tcl *break* command will exit the while loop that is performing the read. We could include a counter to ensure that we don't loop through the whole file if all five values have been checked. This is done by using the counter variable *caught*. The counter increments if the value is valid. Once the counter reaches the number of caught items that we want, it will allow the loop to be broken, saving us from having to process every record in the file after we have all the records we need.

The value of the variable caught is set to 0 prior to entering the read loop and is incremented each time a value is examined in the test. The value of preimflag is set to F, but will be set to true if we have a keyword hit. This flag is output in the log file that the customer requested so we know when we hit on a keyword match verses a truly random display.

```
if {[regexp "\ $cnt\ " $rannum]} {
  if {[string compare [lindex $rannum 0] $cnt] == 0} {
    set dispval [lindex $inline 1]
  }
  if {[regexp "$urlkey" [lindex $inline 0]} {
    set dispval $inline
    set preimflag "T"
    break
  }
  incr caught
  if {caught == 5} {
    break
  }
}
```

If we hit the first value, it is shoved into the dispval variable for display, only if there is not already a value in there. Otherwise, the loop will be broken once any value that matches the urlkey is inserted into the dispval variable.

This single array method, although more complex, is much more effective than creating two loops: one to load an internal array and another to read it.

Once we have a display value, we can display it, open and write the log file record (remember item seven: open and update a log file with the date/time - uri - advertiser - premierflag - user name (if known)), and exit the processor.

Plopping the Advertisement Into the HTML

At this point, we can look at the entire program in Listing 8.1. The program will support all the things the customer would need to allow advertisements to be displayed on a page. The method also allows for the advertisements to be tweaked so they can be weighted to land on certain pages with a higher propensity. Later on, in Listing 8.3, we will provide the same basic concept, but without weighting. If you are having trouble understanding the code, jump ahead and look at Listing 8.3 which is a non-weighted procedure, and then review this listing again. You should then have no trouble seeing where additional code was used to support the weighting of the randomization.

Listing 8.1: plopad.tcl

```
#!/usr/local/bin/tclsh
##
##
## plopad.tcl
##    used to plop an advertisement on a page.
##
##
## This procedure will open a file, see if the URL is
## in it, if so extract it, if not, get a random line
## and display it, if so, get 5 random lines, do a
## keyword search, if there is a hit, display it, if
## there is no hit, display the first item.
```

```
##
puts "Content-type: text/html\n\n"
##
## The variables urlfil, adfil and logfil should
## be changed to meet your needs
##
##
## urlfil is the file which lists the "uri" and the
##     associated keywords (if any)
##
## Format:
##    /~username/the/path/thefile.shtml  {keywords}
##
## the {}'s are required and no other {}'s are
## permitted 1-n keywords, space deliniated, no
## spaces between the {}'s and the text
##
set urlfil /home/public_html/.data/urlfil.dat
##
##
## adfil: the HTML and keywords to place the advert.
##
## Format:   keyword {HTML}
##
## where the keyword is a valid keyword that you will
## search for. In the case of no keyword use an
## astric (*). In the case where there are multiple
## keywords use a dash (-) between each word. The
## {}'s are again required as they permit spaces and
## quote marks to be within the line. The HTML code
## must be valid code. The sample code below shows
## how you can format it (note: the sample below has
## been broken up to fit within 60 characters... you
## don't have to do that, and you shouldn't).
##
## {<a href="/cgi-bin/uncgi/trackit.cgi?
##     loc=http://www.examp.com/adspot.shtml">
##     <img src="/yourpath/thegiffile.gif"
#       alt="always use an alt" border=0></a>}
##
## this was designed to work with trackit, you don't
## have to use it, but it is recommended. Working
## together they provide a clear concise picture of
## what's getting displayed where, and when those
## items are being followed. This provides for a
## method of determining payment, and enhancing what
## ads get shown on certain pages, to increase site
## profitability.
##
set adfil  /home/public_html/.data/adfil.dat
##
```

```
##
## The place where you log the hits. You must make
## sure that the owner of the HTTPd process has write
## capability to this log file.
##
set logfil /home/public_html/.data/adlog.fil
##
## Preset some base values
##
set preimflag "F"
set dispval "Error in processing"
##
## the randomizer routine and some base data that it
## needs (ran)
##
global _ran
set _ran [pid]
proc rand {range} {
  global _ran
  set _ran [expr ($_ran * 9301 + 49297) % 233280]
  return [expr int($range * \
          ($_ran / double(233280)))]
}
##
## count the number of items to randomize from
##(the "range")
##
## note that the counter is init'd to a -1. this has
## to do with a Tcl'ism that will cause the loop to
## run through one more time after it reads all the
## data. That last read is when it gets
## the end-of-file and knows to exit the loop. In
## order to offset for the counter getting
## incremented one additional time, it starts at -1
## instead of 0.
##
set knt -1
set f1 [open $adfil]
while {![eof $f1]} {
  gets $f1 i
  incr knt
}
close $f1
##
## get URI and if we have a "match" load the key
## value to the urlkey variable
##
set uri $env(DOCUMENT_URI)
set f1 [open $urlfil]
while {![eof $f1]} {
  gets $f1 chkurl
```

```
      if {[regexp "$uri" [lindex $chkurl 0]]} {
        set urlkey [lindex $chkurl 1]
        break
      }
  }
  close $f1
  ##
  ## get a single random number (will only be done if
  ## the urlkey is not there which means that we didn't
  ## get a match)
  ##
  if {![info exists urlkey]} {
  ##
  ## we start all of our counts at 0 (unix style ;-) )
  ##
    set tnum [random $knt]
  ##
  set f1 [open $adfil]
    set cnt 0
  ##
  ## loop until we get the right random number value,
  ## then stuff it in the dispval
  ##
    while {$cnt <= $tnum} {
      gets $f1 inline
      set dispval [lindex $inline 1]
      incr cnt
    }
    close $f1
  } else {
  ##
  ## we have to do a search based on a keyword - first
  ## make sure the expression is a regexp (if there is
  ## more than one value, put "or"'s in)
  ##
    if {[llength $urlkey] > 1} {
      regsub -all " " $urlkey "|" urlkey
    }
  ##
  ## load up the array of five random numbers open the
  ## file and set the counter variable to an initial 0.
  ##
    set rannum " [rand $knt] [rand $knt] \
          [rand $knt] [rand $knt] [rand $knt] "
    set f1 [open $adfil]
    set cnt 0
  ##
  ## while not at the end of the file, get the next
  ## line in the file see if it has the current "count"
  ## number in the random number list if so, and it is
  ## the first number in the chosen list, shove it into
```

```
## a special variable for first random. This will be
## used if there is no keyword match.
##
## Do the keyword match. No match, continue, if a
## match, set the dispval with the display string and
## exit the loop.
##
  while {![eof $f1]} {
    gets $f1 inline
    if {[regexp "\ $cnt\ " $rannum]} {
      if {[string compare [lindex $rannum 0] \
          $cnt] == 0} {
        set dispval [lindex $inline 1]
      }
      if {[regexp "$urlkey" [lindex $inline 0] ]} {
        set dispval [lindex $inline 1]
        set preimflag "T"
        break
      }
    }
    incr cnt
  }
  close $f1
}
##
## Take the display variable and put it to standard
## output (the user)
##
puts "$dispval"
##
## log it. First get the URL portion of the ad, then
## the remote user info if it is available. Then open
## the logfile and write the following:
##      date uri ad's-URL weighted-ad-flag user-name
##
set adv [lindex [split [lindex [split $dispval : \
        ] 1] {\"} ] 0]
if {![info exists env(REMOTE_USER)]} {
  set user "non-registered"}
} else {
  set user $env(REMOTE_USER)
}
set ll [open $logfil a+]
puts $ll "\[[exec date]\] $uri $adv $preimflag $user"
close $ll
exit
```

Perl Code

Now let's look at doing the same thing in Perl. The algorithm used in the Tcl code is summarized in these steps:

1. Use the DOCUMENT_URI value as the current document as the referrer.
2. If the user has selected a keyword, select 5 random items otherwise just use one random item.
3. If we have one random item, just use it to create the URL.
4. If we have five (5) random items from the adfile.txt file.
5. Now check if the keyword matches any one of these file selections.
6. If there is such a match use the first such random match as the URL to use, otherwise,
7. Use the URL from the first random hit from the list of 5 entries.

Steps 1 and 3 are straight forward. If there are no keywords to match on, get an entry at random from adfile.txt and use it. In steps 4 through 7, we have to use the Tcl cloned code. First, create an array of 5 random numbers:

```
for ($i=0;$i<5;$i++) {
    $myrand[$i] = int rand $knt;
    print "RND = $myrand[$i]\n";
}
```

You have to modify the code to the correct locations of the readable files pgfile.txt and adfile.txt:

```
$pgfile = "/your/file/path/pgfile.txt";
$adfile = "/your/file/path/adfile.txt";
```

Now find this referrer file in the list of keywords and filenames in the pgfile.txt file. The search extracts the filename as the first word per line. The rest of the line is treated as a list of keywords and is placed in the @keys array after stripping off any trailing end curly braces ({}). The file handle PGFILE should be closed, now that all we need from it is in memory. If no matched file was found, then $name is set to an empty string.

```
open (PGFILE,$pgfile) || die "Cannot open $pgfile";
while (<PGFILE>){
    ($fname)= split(' ', $_);
    if ($fname =~ /$referer/) {
      $name = $referer;
      $_ =~ s/}//;
      ($fname,@keys) = split('{',$_);
      last; # just use the first entry
    }
}
close PGFILE;
```

Now that we have the name of the file to show, let's see which keywords match to show which advertisement. We open the file adfile.txt
and read in lines from it into the @ads array to get an idea of the
range of random numbers to use. Conveniently, we use the $knt vari-
able to track this number.

```
open (ADFILE,$adfile) || die "Cannot open $adfile.txt";
$knt = 0;
while (<ADFILE>) {
    $knt++;
}
close ADFILE;
```

Then get entries from the ad file. On each random entry listed in
your list of random numbers, see if any keywords match. If they do,
great, use this URL. If none of the keywords match in any of the five
random entries you picked up, then simply use the first random entry
listed in the array of random numbers.

The default random number generator in Perl works sufficiently
well in this application. The srand() call seeds the random number
generator with process ID or-ed with the current time in seconds.
The rand($i) call returns a number from 0 to $i (the number passed
into the function), of which we only use the integer portion with
the int function.. Listing 8.2 shows how the perl script to generate
these URLs.

Listing 8.2: plopad.pl

```
#!/usr/local/bin/perl

srand($$|time);
# ==========================================
```

```perl
# You must modify these values for your system
# =================================================
$pgfile = "/home/khusain/httpd/logs/pgfile.txt";
$adfile = "/home/khusain/httpd/logs/adfile.txt";


# =================================================
# Extract the name in the current page.
# =================================================
$referer  = $ENV{'DOCUMENT_URI'};
$referer  =~ s/http:\/\///;   #remove header
if (referer eq "") {
  print "\n <B> No referer </b> " ; #  modify it!
    exit(0);
}


# =================================================
# Count the number of lines in adfile.txt
# =================================================
$knt = 0;
open (ADFILE,$adfile) || die "Cannot open $adfile.txt";
while (<ADFILE>) {
    $knt++;
}
close ADFILE;
# =================================================
# Now find this file in the list of keywords and filenames
# =================================================
$name = "";
$keys = "*";
@keywds = ();
open (PGFILE,$pgfile) || die "Cannot open $pgfile";
while (<PGFILE>){
    ($fname)= split(' ', $_);
    if ($fname =~ /$referer/) {
      $name = $referer;
      $_ =~ s/}//;
      $keys = substr($_,length($fname)+1);
        # remember keywords are separated by dashes.
      @keywds = split($keys,'-'); # get keywords
      last; # stop processing.
    }
}
close PGFILE;

#
# Using the keywords determine the ad to place up
there.
#
open (ADFILE,$adfile)||die "Cannot open $adfile.txt";
if ($name eq "") # no name with matched keywords?
    { # that's fine we'll use any random record
```

```perl
      my ($count,$i);  # use a random record.
    $count = int rand $knt;  # get any record
    while (<ADFILE>) {
       if ($i == $count) { # got it!
         $useURL = $_;
         last;
       }  # if found
         $i++;  # count input lines…
    } # while loop
}else { # choose five random numbers ..
    my ($i,@myrand,$count,$first,$found);
    for ($i=0;$i<5;$i++) { #create 5 random numbers
      $myrand[$i] = int rand $knt;
      print "RND = $myrand[$i]\n";
    }
    $count = 0;
    $first = "";  # start with nothing
    while (<ADFILE>) {
         for ($i=0;$i<5;$i++) {
        # check random number list
        if ($myrand[$i] == $count) {
        if ($first eq "") { # 1st random item default
          $useURL = $_; # with or w/out match
                }
      my $upto = index($_,"{"); # get open curly brace
      # examine all up to open brace
      my $theseKeys = substr($_,$upto-1);
      foreach $k (@keys) { # any keywords
        if ($theseKeys =~ /$k/) { # in here?
          $useURL = $_; # use this URL!
          $found = 1;  # set up exit motion
          last; # from inner most loop
          }
          } # for keys.
      last if $found;  # break out
            }   # if random hit made.
          } # for the list of random numbers
    last if $found; # break out if found.
    $count++;   # count lines
    } # while loop
} # end of else clause for keyword hits…
close ADFILE;

# ===============================
# print out URL for SSI output
# ===============================
$upto = index($useURL,"{"); # get open curly brace
$href = substr($useURL,$upto+1); # exclude all up to
it
$href =~ s/}//;  #  then remove end curly brace.
print "$href \n";
```

A Simple Random Number Generator

For those of you who feel a need to know how to make the Unweighted Randomizer for *What's new* on an Intranet, the following code in Listing 8.3 will read an unweighted file and display a random item back to the reader. Remember to use valid HTML in the line within the data file.

Listing 8.3: intranet.tcl

```
#!/usr/local/bin/tclsh
##
## I call this intranet.tcl. This is much like the
## plopad.tcl procedure in that it uses random
## numbers to generate displays back to the user.
##
## in this case I would suggest that you could use
## this to display a reminder of the day note, or a
## link to what's new, a funny line of the day, a
## fortune cookie, or any random text or image (using
## the proper HTML).
##
## The file must only contain the item to be sent
## back in {}'s and one per line
##
##
puts   "Content-type: text/html\n\n "
set fname /the-path-to-the-datafile/data.file
global _ran
set _ran [pid]
##
## The random Procedure
##
proc rand {range} {
global _ran
  set _ran [expr ($_ran * 9301 + 49297) % 233280]
  return [expr int($range * ($_ran / \
          double(233280)))]
}
##
## count the entries
##
set knt -1
set f1 [open $fname]
```

```
while {![eof $f1]} {
  gets $f1 i
  incr knt
}
close $f1
##
## set the random number
##
set tnum [random $knt]
##
## open the loop and continue until you get to the
## random number
##
set f1 [open $fname]
set cnt 0
while {$cnt <= $tnum} {
  gets $f1 oline
  incr cnt
}
close $f1
##
## put it into the standard output stream.
##
puts "$oline"
##
## That's all there is to it. You can use this to
## load a random image a random URL, random text,
## whatever you want. Have fun with it.
##
```

In this chapter, we have tied up the pieces of code that we started with in Chapter 6 when we talked about counters. In the code examples here we have built on the software we provided in redirection (Chapter 7), and have shown you how the same basic concepts from business applications can be reused in intranets for non-business applications.

In much the same way, the focus will remain fixed on providing software that is reusable, modular, and easy to modify to meet your needs as we move on to calendars in the next chapter.

We will also continue to build on things that we have already used. In this chapter, we learned how to utilize keywords and in the next we will utilize them again, but the application and the way they will be applied change to meet new circumstances. The focus is again on building on the items that we talked about in this chapter and reusing constructs and concepts, even if the application looks substantially different.

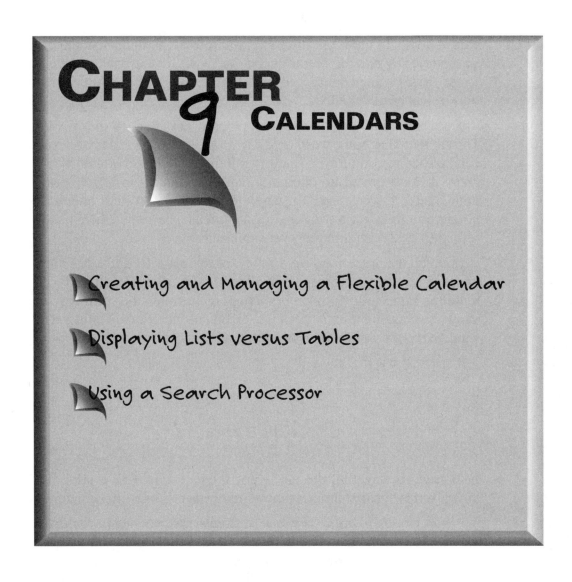

CHAPTER 9 CALENDARS

- Creating and Managing a Flexible Calendar

- Displaying Lists versus Tables

- Using a Search Processor

Providing and receiving information in a simple-to-use format is the primary concern for people on an Intranet and the Internet. For many people, that format is one they use everyday—a calendar. Calendars present data to us in a format that is easy to use and understand by maintaining an ordered and structured relationship between the data/events and dates.

This chapter introduces some basic concepts in using a calendar within a Web-based environment and CGI development to support that model of information distribution. The chapter also focuses on meeting a customer's need for flexibility in a calendar utility. This utility allows the same code to service any number of functioning calendars at a site. In addition, the styles and formats of the calendars can be modified by *passing in* parameters to the CGI. This makes the calendar utility a high reuse program that requires little maintenance once it has been installed.

This particular piece of software was designed to be reused. Throughout this book we have tried to show how similar concepts can be used over and over again in different ways to create new programs and integrated functionality. This was evident in the way random numbers were used to generate a counter, to pick an image library and to select a weighted display item. The same concepts are reused to deal with different, yet similar problems.

In much the same way, we don't want to create 10 different calendar utilities for 10 different customers or departments. In order to reuse the same code decision branches are placed in the software and allow the various users switch on or off the functionality that they want. Here the same piece of software is used to meet the needs of many varied people.

Creating a Calendar

Let's begin by creating the model for the calendar. This model outlines a series of capabilities, wants, and needs of a potential customer.

- *The calendar must support Netscape tables or lists for users without Netscape.* The calendar should look like (you guessed it) a calendar. Using tables is fine, but I also want people using a browser that can't read tables to have the option to get the items by list. Most of the code provided in this chapter creates Netscape-type tables. By that I mean a table within a table. At the time of this writing, Netscape 2.0 or greater and the Microsoft Internet Explorer 3.0 have no problem supporting this format. However, NCSA Mosaic cannot display tables in tables and some users have had problems with Netcom and AOL software.

- *The calendar must allow a title to be unique, support a default, and allow a user to define, omit, or modify the title.* The person setting up the calendar should be able to use a hidden field in the form to use a default page header showing the month and year or have the option of specifying them to be whatever they so desire. As for that title, the owners of the calendar shall also be able to name it as they choose (like *My Calendar*, for instance). In addition, the calendar owner may want to be able to give the calendar a "<h1>" level heading. The default should give the same heading that the page title gets with the month and year. The program should also support not having a heading at all.

- *The calendar must allow the user to insert a description/text file* before *the calendar and append a description/text file* after *the calendar.* For instance, an appendable About file with copyright information. As not every system supports SSI's it is important that this file not be expected to be included using the SSI include formats (see Chapter 3).

- *The calendar must support the use of HTML included as data for any date.* An example of this would be the ability to generate links from the information that is in the data file. In addition, the calendar owners shall be able to place an image on the calendar, like a big American flag on the 4th of July or a Mexican flag on Cinco De Mayo. In this case, the calendar owners could also add links from that image to Web pages on local festivals, etc. In simple terms, if there is HTML in the data file, the calendar must be able to properly display the HTML within the calendar.

- *The calendar must be able search for keywords.* You may want to limit what is seen on the calendar and/or select required information. This is easily done by allowing the use of keywords within the database file. In this way you can create a calendar that is specific to various topics. An example of this would be a corporate training calendar. The data file could list all training that is available, but users would be able to use a checkbox on the page that calls the calendar to limit the display to show only those items that are of interest to them. In this way a person would be able to reduce the data on the calendar to show a view that is more in line with their training needs.

- *The calendar must support a prior/next month capability with a single selection from the calendar.* It would be nice to be able to *turn the pages* of the calendar without going back to a previous form. That way, selections don't have to be reset each time.

- *The calendar must support leap year processing.* It may not sound like a big deal now, but every fourth year it will be.
- *The calendar should be able to support anniversaries.* Anniversaries are events that happen at given dates and/or times. Each year Valentines Day will fall on 2/14. There has to be a way to indicate when that is in the data file so that data re-entry won't be required by the calendar maintainer.

Getting Started

When a request gets this complex, the hardest part is deciding where to start. Experienced developers know data modeling is crucial, so let's first define the data file first. We know it will have to support HTML text and that it should support a unique method of describing a date. The date is easy. The date description will be in the format YYMMDD. That format permits the ability to sort the file on a known key that will generate consistent results. We also have to come up with a unique way of delineating the start and end points of the string to be displayed. Since the brackets are not used much, they will be established as keywords for enclosing the text. This allows comments to be appended after that text to describe the item, if so desired.

This clearly defines a data record to look like the ones we used in the anniversary example. Valid strings could be:

```
961115 {Due Date} ptrph
AA1223 {<a href="http://www.florist1.com">Don't forget the
⇒  wife</a>} bday
961221 {<a href="/gen/autosched.html"><img
⇒  src="/giflib/van.gif"></a>}
```

If I was searching for *Prentice Hall* items for the month of November in 1996, the first item in this list would come up. The second item would come up on birthday searches in the month of December, no matter what year as it is prefixed with a special code for anniversaries.

Both the first and the second would be shown on any standard calendar as searches limit the set, not expand it.

The first item would appear as plain text in the day selected. The second item would appear as a hypertext link to a florist. The third and final example would not be searchable by a keyword (that doesn't mean that it is not searchable, just that we haven't associated a keyword to the data item). The third item will display a picture of a van (based in the name of the .gif image file that it says to display) and a link from that image to another page on the site.

The data model allows for a number of key features. Let's clearly define the requirements we have so far. Table 9.1 uses the statements and the data model just discussed to define the scope of the program.

Table 9-1: Mapping out calendar requirements

Required Features

Support Netscape tables or lists for those without Netscape table support

Allow a title to be unique (user defined or omitted), support a default

Allow the user to insert a description/text file *before* the calendar and append a description/text file *after* the calendar

The calendar must load the data from a data file that can be hand modified (although the next chapter will supply the software to modify the data file).

Support HTML included in the calendar as data for any date

Allow for a search capability on keywords

Allow the user to use multiple unique methods of showing the day number in the calendar

Support a prior/next month capability with a single selection from the calendar

Support leap year processing

Optional support for anniversaries

Testing Options Within the Calendar

The Tcl script shown in Listing 9.1 can be used to generate the date value defaulting to the current month (with a minor change you can also use the same basic script to create the default for the year).

Tip Remember the cookie examples in Chapter 3 that demonstrated how to obtain the current date using the clock functions in TCL? In that chapter a copy of the program mon.tcl was included in the [exec date] format (commented out, but also included here) to get the month instead of the clock method. Both of these work, but in Tcl 7.5 the [exec date] can be replaced with the more generic clock function. In Listing 9.1, we will use the clock method.

Listing 9.1: mon.tcl

```
#!/usr/local/bin/tclsh
puts "Content-type: text/html\n\n"
##
## gets and returns month data for the calendar
## program.
## sets the select statements to default to the
## current month
## requires that it be called as /cgi-bin/mon.tcl
##
set molst "<option>Jan <option>Feb <option>Mar "\
"<option>Apr <option>May <option>Jun <option>Jul"\
" <option>Aug <option>Sep <option>Oct <option>Nov"\
" <option>Dec"
set cmo [clock format [clock scan now] -format %b]
## the line below uses the exec format:
## set cmo [ lindex [exec date] 1 ]
##
regsub <option>$cmo $molst "\"<option \
    selected>$cmo"" newmolst
foreach mon $newmolst {
puts "$mon"
}
exit
###
```

The following HTML will generate a page that can be used to test the various options within the calendar program. Figure 9.1 shows the textual output. At the end of the form for user entry is a listing of all the parameters that were passed and descriptions of the values passed into the CGI script.

```
<TITLE> Calendar Request Sample</TITLE>
<h1> Calendar Request Processor Sample</h1>
This is a form that allows you to create a calendar
on the fly. Steal this page, and copy the database
format as well. Make sure you follow the directions
below...
<p>
<hr>
<!- make sure that you have placed uncgi into the
cgi-bin and place cal.tcl there too ->
<FORM METHOD="POST" ACTION="/cgi-bin/uncgi/cal.tcl">
<p> Month:
<select name="mon">
<!- here you would use the CGI above to generate the
select options - remember to name it .shtml to use
SSI's ->
<!- the <option> tags would be replaced with the SSI
statement:  #exec cgi="/yourcgibin/mon.tcl"    ->
<option> Jan
<option> Feb
<option> Mar
<option> Apr
<option> May
<option> Jun
<option> Jul
<option> Aug
<option> Sep
<option> Oct
<option> Nov
<option> Dec
</select>
<p> Year:
<select name="yr">
<!- again, you can use an the SSI to replace the
options for the year ->
<option> 1995
<option selected> 1996
<option> 1997
</select>
<p>
Please check the city you're interested in (to get
all cities, please do not check any).
<p>
<ul>
<li> <input type=radio name=strsea value="LA"> Los
Angeles<br>
<li> <input type=radio name=strsea value="SF"> San
Francisco<br>
```

```
<li> <input type=radio name=strsea value="CHI">
Chicago<br>
<li> <input type=radio name=strsea value="LON">
London<br>
<li> <input type=radio name=strsea value="NY"> New
York<br>
<li> <input type=radio name=strsea value="BOS">
Boston<br>
<li> <input type=radio name=strsea value="NY|BOS">
East Coast<br>
<li> <input type=radio name=strsea value="LA|SF">
West Coast<br>
</ul>
<p>
```

The system allows display via list or tables. Please
select the type you want (default: Netscape Tables).

```
<p>
<ul>
<li> <input type=radio name=nscapoff value="T">
List<br>
<li> <input type=radio name=nscapoff value="F">
Netscape Tables<br>
</ul>
<p>
```

The system allows display with the dates boxed or
not... Please select the type you want (default:
Boxed dates).

```
<p>
<ul>
<li> <input type=radio name=boxday value="T"> Boxed
<li> <input type=radio name=boxday value="F"> Not Boxed
</ul>
<p>
```

Use this to turn on the "prior" and "next" month
links.

```
<p>
<ul>
<li> <input type=radio name=priornext value="T">
Links on
<li> <input type=radio name=priornext value="F">
Links off (Default)
</ul>
<p>
```

You can change these text values to change the
printed text. Generally this information is hidden.
Remember to fix the path to the database...

```
<p>
Prepend File: <input type=text name=prefile
value="/path/to/the/filename"> <br>
Append File: <input type=text name=postfile
value="/path/to/the/filename"> <br>
Page Title: <input type=text name=title value="Test
```

```
001"> <br>
Table Title: <input type=text name=tabtitle
value="Table 1"> (none will omit)
<input type="hidden" name=db
value="/the/path/of/the/datafile/dbase.txt">
<p>
To submit, press this button: <inPUT TYPE="submit"
VALUE="Submit">
</form>
<hr>
```

Here are the "names" for the variables that are
expected. They are either required(R) or optional(O).

```
<ul>
<li>(R) mon : The month in a 3 character (cap) for-
mat [ex: Jan]
<li>(R) yr : The year in a format YYYY  [ex: 1996 ]
<li>(R) db : The datafile name in a full pathname
format
<li>(O) title : The title for the response page.
```
Default: Calendar of dbase for mon yr".
```
<li>(O) tabtitle : the h1 title over the table. The
```
keyword "none" will omit this, an omission will
default it to "Calendar for mon yr".
```
<li>(O) seastr : a string to search for with the
```
date elements. In this example we are searching for
the cities that training is being led in. By select-
ing one you limit the displayed data. The value can
be any regular expression (note that we use the "|"
or in the examples to get both CT and CA records).
```
<li>(O) prefile : The full path to an HTML file to be
```
prepended to the calendar
```
<li>(O) postfile : The full path to an HTML file to be
```
appended to the calendar
```
<li>(O) nscapoff : Netscape Tables or a list.
```
Default: Tables. To set to list set value to "T"
```
<li>(O) boxday : Put a box around the day, or have
```
the date tiny. Default: Boxed. To set to tiny dates
set value to "F"
```
<li>(O) priornext : Allow the "prior month" "month
```
year datestamp" and "next month" to be placed in a 3
cell area at the top of the table (on nscapoff it
puts "prior month" and "next month" links at the foot
of the page). The links carry all the user information with them. In addition, if the user puts "none"
in the tabtitle, it will enforce the date on the top
of the table, and if the user uses the default, it
will enforce the date at the top of the table.
Default: OFF. To turn on, set the value as a "T".
```
</ul>
<hr>
<address>&#169; Copyright 1996, Infobahn Xpress, Los
Alamitos, CA. All Rights Reserved.</address>
```

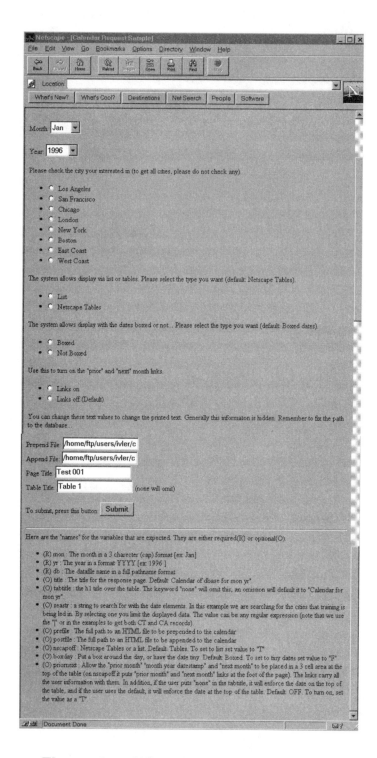

Figure 9.1: What else, but a sample form?

This section contains a sample data file that will work well with the HTML form just mentioned.

Anything is permissible in the brackets except the use of brackets "{}". Dates using standard sort date format (YYMMDD) can be anywhere in the file as long as they appear as the first six characters of the line. Anything other than a six-character date format as the first field of the line will not be processed by the program. You can bundle like things together by topic like this:

```
960110 {<b>NY</b>: <a href="/add/ixprs.html">Infobahn
⇒ Xpress Tcl Training Seminars</a>}
960116 {<b>LON</b>: <a href="/add/ixprs.html">Infobahn
⇒ Xpress Tcl Training Seminars</a>}
960122 {<b>SF</b>: <a href="/add/ixprs.html">Infobahn
⇒ Xpress Tcl Training Seminars</a>}
960126 {<b>LA</b>: <a href="/add/ixprs.html">Infobahn
⇒ Xpress Tcl Training Seminars</a>}
```

Or you can just do it by date like this:

```
960106 {<b>NY</b>: Opening: <i>My Fair Lady</i>}
960107 {<b>CHI</b>: <a href="/add/ub/dinner-
⇒ special.html">Uncle Bucks Rest.</a>}
960108 {<b>BOS</b>: <a href="/add/ub/specials.html">
⇒ Uncle Bucks Rest.</a>}
960109 {<b>LA</b>: <a href="/add/ub/grop.html"><b>
⇒ Grand Opening</b> Uncle Bucks Rest.</a>}
```

Multiple items on a single date are acceptable and will be displayed in the calendar with a <br> between them.

Only values with a matching YYMMDD are processed meaning a comment can be anything but YYMMDD in the first six characters. Additionally, comments can also be added to the line behind the display text in the {} as shown here:

```
960505 {Mexican Independence day} Cinco De Mayo
```

This will allow you to place search keys on a line, but not have those keys displayed in the HTML document the calendar program creates.

It is also possible to create search keys that are nondisplayed but are part of the HTML document by putting the search key into the document that the calendar program creates as an HTML comment:

```
960505 {<!- Festival -> Mexican Independence Day}
```

In this example, the keyword Festival is captured within HTML comments, but will be in the searchable portion of the text line that could be viewed in the *View Source* of the browser for validation of the search.

Finally, any text on the line, like the city identifiers in the examples above, can also be used as a search key. Therefore, since any text on a line can be a searched value, it is very important to make search keys unique.

In order to support the *calendar must support anniversaries* requirement, the year portion of the date in the database would be filled in with the value AA so a record would look like:

```
AA1225 {Christmas Day} hday
```

The following line of code from the cal.tcl program would have to change to allow AAmm as well as yymm formats.

```
if {[string range $inrec 0 3]==  $first4} {
```

The changes include commenting out the if statement and adding the following three lines. The first two lines set the search values for the regular expression, the third line is the new if statement that includes the two search values.

```
set reg1 AA$[string range $inrec 2 3]
set reg2 [string range $inrec 0 3]
if {[regexp $reg1|$reg2 $first4]} {
```

In Chapter 10, there is some discussion on adding and removing data from the database. There are two programs that we will be covering that will allow data items to be manipulated without having to hand edit the database.

Data Display Design: Building a Calendar

There are a number of areas to focus on in the design of the code. In this discussion, we'll deal with the following ones:

- Processing the input to generate the get strings for prior and next month links
- Using the search processor
- Determining the first day of month
- Processing file prefixes and suffixes
- Designing a table

Processing Get and Post to New Get Strings

The only portion of the code in which to avoid tinkering, unless you are willing to break it, is the prior-next code. This was supposed to be an easy feature to test and debug. It ended up taking almost three man days. It may look simple enough, but is actually far too easy to break the POST-GET processing. Debugging that particular piece of code is very difficult.

In order to support the ability to perform the POST-GET transition and process both the POST and GET passed data (in next/prior processing we will be changing the month, and possibly the year data - so we will have to be able to manipulate it as well) we will have to modify the way that we get the data from the foreach loop.

We will also need to concatenate all data obtained in the processing of the uncgi variables into a string that can have reverse character substitution performed on so it can be output as a properly encoded URI for the next calendar.

```
foreach envvar [lsort [array names env] ] {
   if {[regexp {^WWW_} $envvar]} {
     set varname [join [lrange [split [lindex [split $envvar =]\
                  0] _] 1 end ] _]
     if {$varname != ""} {
       set $varname $env(WWW_$varname)
       lappend passapp &$varname=$env(WWW_$varname)
     }
   }
}
```

POST-POST versus POST-GET

In general we have attempted not to put in code that would confuse the reader, but the concept of being able to move from POST to GET and back was important to detail somewhere. This is the first chance that we have had to provide that level of detail. An easier method of doing prior-next is to create a form with hidden variables where the only thing visible would be the button. This button would then be used if the proper flag was set.

One key advantage to the use of a POST-POST over the POST-GET processing is the fact that a POST-POST would not display the GET URI in the location field when returned. This provides some visual comfort for those that don't like the yuckie URI display.

It is easier to keep a post as a post with the prior and next buttons acting as mini-forms with all the data passed back and forth using hidden fields and using the submit button of the post form for the forward/next button Code available at the **Prentice Hall** Web site will be able to be used instead of this complex and, in some ways, confusing post-get transition method.

Again, this method was chosen to show that it could be done, and how it could be done. While this particular instance of software did not need to use this method, there may be times when knowing how to build a complex get stream from simple data formats will be required. Within the scope of the text, this was the best opportunity to provide that information.

The start of this looks like a standard *get the uncgi variables* process. The key difference is that we create a variable called passapp. This variable is the concatenation of the variables that were passed into the procedure. Each variable has an ampersand placed between it and the variable before it.

```
set strmon $mon
set numyr $yr
set dbase $db
```

Now extract all the required variables.

```
set nummon [lsearch \
  "none Jan Feb Mar Apr May Jun Jul Aug Sep Oct Nov Dec"\
  $strmon]
```

Then pull off the month string value for the current month.

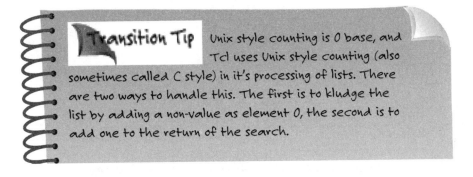

Transition Tip   Unix style counting is 0 base, and Tcl uses Unix style counting (also sometimes called C style) in it's processing of lists. There are two ways to handle this. The first is to kludge the list by adding a non-value as element 0, the second is to add one to the return of the search.

In the second case the code would have been:

```
set nummon \
  [expr 1+\
  [lsearch "Jan Feb Mar Apr May Jun Jul Aug Sep Oct \
  Nov Dec"\
    $strmon] ]
```

While both work, the first method shown is a kludge and is not the preferred method.

```
if {![info exists priornext]} {
  set priornext F
}
if {$priornext == "T"} {
  if {[info exists tabtitle]} {
    if {"$tabtitle" == ""} {
      set tabtitle "none"
```

```
      }
    }
    if {![info exists tabtitle]} {
      set tabtitle "none"
    }
```

If we are not asked to do prior/next processing, set a flag to not process (the default). Then, process the flag as it was set. If we are doing prior/next processing, override the tabtitle variable. This is done so we can place the default tabtitle data into the title bar of the table (where we will also be placing the prior/next selections).

```
if {$nummon == 1} {
  set lmon 12
  set lyr [expr $yr -1]
  set nmon [expr $nummon + 1]
  set nyr $yr
} else {
```

Special case processing: Handle January so that prior month is set to December of the prior year.

```
  if {$nummon == 12} {
  set nmon 1
  set nyr [expr $yr + 1]
  set lmon [expr $nummon - 1]
  set lyr $yr
} else {
```

Special case processing: Handle December so that next month is set to January of the next year.

```
    set lmon [expr $nummon - 1]
  set lyr $yr
  set nmon [expr $nummon + 1]
  set nyr $yr
  }
}
```

It wasn't a special case, so we increment and decrement the month as required and keep the year the same.

```
if {$env(REQUEST_METHOD) == "GET" } {
  set passapp $env(QUERY_STRING)
} else {
  regsub -all \{|\} $passapp "" passapp
  regsub -all {\ \&} $passapp {\&} passapp
  regsub -all {\ } $passapp {+} passapp
  set passapp [string range $passapp 1 end]
}
```

Here we process all the passed-in data. Note that we cheat a bit and use the QUERY_STRING if it was a GET. That saves us from doing regular expression substitution on GET processing.

In the substitution, we eliminate all {} (there are put on in the lappend command that was used to get the POST data). Close up any spaces between variables by replacing any " &" (space with an ampersand) with "&" (the ampersand without the space). And, finally, replace all remaining spaces with the standard + sign, thereby completing the encode procedure. The final set just rewrites the variable space.

```
set npassapp $passapp
regsub -all mon=$strmon $passapp mon=[expr 1+[lindex \
  {Jan Feb Mar Apr May Jun Jul Aug Sep Oct Nov Dec}\
  $lmon] passapp
  regsub -all yr=$yr $passapp yr=$lyr passapp
  set lmonstr "<a href=\"[string range
$env(SCRIPT_NAME)\
  [string first {/cgi-bin} $env(SCRIPT_NAME)] \
  end]?$passapp\">Last Month</a>"
```

Here we substitute the Month and Year variables with the ones that we want associated in the prior month URI. Once again, we can go with either the expression computation (above) or the additional list item to offset for 0 based indexing.

```
regsub -all mon=$strmon $npassapp mon=[lindex \
  {none Jan Feb Mar Apr May Jun Jul Aug Sep Oct Nov Dec} \
  $nmon] npassapp
regsub -all yr=$yr $npassapp yr=$nyr npassapp
set nmonstr "<a href=\"[string range $env(SCRIPT_NAME) \
  [string first {/cgi-bin} $env(SCRIPT_NAME)] \
    end]?$npassapp\">Next Month</a>"
} else {.
set lmonstr ""
set nmonstr ""
}
```

Regexp and the Search Processor

In this case, we want to allow the users to perform specific searches against the date selected items in the database. This allows for keywords to be used and searched from within a line of database text. In the sample form and the sample data file, we used the *city designators* to be search keys for the form, and we used the same keys as part of the displayed data.

Open the data file (as shown here) and start a loop to process every record in the file, until end of file.

```
set f1 [open $dbase r]
while {![eof $f1]} {
gets $f1 inrec
if {[string range $inrec 0 3]==  $first4} {
if {[info exists strsea]} {
if {[regexp $strsea $inrec]} {
```

Once again, we have the problem with Tcl's use of the EOF statement. The EOF will not be reached until after the last record has been read in the file. This will cause the program to perform an additional, unnecessary pass through the file at the end of the loop. To avoid that additional pass, include the read within the while and look for a string size of 0. This won't work in this case because there is the possibility that the file may contain null lines within it

Just a reminder: if you wanted to modify the procedure to handle the AA processing of anniversaries, the second line from this snippet is the place to make the change. If the record is valid for the YYMM that we are working with, then determine if we need to perform a string search on the record. Note that this is where all records that don't use the YYMMDD format will be ignored. If we do process the record and the value has been set to perform the search for a keyword, process the entire record through a regular expression.

By not parsing the record in any way or form, we open up the option that allows the database designer to include keywords or comments after the bracketed data. Consider the following record:

```
960510 {Sunny and Steve's Anniversary} friends dtr
⇒  imp aniv
```

Here, I have used a keyword that can be searched for using regexp. I have used full words (friends), keywords (dtr is a keyword for Dates To Remember (dtr)) and short key terms (imp stands for important and aniv for anniversaries). Each of these terms can be used in a regexp search. For instance a seastr of aniv|dtr will catch this as both an anniversary or as a date-to-remember. As the data from the prior section shows, we permit any value anywhere in the string in the file to be considered a valid search value.

```
lappend valrec([string range [lindex $inrec 0] 4 5]) \
    [string trim [lindex $inrec 1] \{\} ]<br>
    }
} else {
lappend valrec([string range [lindex $inrec 0] 4 5]) \
    [string trim [lindex $inrec 1] \{\} ]<br>
    }
    }
}
close $f1
```

Here we append the data to the date-value associative array we established that permits us to output the data for each date. We choose to use the lappend as the syntax that allows us to append any new data to the current variable, yet it will create the variable if it doesn't already exist.

Determining the First Day of Month

One of the more important elements in creating a calendar table is determining the first day of the month. There are two approaches to this: Unix-specific and Generic. The Unix-specific approach, shown here, was part of the initial release of the software.

```
regsub -all  "\ " [lindex [split [exec cal $nummon \
   $numyr ] \n] 2] "" b
set fsat [string length $b ]
set stday [expr 7-$fsat]
set stdow "[lindex "Sun Mon Tue Wen Thu Fri Sat" $stday]"
set value "$stdow $strmon 1"
```

In this case, we specifically called the Unix utility cal. This utility returns a calendar with a title row, and then with days, followed by the dates. This program example performs an exec (external call) to the Unix cal utility and then parses the known format response by indexing to the third line of the returned data. This is the same as stripping off the first two lines.

That leaves us with a series of numbers. We then determine the number of items in the list (how many days had numbers) . That number is subtracted from the number of days in the week to establish the location of the first numeric value for the line, which should be the first day of the month. We then use that to index a "week" of day string to set the proper day string on.

The generic approach was recommended by John Haxby (<jch@ hazel.pwd.hp.com>) in the Usenet newsgroup comp.lang.tcl. This was such a powerful approach (saving the time to create the subprocess, as well as making the Tcl procedure generic enough to cross platforms) that cal.tcl was immediately modified to use this method.

```
#
proc DayOfWeek {d m y {dayOffset 1}} {
set m [expr ($m+9)%12 + 1]
if {$m >= 11} {
incr y -1
      }
set c [expr $y/100]
set y [expr $y%100]
expr abs($d - $dayOffset + \
(13*$m-1)/5 - 2*$c + $y + $y/4 + $c/4) % 7
}
```

This procedure calculates the day of the week on the Gregorian Calendar. The dayOffset is the day offset from Sunday (=0) in which we want to start the week. A day offset of 1 (default) means we start the week on Monday.

```
set stday [DayOfWeek 01 $nummon $numyr 0]
set stdow "[lindex "Sun Mon Tue Wen Thu Fri Sat" $stday]"
set value "$stdow $strmon 1"
```

In this case, we don't make an external call using the exec, saving us the overhead of instantiating another process. But we do call the procedure passing it the numeric value for the month and year, along with the start day (0 = Sunday) for the calendar layout and the day we want (the first day of the month). It will return an index into the week pointing to the day-of-the-week that we want (a 5 would be the fifth day of the week, or Thursday).The following code would also been valid, but debugging it would have been painful:

```
set value "[lindex "Sun Mon Tue Wen Thu Fri Sat" \
    [DayOfWeek 01 $nummon $numyr 0] ] $strmon 1]"
```

Then, after we have the value, repeat what has gone before with the nongeneric procedure. We will index the weekday name string by the returned value, and then load up the value variable with the first-day-of-the-month data.

Processing File Prefixes and Suffixes

One of the key features in creating this calendar is to provide a level of complexity that permits the user to define a custom response. This concept allows the calendar to have a high reuse and be applicable to any number of situations. To provide this functionality the program has to support the process of including HTML as part of the pre- and post-processing of the data file.

This permits a file to be presented to the user that has an explanation of the calendar data and how to read it (a pre-calendar file), as well as the ability to include a unique copyright notice at the end of the file, or other post-processing features

There are two basic ways that this feature could be supported. The first is to require that SSIs be implemented. This means that anyone who wants to use the calendar utility must be able to use the SSI *include file* capability. While this would work well for a site that allows these features, not all sites allow SSIs. To keep the process generic enough for any site to implement, SSIs couldn't be used.

The second possible method is to provide support for including a text file by allowing the *true path* of the file to be processed. This means that an actual path has to be passed to the procedure, and the CGI script must access and process that file.

Warning! This also leads to a security concern. When the initial POST to the calendar is processed with the prior/next options active, anyone using a GET or even moving the mouse over the hyperlink would be able to see the path on your system to the file that will be used for pre- or post-addition to the output. For this reason, it is suggested that you put the files in a location where it won't matter if the person browsing knows the location (/temp/prepost/...) and set the directory at the location as executable only, while the files have read permissions on them.

Once we have the path, there are two ways to process the file. The first involves using the exec command. In this method, we would exec a cat command to dump the file out to stdout. This would have displayed the data to the screen. This method works just fine, but like other things we dealt with here, we wanted to move to a less platform specific implementation.

The second method has a bit higher overhead in processing time (due to the file open), but doesn't require a subprocess (saving us the overhead of subprocess creation) or the use of the Unix specific cat command. In this second case, we open the file and read and write each line, until the file completes. The overhead associated to the file open is much less than that required in creating an exec'd process; therefore, the second method was chosen even without the platform concern.

```
if {[info exists prefile]} {
if {[file exists $prefile]} {
set f1 [open $prefile r]
while {![eof $f1]} {
gets $f1 inrec
puts "$inrec"
     }
close $f1
   }
}
```

and

```
if {[info exists postfile]} {
if {[file exists $postfile]} {
set f1 [open $postfile r]
while {![eof $f1]} {
gets $f1 inrec
puts "$inrec"
     }
close $f1
   }
}
```

In both cases, a check is made to see if there is a file requested and, if so, it is opened and each line is processed by a read-write loop. If the file didn't exist, there is no error processing performed. As you may have noticed, these two pieces of code are almost identical. In cases like these the code is screaming to be placed in a procedure. Within the code the procedure is called out instead of separate routines.

For a moment, close your eyes and visualize a calendar. Great. Now you have an image in your mind on what a calendar is to you. Was it:

- A wall calendar (with or without a pretty picture)?
- A desk pad calendar with a month at a time showing?
- A desk flip a day at a time calendar?
- A year at a glance calendar (from the back of a checkbook)?
- A calendar that comes up on a PC?
- A calendar that comes up with the Unix cal command?
- What anyone else who read this book may have thought of as a calendar?

See, the problem is we all associate our vision of a calendar to what we visualize a calendar to be. Without a clear definition of what the calendar is, there are too many opportunities to misunderstand what we are going to display.

Making the assumption that we all agree to what a calendar is and, therefore, agree to what one should look like is a recipe for disaster. A calendar has two distinct parts. The first part is the functionality. I think that in that area there can be some level of common agreement. The second part is presentation; such as, how that shared common concept of functionality can be visualized in the physical realm.

Before discussing making the calendar with tables, first define the calendar's physical appearance.

We begin by picking a common model so there is a base from which to work. In this case, the model chosen is the desktop month-at-a-glance pad.

Here are some issues that are raised by the selection and the associated decisions made when developing the software.

How will blank days at the beginning and end of the calendar be filled?

In the beginning, there are actual days there from the prior month. These will be indicated by the boxing of the day, but no dates will be inserted into the boxes. At the end of the month, there are no more known days and so the last day of the month is the last date to be indicated by being boxed. This shown in Figures 9.2 and 9.3.

Sun	Mon	Tue	Wed	Thu	Fri	Sat
	1 NA	2 NA	3 NA	4 NA		

Figure 9.2: *Beginning of the month . . .*

| 28 NA | 29 NA | | | | | |

Figure 9.3: *. . . and end of the month*

How will days without data within them be indicated?

As we can see in Figure 9.4, any date without data will be indicated by an NA (for No Available data). Why put anything at all? To ensure that the computer read all the data for that month and there was none to display.

When we display prior/next, just where will they be displayed?

When we turn on the context switch to allow for prior/next, we also will add a new line to the top of the calendar. That line will be broken into thirds, as shown in Figure 9.5. The center third, covering the three middle days, will be the month and year for the display. The right and left two thirds will be the prior (left) and next (right). In non-table display mode, the list will support having the prior/next at the end of the month.

In general, these issues are caught when the requirements gathering process takes place. During the intake, when discussions are ongoing between the people who are taking the customers requirements and the customers, what should happen is the screen that was being displayed be drawn for the person requesting the calendar.

In this case, certain rules were established. Using these rules allowed for a consistent display to be made.

Figure 9.4:

A month without data

Sun	Mon	Tue	Wed	Thu	Fri	Sat
						1 NA
2 NA	3 NA	4 NA	5 NA	6 NA	7 NA	8 NA
9 NA	10 NA	11 NA	12 NA	13 NA	14 NA	15 NA
16 NA	17 NA	18 NA	19 NA	20 NA	21 NA	22 NA
23 NA	24 NA	25 NA	26 NA	27 NA	28 NA	29 NA
30 NA	31 NA					

Last Month		Jan 2000			Next Month	
Sun	Mon	Tue	Wed	Thu	Fri	Sat
						1 NA
2 NA	3 NA	4 NA	5 NA	6 NA	7 NA	8 NA
9 NA	10 NA	11 NA	12 NA	13 NA	14 NA	15 NA
16 NA	17 NA	18 NA	19 NA	20 NA	21 NA	22 NA
23 NA	24 NA	25 NA	26 NA	27 NA	28 NA	29 NA
30 NA	31 NA					

Figure 9.5:
Calendar with Prior/Next

A nice alternative model to the one we will be building has the month-at-a-glance, but with no data displayed on it. If there is data associated to a day (an event) then the day number becomes a link to a secondary day page that displays all the day information. To really fancy that model up, you could also have the day subpage launched as a new browser window.

What we will be doing in this chapter is providing the basic month-at-a-glance calendar without all the bells and whistles formerly described. The great part of all this is that the code provides a starting point to go on and develop a fancy calendar.

So, let's start by looking at how the table comes together. We start with the command to set up the table.

```
puts "<table border=1>"
```

Next, if prior/next processing is called for, create the top-most line of the table. This is following the rule established earlier. It breaks the top-most line down into three sections of 2 columns, 3 columns and 2 columns and loads them with prior URI, date in the form of Month Year, and next URI.

```
if {$priornext == "T"} {
puts "<tr><td align=left colspan=2 \
    nowrap>$lmonstr</td> \
    <td align=center colspan=3 nowrap><b>$strmon \
    $numyr </b></td><td align=right colspan=2 nowrap> \
    $nmonstr</td></tr>"
}
```

Then place the days of the week across the top, like this:

```
puts "<tr> <th>Sun</th> <th>Mon</th> <th>Tue</th> \
    <th>Wed</th> <th>Thu</th> <th>Fri</th> \
    <th>Sat</th></tr>"
```

This line can also be replaced with images containing the day names. In that case, it would look like:

```
puts "<tr> <th><img src=\"/giflib/sun.gif\" alt=\"Sun\"></th>…
```

It should be noted that this will create a calendar with standardized fields when there is no data. While some may look at that as a positive point, I tend to feel that the calendar should be the size it needs to be to display the data. That way, if there is no data for the month on a Saturday, the calendar shouldn't output a large empty column for that day. Once again, since the look wasn't pre-defined, be prepared to create a calendar that has standardized field sizes. To do that, you would be able to use the code above, with images, or you could use the *width* option that comes with tables.

The following line is the main loop and will ensure that each day will be processed:

```
while {$dayct < $initv} {
```

This next line starts a new row in the table.

```
puts "<tr valign=top>"
```

weekcnt is a counter for the day of the week. If it is set to 99 then we have reached the end of the month and we break out of the procedure that builds the weekdays into table format.

```
while {$weekcnt < 7} {
if {$dayct == $initv} {
set weekcnt 99
break
  }
```

If we haven't hit the start day for the month, we need to fill the value from the start of the week with a blank date, like this.

```
incr weekcnt
if {$dayct == 0} {
if {$weekcnt <= $stday} {
puts "<td><table border=0><tr><td></td> \
    <td rowspan=2></td></tr><tr><td></td></tr></table></td>"
```

We have hit a valid date. In that case, we have to make sure that we *zero fill* the value we will be using as an index (the index into the value array for a day is always two characters(it was generated when we extracted the *day* value from the YYMMDD portion of the incoming record).

```
} else {
incr dayct
if {[string length $dayct] == 1} {
set ldcnt [format %02d $dayct]
} else {
set ldcnt $dayct
    }
```

If there is information for that day to be displayed, we must first clean up the {} that are put into the value to separate the list elements (as we now want this to be a string, not a series of list elements).

```
if {[info exists valrec($ldcnt)] } {
regsub -all \{|\} $valrec($ldcnt) "" valrec($ldcnt)
```

Then, based on whether there is a value, we will write out the day record or the value NA. The table is written using a table within the table item. This allows for the day number to be placed in the upper right corner of the day cell, with the text to its right.

```
puts "<td><table border=0><tr valign=top> \
    <td>$predate$dayct$postdate</td> <td> \
    $valrec($ldcnt)</td></tr></table></td>
} else {
puts "<td><table border=0><tr valign=top> \
    <td>$predate$dayct$postdate</td> <td> NA \
    </td></tr></table></td>"
    }
  }
```

We are not on the first week any longer. We can now process all the following weeks alike. This is done by using the same code as had been used above.

```
} else {
```

The following ends the processing for each day:

```
incr dayct
if {[string length $dayct] == 1} {
set ldcnt 0$dayct
} else {
set ldcnt $dayct
 }
if {[info exists valrec($ldcnt)] } {
```

```
regsub -all \{|\} $valrec($ldcnt) "" valrec($ldcnt)
puts "<td><table border=0><tr valign=top> \
    <td>$predate$dayct$postdate</td> <td>
$valrec($ldcnt) \
    </td></tr></table></td>"
} else {
puts "<td><table border=0><tr valign=top> \
    <td>$predate$dayct$postdate</td> <td> NA \
    </td></tr></table></td>"
  }
 }
}
```

The following ends the processing for each week:

```
puts "</tr>"
set weekcnt 0
}
```

This line ends the processing for the table.

```
puts "</tr></table></center>"
```

Why have lists at all? Why not use the browser to determine if a list is required and make the decision?

In some cases people may not want a table. They may want a list that they can dump to a file for later processing, or they may not be able to display a table on the browser that they are using. This code also creates a list as described in the code itself. While this functionality was originally added because many browsers couldn't handle tables within tables, it should be noted that as time marches on more browsers will handle embedded tables and this code may be thought of as expendable.

If you want to distribute this data so that a robot could read it, parse it and then utilize it in another application. This mode of creating lists would make development of the robot, and the parsing all that much easier. Once again, the list code has not been called out here, but is clearly commented in the code itself.

Listing 9.2 provides the core software for this section. In some case, we used different algorithms in the software. Again, this text is both a working text, in that all the software we have used works in the real world, and a teaching text. We want you to see that there are any number of ways to accomplish tasks, know that some are better than others, and why.

Listing 9.2: cal.tcl

```tcl
#!/usr/local/bin/tclsh
##
## cal.tcl
##
puts "Content-type: text/html\n\n"
##
##
## Required Variables to be passed in:
##
## mon = the month in three character string format
## (first character caps)
## yr  = the year as a four digit number
## db  = the full pathname of the datafile
##
##  examples:
##  mon = Jan
##  yr  = 1996
##  db  = /users/brooke/database/mydata.db
##
##
## Optional Variables:
##
## title = the html <title></title> value
##     Default: <title>Calendar of $dbase for
##       $strmon $numyr</title>
## tabtitle = the title on the table <h1></h1>
##     Default: <h1>Calendar for $strmon $numyr</h1>
##   Keyword:  use of the keyword "none" will put no
##        table title
##     SPECIAL RULE: If tabtitle is default and
##          priornext is on tabtitle is set to "none"
## prefile = file to prepended to the table
## postfile = file appended to the table
## seastr = search string. Allows for table data to
##     be chosen based on a string in the data. Thus
##     a datafile can use keywords and the form can
##     pass in the keyword to search for.
## nscapoff = Netscape-off : use list not tables ("T"=off)
## boxday = determines if the day is "boxed" or small font
##     Default: days are boxed
## priornext = put up a next month / prior month
##   selection item
##     Default: *NONE* must be set "T" to run.
##
##
##   ***NEW*** Because 8 of 10 beta testers asked for
## it we have included the functionality for the
## user to pass in:
```

```
##   emptyval = determine what the empty day text will be:
##     Default: NA
##     Keyword: noval = no value (it will be blank)
##        Text: a text string (in quotes) can be passed
##              and it will use that string as the
##              empty date value.
##
## The code has been included below. It was not part
## of the original requirements and is not documented
## in the html sample we use.
##
##
## Some closing comments:
##
## The data files are simple. I designed them that
## way because I thought that they would be easy to
## maintain (by hand). Well, one key thing that has
## been asked for is a processor to allow people to
## add and remove database entries. This program
## is a viewer, and I want to keep it that way so the
## add/remove programs are separate.
##
## Database format:         yymmdd {entry}
##
##   Required: yymmdd - the first six characters are the
##                          date in that format
##   Required and Reserved: {} - also known as
##                       "braces" and "curley brackets"
##   Required: entry - the text can be in HTML or
##                         plain text
##
## One final word of warning... I am assuming that
## this is being installed by a webmaster or someone
## who can look at the error_log, as there is no
## error recovery whatsoever. Either you get a
## calendar or you get a broken page. Since everything
## in here is "controlled" there should be no problem
## with this. Even if there is no data, an empty
## calendar is returned. The only time there will be
## a problem is if the required data is sent in a
## way that doesn't match what is expected (full path,
## capitalized months and full four character years).
## So, follow directions and you should be rewarded
## with a working script.- also, make sure the data
## file is readable.
##
##—
## The following code will obtain every environment
## variable preceded with WWW_ (all uncgi variables
## have that) and process it to be a variable name
## with the value in it.
```

```
##
foreach envvar [lsort [array names env] ] {
  if {[regexp {^WWW_} $envvar]} {
    set varname [join [lrange [split [lindex [split \
              $envvar =] 0] _] 1 end ] _]
    if {$varname != ""} {
      set $varname $env(WWW_$varname)
      lappend passapp &$varname=$env(WWW_$varname)
    }
  }
}
##
## pull the three required variables into special
## variable names
##
set strmon $mon
set numyr $yr
set dbase $db
##
## change the string value for the month to a numeric
##
set nummon [expr 1+[lsearch \
  "Jan Feb Mar Apr May Jun Jul Aug Sep Oct Nov Dec"\
          $strmon] ]
##
##
## Recommendation: Don't pull on superman's cape,
## don't spit into the wind, don't mess around with
## priornext code.
##
## create the strings for priormonth and nextmonth:
##     Make sure the var is set
##
if {![info exists priornext]} {
  set priornext F
}
##
## if set, make sure the tabtitle is set off if it
## is default
##
if {$priornext == "T"} {
  if {[info exists tabtitle]} {
    if {"$tabtitle" == ""} {
      set tabtitle "none"
    }
  }
  if {![info exists tabtitle]} {
    set tabtitle "none"
  }
##
## if it's Jan then do processing to set for Dec -
```

```
## prior year
##
  if {$nummon == 1} {
    set lmon 12
    set lyr [expr $yr -1]
    set nmon [expr $nummon + 1]
    set nyr $yr
  } else {
##
## if it's Dec do processing to set next for Jan -
## next year
##
    if {$nummon == 12} {
      set nmon 1
      set nyr [expr $yr + 1]
      set lmon [expr $nummon - 1]
      set lyr $yr
    } else {
##
## do normal processing
##
      set lmon [expr $nummon - 1]
      set lyr $yr
      set nmon [expr $nummon + 1]
      set nyr $yr
    }
  }
##
## we need to keep passing the user data back and
## forth this will ensure that we get it all and
## that it is properly formatted in GET protocol format
##
  if {$env(REQUEST_METHOD) == "GET" } {
    set passapp $env(QUERY_STRING)
  } else {
    regsub -all \{|\} $passapp "" passapp
    regsub -all {\ \&} $passapp {\&} passapp
    regsub -all {\ } $passapp {+} passapp
    set passapp [string range $passapp 1 end]
  }
##
## build the output for last month
##
  set npassapp $passapp
  regsub -all mon=$strmon $passapp mon=[expr 1+ \
      [lindex {Jan Feb Mar Apr May Jun Jul Aug Sep \
      Oct Nov Dec} $lmon] passapp
  regsub -all yr=$yr $passapp yr=$lyr passapp
  set lmonstr "<a href=\"[string range \
      $env(SCRIPT_NAME) \
      [string first {/cgi-bin} $env(SCRIPT_NAME)] \
```

```
                end]?$passapp\">Last Month</a>"
##
##  build the output for next month
##

     regsub -all mon=$strmon $npassapp mon=[lindex \
         {none Jan Feb Mar Apr May Jun Jul Aug Sep \
         Oct Nov Dec} $nmon] npassapp
     regsub -all yr=$yr $npassapp yr=$nyr npassapp
     set nmonstr "<a href=\"[string range \
         $env(SCRIPT_NAME) [string first {/cgi-bin}\
         $env(SCRIPT_NAME)] end]?$npassapp\">Next \
         Month</a>"
  } else {
##
##  set these to null, just in case :-)
##

     set lmonstr ""
     set nmonstr ""
  }
##
##
##  ─────────────────────────────────
##  Thanks to John Haxby <jch@hazel.pwd.hp.com> for
##  the following procedure that can replace the Unix
##  specific code that required the cal command.
##  ─────────────────────────────────
##  Calculate the day of the week on the Gregorian
##  Calendar. The dayOffset is the day offset from
##  Sunday (=0) that we want to start the week on. A
##  day offset of 1 (default) means we start the week
##  on Monday
##
  proc DayOfWeek {d m y {dayOffset 1}} {
    set m [expr ($m+9)%12 + 1]
    if {$m >= 11} {
      incr y -1
    }
    set c [expr $y/100]
    set y [expr $y%100]
    expr abs($d - $dayOffset + (13*$m-1)/5 - 2*$c + \
             $y + $y/4 + $c/4) % 7
  }
##
##
##
  set stday [DayOfWeek 01 $nummon $numyr 0]
  set stdow "[lindex "Sun Mon Tue Wed Thu Fri Sat" \
      $stday]"
  set value "$stdow $strmon 1"
##
##  if the month is a single numeric character,
```

```
## prepend a "0" There are two ways to do this. The
## way shown here, or we could have used the format
## command. In that case we wouldn't do the check,
## but would force the format with:
##   set nummon [format %.2d $nummon]
##
  if {[string length $nummon] == 1} {
    set nummon 0$nummon
  }
##
## build the search value of YYMM for processing the
## database remember that this is the line of code
## we want to change if we do processing for
## anniversaries (to do AAMM|YYMM)
##
  set first4 [string range $numyr 2 3]$nummon
##
## Database processing:
## open the file and parse each records first four
## characters. If we get a match, then either append
## it to a variable for that specific date, or if
## seastr is set, do a subsearch on the data portion
## of the string and append it if it matches.
##
  set f1 [open $dbase r]
  while {![eof $f1]} {
    gets $f1 inrec
    if {[string range $inrec 0 3]==  $first4} {
      if {[info exists strsea]} {
        if {[regexp $strsea $inrec]} {
##
## Now, we have used a regexp to perform matching.
## This is special as the substitution will be
## somewhat complete. This allows us to pass in values
## with rules in them. For instance, if we wanted a
## list of all calendar items in the database that
## had the keywords "BDAY" and "ANIV" (all birthday
## and anniversary references) we could fill substr
## in with the value "BDAY|ANIV" and all strings
## with either of those values will be taken.
##
          lappend valrec([string range [lindex \
              $inrec 0] 4 5]) [string trim \
              [lindex $inrec 1] \{\} ]<br>
        }
      } else {
        lappend valrec([string range [lindex \
            $inrec 0] 4 5]) [string trim \
            [lindex $inrec 1] \{\} ]<br>
      }
    }
```

```
    }
  close $f1
#
##
## Database processing completed. Why did we do this
## instead of using a "grep"? Because the idea was
## to make this as generic as possible, not Unix
## specific.
##
## If a title was passed in use it, otherwise use
## the default
##
  if {[info exists title]} {
    puts "<title>$title</title>"
  } else {
    puts "<title>Calendar of $dbase for $strmon \
        $numyr</title>"
  }
##
## A table on the page could be confusing, this
## procedure allows files to be added to the
## calendar. It is used here to allow for
## preprending a file or appending a file.
##
  proc dofile {filnam} {
    if {[file exists $filnam]} {
      set f1 [open $filnam r]
      while {![eof $f1]} {
        gets $f1 inrec
        puts "$inrec"
      }
      close $f1
    }
  }
##
## call the file include procedure above if necessary
##
if {[info exists prefile]} {
  dofile $prefile
}
##
## if emptyval not used place an NA in it, if noval
## make it empty, or if used but not noval, use the
## text as the fill
##
  if {[info exists emptyval]} {
    if {$emptyval == "noval"} {
      set NA " "
    } else {
      set NA $emptyval
    }
  } else {
```

```
        set NA NA
    }
##
## Here we start to build the table. set the number
## of days in the month. if it's a leap year, pop
## the right number in for Feb. Elsewhere in the
## text we have a leap-year algorithm - this is the
## leap-year kludge.
##
  set initv [lindex "31 28 31 30 31 30 31 31 30 31 30 31" \
        [lsearch "Jan Feb Mar Apr May Jun Jul Aug Sep \
        Oct Nov Dec" [lindex [string trim $value] 1 ] ] ] ]
  if {[lindex [string trim $value] 1 ] == "Feb"} {
    if {[lsearch "1996 2000 2004 2008 2012 2016 2020" \
        $numyr] > -1 } {
        set initv 29
    }
  }
##
## initialize the counters to 0
##
  set weekcnt 0
  set dayct 0
##
## If the user asked for small titles - get them for
## the user
##
  set predate "<table border=1
cellspacing=0><tr><td><b>"
  set postdate "</b></td></tr></table>"
  if {[info exists boxday]} {
    if {$boxday == "F"} {
      set predate "<table border=0 \
          cellspacing=0><tr><td>" "<font size=1><b>"
      set postdate "</b></font></td></tr></table>"
    }
  }
##
## insert the <h1> table header if it exists
## (support the keyword "none" to not use a h1
## header in this location).
##
  if {[info exists tabtitle]} {
    if {!("$tabtitle" == "none")} {
      if {"$tabtitle" == ""} {
        puts "<h1>Calendar for $strmon $numyr</h1>"
      } else {
        puts "<h1>$tabtitle</h1>"
      }
    }
  } else {
```

```
        puts "<h1>Calendar for $strmon $numyr</h1>"
  }
##
##   do the list only?
##
  set listout 0
    if {[info exists nscapoff]} {
      if {("$nscapoff" == "T")} {
        set listout 1
##
## if so, require a header!
##
        if {[info exists tabtitle]} {
          if {"$tabtitle" == "none"} {
           puts "<h1>Calendar for $strmon $numyr</h1>"
          }
          if {"$tabtitle" == ""} {
           puts "<h1>Calendar for $strmon $numyr</h1>"
          }
        } else {
          puts "<h1>Calendar for $strmon $numyr</h1>"
        }
##
## This is the code that creates the list rather
## than a table. Note that it is *much* shorter than
## the table code... ;-). Also, we set a value
## "listout" this is set so that we will know we
## did a list and won't also do a table.
##
          puts "<ul>"
            while {$dayct < $initv} {
              while {$weekcnt < 7} {
                if {$dayct == $initv} {
                  set weekcnt 99
                  break
                }
                incr weekcnt
                set dow "[lindex "Sun Mon Tue Wed Thu \
                  Fri Sat" [expr $weekcnt-1]]"
                if {$weekcnt > $stday} {
                  incr dayct
                  if {[string length $dayct] == 1} {
                    set stday 0
                    set ldcnt 0$dayct
                  } else {
                    set ldcnt $dayct
                  }
                    if {[info exists valrec($ldcnt)] } {
                      regsub -all \{|\} $valrec($ldcnt) ""\
                        valrec($ldcnt)
                          puts "<li>$dow, $dayct :<dl> \
```

```
                                  <dd>$valrec($ldcnt)</dl><p>"
                     } else {
                       puts "<li>$dow, $dayct :<dl><dd>No \
                            Data</dl><p>"
                     }
                 }
             }
          set weekcnt 0
          }
        puts "</ul>"
        if {$priornext == "T"}
         puts "$lmonstr"
         puts "$nmonstr"
         }
## this bracket closes the listout if-then statement
       }
      }
   if {!$listout} {
##
## This is the code that actually creates the table.
## It will check to see if we are using the
## priornext header, and if so will slap it on the
## top of the table. It puts the day headers
## (in text, although one person asked for the
## ability to put a day graphic up there instead) on
## the top for the days of the week, and then
## processes blank days until the first day of
## the month is hit. Then processes the each day
## rotating to a new row with each new week. The
## processing of each day places the date in a small
## box or teni-text at the top of the day-table for
## that date, and then the data in the balance of
## that day-table (each row is made up of seven day-
## tables - same as the number of days :-) ). If no
## data is available an NA is placed in the table.
##
     puts "<table border=1>"
     if {$priornext == "T"} {
       puts "<tr><td align=left colspan=2 \
            nowrap>$lmonstr</td><td align=center \
            colspan=3 nowrap><b>$strmon \
            $numyr</b></td><td align=right colspan=2 \
            nowrap> $nmonstr</td></tr>"
     }
       puts "<tr> <th>Sun</th> <th>Mon</th> <th>Tue</th> \
            <th>Wed</th> <th>Thu</th> <th>Fri</th> \
            <th>Sat</th></tr>"
        while {$dayct < $initv} {
          puts "<tr valign=top>"
          while {$weekcnt < 7} {
             if {$dayct == $initv} {
```

```tcl
        set weekcnt 99
        break
    }
    incr weekcnt
    if {$dayct == 0} {
        if {$weekcnt <= $stday} {
            puts "<td><table border=0><tr><td></td> \
                <td rowspan=2></td></tr><tr><td></td> \
                </tr></table></td>"
        } else {
            incr dayct
            if {[string length $dayct] == 1} {
                set ldcnt 0$dayct
            } else {
                set ldcnt $dayct
            }
            if {[info exists valrec($ldcnt)] } {
                regsub -all \{|\} $valrec($ldcnt) ""\
                    valrec($ldcnt)
                puts "<td><table border=0><tr \
                    valign=top><td> \
                    $predate$dayct$postdate</td><td> \
                    $valrec($ldcnt)</td></tr> \
                    </table></td>"
            } else {
                puts "<td><table border=0><tr \
                    valign=top><td> \
                    $predate$dayct$postdate</td> \
                    <td> NA </td></tr></table></td>"
            }
        }
    } else {
        incr dayct
        if {[string length $dayct] == 1} {
            set ldcnt 0$dayct
        } else {
            set ldcnt $dayct
        }
        if {[info exists valrec($ldcnt)] } {
            regsub -all \{|\} $valrec($ldcnt) ""\
                valrec($ldcnt)
            puts "<td><table border=0><tr valign=top> \
                <td>$predate$dayct$postdate</td> \
                <td> $valrec($ldcnt) \
                </td></tr></table></td>"
        } else {
            puts "<td><table border=0><tr valign=top> \
                <td>$predate$dayct$postdate</td> \
                <td> NA </td></tr></table></td>"
        }
    }
    }
}
```

```
            puts "</tr>"
            set weekcnt 0
        }
        puts "</tr></table></center>"
## this bracket closes the listout if-then statement
    }
##
## insert a footer file. This could be the "copyright"
## information on the table data.
##
    if {[info exists postfile]} {
        dofile $postfile
    }
}
##
## Fini! -> exit gracefully
##
puts "<hr><address>Document created when requested</address>"
exit
```

Figure 9.6: *A sample calendar (table format)*

Last Month			Jan 1996				Next Month
Sun	Mon	Tue	Wed	Thu	Fri	Sat
	1 NA	2 NA	3 NA	4 NA	5 NA	6 NY: Opening: *My Fair Lady*
7 CHI: Uncle Bucks Rest.	8 BOS: Uncle Bucks Rest.	9 LA: Grand Opening Uncle Bucks Rest.	10 NY: Infobahn Xpress Tcl Training Seminars	11 NA	12 NA	13 NA
14 NA	15 NA	16 LON: Infobahn Xpress Tcl Training Seminars	17 NA	18 NA	19 NA	20 NA
21 NA	22 SF: Infobahn Xpress Tcl Training Seminars	23 NA	24 NA	25 NA	26 LA: Infobahn Xpress Tcl Training Seminars	27 NA
28 NA						

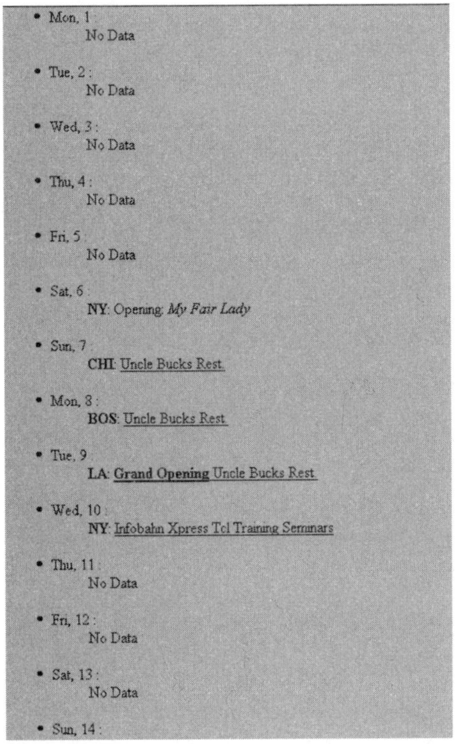

- Mon, 1 :
  No Data

- Tue, 2 :
  No Data

- Wed, 3 :
  No Data

- Thu, 4 :
  No Data

- Fri, 5 :
  No Data

- Sat, 6 :
  NY: Opening: *My Fair Lady*

- Sun, 7 :
  CHI: Uncle Bucks Rest.

- Mon, 8 :
  BOS: Uncle Bucks Rest.

- Tue, 9 :
  LA: **Grand Opening** Uncle Bucks Rest.

- Wed, 10 :
  NY: Infobahn Xpress Tcl Training Seminars

- Thu, 11 :
  No Data

- Fri, 12 :
  No Data

- Sat, 13 :
  No Data

- Sun, 14 :

Figure 9.7: *A sample calendar (list format)*

Managing a Web Site Calendar with Perl

The Perl scripts that follow let you manage a calendar on your Web site. You will be given the basic code to do this. You can then add the functionality as you see fit. The basic functionality provided by these scripts is the same as the Tcl code discussed in this chapter.

Note There isn't a provision for editing, deleting or adding events via HTML FORMs. The primary reason for this is security. This prevents anyone coming to my Web site from arbitrarily doing things that would write information to disk. A misguided user may write a robot that can simply add events to my calendar! If there **is** an error in listing events, simply send a mail message to the calendar manager and be done with it. Separate programs to add and delete entries are in Chapter 10.

The full script cal.pl is shown here in Listing 9.3. A discussion on the individual components follows.

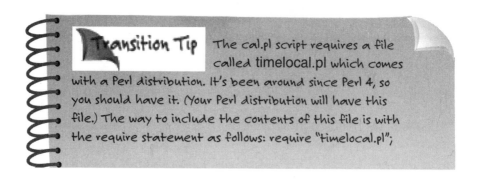

Transition Tip The cal.pl script requires a file called **timelocal.pl** which comes with a Perl distribution. It's been around since Perl 4, so you should have it. (Your Perl distribution will have this file.) The way to include the contents of this file is with the require statement as follows: require "timelocal.pl";

Listing 9.3: cal.pl

```perl
#!/usr/local/bin/perl
require "timelocal.pl";
$| = 1;
print "Content-type: text/html\n\n";
# =========================================================
#            Handling POST queries from the FORM.
# =========================================================
# This following lines of code are used to collect
# data from the standard input. The length of the
# standard input is in the environment variable
# CONTENT_LENGTH.
# =========================================================
#
if ($ENV{'REQUEST_METHOD'} eq "POST") {
read(STDIN,$buffer,$ENV{'CONTENT_LENGTH'});
} else {
$buffer = $ENV{'QUERY_STRING'};
}
@pairs= split(/&/,$buffer);
foreach $pair (@pairs) {
($name,$value) = split(/=/,$pair);
$value =~ tr/+/ /;
$value =~ s/%([a-fA-F0-9][a-fA-F0-
9])/pack("C",hex($1))/eg;
$contents{$name} = $value;
    }

#
# =========================================================
# Great, now we have all our input in the @contents
```

```
# associative array.
# =======================================================
@weekdays = ("Sun","Mon","Tue","Wed","Thu","Fri","Sat");
@daysInMonth = (31,28,31,30,31,30,31,31,30,31,30,31);
@months = ("Jan","Feb","Mar","Apr","May","Jun",
"Jul","Aug","Sep","Oct","Nov","Dec");
@activity = ();
#
# Get the current time if month and date are missing.
#

$mon = $contents{'mon'};
$year = $contents{'year'};

$usingTime = 0;
if (($mon == 0) && ($year == 0)) {
$usingTime = 1;
$time = time;
($sec,$min,$hour,$mday,$mon,$year,$wday,$yday,$isdst) =
localtime($time);
}
else {
$time = &timelocal(1,1,1,1,$mon,$year) ;
$wday = (localtime($time))[6];
}

$nextyear = $year;
$nextmonth = $mon + 1;
if ($nextmonth >= 12) { $nextmonth = 0; $nextyear++; }
$prevmonth = $mon - 1;
$prevyear = $year;
if ($prevmonth < 0) { $prevmonth = 11; $prevyear-; }
#
# Adjust for leap year.
#
if (&isLeap($year)) {
$daysInMonth[1] = 29;
}
@cachedItems = ();
# &setActivity($mon+1);
cacheCalendar();
$ntime = &timelocal($sec,$min,$hour,1,$mon,$year) ;
($sday) = (localtime($ntime))[6];
#
# ($sday,$mon,$year,$wday,$yday) =
(localtime($time))[3,4,5,6,7];
#
$daysToDo = $daysInMonth[$mon];
$rows = ($daysToDo + $wday) / 7;
# print "<HTML><TITLE>A Calendar</TITLE><BODY>\n";
```

```
# printf "<H1><center> %s %d </center> </H1>\n",
$months[$mon], $year + 1900;
# printf "<H2>Using time </H2>\n" if $usingTime;
$pageTitle = $contents{'title'};
if ($pageTitle eq "") {
$pageTitle = "A Calendar";
}
print "<HTML><TITLE>$pageTitle</TITLE><BODY>\n";
$headerTitle = $contents{'tabtitle'};
if ($headerTitle eq "") {
printf "<H1><center> Calendar for %s %d </center>
</H1>\n", $months[$mon], $year + 1900;
} else {
print "<H1><center>$headerTitle</center> </H1>\n";
}
if ($contents{'prefile'} ne "") {
open (PREF, "<".$contents{'prefile'})||die "<H1>Prefile
Error</h1> </BODY></HTML>";
while (<PREF>) {
print $_;
    }
close PREF;
}

if ($contents{'priornext'} ne "OFF") {
print   << "HTMLHEAD";
<HR>
<A HREF="http://www.company.com/cgi-
bin/cal4.pl?mon=$prevmonth&year=$prevyear"> [ Go to
Prev month ] </A>
<A HREF="/cgi-bin/xdocal.pl?mon=$nextmonth&day=-
1&year=$nextyear"> [ List This Month's Events ]</A>
<A HREF="http://www.company.com/cgi-
bin/cal4.pl?mon=$nextmonth&year=$nextyear">[ Go to
Next month ] </A>
HTMLHEAD
}
# print lists or tables?
if ($contents{'nscapoff'} ne "T") {
print "<TABLE BORDER WIDTH=\"50%\">\n";
foreach $i (@weekdays) { print "<TH>$i</TH>\n"; }
$jday = $sday;
$doCalYear = $year;
if ($year < 100) { $doCalYear += 1900; }
print "<TR>\n";
for ($i= 0; $i < $sday ; $i++) { print "<TD>
</TD>\n"; }
for ($i= 0; $i < $daysToDo; $i++) {
if ($contents{'boxDay'} eq "F") {
$myuri = sprintf "<b>%d</b>", $i+1;
}else {
```

```perl
$myuri = sprintf "<table border=1
valign=top><tr><td><b>%d</b></td></tr></table>",$i+1;
    }
$boxstr = sprintf "\n<A HREF=\"/cgi-
bin/xdocal.pl?mon=%d&day=%d&year=%d\">%s</A>"
,$mon+1,$i+1,$year,$myuri;
printf "\n<TD>%s<A HREF=\"/cgi-
bin/xdocal.pl?mon=%d&day=%d&year=%d\">%s</A></TD>"
,$boxstr,$mon+1,$i+1,$year,&showAppt($mon+1,$i+1,$yea
r,$i+1);
$jday++;
if ($jday > 6) { $jday = 0;  print "</TR>\n<TR>\n";}
    }
} else {
print "<BL>\n";
for ($i= 0; $i < $daysToDo; $i++) {
printf "\n<LI><A HREF=\"/cgi-
bin/docal.pl?mon=%d&day=%d&year=%d\">%d",
$mon+1,$i+1,$doCalYear,$i+1;
    }
print "</BL>\n";
}
print "<TR>\n";
print "</TABLE>\n";


#
# Now append the contents of the post file.
#
if ($contents{'postfile'} ne "") {
open (PSTF, "<".$contents{'postfile'})||die
"<H1>Prefile Error</h1> </BODY></HTML>";
while (<PSTF>) {
print $_;
    }
close PSTF;
}
# end the document and bailout
print "</BODY>\n";
print "</HTML>\n";
# ==========================================
sub isLeap() {
local $y = shift @_;
if (($y % 4) == 0) { return 1; }
if (($y % 100) == 0)
     {
if  (($y % 400) == 0) { return 0; }
return 1;
     }
return 0;
}
# ==========================================
```

```perl
sub showAppt() {
my ($mon,$day,$year,$wday) =  @_;
my ($xmon,$xday,$xyear);
my $ans;
my $date;
my $lindex;
my $rindex;
$ans =  "";
$count = 0;
my $count =  @cachedItems;
my $k;
for ($k=0;$k<$count;$k++) {
$input = $cachedItems[$k];
# ($xmon,$xday,$xyear,$key,$desc) =
split(':',$input);
# =========================================
# Get item for calendar
# =========================================

$lindex = index($input,"{");
$date = substr($input,0,$lindex-1);
$rindex = index($input,"}");
$desc = substr($input,$lindex+1,$rindex-$lindex-1);
$key = substr($input,$rindex+1);
$xyear = substr($date,0,2);
$xmon = substr($date,2,2);
$xday = substr($date,4,2);
if ($xyear eq "AA") {
$xyear = $year;
    }
    # =========================================
# found it?
if(($xmon == $mon) && ($xday == $day) && ($year ==
$xyear)) {
$ans .= $desc . "<BR>";
    }
   }

return $ans;
}

sub cacheCalendar() {
@cacheItems=();
open (MYCAL,"xcal.dat") || die "<H1>Cannot open
it</h1> </BODY></HTML>";
my $count =  0;
while(<MYCAL>) {
$cachedItems[$count++] = $_;
    }
close(MYCAL);
}
```

The usual scheme of grabbing the incoming parameters is done next to return an HTML page back to the browser. The two items in the %contents array to display the calendar for are mon (month) and year (year). The values are set in the following code:

```
$mon = $contents{'mon'};
$year = $contents{'year'};
```

Then, we set up some defaults for displaying the day of the week, the month and the number of days in the month. This is done with the following statements:

```
@weekdays = ("Sun","Mon","Tue","Wed","Thu","Fri","Sat");
@daysInMonth = (31,28,31,30,31,30,31,31,30,31,30,31);
@months = ("Jan","Feb","Mar","Apr","May","Jun",
"Jul","Aug","Sep","Oct","Nov","Dec");
```

The @cachedItems array is used to record any events per day. For the moment, it's set to an empty list.

```
@cachedItems = ();
```

If the calendar file you are working with is not large, (i.e. < 64K or something), you may as well cache it in memory for the Perl script. For requirements, we were using simple text files and did not have to do too much work with the disk so we can cache this away in memory for later use. The subroutine to do the caching for us is shown below:

```
sub cacheCalendar() {
@cacheItems=();
open (MYCAL, "xcal.dat") || die "<H1>Cannot open
it</h1> </BODY></HTML>";
my $count = 0;
while(<MYCAL>) {
$cachedItems[$count++] = $_;
    }
close(MYCAL);
}
```

If neither month nor year is specified, we will use the current date at the server. The $usingTime flag is set to determine if (who/what) are using the current time at the server or whether the time was specified at the prompt. Using the forms that were described earlier, this default case should never happen. But having this default action here allows the user to not pass in the values and has the software compute them. This could be used in place of the SSIs to get the current month and year that were discussed earlier in this chapter.

The localtime function returns a lot of information given the number of seconds since midnight, Jan 1, 1970. The returned information includes the time, the date, the weekday, the day of the year and whether we are in daylight savings time. All indices start at 0 or 1, with Sunday equal to 0. Months start at 0 and the first day starts at 1. The time function returns the number of seconds for the server.

```
if (($mon == 0) && ($year == 0)) {
$usingTime = 1;
$time = time;
($sec,$min,$hour,$mday,$mon,$year,$wday,$yday,$isdst) =
localtime($time);
}
```

If the month was specified in the request, the timelocal function is used to convert from a time, a day, a month and a year back to a value containing the number of seconds from Jan 1, 1970.

```
$time = &timelocal(1,1,1,1,$mon,$year) ;
```

Then, we get the day of the week from this number of seconds, but we only get the seventh item from this function call's return value.

```
$wday = (localtime($time))[6];
```

To set up the links to the next and previous month's calendar, we can set up the variables now:

```
$nextyear = $year;
$nextmonth = $mon + 1;
if ($nextmonth >= 12) { $nextmonth = 0; $nextyear++;  }
$prevmonth = $mon - 1;
$prevyear = $year;
if ($prevmonth < 0) { $prevmonth = 11; $prevyear-;  }
```

These variables will be used later depending on the 'priornext' option set on the calendar. The leap year is adjusted for to get the number of days in February:

```
if (&isLeap($year)) { $daysInMonth[1] = 29; }
```

You should note that the formula for determining the leap year is as designed with the same command as the Unix cal(1) command. This formula is described in the file on the web site at

The code for description roughly translates to the following as encoded in the isLeap() function:

- If the year modulo 400 is zero, it's a leap year
- If the year is before 1752, a modulo four of 0 means a leap year
- Otherwise it's a leap year only if modulo for is 0 AND modulo 100 is not

Once we determine what year it is, we get the local time. The $ntime variable is set to the time for the first day of the month. The $sday variable is set to the day of the week for the first day of the month.

```
$ntime = &timelocal($sec,$min,$hour,1,$mon,$year) ;
($sday) = (localtime($ntime))[6];
```

Next, we determine the number of days for which we have to show the calendar. This will tell us how many table rows we have to show.

```
$daysToDo = $daysInMonth[$mon];
$rows = ($daysToDo + $wday) / 7;
```

Now we can print the header for the calendar and the links for the next and previous months along with the link to list of activities for that month.

```
<A HREF="http://www.company.com/cgi-
bin/cal.pl?mon=$prevmonth&year=$prevyear">
[ Go to Prev month ] </A>
<A HREF="/cgi-bin/docal.pl?mon=$nextmonth&day=
-1&year=$nextyear">
[ List This Month's Events ]</A>
<A HREF="http://www.company.com/cgi-
bin/cal.pl?mon=$nextmonth&year=$nextyear">
[ Go to Next month ] </A>
HTMLHEAD
print "<TABLE BORDER WIDTH=\"50%\" >\n";
foreach $i (@weekdays) { print "<TH>$i</TH>\n"; }
```

Now adjust the value of the year to be in the 1900s. We are too close to the millennium to use two- digit year codes, so we will avoid them as best we can. Unfortunately, old habits die hard, so we have to know how to work with both types of values for the year.

```
$jday = $sday;
$doCalYear = $year;
```

```
if ($year < 100) { $doCalYear += 1900; }
print "<TR>\n";
```

Print blank elements for those calendar elements that do not exist.

```
for ($i= 0; $i < $sday ; $i++) { print "<TD> </TD>\n"; }
```

Now print out each element of the calendar. If there is an activity for that day (cached in cacheItems array), print a link to the docal.pl script. If there is no activity, simply print the day of the week out.

```
for ($i= 0; $i < $daysToDo; $i++) {
if ($activity[$i+1]) {
# we will print out values as numbers or boxes.
    }
else {
printf "\n<TD>%d</TD>",$i +1;
    }
$jday++;
if ($jday > 6) { $jday = 0;  print "</TR>\n<TR>\n";}
    }
```

Now what you have to do is determine whether to display a box around the date or just draw it the way it is as bold text. This is done by examining the 'boxDay' environment variable and using it's value to determine what to print out. The value of the $myuri variable will be set to whatever is found in the curly braces in the data file.

```
if ($contents{'boxDay'} eq "F") {
$myuri = sprintf "<b>%d</b>", $i+1;
}else {
$myuri = sprintf "<table border=1
valign=top><tr><td><b>%d</b></td></tr></table>",$i+1;
    }
$boxstr = sprintf "\n<A HREF=\"/cgi-
bin/xdocal.pl?mon=%d&day=%d&year=%d\">%s</A>"
,$mon+1,$i+1,$year,$myuri;
printf "\n<TD>%s<A HREF=\"/cgi-
bin/xdocal.pl?mon=%d&day=%d&year=%d\">%s</A></TD>"
,$boxstr,$mon+1,$i+1,$year,&showAppt($mon+1,$i+1,$year
,$i+1);
```

The showAppt() function call returns a string of keywords for a given month, a day and a year. It's a bit of a memory hog for large calendar file. Using the disk directly would make it very slow. Another disadvantage is that individual cells of the table, especially for those days with many activities, will be bigger than those cells with no activities. However, the advantage is that one glance will tell the reader about the set of activities on a particular day. The code for this function relies on looking up the input cache and determining if there are any appointments for a given day, month and year. Anniversaries are handled by setting the search year equal to the current year. The values of the date, comments, etc to use in the calendar are extracted from each cachedItem.

```
my ($mon,$day,$year,$wday) =  @_;
my ($xmon,$xday,$xyear);      # declare used local [sic]
my ($ans,$date,$lindex,$rindex); # variables.
$ans = "";
$count = 0;
my $count =  @cachedItems;
my $k;
for ($k=0;$k<$count;$k++) {
$input = $cachedItems[$k];  # get Item
$lindex = index($input,"{");      # look up date
$date = substr($input,0,$lindex-1); # description
$rindex = index($input,"}");       # extract comments
$desc = substr($input,$lindex+1,$rindex-$lindex-1);
$key = substr($input,$rindex+1);
$xyear = substr($date,0,2); #get date
$xmon = substr($date,2,2);   #from YYMMDD
$xday = substr($date,4,2);
if ($xyear eq "AA") { # allow for anniv.
$xyear = $year;
    }
# if matched, then add to output string
if(($xmon == $mon) && ($xday == $day) && ($year == $xyear)) {
$ans .= $desc . $key . "<BR>";
    }
  }

return $ans;
```

So once the activities for a day are derived from the cached data file, they are strung together in the response to the text for table cell being generated. In this manner, each cell of the calendar is populated with the activity for the day.

Of course, based on the original Tcl code requirements, we may have to adjust the output based on the settings in some environment variables. For example, If the nscapoff environment variable is set to "T," then we will generate lists using bulleted lists. Also, the title and tabtitle variables will be used to determine the TITLE and the first header of the output file.

The other requirements we have to honor are the ability to include HTML text before and after this table. This is done quite easily by examining the prefile and postfile environment variable settings and including the file listed there. You must have the ability to read the files listed in these variables for this to work. For example, the post-file is included in the output with this section of code:

```
if ($contents{'postfile'} ne "") {
open (PSTF, "<".$contents{'postfile'})||die
"<H1>Prefile Error</h1> </BODY></HTML>";
while (<PSTF>) {
print $_;
    }
close PSTF;
}
```

The priornext environment variable is used to put up links for traversing calendar events by month. The code basically introduces links to the same script given a previous and next month. The code discussed earlier for determining these months is therefore enclosed in between an if clause that is True if the value of priornext is set to something that is not equal to string OFF

So what's this docal file? This is used to perform searches given dates and can be easily modified to search for keywords. The program shown in Listing 9.4 takes a month and a year, opens that xcal.dat file and lists all the entries with matching month and year entries. The day value passed into the docal.pl script can assume two values. If $day is set to -1, the script will print all activities for that month. If set to a particular day of the month, not -1, only activities for that day are listed. This is why the link for the *all events* sends a value of -1 for the day, whereas each link in the table sends that particular day number to the docal.pl script. To make this code work with a string for key-words, you can simply modify comparison operator for month, day and year to something that matches on this ($input =~ /seastr/) where $seastr is set to the value in the environment variable seastr.

Listing 9.4: xdocal.pl

```
#!/usr/bin/perl
#
#
$|=1;
print "Content-type: text/html\n\n";
if ($ENV{'REQUEST_METHOD'} eq "POST") {
read(STDIN,$buffer,$ENV{'CONTENT_LENGTH'});
```

```perl
} else {
$buffer = $ENV{'QUERY_STRING'};
}
@pairs= split(/&/,$buffer);
foreach $pair (@pairs) {
($name,$value) = split(/=/,$pair);
$value =~ tr/+/ /;
$value =~ s/%([a-fA-F0-9][a-fA-F0-9])/pack("C",hex($1))/eg;
$contents{$name} = $value;
}
$mon = $contents{'mon'};
$day = $contents{'day'};
$year = $contents{'year'};
#
print "<HTML><HEAD><TITLE>Calendar</TITLE><HEAD><BODY>\n";
if ($day != -1) {
printf "<H1><center>All Events on %d/%d/%d
</center></H1>\n",$mon,$day,$year;
}
else {
printf "<H1><center>All Events for  %d, %d
</center></H1>\n",$mon,$year;
}
open (MYCAL, "./cal.dat") || die "<H1>Cannot open
it</h1> </BODY></HTML>";
while($input = <MYCAL>) {
my $date;
my $lindex;
my $rindex;
$lindex = index($input,"{");
$date = substr($input,0,$lindex-1);
$rindex = index($input,"}");
$desc = substr($input,$lindex+1,$rindex-$lindex-1);
$key = substr($input,$rindex+1); # get index ID
$xyear = substr($date,0,2); #extract year
$xmon = substr($date,2,2); # extract month
$xday = substr($date,4,2);   #extract day
if ($xyear eq "AA") { # allow for anniversaries
$xyear = $year;
    }
if(($xmon == $mon) && (($xday == $day) || ($day ==
-1)) && ($year == $xyear)) {
printf "\n %d-%d-%d : (%s)
%s<BR>",$xmon,$xday,$xyear,$key,$desc;
    }
}
close MYCAL;
print "\n</BODY></HTML>";
```

There you have it. A simple and extensible Perl script to dynamically create a custom calendar. Just remember that adding more functionality to this script may cause it to be more complicated. Features that you can add include buttons to create, to delete, or to modify existing entries. Such features would be useful in a group environment. However, the complexity of managing the cal.dat file with appropriate locks would certainly make the code more complicated and possibly even slower. Sometimes a simple text editor and one human event manager may be the best solution.

Note that the format for the xcal.dat file is simple and easily editable by a human. Using the DBM (for managing databases in Perl) file format built into Perl may provide a faster solution, but would require Perl scripts to do error recovery. The present format for the xcal.dat file makes it very easy to update, to modify and to maintain. After all, simplicity is not a bad thing.

Summary

As with any complex piece of software, there are drawbacks to this program. However, properly implemented, it does most of what not only a person *wants* it to do, but, also, what it *should* do. It provides basic functionality for a calendar and provides the ability for users to tune the software without having to get in and muck around with the code.

This high level of code reuse means that there will always be someone who wants something different. In most cases the software can be modified to see that they have access to that functionality without having to toss the baby out with the bath water and recreate the wheel.

The larger the code, the greater the functionality, the more it will be used and the more often enhancements will be demanded. The more enhancements added to the code, the larger the number of bugs that are created in developing the software (complexity issues) and then the more enhancements and bug fixes that will be wanted.

This is already a monster piece of code. In beta testing there were enhancement requests. For instance, the nice feature that was put in to make sure that the file was getting processed (the NA). Some people don't want NA; they just want it blank. Beta testers asked for that feature so much that we added it to the original code we included in this text. A less asked-for item was *fixed width* days. We didn't implement that here, but it could have been done by allowing a "fixedday" flag to be used, and when it was sent then we would have used a different "<th>" line, one that would have fixed the day size to a percentage of the screen (about 14% of the screen for each day column). This would have created fixed day width fields and not required that the entire program be recreated to support the new functionality.

Another major request is for a piece of code that allows for people to add or to remove calendar entries without having to get onto the machine with the data files and then hand edit them. As the techniques that would be used to do that are the same ones that are used in guest book and threaded discussion groups, the next chapter looks like a good place to start with managing data files via the Web.

CHAPTER 10
ADDING TO AND DELETING FROM A DATA FILE

- Writing to a Flat Data File

- Speed Reading a Flat Data File

- Deleting a Record from a Flat Data File

- Differences Between Data Files and Databases

A data file can be maintained manually or by a program designed to add and to remove (or update) items. The code included in this chapter deals with adding and removing entries from a calendar data file (the program in Chapter 9). This code was not defined in Chapter 9, but has been included here to support additional functionality for the calendar section. This section should also provide a simple to understand, single location reference on how to work with data files in the Web-based environment.

A data file and a database are really two separate entities. As was stated at the beginning of this section, the book will utilize data files, not databases. This is done as to maintain levels of portability. The data file that we will be using in this section has been created to be portable and modifiable by hand. It is a simple, uncomplicated format that is easy to parse and to work with, without requiring software to add or to remove elements.

As you've most likely noted by now, we aren't including a guestbook application in this text. The key reason for this is that there are so many already available on the Internet that having yet another one seemed like overkill. But for a moment, consider the guestbook application itself. In it you are using a form to add an entry to a data file. This entry may be a series of fields and then a pointer to a separate text file where the text of your guestbook entry actually resides. Or, the entire guestbook entry may be maintained within the data file. In either case, the software for a guestbook application would function in many the same ways as the software we will be using here.

So, while this text lacks a guestbook applications per se, all that you need to build one is right in this chapter.

Using the .htaccess File for Secure Writes

One key concern when people are permitted access to write/add to and delete/remove records from a data file is the need to secure who has access to the data file for writes. This concern can be addressed in any number of ways, but one of the easiest is to use the security features built into the HTTPd protocols, in this case, the .htaccess file. This chapter details with how one can create and maintain the .htaccess file, as well as how one could use it. Since this is an area where it could become useful, here is a very brief overview of how to leverage the .htaccess file to perform some security on just who can write to the data file.

In some cases, it is useful to enable the user's name in the REMOTE_USER variable, as in Chapter 7, when the user's name was captured on the click-through and saved to the redirection log. The .htaccess file is used to perform that action. In much the same way, the .htaccess file can be used to limit access to the forms that are used to add and to delete entries in the data file.

In most cases, world write access to the data file is not what a site would like. This means that anyone could, if they knew the location of the data file, actually overwrite the data file. As the FBI and IRS has discovered, proper directory protections are a must if the system is to be maintained. That is especially true when people are given permission to write to a file on the system (a delete is, by the fact that the file is being modified, a write to the file).

To ensure that a visitor cannot obtain access to the data file, that file could be inserted into a protected directory. But what about the person who wants to use a program that exists on the site that was created to allow people the ability to modify by a write or delete the data file? In this case, the .html file used to access the data file must also be protected.

This protection, as provided by the .htaccess, allows the .html file that calls the data file add/remove capabilities (the form) to be protected. If the .html file is in a directory called cal01, that directory can be protected by using an .htaccess file within this directory. Another directory can be the location for the program's data file, say /cal01/.caldata. To allow anyone on the local host (mymachine.myco.com) to access the add and remove data html files, there only needs to be a line providing for that level of access within the .htaccess file. Doing this ensures that only local users will be able to access the data in the data file using the add or delete HTML forms.

Further detailed information on .htaccess is provided in Chapter 15.

The Individual Pieces

As the title implies, here we uncover the various pieces that make up a calendar application beyond the display that was covered in Chapter 9. Although not mentioned as requirements in Chapter 9, the procedures for inputting an entry into the data file (and the associated HTML code) and removing data from the data file (and the associated HTML code) have been included here.

It is important to note that the techniques here are being associated with the prior chapter, but they don't have to be used that way. These techniques can also be used to implement guest books (as just discussed), threaded discussions, or any other number of processes that deal with data exchange (see the discussion on how cookies could be used in a cigar shop in Chapter 3 for yet another idea). The important part of this chapter is to understand a bit about how you can use data files, and then let your needs define the applications for which they would be properly used.

The examples we are using for this exploration into the addition and the deletion of data file records are specific to the data file that was detailed in Chapter 9. In that chapter, we were dealing with calendar records and the data file we will be accessing will be using a complex key based on year + month + day

The Make Data CGI

This CGI and the associated form will provide users the ability to add an item to the database. Table 10.1 lists the fields CGI expects to receive from the form.

Table 10.1: Passed Fields

Field	Description
db	The path to the data file to be modified (hidden field)
mon	A two-field numeric for the month (01-12)
day	A two-field numeric day value (01-31)
yr	A two-field year value (00-99)
data	A string; the data to be displayed
com	A string; comments to be in the database, but not displayed

The sample form for creating the HTML input is shown at the end of this paragraph. This form generates a base screen shown in Figure 10.1 that can be used to import data items into the database. There is also some bounds checking and some error handling.

```
<TITLE> Calendar Data Entry Sample</TITLE>
<h1> Calendar Data Entry Sample</h1>
This is a form that allows you to add a data element
to the calendar database. Steal this page. Make sure
you follow the directions below...
<p>
<hr>
<!— place uncgi into the cgi-bin and place decal.tcl
there too —>
<FORM METHOD="POST" ACTION="http://www.com/cgi-
bin/uncgi.cgi/decal.tcl">
<table border=1>
<tr><td>Month</td><td>Day</td><td>Year</td></tr>
<tr>
<td>
<select name="mon">
<option> Jan
<option> Feb
<option> Mar
<option> Apr
<option> May
<option> Jun
<option> Jul
<option> Aug
<option> Sep
<option> Oct
<option> Nov
<option> Dec
</select>
</td>
<td>
<select name="day">
<option> 01
<option> 02
<option> 03
<option> 04
<option> 05
<option> 06
<option> 07
<option> 08
<option> 09
<option> 10
<option> 11
<option> 12
<option> 13
<option> 14
```

```
<option> 15
<option> 16
<option> 17
<option> 18
<option> 19
<option> 20
<option> 21
<option> 22
<option> 23
<option> 24
<option> 25
<option> 26
<option> 27
<option> 28
<option> 29
<option> 30
<option> 31
</select>
</td>
<td>
<select name="yr">
<option> 1996
<option> 1997
<option> 1998
<option> 1999
<option> 2000
<option> 2001
<option> 2002
<option> 2003
<option> 2004
<option> 2005
</select>
</td>
</tr>
</table>
<p>
Calendar Display (Text or HTML): <textarea cols=65
rows=5 name=data></textarea> <br>
Comments/Keywords: <textarea cols=65 rows=5
name=com></textarea>
<input type="hidden" name=db
value="/the/path/to/the/data.file">
<p>
To submit, press this button: <input type="submit"
VALUE="Submit">
</form>
<hr>
Here are the "names" for the variables that are
expected. They are either required(R) or optional(O).
<ul>
<li>(R) mon : The month in a  3 character (cap) for-
mat [ex: Jan]
<li>(R) day : The day in a format DD  [ex: 04 ]
```

```
<li>(R) yr : The year in a format YYYY  [ex: 1996 ]
<li>(R) db : The datafile name in a full pathname format
<li>(R) data : The display text. This can be
straight text or HTML.
<li>(O) com : The comment (displays at end of line
in the data file. This text is used for keyword
searching, or as comments in the raw data file.
</ul>
```

Figure 10.1 *This data entry allows you to add a data element*

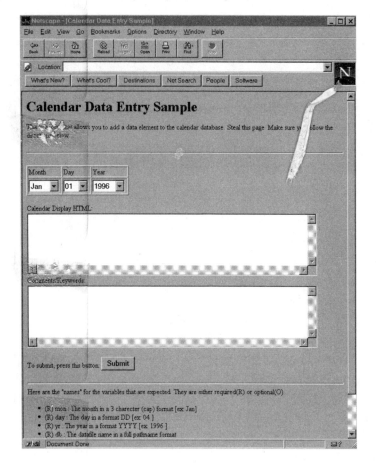

Data Entry for the Calendar Program

The Tcl code in Listing 10.1 will generate a data file entry. It will *not* create the file if it doesn't exist. The program appends the entry to the existing data file. It is important to remember that the data file must be secured in such a way as to allow the processor to write to it.

The code uses some very simple validation routines to process for error checking. These include a hard-coded processor for leap year checking and minimal validation on the year. The padded-in data is not checked to validate that it meets any standards. That means that special characters could be passed into this procedure. These characters won't be escaped out when inserted into the database and could prove to be a problem in the display of data from the calendar. The best example of this is someone passing in a close-brace }. The {} are keywords within the data file.

Note This escaping issue is something that it is important to remember whenever you are working with data and reading and writing it to a file from an interpretive language. It is important to ensure that the data written to the file will be able to be parsed properly as data to be displayed. In cases where the amount of data is small, but the information needs to be kept intact, some programmers have gone so far as to hexify the data before writing it to a file. In this instance, every character is turned into its hex-based equivalent and then stored in the data file. The program that reads the data then de-hex's the line when it's read in by that program. This method expands the amount of room that a data file takes up by 200 percent, but guarantees that the data in the file is character-by-character accurate to what was originally put into the file. Additional advantages are: Browsers understand hex, so there is no need to de-hex display items and the data in the file looks to be encrypted (and in a way it is) and cannot be useful without decryption (de-hex).

Listing 10.1: decal.tcl

```
#!/usr/local/bin/tclsh
##
foreach envvar [lsort [array names env] ] {
  if {[regexp {^WWW_} $envvar]} {
```

```
      set varname [join [lrange [split [lindex \
         [split $envvar =] 0] _] 1 end ] _]
      if {$varname != ""} {
         set $varname $env(WWW_$varname)
      }
   }
}
##
## data expected (R = required O = optional)
## db = database name (R)
## mon = a two-digit numeric for the month (R)
## yr = a two-digit numeric for the year (R)
## day = a two-digit numeric for the day (R)
## data = a string to be processed in as the entry to
##          the database (R)
## com = a string to be processed in as the comment
##          to a database entry    (O)
##
##
## Let's follow "good coding practice" -one exit! :-
)
##
proc doexit {} {
puts "<address>Please use your back key (twice) \
      to exit this page.</address>"
exit
}
##
##
puts "Content-type: text/html\n\n <title>Calendar \
      Update Response</title>"
##
## place a check for the database here
##
if {![file exists $db]} {
   puts "<h1>ERROR</h1>"
   puts "$db doesn't exist"
   doexit
}
##
## place a check for the month validation here
##   - if you use a correct three-character value,
##        this should never be set
##

set nummon [format %02d [expr [lsearch \
   "Jan Feb Mar Apr May Jun Jul Aug Sep Oct Nov Dec"\
   $mon] +1] ]
if {$nummon < 1} {
   puts "<h1>ERROR in the month value</h1>"
   puts "$nummon is out of range - you passed in \
```

```
        $mon."
    doexit
}
##
## place a check for the year validation here
##    - if you blew this, it's in the form
## Year 2000 note: we are using 2 character
##                      years... warning... beware...
##
set numyr [string range $yr 2 3]
if {$numyr < 0 || $numyr >= 100} {
  puts "<h1>ERROR in the year value</h1>"
  puts "$numyr is out of range in $year."
  doexit
}
##
## place a check for day validation here
## note: lazy mans leapyear check. Better
##       methods are used in cal.tcl
##
set emon [lindex \
    "0 31 28 31 30 31 30 31 31 30 31 30 31" $nummon ]
if {$nummon == "02"} {
  if {[lsearch "96 00 04 08 12 16 20" $numyr] > -1 } {
    set emon 29
  }
}
if {$day < 0 || $day > $emon} {
  puts "<h1>ERROR in day selected</h1>"
  puts "$day is out of range for $mon/$yr."
  doexit
}
##
## Do the work, and tell the user
##
set f1 [open $db a+]
puts $f1 "$numyr$nummon$day {$data} $com"
close $f1
puts "<h1>Database Update Completed</h1>"
puts "The following record was added to \
    the database. It will be displayed on:"
puts "<p>$mon/$day/$yr<p>"
puts "$data"
puts "<p>In addition a comment was added to the \
    record:<p>$com<p><hr>"
doexit
```

The Delete Data CGI

This CGI and the associated forms provide users with the ability to delete data items for a certain day from the data file. The CGI uses two forms: the first is user-generated (in HTML and not generated by a program, but by a person); the second is generated by the CGI procedure.

Table 10.2 defines the fields that CGI expects to be passed to it from the form that was generated by the user. The generated form, being built from the data that is passed into it, will process fields as they are supplied. The values passed in to the generated form are val0 through valN where N is the total number of items that the form has on it.

Table 10.2: Just Passing Through

Fields	Description
db	The path to the data file to be modified (hidden field)
val	A value that tells if this is the delete request or the search request (S or D)
Initial Form	On the initial form:
mon	A two-digit month value(01-12)
day	A two-digit day value (01-31)
yr	A two field year value (00-99)

After the submit button is pressed, the process will search the datafile and return a list of events that are scheduled for the day requested. This is called the *search* request. The events will have a checkbox in front of them that can be used to select those events to be deleted. If there are no events, the program will say so. Once events are selected for deletion and the submit button is pushed, the delete request will be processed.

It is important for the CGI developer to understand what a delete is when done from a data file (verses a database). A delete from the data file is not as simple as saying "delete this line." With a delete, the entire data file gets copied, minus those lines, and then is used to replace the old version. This could, depending on the size of the data file, be time consuming.

As previously mentioned, there are actually two HTML screens used in this process. The first is shown in the following code (and in Figure 10.2). The second is generated by the search pass through the data file in Listing 10.2.

```
<TITLE> Calendar Data Deletion </TITLE>
<h1> Calendar Data Deletion Sample</h1>
This is a form that allows you to delete elements
from the calendar database. Steal this page. Make
sure you follow the directions below...
<p>
<hr>
<!- place uncgi into the cgi-bin and place rical.tcl
there too ->
<FORM METHOD="POST" ACTION="http://www.com/cgi-
bin/uncgi.cgi/rical.tcl">
<table border=1>
<tr><td>Month</td><td>Day</td><td>Year</td></tr>
<tr>
<td>
<select name="mon">
<option> Jan
<option> …        ***see the example above***
<option> Dec
</select>
</td>
<td>
<select name="day">
<option> 01
<option> …      ***see the example above***
<option> 31
</select>
</td>
<td>
<select name="yr">
<option> 1996
<option> … ***see the example above***
<option> 2005
</select>
</td>
</tr>
</table>
<input type="hidden" name=db
value="/path/to/the/data.file">
<input type="hidden" name=val value="S">
<p>
To submit, press this button: <inPUT TYPE="submit"
VALUE="Submit">
</form>
<hr>
```

```
Here are the "names" for the variables that are
expected. They are either required(R) or optional(O).
<ul>
<li>(R) mon : The month in a  3-character (cap) for-
mat [ex: Jan]
<li>(R) day : The day in a format DD   [ex: 04 ]
<li>(R) yr : The year in a format YYYY  [ex: 1996 ]
<li>(R) db : The datafile name in a full pathname
format
<li>(R) val : (S) Search or (D) Delete (Always S,
the code creates a D)
</ul>
<b>WARNING</B>
<p>
If you have two matching entries in the data file,
they will both be deleted by this procedure.
```

The code in Listing 10.2 is used to generate a second deletion screen (Figures 10.3 and 10.4) for the user to make a selection of items to be deleted. To support multiple items to be deleted as well as multiple items to be displayed, the software has been modified to perform both actions.

Figure 10.2: *The data deletion initial screen*

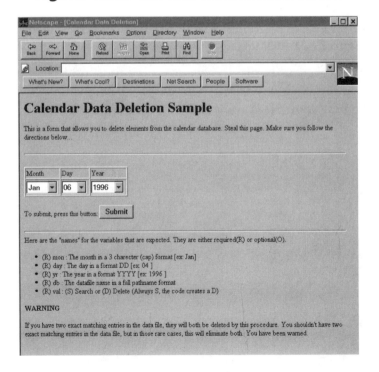

The first time this routine is called it will be passed a flag value of an S. This value is telling the software that it is supposed to perform a search against the data file and generate a secondary selection page. This page will create a form that, when submitted, will submit the passed flag value with a D for delete. When the CGI is called and a D value is sent to it, the program will know that certain values will be passed with the D.

For a deletion to actually be performed against the data file, the first and the second forms must both have been submitted.

The first pass through this code, with the S option, will generate a list of items that have met the search criteria and can be selected for deletion. The program then run creates a selection form allowing those items, that met the search criteria from the first form, to have a selectable checkbox (allowing for multiple item selection) so the user can indicate what items are to be deleted from the selection list. This form is then generated and displayed to the user.

Remember the problems we talked about in Part 1 of the book? One of the greatest problems in the HTTPd protocol is maintaining state in a process across transactions. In this case, we have two transactions; one to select matching criteria, and another to remove selected items. Rather than writing the same code twice, the selection section is kept and the S/D flag is used to determine what is to be done at the point after all matching selections from the data file are made.

When the process is run the second time and the D value is sent, all selected items' codes are associated to the flag value as well. The in-line comments explain how and why this approach was chosen.

Listing 10.2: rical.tcl

```tcl
#!/usr/local/bin/tclsh
##
## rical.tcl (remove item from the cal data file)
##
foreach envvar [lsort [array names env] ] {
  if {[regexp {^WWW_} $envvar]} {
    set varname [join [lrange [split [lindex \
        [split $envvar =] 0] _] 1 end ] _]
    if {$varname != ""} {
      set $varname $env(WWW_$varname)
    }
  }
}
```

```
}
##
## data expected (R = required O = optional)
## db = database name (r)
## mon = a two-digit numeric for the month (r)
## yr = a two-digit numeric for the year (r)
## day = a two-digit numeric for the day (r)
## val = S or D
##
##
## Let's follow "good coding practice" -one exit! :-)
##
proc doexit {} {
  puts "<address>Please use your back key to exit \
      this page/process.</address>"
  exit
}
##
## we always use the same title... for every page...
## no matter what...
##
puts "Content-type: text/html\n\n <title>Calendar \
    Update Response</title>"
##
## The big loop... if it's an S do the search, if
## it's a D do the delete
##
if {$val == "S"} {
##
## check for the database here
##
 if {![file exists $db]} {
  puts "<h1>ERROR</h1>"
  puts "$db doesn't exist"
  doexit
 }
##
## check for the month validation here
##  - if you use a correct three-character value,
##     this should never be set
## note: here we are validating and getting the month
##       using a complex format. The format statement
##       ensures that the value is always 2 character
##       0 leading. The [expr 1+…] offsets the 0 base
##       that Tcl counts with and the lsearch will
##       obtain a 0-11 value based on the month
## a value of less than 1 is an error
##
 set nummon [format %.2d [expr 1 + [lsearch "Jan Feb \
    Mar Apr May Jun Jul Aug Sep Oct Nov Dec" $mon
 ] ] ]
```

```
if {$nummon < 1} {
  puts "<h1>ERROR in the month value</h1>"
  puts "$nummon is out of range - you passed in \
     $mon."
  doexit
}
##
## check for the year validation here
##  - if you blew this, it's in the form
##
 set numyr [string range $yr 2 3]
if {$numyr < 0 || $numyr >= 100} {
  puts "<h1>ERROR in the year value</h1>"
  puts "$numyr is out of range in $yr."
  doexit
}
##
## check for day validation here
## again, this is a kludgey way to check
## for leapyears, but it does work
##
 set emon \
    [lindex "0 31 28 31 30 31 30 31 31 30 31 30 31" \
     $nummon ]
 if {$nummon == "02"} {
  if {[lsearch "96 00 04 08 12 16 20" $numyr]> -1 } {
   set emon 29
  }
}
 if {$day < 0 || $day > $emon} {
  puts "<h1>ERROR in day selected</h1>"
  puts "$day is out of range for $mon/$yr."
  doexit
}
##
## Do it, search the database for all occurrences
## of that date
##
set knt 0
 set f1 [open $db r]
 while {![eof $f1]} {
  gets $f1 inline
  if {"[lindex $inline 0]" == "$numyr$nummon$day"} {
   set rec$knt $inline
   incr knt
  }
}
 close $f1
 if {$knt == 0} {
  puts "<h1>ERROR in processing - no matched dates \
     in data file</h1>"
```

```
  } else {
    puts "<title>Delete Data - Part \
        2</title><h1>Continue with data deletion</h1>"
    puts "Please select the items that are to be \
        deleted from the database for \
        $mon/$day/$yr. <p>"
    puts "<hr><FORM METHOD=\"POST\" ACTION= \
        \"http://www.com/cgibin/uncgi.cgi/rical.tcl\" \
        ><input type=hidden name=val value=D~$knt>"
    puts "<input type=\"hidden\" name=db \
        value=\"$db\">"
    puts "<dl>"
    for {set cnt 0} {$cnt < $knt} {incr cnt} {
puts "<dd><input type=checkbox name=val$cnt \
    value=\"[set rec$cnt]\">[set rec$cnt]"
    }
    puts "</dl><p> To <b>delete</b> the selected \
        entries, press this button: <input \
        type=submit value=\"Delete\"> </form>"
  }
  doexit
##
## end the search (S) portion
##
} else {
##
## We have a D and we are going for it.
##
## Okay, here is a cheat of sorts. I say that the
## value of "val" must be an S or a D, but I also
## throw some additional data along if it is a D.
## That data is the number of items that were
## processed to the user. Since I don't do this
## anywhere else in the book, let me take a moment to
## explain why it is done here. Since only "the
## program" should set the "D" value, it is of
## only interest to the program what's in it. Rather
## than create and document another value, we just
## pass the numeric along as an appended value to the
## "val" variable. We use a tilde "~" to separate the
## values, although we could have just used a string
## range since we know the first value is a single
## character, and the second is from position 2->end.
##
  if {[lindex [split $val ~] 0] != "D"} {
    puts "<h1>Internal Error</h1> Passed value not \
        a valid value (S or D)!<p>"
    doexit
  }
  set rknt 0
  set tknt [lindex [split $val ~] 1]
```

```
##
## let's make sure that there is something checked
##   before we go deleting stuff
##
 for {set cnt 0} {$cnt < $tknt} {incr cnt} {
  if {[info exists val$cnt]} {
  set dt [lindex [set val$cnt] 0]
  set rknt 1
  }
 }
##
## No checkboxes set
##
if {$rknt == 0} {
  puts "<h1>No Data Passed</h1> Did you forget to \
      check a checkbox?<p>"
  doexit
 }
##
## Okay, we have a valid delete request -- lets open
## a temp file and process every record to it
## (special process those that match a delete record
##
 set f1 [open /tmp/[pid].tmp w+]
 set f2 [open $db r+]
##
## while there are still records to be processed
##
 while {![eof $f2]} {
  set inline ""
  gets $f2 inline
##
## if we don't have a date match process the line
##
  if {$dt != [lindex $inline 0]} {
   puts $f1 "$inline"
  } else {
##
## we have a date match, let's see if it's to be
## deleted, and if so don't write it out to the
## temp file
##
   for {set cnt 0} {$cnt < $tknt} {incr cnt} {
    if {[info exists val$cnt]} {
     if {$inline != [set val$cnt]} {
      puts $f1 "$inline"
     }
    }
   }
  }
 }
##
## we have completed the processing of the files -
```

```
## let's swap and advise the user that the actions
## have been completed.
##
 close $f1
 close $f2
exec cp /tmp/[pid].tmp $db
exec rm /tmp/[pid].tmp
puts "<h1>Deletion Completed</h1>The deletion you \
     requested has been completed. The data file \
     has been updated to reflect the changes.<p>"
##
## end the D (deletion) portion
##
 doexit
}
```

Figure 10.3: HTML screen for a single item delete

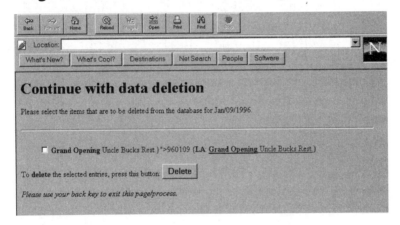

Figure 10.4: HTML screen for a multiple item delete

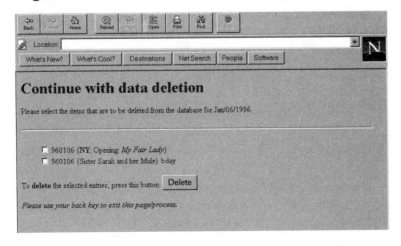

Adding and Deleting Data Using Perl

The Perl code shown in this section handles the input from the HTML files shown in the previous sections. There are two CGI scripts shown here, one to perform additions, and the other to do the search and delete operations. The functionality for each action is placed in a subroutine allowing you the future ability to consolidate them into one CGI script that handles all the actions thus reducing maintenance problems.

The only adjustment done in the Perl code is to use a four-digit year. It sounds a bit trite now, but it's better to be prepared for the millennium by using four-digit year codes. Supposedly, a lot of software will break when the year 2000 rolls around and we should really be careful to code for the event. If you want to work with two digit year codes, you will have to modify the Perl code to accommodate it by changing the %04d format codes into %02d and check for years between 0 and 100. However, I advise against this move in your coding scheme simply because you may have to maintain that piece of code after 2000 CE!

The code for the decal.pl script takes these actions:

- Extract the values for the month, day, year, data, comments and the action to take.
- Validate the input (month, day and year within limits?)
- If input to this point looks good, construct a data entry item and append it to the datafile. Don't create a data file if it does not already exist.
- Display an error message in case of errors.

The extraction of data from the query and its validation is done in the same way as in Chapter 9. The code calls the appendItem() function to add the item to the end of the fie. The error messages and headers are sent back with function calls to the bailOut and printHeader functions respectively. (At times like these, I use the CGI.pm modules in Perl 5 to make the code a bit simpler to use. For consistency, we have to stick with simple Perl code at this point.) The thing to keep in mind is that all the output that script in writing to its standard output is really being handled by a browser and therefore has to be tagged appropriately. See Listing 10.3

Listing 10.3 decal.pl 315

```perl
#!/usr/local/bin/perl
# Filename: decal.pl
$| = 1;
print "Content-type: text/html\n\n";

# =====================================
# Collect CGI input
# =====================================
if ($ENV{'REQUEST_METHOD'} eq "POST") {
    read(STDIN,$buffer,$ENV{'CONTENT_LENGTH'});
} else {
    $buffer = $ENV{'QUERY_STRING'};
}
# =====================================
# Split it all up into pairs!
# =====================================
@pairs= split(/&/,$buffer);
foreach $pair (@pairs) {
    ($name,$value) = split(/=/,$pair);
    $value =~ tr/+/ /;
    $value =~ s/%([a-fA-F0-9][a-fA-F0-9])/pack("C",hex($1))/eg;
    $contents{$name} = $value;
    }
# =====================================
# Now we have all our input in the @contents
# associative array.
# =====================================
@daysInMonth = (31,28,31,30,31,30,31,31,30,31,30,31);
@months = ("Jan","Feb","Mar","Apr","May","Jun",
        "Jul","Aug","Sep","Oct","Nov","Dec");
# =====================================
# Get the variables that concern us.
# =====================================

$val = $contents{'val'};
$action = substr($val,0,1);
$day = $contents{'day'};
$mon = $contents{'mon'};
$year = $contents{'year'};
$data = $contents{'data'};
$comment = $contents{'com'};
$filename = $contents{'db'};
if ($filename eq "") { ### CUSTOMIZE THIS LINE
    $filename = "/your/path/name/here/flatfile.txt";
}

# =======================================================
# Check month, year and adjust the Feb 29th day values
# =======================================================
```

```perl
    if ($year <= 0) { &bailOut("Invalid Year. "); }
      if (&isLeap($year)) { $daysInMonth[1] = 29; }
      $mon -= 1;  # normalize for array access.
      if (($mon <= 0) || ($mon >= 12))
        { &bailOut("Invalid Month. "); }
      if (($day <= 0) || ($day > $daysInMonth[$mon]))
        { &bailOut("Invalid day of month. "); }

      $sstr = sprintf "%04d%s%02d {%s} %s\n",
        $year,$months[$mon],$day,$data,$comment;

&appendItem($sstr);
print "</BODY></HTML>";
exit(0);


# =========================================
#   Print a standard HTML Header
# =========================================
sub printHeader() {
my $title = shift @_;
print  << "HTMLHEAD";
<HTML>
<HEAD>
<TITLE>$title</TITLE>
</HEAD>
<BODY>
<H2>$title</H2>
<HR>
HTMLHEAD
}
# =========================================
#   Print out an error message and bailout
# =========================================
sub bailOut() {
my $err = shift @_;
&printHeader("!!Error!!");
printf "\n Condition: %s <P></BODY></HTML>", $err;
exit(-1);
}

#=============================
#   Check if you have a leap year.
#=============================
sub isLeap() {
my $y = shift @_;
if (($y % 400) == 0) { return 1; }
if (($y % 4)== 0) {
    if ($y < 1752) { return 1; }
    return ($y % 100) ? 1 : 0;
    }
return 0;
```

```
}

#===============================
#  Append a date to the flat data file
#===============================
sub appendItem() {
my $fmtstr = shift @_;
&printHeader("Append Item");
print "Append [ $fmtstr ] <BR> to the data file:
[$filename]<BR>";
open (FH,">>$filename") || die "Cant Open [$file-
name]$!</BODY></HTML>";
print FH $fmtstr;
close FH;
}
```

Now comes the search and destroy functionality that is present in the rical.pl script. Basically, we search for and present a list of check boxes that are items which match a given date. The user can then tick off all the items they want deleted and press a delete button. The function to search for these items is called findItems(). The findItems() function takes a string in the same format as used in the appendItem() function and uses it to search for items. All found items are displayed as a list of check boxes that returned back to the user at the browser along with a delete button. When the delete button is pressed, the values of the checkboxes are sent back to the same rical.pl script with the value of the $val variable set to D followed by a count of the number of checkboxes to use.

The D value of $val is handled by the removeItems() function which deletes items given a specific date and topic. The number of items to remove are in the environment variables $val0, $val1, and so on up to the number of checkboxes. The code for this function looks like the findItems() function except that it separates the items into two arrays: one for all matched items and the other for items that did not match. The data file is then closed and reopened for writing, and only the items that did not match are written back to disk.

The search routine requires the validation tests for the dates, the delete routine does not since is it uses input that is setup up the search routine. Got that? The search routine presents a list of items to delete when given a date. (The output for deletion in the Perl routine is slightly more verbose than its Tcl cousin, though you can modify it to suit to your heart's content.) The name of CGI script being set up in the CGI routine will have to be modified to the name of this script, rical.pl. (You can also use $0 but I prefer to code the complete path name instead of a variable.) The value of $val in the script will be set to include D and the number of checkboxes with this line:

```
<input type=hidden name=val value="D~$counter">
```

After this set up, we send back a list of the checkboxes in a loop and terminate the list with a delete button. The displayed message for each checkbox is what is in the data file. You will probably want to modify the message to include a record number.

When the delete button is pressed, the same rical.pl script is called. This time we do not check for dates, etc. and simply process the variables $val0, $val1, . . . up to the number (minus 1) specified in the counter following D. Then we construct two arrays matched and unmatched to hold the strings that match those being input and those that do not match. The list of items to match are constructed in the removeItems() function in the @items array. The $items are matched with each line being input from the file and placed in the @matched array if the date and contents match. If no match occurs, the input string is placed in the @unmatched array. After the file has been read from, the unmatched items are flushed off to disk after being alphabetically sorted and the matched items are displayed for the user's viewing pleasure. Note that the Perl code in Listing 10.4 does not use any temporary files to do the sifting and sorting of items so no locks on files are necessary nor is any disk space required for temporary files.

Listing 10.4 rical.pl

```perl
#!/usr/local/bin/perl
# Filename: rical.pl
$| = 1;
print "Content-type: text/html\n\n";
# =========================================
# The following lines of code are used to collect
# data from standard input. The length of the
# standard input is in the environment variable
# CONTENT_LENGTH.
# =========================================
#
if ($ENV{'REQUEST_METHOD'} eq "POST") {
```

```perl
read(STDIN,$buffer,$ENV{'CONTENT_LENGTH'});
} else {
$buffer = $ENV{'QUERY_STRING'};
}
#=========================================
# Split it all up into pairs!
#=========================================
@pairs= split(/&/,$buffer);
foreach $pair (@pairs) {
    ($name,$value) = split(/=/,$pair);
    $value =~ tr/+/ /;
    $value =~ s/%([a-fA-F0-9][a-fA-F0-9])/pack("C",hex($1))/eg;
    $contents{$name} = $value;
    }
# =============================================
# Now we have all our input in the @contents
# associative array.
# =============================================
@daysInMonth = (31,28,31,30,31,30,31,31,30,31,30,31);
@months = ("Jan","Feb","Mar","Apr","May","Jun",
        "Jul","Aug","Sep","Oct","Nov","Dec");
#=========================================
# Action value: 'D' for delete and 'S' for search.
# In the case of 'D', it will contain a counter of
# the items to delete from the database.
#=========================================
$val = $contents{'val'};
$action = substr($val,0,1);
$day = $contents{'day'};
$mon = $contents{'mon'};
$year = $contents{'year'};
$data = $contents{'data'};
$comment = $contents{'com'};
$filename = $contents{'db'};
if ($filename eq "") { ##### MODIFY DEFAULT HERE
    $filename = "/your/path/name/here/flatfile.txt";
}

# =========================================
# Check month, year and adjust the Feb 29th day values
# =========================================
if ($action eq 'S') {
    if ($year <= 0) { &bailOut("Invalid Year. "); }
    if (&isLeap($year)) { $daysInMonth[1] = 29; }
    $mon -= 1;  # normalize for array access.
    if (($mon <= 0) || ($mon >= 12))
        { &bailOut("Invalid Month. "); }
    if (($day <= 0) || ($day > $daysInMonth[$mon]))
        { &bailOut("Invalid day of month. "); }
  # search given date
    $sstr = sprintf "%04d%s%02d",$year,$months[$mon],$day;
```

```
        &findItems($sstr,$year,$mon,$day); # Set up HTML
        # for output.
        }
    elsif ($action eq 'D') {  # remove all items on a date.
        # $sstr = sprintf
"%04d%s%02d",$year,$months[$mon],$day;
        &removeItems($val);
        }
    else { &bailOut("Invalid Command Request"); }

        print "</BODY></HTML>";
exit(0);

# =========================================
#  Print a standard Header
# =========================================
sub printHeader() {
    my $title = shift @_;
print   << "HTMLHEAD";
<HTML>
<HEAD>
<TITLE>$title</TITLE>
</HEAD>
<BODY>
<H2>$title</H2>
<HR>
HTMLHEAD
}
# =========================================
#  Print out an error message and bailout
# =========================================
sub bailOut() {
    my $err = shift @_;
    &printHeader("!!Error!!");
    printf "\n Condition: %s <P></BODY></HTML>", $err;
    exit(-1);
}


#=========================================
#  Find all the items in the flat data file and setup
#  a list of checkboxes
# =========================================
sub findItems() {
    my ($fmtstr,$y,$m,$d) = @_; # find match substr
    my $counter = 0;
    my @matched = ();    # empty matches

    &printHeader("Delete Data - Part 2");
    open (FH,"$filename") || die " Cant Search $!
</BODY></HTML>";
    while ($instr = <FH>) {
```

```
        if ($instr =~ /$fmtstr/) {
            $matched[$counter++] = $instr;
        }
    } # end of while loop
    close FH;

    if ($counter == 0) {
        print "<P>ERROR in processing -  no matched
dates<HR>\n";
    } else {
print << "ASK4DELETE";
<P>
Please select the items that are to be deleted
from the database for $m/$d/$y.
<P>
<HR>
<FORM  method="POST" ACTION="/cgi-bin/rical.pl">
<input type=hidden name=val value="D~$counter">
ASK4DELETE

    for($i=0;$i<$counter;$i++) {
    $dstr = sprintf "[%2d/%2d/%d]", $m,$d,$y;
    # $vstr = substr($matched[$i],0,9);
    $vstr = "\"" . $matched[$i] . "\"";
    print "<dd><input type=checkbox name=val$i value=$vstr>";
    print "$dstr -  $matched[$i]";
} # end of for loop

print << "QUERYDEL";
<dl><p>To <b>delete<b> the selected entries press
this button
<input type=submit value="Delete"> </form>
QUERYDEL

    } # end of else loop
    print "</dl></BODY></HTML>";
}

#=====================================
# Delete all matched date items from the flat data file
#=====================================
sub removeItems() {
my ($delList) = @_; # find match substr
my $found = 0;    # count matched
my $notfound = 0; # count not matched
my @matched = ();   # matches only
my @unmatched = ();   # not matched items

my ($code,$count) = split('~',$delList);
my $fmtstr;    # temporary variable
my $item; # for matching loop ctr
```

```perl
my @items = ():  # items to hunt
my $itemcount = 0;  # tracking counter

#=======================================
# make the list of items to check for
#=======================================
for($item=0;$item < $count;$item++) {
    $fmtstr = "val" . $item;
    if ($contents{$fmtstr} ne "") {
    $items[$itemcount++] = $contents{$fmtstr};
    }
}
#=======================================
# Echo it back, good for feedback
#=======================================
        foreach $item (@items) {
      print "<P>To remove $item<HR>\n";
    }
#=======================================
# Do the sifting and remove all the items into the
# match and unmatched arrays.
#=======================================
    &printHeader("Remove Item");
    open (FH,"<$filename") || die
"$![$filename]</BODY></HTML>";
    while ($instr = <FH>) {
       $deleted = 0;
       foreach $item (@items) {
            $fmtstr = $item;
      if ($instr =~ /$fmtstr/) {
      $matched[$found++] = $instr;
      $deleted = 1;
      print "<P>To be deleted $instr\n";
      last;
      }
            } # foreach loop
      if ($deleted == 0) {
      $unmatched[$notfound++] = $instr;
      }
    } # end of while loop
    close FH;
#=======================================
# Tell the user what happened.
#=======================================
    if ($found == 0) {
      print "<P>No matches were found<HR>\n";
      print "<P>Nothing was deleted..<HR>\n";
        }
    else {
    printf "<P>%d matches were removed<BR><OL>", $found;
    for($i=0;$i<$found;$i++) {
```

```
        print "<LI>", $matched[$i];
      } # end of for loop
    print "</OL>";
            } # end of else loop
# ==================================
# flush the rest of items to disk.
# ==================================
open (FH,">$filename") || die "Cant write $filename
$!</body></html>";
for (@unmatched) { print FH $_ ; }
close FH;
print "</BODY></HTML>";
}


#===============================
#   Check if you have a leap year.
#   Returns 0 if not, 1 if it is leap year
#   Based on formula used for cal(1) in
#   Unix…..
#===============================
sub isLeap() {
my $y = shift @_;
if (($y % 400) == 0) { return 1; }
if (($y % 4)== 0) {
   if ($y < 1752) { return 1; }
   return ($y % 100) ? 1 : 0;
   }
return 0;
}
```

A parting note about the code in the above files: decal.pl and rical.pl files. They can be combined into one file by using the first character of the $val variable as an action item. This will keep you from having two separate files to maintain. By using one CGI script, two separate HTML forms can be set up to call the same script to perform the requisite action by setting the first character of $val to A, S or D. The section of code required to perform this action would simply check the value of $val and then call the appropriate subroutine. An excerpt of this would be done is shown here;

```
if (($action eq 'S') || ($action eq 'A')) {
    # Check dates when searching or appending
    if ($year <= 0) { &bailOut("Invalid Year. "); }
    if (&isLeap($year)) { $daysInMonth[1] = 29; }
    $mon -= 1;  # normalize for array access.
    if (($mon <= 0) || ($mon >= 12))
      { &bailOut("Invalid Month. "); }
    if (($day <= 0) || ($day > $daysInMonth[$mon]))
```

```
                          { &bailOut("Invalid day of month. "); }
    }
```

When the dates check out to be okay, you have to know what action to take. Then you take action based on what value of $action is based on the value of $action is set:

```
if ($action eq 'A') { # append full record
    $sstr = sprintf "%04d%s%02d {%s} %s\n",
       $year,$months[$mon],$day,$data,$comment;
    &appendItem($sstr);
    }
elsif ($action eq 'S') {  # search given date
    $sstr = sprintf
"%04d%s%02d",$year,$months[$mon],$day;
    &findItems($sstr,$year,$mon,$day); # Set up HTML
    # for output.
    }
elsif ($action eq 'D') {  # remove all items on a date.
    # $sstr = sprintf "%04d%s%02d",$year,$months[$mon],$day;
    &removeItems($val);
    }
else { &bailOut("Invalid Command Request"); }
```

Of course, the choice is really up to you as how to handle this functionality. The functions shown here to manipulate the datafile are very simple to use.

So why did I not use the DBM database functions that are available in Perl? Well, they do not generate the easily edited text files that I get with this simple approach. Yes, the code to extract and to insert data into a DBM file may turn out shorter, but the general idea of this exercise was to use text files. It's easy to edit these text files with an editor and even sort them out without having to resort to a Perl program to extract the data. For the simple application used in this book, this is all we need.

Data Files or Databases

Throughout this chapter we used the term and the concept of *data files*. These are flat files that contain delineated fields within them. We chose to use this method throughout the book so that we would be working with the lowest common denominator, as was stated in the section opening and the Introduction.

If you are using a database instead of a datafile, many of the operations that we did could be moved to a relational environment with ease. In the cases where the code does such file operations as opens, reads, and writes, SQL commands could be issued to perform the same operations on relational databases.

There are any number of ways that this integration could be done within both Tcl and Perl. It should be noted that many, if not all, the popular relational database products are developing interfaces that permit them to be Web-enabled. This makes the integration between databases and Web-based environments very tight and, in most cases, unless you really feel a need to work outside these highly integrated environments, there is no need to use programs like the two described herein.

Summary

While reading this chapter, if you started to have visions of how to make a guest book or a threaded discussion area, you are right on track. All the methods for creating those two applications were covered in Chapters 9 and 10 . In general, you wouldn't want to give the delete capability to outside users of either application, but it would prove to be a useful tool for permitting the person managing a public data file to have on hand for remote cleanup of the data file.

This would permit you to allow people to manage threaded discussion groups and relieve some of the Webmaster duties from the tired old Webmaster and put them back on to the user community who wants these applications.

Making the Webmaster's job easier is always a bit of a challenge. In the paragraph above there was a hint that delegation might be the way to do it, but that is only part of the way. The rest is through automation. In the next chapter, we will focus on an SSI that will help relieve the "directory indexing" tasks and allow someone to make and to maintain specialized directories that require a very low amount of Webmaster overhead.

CHAPTER 11

ACTIVE PAGES USING SSI

- Server Side Includes
- Regular Expressions
- Date Validation and Parsing

In this chapter we will be dealing with Server Side Includes (SSIs). These are commands embedded in the HTML that cause the HTML document to be processed. Chapter 3 discusses the positive and negative effects of SSIs. Issues involving how to set them up and use them on an NCSA HTTPd server are discussed further in Chapter 16.

When you have completed this chapter, you will be able to index a directory determining the following:

- What is a file link
- What is a directory link
- How to display that index to an HTML page

- How to modify unique month filenames into a usable format
- How to create links using that format
- How to create HTML documents that use SSIs.

To do so, we'll discuss a search processor that searches directories and builds indexed lists from information obtained by the directories. This processor allows for documents to be active. A sample application would be a directory of date-sensitive items, like a single location for weekly departmental status reports as shown in Figure 11.1. You probably don't want to maintain this type of index by hand. This program allows for a directory to be created that contains a separate directory for each week's reports.

Our program permits the second directory's index to be created on the fly as well. For instance, a department called Software Engineering can create its report called Software-Engineering.html. The index processor will then create a hypertext listing in the index with the department name and a link to the proper .html file. A directory listing of a file directory is seen in Figure 11.2.

This allows the index to be as active as the fancy indexing of the server, but with a higher level of user control (the way dates are handled, for instance). It also allows for the index.shtml file to be used to pass along the other static information.

Figure 11.1:

Indexed directory based on dates

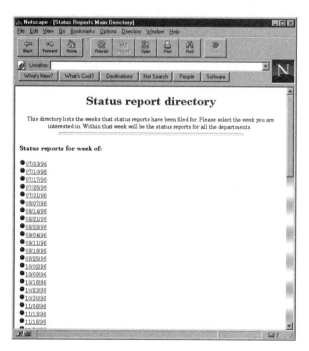

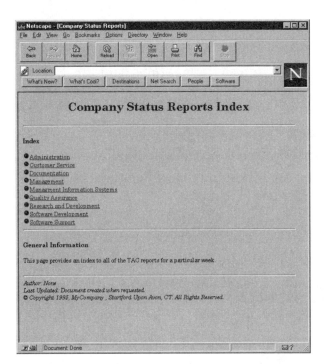

Figure 11.2:
Indexed directory
of files

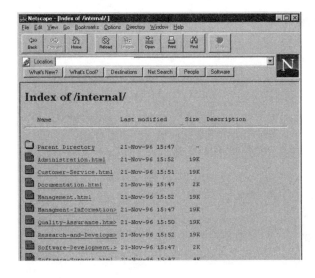

Figure 11.3:
Standard indexing

Running a Program as a SSI

Figure 11.3 shows what a standard directory indexing looks like. As
we have seen in Figures 11.1 and 11.2, there is a better way to do
indexed listings. In order to be able to generate nice indexed listings
that support date formatted files (as well as listings with spaces in the
names), there will have to be some processing that takes place.

Here are the requirements for the software that is needed to produce the output in Figures 11.1 and 11.2.

- Dated files using a standard date format (internal format: yymmdd) can be displayed with an easy to use standard date format (external format: mm/dd/yy)
- All files in a directory will be indexed
- All files will be sorted using a simple a-z descending sort
- Image bullets will be used in front of each item with different colored bullets for files and directories
- Directory bullets will use the bluebullet image from the image library
- All files will use the yellowbullet image from the image library.
- All files will use a process of substitution on the filename of the file. If the filename was this-is-the-filename.html the text hyperlink will be this is the filename.
- Only .html files and directories should be on this list.
- A - in the name of a directory will not be processed to a space
- If the directory is a date directory, then the index file within will be an index.shtml
- If it is directory (but not a date directory) it will use no file reference when building the link, but will index the directory raw, and let the server determine what file is to be served to the viewer.

Putting it all Together

In a nutshell, the requirements for this program are to generate the following output:

- A bulleted list of directories that: use blue bullets from the image library; change the format from yymmdd to MM/DD/YY on date directories; use the hyperlink to index.shtml on date directories; and use the hyperlink to a null value (/) on non-date directories
- Directories that are alpha sorted
- A list of .html files by filename that appear after a directory. (Use filename " " for "-" substitution rule for filenames only)
- An error message if there are no directories or files

HTML Design

There are numerous ways that SSIs can be utilized in code. To build index lists in the first program, SSIs are called out with the exec command. Additionally, the following HTML code allows and uses the "include" directive. This allows for a descriptive text to be included in the index.

```
<title>Index of directory</title>
<center><h1>Index of Directory</h1></center>
<hr>
<h3>Index</h3>
<p>
<!-#exec cgi="/cgi-bin/getidx.tcl" - >
<p>
<hr>
<h3>Description</h3>
<p>
<!-#include file="descript.txt" - >
<p>
<hr><address>Author: The Computer <br> Copyright:
None <br> This output built "on the fly"</address>
```

Tcl design for the Directory Lister

The design for this program breaks down into the following items:

1. Getting the file list
2. Determining if it's a date directory
3. Determining if it's an .html file
4. Building the directory list in sorted order
5. Redoing the name on date directories
6. Building the hypertext links for directories
7. File "-" to " " substitution on .html files only
8. Building the hypertext links for files
9. Outputting the listing or the error message

In Tcl, the following command will return a list of all the files in the directory:

```
set filelist [glob *]
```

This takes care of item 1. The key is to differentiate between what is a file and what is a directory. So, what the program should do is go through the list of files and create a list of two types. The first, called directories and the second, called files.

```
foreach fname [glob *] {
  if {[file isfile $fname]} {
    lappend flist $fname
} else {
    lappend dlist $fname
}
```

This will provide a list for files and directories (item 2). At this point, we can also clear item 9 by using an if around the rest of the procedure.

```
if {![info exists flist]  && ![info exists dlist]} {
  puts "error - no files or directories"
} else {
— insert balance of code here —
}
```

The next thing we want to do is sort and process the directories (items 4-6).

```
if {[info exists dlist]}  {
```

The sort is easy. Make sure the list exists, then lsort on it. That could be done by loading the value into a new variable (set wlist [lsort $dlist]). or, by placing the lsort code in the foreach loop that will be used in processing.

Process each item to a hyperlink, and rename all date directories to the new format (from yymmdd to mm/dd/yy) (items 4 and 5). The easiest way to do that is to use the code:

```
if { [file isdirectory $itm]}
  if { [regexp {^[0-9]+$} $smallitm] } {
    set yr [string range $smallitm 0 1 ]
    set mo [string range $smallitm 2 3 ]
    set dy [string range $smallitm 4 5 ]
    set linkval [join "$mo $dy $yr" /]
  } else {
set linkval [split $smallitm "-"]
  }
```

On the other hand, if you desire you could also put in some date validation information. That would add some additional functionality and make the display a bit cleaner in terms of not outputting an invalid date. This validation isn't required and has been included so you can see how it would be accomplished.

```
foreach direct {[lsort $dlist]} {
  set linkval $direct
  if { [regexp {^[0-9]+$} $direct] } {
     if {[string length $direct] == 6} {
        set yr [string range $direct 0 1 ]
        set mo [string range $direct 2 3 ]
        if {$mo > 0 && $mo < 13} {
           set dy [string range $direct 4 5 ]
           if {$dy > 0 && $dy < 32} {
              set linkval [join "$mo $dy $yr" /]
           }
        }
     }
  }
## [insert print statement here]
}
```

The code uses regular expression to determine if the name is all numeric. If it is, the processor will assume that the item is to be treated as a date directory. There is another check in here for the length of the item. This ensures that it was six characters (if {[string length $direct] = 6} {...}.

In the validation routine a check is made to ensure that the month's extracted value is between 01-12 and that the day to ensure that the date range is between 1-31.

An additional series of checks could be made to ensure that the day range didn't exceed the month maximum. We could also add a computation in for handling leap years. But the requirements were to display the information from the internal date format of yymmdd to mm/dd/yy and there are no requirements that the date be valid.

The regular expression looks at the beginning of the line and says that the passed in value must start with "^" and have 1 or more of the defined set [0-9]+ and then the string must end "$". Therefore anything that has a non-numeric would fail the regular expression. Since we are expecting yymmdd, we extract the fields out in 2 item sets, and then use the join command to rejoin the sets in the new order with the new separator.

If the value is not a numeric, drop through.

At this point, let's skip down and look at how the files will be processed.

Here we want to validate that we are only using HTML file references (so a file called abc.txt won't be processed to the list). This code will address items 3 and 7.

```
if {[info exists flist]}  {
   foreach itm {[lsort $flist]} {
      if { string match [file extention $itm] .html] } {
      set linkit [lindex [split $itm .] 0 ]
      set linkval [split $linkit "-"]
##    [insert print statement here]
      }
   }
}
```

Again we have sorted the list and are processing each item. The items are validated to have .html extensions. Then the extension is stripped and the item is split at each "-" with the "-" being replaced with a " ". It should be noted that some systems use the .htm extension. This portion of the code should be modified to the proper three or four character extension that is being used.

The only things left undone at this point are items 6 and 8, building and generating the individual output strings in HTML. The code samples just given show where to insert the statement to output the HTML strings. Rather than outputting the strings, an array could be created internally to store the data, and a separate procedure could be used to dump the stored structures. Either method would be functional. If there is no reason to load up memory and we can dump to standard output, that is generally preferred. So the completed code will do that.

The Listing 11.1 will. Note that it does most of what was discussed. The assumptions about the date have been retained.

Listing 11.1: getidx.tcl

```
#!/usr/local/bin/tclsh
##
## getidx.tcl
##
## This program is designed to index a directory and
## present the indexed directory to the user with
## directories first, then files. All will be link
## references with the directories getting one
## bullet, the files another. Finally, any directory
## in the format YYMMDD will be displayed as
## mm/dd/yy to the user.
##
puts "Content-type: text/html\n\n"
##
```

```
##  we want to use the DOCUMENT_URI value, but in
##  some cases we have seen that returned in a way
##  that is not usable. If we get a ~username return,
##  and the server is doing ~ substitution we must
##  fix that. This is done by seeing if the value
##  exists (~) and if so using a substitution process
##  to point to the proper directory structure. This
##  may require modification for your site. In the
##  case of the test code, we have users in
##  ~username/public_html so we substitute /~username/
##  to that so we can perform the "glob" on the
##  directory.
##
if { [regexp {~} $env(DOCUMENT_URI) ] } {
 regsub /[lindex [split $env(DOCUMENT_URI) /] 1] \
   $env(DOCUMENT_URI) [lindex [split $env(DOCUMENT_URI) /] \
   1]/public_html uri
} else {
   set uri $env(DOCUMENT_URI)
##
##  In some cases you may wish to have a separate
##  rooted directory that isn't part of the standard
##  tree. In those cases you would have to add a line
##  like this that would search that directory spec
##  for a keyword value and then prepend the full
##  directory spec information to the directory so it
##  can be properly glob'd
##
  if {[regexp "fifree" $uri]} {
   set uri /home/ivler/wwinfo/$uri
  }
}
##
##  This process will grab and process each directory
##
foreach itm [lsort [glob [file dirname $uri ]/* ] ] {
  set smallitm [file tail $itm]
##
##  If the file is a directory, then process it - and
##  special process it if the file was a date
##  directory. It should be noted that this code
##  doesn't perform any of the validation
##  testing that the "design" portion did.
##
  if { [file isdirectory $itm]} {
    if { [regexp {^[0-9]+$} $smallitm] } {
      set yr [string range $smallitm 0 1 ]
      set mo [string range $smallitm 2 3 ]
      set dy [string range $smallitm 4 5 ]
      set linkval [join "$mo $dy $yr" /]
    } else {
```

```
        set linkval [split $smallitm "-"]
        }
    puts "<img src=\"/giflib/blueball1.gif\" alt=\"*\"> \
        <a href=\"[file dirname \
        $env(DOCUMENT_URI)]/$smallitm/index.shtml\"> \
        $linkval </a><br>"
    }
}
##
## Process each of the .html files in the directory.
##
foreach itm [lsort [glob [file dirname $uri ]/* ] ] {
  set smallitm [file tail $itm]
  if { [file isfile $itm]} {
##
##
## Note that we are using a string match to see if
## it is an HTML file based on the extension of the
## file. If you are using files from a pc, you may
## want to check for a match on .htm (the three
## character limitation)
##
    if { [string match [file extension $itm] .html] } {
      set shitm [lindex [split $smallitm .] 0 ]
      set linkval [split $shitm "-"]
      puts "<img src=\"/giflib/greenball.gif\" alt=\"-\"> \
          <a href=\"[file dirname \
          $env(DOCUMENT_URI)]/$smallitm\">$linkval</a><br>"
    }
  }
}
exit
```

Displaying Listings in Perl

In the Perl version of this program we will be working with displaying the listings of a directory with green and blue bullet images. The value of the DOCUMENT_URI environment variable is used in this example. You are, of course, at liberty to allow the send user to pass in the directory name via a FORM too. Security issues may prevent you from allowing anyone to look in the /home directory.

The $uri is picked directly from the working environment of the Perl script. If this value is NULL, we will use the DOCUMENT_ROOT value, though this will limit the searches off the root of where the original HTML file resides. (This step is only necessary if you are dealing with old http servers from NCSA.)

```
$uri = $ENV{`DOCUMENT_URI'};
if ($uri eq "") { $uri = $ENV{`DOCUMENT_ROOT'}; }
```

Then we check to see if the value in $uri is using the tilde (~) expansion. If so, then we direct our searches from the /public_html directory instead.

```
if ($uri =~ /\~/)  {
    $index = index($uri,'~');
    $urifilename = substr($uri,$index);
    $uri = "/public_html" . $urifilename;
    }
```

Now comes the fun part of taking a directory listing of the name specified in the $uri variable. The $all variable contains the list of all the names separated by carriage returns. We split them accordingly with the /\n/ qualifier to split() and place the results in the @input array.

```
$all = `ls $uri';
@input = split(/\n/,$all);
```

We track the names of the files and directories in arrays @flist and @dlist, respectively. Both are initialized to be empty lists. For each line of input, if the name in the @input array entry is a directory, place the name in the @dlist array. If the name is not a directory, check to see if it has an .html in its name. To check if the name ends in '.html', you would have to change the comparison string to /\.html$/, where the $ implies the end of string for the name. Items are added to the end of the @dlist or the @flist by pushing the name to the end of the appropriate list. The push command in Perl appends items to a list. (Conversely, the pop() command in Perl will remove the first item from an array, reducing its size by the number of popped items.)

```
foreach (@input) {
    if (-d $_) { push(@dlist,$_); }
    else {
        if ($_ =~ /\.html/) {
        push(@flist,$_);
    }
        }
    }
```

Note that we are not checking if this name could be a link, a pipe, a socket or a binary file. All of these checks may be done with the -l, -p, -S or -b flags to the if statement, respectively. Normally, you would not allow links to be listed to prevent security breaches.

The names in the @dlist and @flist will already be sorted since the names in the @input will be sorted by name in the output from the 'ls' command. Once the lists are created in @dlist and @flists, it's simply a matter of printing them out in an HTML page:

```
foreach (@dlist) {
$dn = $uri . $_;   # construct path name
print "<img src=\"blueball.gif\" alt=\"-\"><a
href=\"$dn/index.shtml\">$_</a><br>\n";
}
```

The file list is a bit trickier in that we have to show the date and size of each file in the listing too. The way to get information given a file name is to use the stat() command. The returned value from the stat function call in Perl is an array of 13 items as follows:

1. $dev - for device ID
2. $inode - for the file
3. $prot - for file protections,
4. $links - for the number of links to this file
5. $uid - UID of the owner
6. $gid - GID of the owner
7. $dtype - Device Type ID
8. $size - of the file in bytes
9. $blocksize - of the file
10. $blocksUsed - used by the file
11. $lastAccess - to the file in seconds
12. $lastModify - time of modification of inode
13. $lastChange - time of last change

To get this information given a file name, you can issue the following call:

```
($dev,$inode,$prot,$links,
  $uid,$gid,$dtype, $size,
  $blocksize,$blocksUsed,$lastAccess,
  $lastModify,$lastChange) = stat ($n);
```

Since we only need the last access time and the size, we can use the indices in the return value of the stat() call like this:

```
($size,$blocksize,$blocksUsed,$lastAccess) = (stat($a))[7,8,9,10];
```

This statement will pick out the 8th to the 10th element from the list returned from the stat call.

In a similar fashion, the date's month, day of the month and year can be derived from the localtime() function call on the lastAccess variable's value. The items we need are indexed at 3, 4 and 5, respectively, in the array, so the call to extract this information would be:

```
($mday,$mon,$year) = (localtime($lastAccess))[3,4,5];
```

Then we can just print the information out in two steps to make it a bit easy to see:

```
$outstr = sprintf "%s %02d/%02d/%d
%d\n",$n,$mday,$mon+1,$year,$size;
print "<img src=\"greenball.gif\" alt=\"-\"><a
href=\"$outstr\">$_</a><br>\n";
```

Actually, you can make it all one print statement, but that would make the line a bit complicated to read and to debug should you run into any problems in the future.

The complete program is shown in Listing 11.2

Listing 11.2: Listings files via Perl

```
#!/usr/local/bin/perl
#--------------------------------------------------------
# Provide a HTML tags to give a pretty interface with
# sorted names of files and directories in a path
# specified by the DOCUMENT_URI environment variable.
#--------------------------------------------------------
$| = 1;
print "Content-type: text/html\n\n";

$uri = $ENV{'DOCUMENT_URI'};
if ($uri eq "") { $uri = $ENV{'DOCUMENT_ROOT'}; }
if ($uri =~ /\~/) {
    $index = index($uri,'~');
    $urifilename = substr($uri,$index);
```

```
    $uri = "/public_html" . $urifilename;
    }

#----------------------------------------------------------
# Get a listing for the current directory in $all. Then
# split the contents of $all by carriage returns and
# store the values into elements of the @input array.
#----------------------------------------------------------
$all = `ls $uri`;
@input = split(/\n/,$all);


#----------------------------------------------------------
# Initialize the repository arrays
#----------------------------------------------------------
@flist = ();
@dlist = ();


#----------------------------------------------------------
# Separate the files from the directories.
#----------------------------------------------------------
foreach (@input) {
    if (-d $_) { push(@dlist,$_); }
    else {
        if ($_ =~ /\.html/) {
        push(@flist,$_);
    }
        }
    }


#----------------------------------------------------------
# Print each file name out with a blue icon
#----------------------------------------------------------
foreach (@dlist) {
$dn = $uri . $_;   # construct path name  + directory
name
print
"<img src=\"blueball.gif\" alt=\"-\"><a
href=\"$dn/index.shtml\">$_</a><br>\n";
}

#----------------------------------------------------------
# Print each file name out with a green icon
#----------------------------------------------------------
foreach (@flist) {

    $fn = $uri . "/" . $_; construct path name  +
file name
# $dev  - for device ID
# $inode - for the file
# $prot  - for file protections,
# $links - for the number of links to this file
# $uid   - UID of the owner
```

```
# $gid    - GID of the owner
# $dtype - Device Type ID
# $size   - of the file in bytes
# $blocksize - of the file
# $blocksUsed - used by the file
# $lastAccess - to the file in seconds
# $lastModify - time of modification of inode
# $lastChange - time of last change


    ($dev,$inode,$prot,$links,
      $uid,$gid,$dtype, $size,
      $blocksize,$blocksUsed,$lastAccess,
      $lastModify,$lastChange) = stat ($n);
    ($mday,$mon,$year) =
(localtime($lastAccess))[3,4,5];

$outstr = sprintf "%s %02d/%02d/%d
%d\n",$n,$mday,$mon+1,$year,$size;
print "<img src=\"greenball.gif\" alt=\"-\"><a
href=\"$outstr\">$_</a><br>\n";
}
```

Summary

Of all the varied SSI programs that we could have used, why this one? We chose this one because you have already seen how to do many of the different things for which SSI programs are used. The most common SSI program around is the counter, and the second most common is the random display program. We wanted you to get a feel for an SSI that is a bit more unusual and focuses in on a possible resource for Intranets. That is why we focused on the concept of a weekly report.

Throughout this section we have tried to provide you with building blocks. We have also tried to provide useful pieces of code that can be plugged right in. And, with a bit of customization, the code can be a bit more.

In the next section, we will provide some of the basic building blocks that are used to create a commercial Web site. We will not provide all the blocks because many of them are owned by the Web site for which they were designed. Again, we want to ensure that you understand that the techniques being used can and should be the starting point for your development. We want you to expand on what we provided, not just to be happy with it.

What's Black and White and Read All Over?

This could also be used for allowing daily reports, like a newspaper. In a case like this, the newspaper would allow you to select dates from a date index generated by this program. The newspaper would most likely want to change some of the default features like page layout, but all that can be done with simple HTML modifications to the lines that do the output.

Once you select a date, it would bring you down to the "sections" for that date's paper. You could then select a "section" of the paper and this program would also be used to index that directory, doing "-" substitution where required.

Would this work for a major daily metropolitan newspaper? Hey, it's not superman, it's Clark Kent, and it could do a nice job with some HTML help. As it stands now, it would work just fine with very little help for a high school or a college newspaper. That little help would be in layout or table design, but not in the functionality of the actual code.

CHAPTER 12 MAKING MONEY ON THE NET

- Integrating Forms and E-mail to a Site

- Integrating SSI and Passive Pages

- Integrating Forms Built on the Fly

- Integrating Tables From Data Files

Up to this point, the programs and systems we have been talking about have all been standalone. These programs have all served needs, yet they didn't work in harmony to a common end. In this section, all the work we have done so far will be pulled together, in some way, shape or form, to evolve as a single site. In addition, we will look at some concepts here that we will delve into further in the upcoming chapters.

To prove that it is actually possible to use these concepts and programs to make a site work, and to make money, it had been necessary to define a business and develop a business plan. Now, before you turn your nose up, it had been determined that there was a limited amount of time to validate that this site and the software would work. Within those restrictions, it was determined that the site would leverage a business plan based upon network marketing as defined by a client.

The site had been developed using the programs that will be included here, as well as some not included in this text. The site is, at the time of this writing, turning a profit for the company that owned the developed site using this code. The network marketing program chosen, the site that is running the software, and other such details have been omitted from the code, the HTML pages, images and the text as it is not the intent to publish the site or in any way promote it from within the text.

It is not the author's position to approve, or to disapprove, a person's method of conducting business; therefore, we won't pass judgment in this case. We will say that, after 90 days of operation, the software is still running strong, and that the site has 135 people within the network with over 60 others in the process of joining it. In network marketing terms, it is doing very well.

So, is it possible to make money on the net? Yes it is. The site had been assembled in 46 man-hours, the code herein had been pulled together from bits and pieces of existing code that had been written for other customers, and much of the code and the concepts are contained in this book. There were some original pieces of software that were written to handle some of the administrative tasks, as well as some specific to the product and the methods that were being used to market the product. In the cases where the software was market specific or product/site oriented, the software has not been included within this text.

To understand how the code had been put together, it is important to understand a bit about the overall application. This will mean delving into network marketing, but no more than we did on advertising and the methods of charging for impressions and click-throughs.

Network Marketing: A Quick Overview

Network marketing is better known by the companies that are involved with it. The most famous of these companies is Amway (note: this was not the company or product for which the site was developed, as that company, at this time, has a no-Internet policy).

Network marketing is based on the fact that each person who joins the company as a product distributor, not only distributes the product, but also recruits other people interested in becoming product distributors into being part of their network of distributors.

Now, it is very important to understand that the words *product distributors* were chosen with care. Running a network marketing program without a product is commonly referred to as a pyramid or Ponzi scheme. There are a number of legal and technical issues that differentiate a network marketing system from an illegal scheme, but this isn't the place to get into that level of discourse. Suffice it to say that one clear indicator is the fact that there is a value-added product going from a producer to a consumer and that there are consumers who are not part of the network (products sold to people who are not in the network of distributors).

There are a great many terms in network marketing for the way the systems are set up. There is the 3X7, the infinity bonus, the overflow, and almost as much jargon as in any other industry. The Web site that had been being built was a form referred to as *3x7 forced overflow*. What that meant to the Web space was a design detail on how the structure looked. Each branch from the root of the tree structure had three branches extending from it (the 7 has to do with commission structures and are not functional in this case).

Since we will be working with this model, there are two ways to view it that are a bit better than thinking in matrices. The first is like a tree in a garden, in which we see a root and then a trunk that breaks into a series of three, and then each branch breaks the same way. The second and best way to view it is as if the tree was a family tree, or an organizational tree in a large corporation. In this second case, the root of the tree starts at the top and the branches extend downward. This gives the terms *downline* and *upline* their meanings. A downline are the people who you bring in below you on the organizational tree, and an upline are the people who brought you into the organization.

Customer Additions to the Network Marketing System

To this basic network marketing plan, the customer wanted to add some additional functionality. In a standard network marketing system, people bring other people into their distribution system under them. In other words, each person builds his own structure or down-line. This has some serious drawbacks and side effects. These are:

- Uneven growth
- Holes in the tree structure and its varied limbs
- People not getting commissions and support
- The greed factor

The customer wanted to eliminate these four drawbacks. That action was accomplished through two processes, empowering the individual and level loading.

To empower an individual a system had to be established where the individual could place himself within the downline structure of the tree. This could be done at any place in the tree, as long as there was someone in the position above him in the tree.

Most commercial enterprises contain some level of the greed factor. It is usually called the profit motive. In this case, the customer created a process they called *level loading*. This process was designed to entice people to help others rather than themselves by making the software show, in a very visible way, when someone wasn't following the level loading system. In addition, level loading also reinforced the elimination of holes in the individual branches, as well as ensured that people saw commission checks and results faster.

> **Tip** Level loading is designed to place the person coming into the distributorship at the next highest (read best) position in the organizational structure. It says that the system loads one level at a time rather than loading the tree structure by depth (building branches).

As this is not a lesson in the finer points of network marketing, other considerations and factors are being omitted, and we will focus on how the software to meet these needs had been developed. In addition, we will talk about maintenance or administrative software. This software will also not be detailed within the scope of this chapter.

The requirements we will look at specifically deal with how the site had dealt with the "sign on" situation. We will be looking at what happened after a customer stated that he was interested in either the product or the network marketing business plan.

When a potential customer arrives at the site, he will reach a page where he can either order the product or join in the business opportunity. The site must offer a way to do either. If the customer chooses the product only, the site must allow him to send an E-mail form to the product fulfillment team. If the customer chooses to accept the business opportunity, he should be sent to a page that allows him to select a currently filling level of the tree to come in on.

To ensure that there is no confusion, the terminology in Table 12.1 will be utilized.

Table 12.1: Terms and Definitions

Term	Definition
level	The grouping of a horizontal set of slots at the same position from the initial slot
slot	Any single position within the tree structure. A slot can have one of four possible states. These are: Open (the slot is available for a customer to sign up for); In-process (the slot is not available for selection as it has already been selected by a customer, but it has not been closed); Closed (the slot was selected by a customer and has been paid for); and Reserved (a slot has been temporarily closed by management).
position	A slot relative to those slots above and below it within the tree structure
location	An identification of any single slot's position within the tree structure
initial slot	The starting point of the initial tree structure

The site should provide a clear indication of the current status of each level that will allow a potential customer to know if there is an open location in which to sign on at within that level. Level status should be graphical. In addition, the lowest possible level with possible open positions on it should be highlighted graphically.

Access to any level will be permitted only if the level below it has at least one location that has moved from Open to In-process or to Closed. (See Figure 12.1). Only slots that have a location directly below them that is not Open or Reserved shall be displayed for any level. Any customer shall be able to select any Open slot and continue forward with the registration process.

Selection of any slot that is not in an Open state will generate an error message relative to the state that the slot is in.

After an Open slot is selected, the page will go to a form that will obtain the information shown in Table 12.2 from the user.

In addition, there should be a way of having a current customer sign up new customers. In these instances, we want to know who will be servicing the customer (providing the initial paperwork) and the person who reserved the location. For that reason, the information shown in Table 12.3 should also be on the form.

Figure 12.1: *Diagram of the rules base*

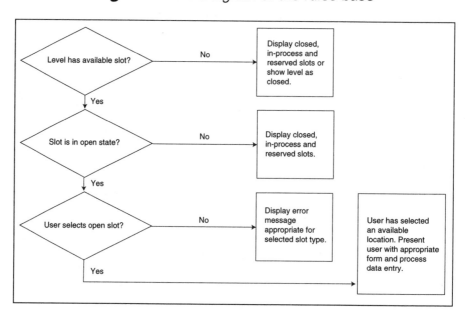

Table 12.2: Information requested when selecting a location

Field	Description
Name	First and last name
Address 1	Line 1 of an address line
Address 2	Line 2 of an address line
City	The city
State	Two-letter state code
Zip	The zip code
Country	USA/Canada/other
E-mail 1	E-mail address
E-mail 2	Backup E-mail address
Product	Information on product sign-up
Phone	Individual's phone number

Table 12.3: Additional information requested during location selection

Who	Who will service the customer
ID	Identification number of the individual who took the location.

To support locations, each location will have a unique identifier. This identifier should allow a person to know the exact path in the tree from the root to that location (see Figure 12.2).

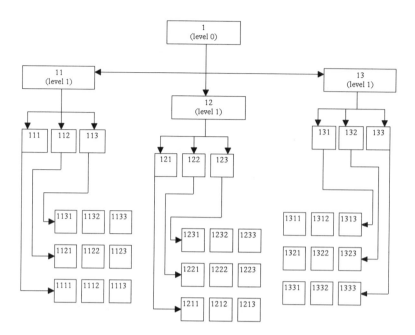

Figure 12.2: *Diagram of a tree (three levels with location specified)*

Once the form has been entered, the user's information will be placed into a data file in an easy-to-use format. This update will also update the proper associated entries in the selected location's level data file, showing the status of the location and the date when taken, as well as creating the proper entries in the next level's data file to allow potential customers the opportunity to access those levels.

The Code in this Chapter

To meet the defined requirements in this chapter, we will have to take some existing code and modify it accordingly.

The easiest one to do is the form for product-only cases. This will use a modified version of e-mail.tcl (Chapter 5). In this case, only the HTML response from inside the code will actually be modified (and the form itself, of course) as can be seen in Figure 12.3.

Display factors to consider are the style of the form and the need to reassure the viewers that the form they are filling out will not turn into yet another request that the users join anything.

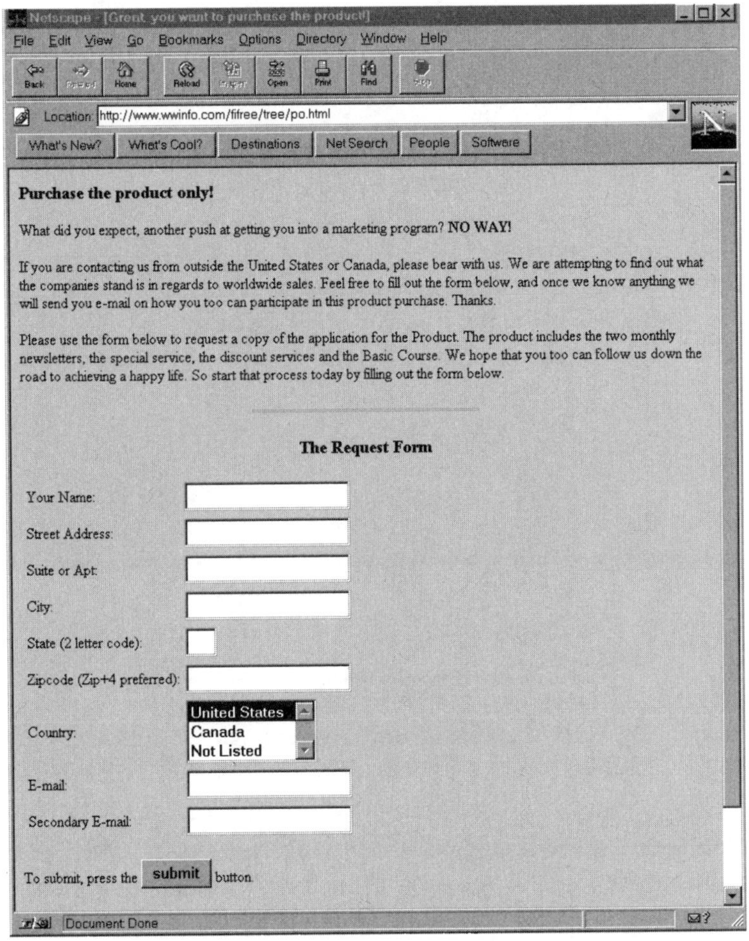

Figure 12.3: *Product request form*

The next four pieces of code perform all the functions required to select the active level, to select the desired slot, to build the form for user data entry for that location and to process the data entry for that location. Each of these pieces of code will be described in detail, both in the design section for the software as well as within the code comments.

The Server Side Include That Displays Levels

To display the open level, there is an SSI that must be run from a .shtml file. This program will open a data file that contains all the currently active levels in it, and each one's current status. This format is shown in Table 12.4.

Table 12.4: A sample level.log data file

level	flag
1	1
2	1
3	1
4	0
5	0
6	0
7	0

In Table 12.4, we can see that the flags say that levels 1, 2 and 3 are closed, whereas levels 4, 5, 6 and 7 are open. When this processes, the system will display the closed indicator for the first two levels (level 1 is not displayed, since it is the initial location or root), the open indicator for the next three levels and then for all levels above that to the maximum allowed, a not-available indicator.

On the screen, this could be indicated graphically as Figure 12.4 shows. The images used would be described on the page in a legend. In this case, the money bag is a closed level, the open door is available, the fire is hot and the stop sign with the hand is not available.

To generate this, the .shtml file should contain the following line:

```
<!-#exec cgi="/cgi-bin/levget.tcl" ->
```

This will call the levget.tcl procedure shown in Listing 12.1 that will access the file and build the table.

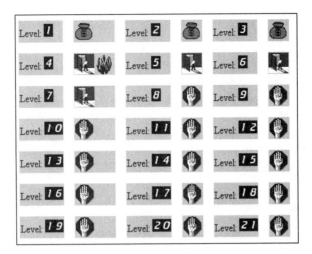

Figure 12.4: *Level selection table provides different graphics*

Listing 12.1: levget.tcl

```tcl
#!/usr/local/bin/tclsh
##
##  levget.tcl
##
##
## get the level information and display it in a table
##
puts   "Content-type: text/html\n\n "
##
## set the path to the data files
##
set path /pathtothe/datafiles
##
## open the level log
##
set f1 [open $path/level.log r]
##
## get all the level data
##
while {[gets $f1 val] >= 0} {
   lappend levls $val
}
##
## close the log and start building the table
## In order to support the "hot" indicator use a flag
## that will add a "hot image" to the first open
## level also, initialize all counters and values.
```

```
##
close $f1
set hot 1
puts "<table bgcolor=pink cellspacing=15> <tr>"
set rknt 0
set rowcnt 0
set oldval ""
##
## the loop. For each item see the state and output
## the appropriate line for the cell, only three
## cells per row.
##
foreach val [lsort $levls] {
  if {$val != $oldval} {
   incr rknt
   set oldval $val
##
## We are working with number to image replacement -
## have to handle single and multiple digits.
## Tcl TIP: In the first "set numimg" below we are
## using the {} method of string encapsulation.
## This means that we don't have to escape our
## quotes as \"  - we have used quote encapsulation
## in the second "set numimg" to show the difference
## between the two methods
##
    if {[lindex $val 0] > 9} {
      set numimg  {<img src="/gif/nlib/[string range \
          [lindex $val 0] 0 0].gif"><img \
          src="/gif/nlib/[string \
          range [lindex $val 0] 1 1].gif">}
    } else {
      set numimg  "<img src=\"/gif/nlib/[lindex \
          $val 0].gif\"> "
    }
##
## Three cells per row
##
    if {$rowcnt == 3} {
     puts "</tr><tr>"
     set rowcnt 1
    } else {
     incr rowcnt
    }
##
## is it open or closed?
##
    switch [lindex $val 1] {
     1 {
    puts "<td>Level: <img src=\"/gif/nlib/[lindex $val \
        0].gif\"></td><td><a href=\"filled.html\"><img \
        src=\"/gif/cashbag.gif\" border=0></a></td> "
```

```
    }
##
##  Open? Is it the first open entry?
##
      0 {
    if {$hot} {
      puts "<td>Level: $numimg</td><td><a href=\
          \"/cgi-bin/uncgi.cgi/levload.tcl?lev=$val\">\
          <img src=\"/gif/exit0a.gif\" border=0></a><img \
          src=\"/gif/fire.gif\"></td>"
      set hot 0
    } else {
      puts "<td>Level: $numimg</td><td><a href=\
          \"/cgi-bin/uncgi.cgi/levload.tcl?lev=$val\">\
          <img src=\"/gif/exit0a.gif\" border=0></a></td>"
    }
      }
    }
  }
}
##
##  It was unavailable. We are going to show up to 21
##  levels available for selection. Considering a
##  3*?? matrix, at level 19, will contain every man,
##  woman and child in the United States, 21 levels
##  should be more than enough as it will contain a
##  total of 3,486,784,401 selection locations on
##  that level alone.
##
while {[expr $rknt < 21]} {
  incr rknt
  if {$rknt > 9} {
    set numimg  "<img src=\"/gif/nlib/[string range \
        $rknt 0 0].gif\"><img src=\"/gif/nlib/[string \
        range $rknt 1 1].gif\">"
  } else {
    set numimg  "<img src=\"/gif/nlib/$rknt.gif\">"
  }
  if {$rowcnt == 3} {
   puts "</tr><tr>"
   set rowcnt 1
  } else {
   incr rowcnt
  }
 puts "<td>Level: $numimg</td><td><a href=\"closedl.html\">\
     <img src=\"/gif/traffc0c.gif\" border=0></a></td>"
}
puts "</tr></table>"
##
##  The table is completed. exit.
##
exit
```

Once the customer has selected a level, based on that selection they will be passed to either a dead-end page (they selected either a closed or unavailable level) or, if they selected an available level, they will be passed to a page that will generate a view of the selected level.

We will be following and documenting the available path. In our case the customer checked level 4, the first available level (as indicated by the hot visual the customer requested), and saw that everything there was either taken, in process or reserved (a thumbs-up, envelope or firecracker image) as in Figure 12.5. In this case, there were no available selections at that level, so the user used the back key and then selected the next available level (level 5) as in Figure 12.6. At this level, the user can see that there are available locations to be selected. The user would then select a location by placing the cursor over the money and indicating that item is to be selected.

When the user selects a level from those available (Figure 12.5), the software will check to see if there is a data file that details the locations that can be displayed, and the value of the selectable fields for those locations. The data file has the format shown in Table 12.5. The table also shows sample data.

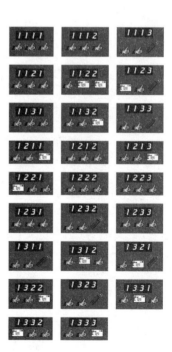

Figure 12.5: Level 4, everything is taken

Figure 12.6: Level 5, selections are available

Table 12.5 A portion of the location file for level 5

Location	State	Date
123121	0	
123122	0	
123123	1	961112
123131	1	961112
123132	2	961110
123133	0	

In the requirements, the user stated that he wanted to be able to trace a line of a tree branch from the root to the current selected slot from an identifier. This identifier is the location identifier; it is what makes each slot unique. In this case, since we are working in a tree, we can define every location relative to its past location within the tree.

In this way, the location of the third person in the organizational tree who is under the second person in the tree who is under the root could be numerically uniquely identified as 123 (root = 1, 2 = number 2 person under root and 3 = number three person under the number 2 person).

Therefore, a slot in the tree structure when identified by its numeric path is a location, since it is a unique slot. Using this method, we can define some of the slots on the fifth level as 12312[1..3] - the first three locations in Table 12.5.

In Table 12.5, we can see that two blocks of three selectable positions have been defined in the data file. The first block is 12312 and it contains elements 1, 2 and 3 below it. The second block is the one that follows it(12313 with its 1, 2 and 3 elements. We can see that the first two elements and the last one in this series have not been selected, as their state remains 0 and there is no activity date. The third and fourth elements of the table are both paid (showing a thumbs-up in the graphics), while the fifth is in process (an envelope in the graphics).

To generate this information, a level file for each level is maintained with the data in the format of Table 12.5 within it.

> **Note** It is important to understand that the data for this file will not be generated unless there is already a selected location in the file for the level below it. If there is a record in the level 5 file for 12312[1..3], there must be a record on level 4 that is either in process or paid (envelope or thumbs-up) for record 12312. When the record 12312 is selected, it generates the records 12312[1..3] in the level 5 data file. This is how we ensure that the rule "there must be someone in the upline before a downline spot can be taken" is enforced. We don't allow a downline slot to be displayed until the upline location has been selected. The methods for doing this are detailed later in Listing 12.4.

The data in the Level file for the level is processed to create the selection tables that are displayed to the user. Listing 12.2 loads the level data file and displays it in table format. This is the procedure that is called when the table item selected by the customer from the levget.tcl SSI is selected. In this case, the level to be processed is passed in to the levload.tcl routine using a GET method.

Listing 12.2: levload.tcl

```
#!/usr/local/bin/tclsh
##
##
## levload.tcl
##
## load a level with information
##
##
## based on the values passed into the procedure a
## file for a level will be opened. The data within
## will be processed and state data will be
## processed as follows:
##
## parent = field 1 - last character
## state = field 2
##   value       state        image           link
##   3          reserved     dynamite2.gif   res.html
##   0          open         money.gif
/cgibin/uncgi/reqslot.tcl?id=
##   1          closed       t_up.gif        closed.html
##   2          in-process   letter.gif      taken.html
##
puts "Content-type: text/html\n\n"
set levls ""
set level $env(WWW_lev)
##
##
## here we are posting out the page information.
## This is as general as need be. There are three
## ways that this can be accomplished. The first way
## is to do it in-line as we have here. The second
## way would be to put the data in a data file
## and then use an [exec cat <filename>]. That, of
## course, is unix specific. The third way would be
## to use the same file, and then to have a read/
## write loop where we read each line of the file in,
## and then write it back out. Any of the three
## methods would be acceptable.
##
##
puts "<title>Level $level</title><body \
```

```
        bgcolor=ffffff><center><h2>Almost There</h2></center> \
        At this point you can view the structure of Level \
        $level. You can also decide to select the \
        <img src=\"/gif/money.gif\"> \
        <b>open location</b> image to join at that location. \
        <p>If you see a <img src=\"/gif/letter.gif\"> \
        image, it means that the slot was selected by \
        someone already, and that it is <b>in-process</b>. \
        When an in-process image becomes a <img \
        src=\"/gif/t_up.gif\"> that means the person \
        in that location has sent their application back \
        in, they are <b>in the downline</b>, and the \
        application is on the way to the parent company. \
        <p>In a few cases you will see a \
        <img src=\"/gif/dynamite2.gif\">. These <b>reserved</b> \
        images mean that there have been issues with the \
        slot (like a person who sent in a request to \
        join, from Germany!) and no slots will be created \
        above it until the issues are settled."
puts "<p>There is the slight possibility that \
        someone selected a <img src=\"/gif/money.gif\"> \
        for the same slot you did at the same time you \
        did. In those rare cases the first to complete the \
        form for the location and submit it will \
        be rewarded with the slot. These are <b>very rare \
        cases</b> and if it happens you should return to this \
        page and issue a browser \"reload\" and then attempt \
        the selection again."
puts "<p><hr width=30%><font size=+2>NOTES:</font> \
        <ul><li>In order to select an item, put your \
        pointer over the image (generally the <img \
        src=\"/gif/money.gif\"> image) and \
        select. <li> Complete the form and submit \
        it (completes the  joining process). Please \
        remember to use the submit \
        at the bottom of the form page"
puts "<li> Again, if you are told that the slot is \
        already taken, please return to this page and use \
        the reload button to refresh the page, chances \
        are you are using a cached page.</ul> <p><hr \
        width=30%>"
##
## general information completed, start the process.
##
set path /pathtothe/datafiles
set f1 [open $path/$level.log]
set rknt 0
##
## read the file and load an internal list
##
while {[gets $f1 val] >= 0} {
```

```
    lappend levls $val
    incr rknt
}
##
## sort the input and close the file
##
lsort $levls
close $f1
set hot 0
##
## the proc used to load the images and links
##
## Here is a yet another good time to note a item
## about strings. Many people do not like to escape
## the quotes in the strings, and Tcl does provide a
## way to avoid that if you so desire. Notice that
## switch item "3" in the switch statement below
## encloses the string in {}'s rather than quotes.
## When this is done Tcl takes the string in as a
## literal list of elements and the quotes are not
## touched by the parser. Switch item "3"
## could have been written as:
##
## 3 {set retimg "<a href=\"/res.html\"><img \
##      src=\"/gif/dynamite2.gif\" \
##      alt=Reserved border=0></a>" }
##
## or the way it was. This is a stylistic issue. I
## prefer to unescape the quotes as it requires me
## to ensure that the HTML is properly written. It
## is not required that you do that, and
## many people prefer to use the {} style instead.
##
proc getimg {val par tail} {
switch $val {
    3 { set retimg {<a href="/res.html"><img \
        src="/gif/dynamite2.gif" alt=Reserved \
        border=0></a>} }
    0 { set retimg "<a href=\"/cgi-bin/uncgi.cgi/reqslot.tcl?\
        id=$par$tail\"><img src=\"/gif/money.gif\" \
        alt=Open border=0></a>" }
    1 { set retimg "<a href=\"/closed.html\"><img \
        src=\"/gif/t_up.gif\" alt=Taken border=0></a>" }
    2 { set retimg "<a href=\"/taken.html\"><img \
        src=\"/gif/letter.gif\" alt=In-Process \
        border=0></a>" }
}
return $retimg
}
##
## If you have used the calendar program, the
```

```
## processing of tables will be very familiar to
## you. This uses many of the same functions that
## cal.tcl used.
##
## the main program - start by initializing
##
puts "<table bgcolor=teal cellspacing=15> <tr>"
set tencnt 0
set rowcnt 0
set oparent 0
set itmcnt 0
##
## outer loop. For every item in the internal array...
##
foreach val $levls {
##
## for speed of display we will build up a ten row
## table and then display that table. This will
## allow the tables to start displaying before we
## have loaded all of them. This should provide the
## user some display before the larger levels have
## completed processing all the data from the data
## file. While we could have used the flush command to
## force the buffer to flush the output to the
## client, it wouldn't have made any difference
## unless we closed the tables first as the browser
## will start filling the tables only after the table
## is completed. This kludge is here to make up for
## the limitations of some of the browsers. Another
## alternative method (and just as much a kludge)
## would have been to limit the number of items
## displayed. This would require that the user page
## through uptene number of "pages" for a level, but
## each page would load fast. In reality, as the
## levels get larger, there is really no way to
## resolve for this problem.
##
  if {$tencnt == 89} {
     set tencnt 0
     puts "</tr></table><table bgcolor=teal \
        cellspacing=15><tr>"
  } else {
     incr tencnt 3
  }
##
## the parent is the numeric identifier for a block of
## three items that are included within it.
##
  set parent [string range [lindex $val 0] 0 [expr \
     [string length [lindex $val 0]]-2] ]
##
```

```
## only three parents per row.
##
  if {$itmcnt == 3} {
    set itmcnt 0
    puts "</tr><tr>"
  }
##
## this routine determines if it is the first time
## through for this <td>
##
  if {$oparent == 0} {
    puts "<td>"
    set numimg ""
##
## load up the location number as an image
##
    foreach num [split $parent ""] {
      set numimg "$numimg<img src=\"/fifree/gif/nlib/$num.gif\" \
        alt=$num >"
    }
  }
##
## build the display output for the table data and
## display it
##
  incr oparent
##   puts "$oparent"
  set img($oparent) [getimg [lindex $val 1] \
      $parent $oparent ]
  if {$oparent == 3} {
    incr itmcnt
    puts " <center> $numimg <br> $img(1) $img(2) $img(3) \
        </center> </td>"
    set oparent 0
  }
}
##
## close the table when we are done
##
puts "</tr></table>"
##
## fini!
##
exit
```

Once a customer has the page of selections before him, he can select on any visual clue. In this case, the "money stack" is the clue that will move him to the subscription form. The processing requires that the selection information be passed along to the routine so we know what location is selected. Because of this, the form will have to be built by a CGI script so the location selected can be passed along to the form processing routine as a hidden variable within the form.

This is one of the best examples of why it is important to know and understand HTML as part of being able to create CGI scripts. The program in Listing 12.3 is nothing more than an HTML file being dumped to the user with one value within the HTML being processed.

There are two ways that this program could have been created to display the form to the customer. The first would have been to break the HTML into two pieces, each in a separate file. In this way, the CGI would then dump the first file to standard output, then process the location identifier into a hidden value and, finally, display the balance of the form by dumping the second file to standard output.

The second way is the way that is shown in Listing 12.3. Either way would be acceptable, and there is no externally visible difference between the two methods.

Listing 12.3: reqslot.tcl

```tcl
#!/usr/local/bin/tclsh
##
## reqslot.tcl
##
## When the person comes in they request a slot.
## This form is built on the fly to permit the person
## to enter the information needed by join.tcl to
## obtain that location. Note that the key pieces of
## the form are the two non "puts" lines below and
## the use of $id in the title and the hidden field
##
puts "Content-type: text/html\n\n"
set levls ""
set id $env(WWW_id)
##
## The only passed data that we care about is the
## slot ID.
##
## Put the form up.
##
puts "<title>Selected location number
$id</title><body \
   bgcolor=ffffff><center><h2>One last thing for you to \
   do here</h2></center>You have requested to join the \
   COMPANY. <b>Welcome aboard</b>. Below this text \
```

```
      is a form that asks you the minimal amount of \
      information we need to get the information you \
      will need to join on its way to you.<p> Please \
      note that it is <b>very</b> minimal. We need your \
      name and mailing address so we can get the mail
      to you. We ask for an e-mail address so we can \
      let you know when it was mailed, and when we expect \
      it back. We don't want your phone number (with one \
      exception), your age, your gender, religion, etc. \
      Like I said, we kept it minimal."
puts "<p> If you are already a COMPANY member, you \
      can use this form to add people to the downline. \
      Make sure that you complete the last section \
      before submitting the form. If you are submitting \
      this for yourself, please leave the last section \
      blank.<p><hr>"
##
## Here is the actual form. Note that it calls
## join.tcl as its action.
##
## Also, note that the form is in table format for
## column and row alignment. If you wanted the form
## to be "tighter" you could have just created two
## cells and put the data in the cells  using <br>
## between the rows. The problem with this method is
## the way the text will adjust if someone sizes the
## window too small (rows will misalign).
##
##
puts "<center><h3>Joining the COMPANY form</h3></center>"
puts "<FORM METHOD=POST \
      ACTION=\"/jmi-bin/uncgi.cgi/join.tcl\">"
##
## here is why we are doing all this
##
puts "<input type=hidden name=location value=$id>"
##
puts "<table>"
puts "<tr><td>Your Name:</td><td><input name=name \
      type=text></td></tr>"
puts "<tr><td>Street Address:</td><td><input \
      name=street type=text></td></tr>"
puts "<tr><td>Suite or Apt:</td><td><input name=apt \
      type=text></td></tr>"
puts "<tr><td>City:</td><td><input name=city \
      type=text></td></tr>"
puts "<tr><td>State (2 letter code):</td><td><input \
      name=st type=text size=2></td></tr><tr><td>Zip \
      (+4 if possible) :</td><td><input name=zip \
      type=text></td></tr>"
puts "<tr><td>Country:</td><td><select name=cntry size=3>"
```

```
puts "<option selected>US"
puts "<option>Canada"
puts "<option>Not Listed"
puts "</select>"
puts "</td></tr>"
puts "<tr><td>E-mail:</td><td><input name=email1 \
   type=text></td></tr>"
puts "<tr><td>Secondary E-mail:</td><td><input
name=email2 \
   type=text></td></tr>"
puts "<tr><td colspan=2><h2>This section must be completed\
   </h2><table><tr><td>Standard (the way we recommend)\
   </td><td><input name=ot value=a32 type=radio \
   selected></td></tr><tr><td>Non-Standard (A bit pricier, \
   not a recommendation)</td><td><input name=ot value=p92 \
   type=radio></td></tr><tr><td>(Phone Number is optional) \
   </td><td>Phone: <input name=mlm-phone type=text>\
   </table></td></tr>"
puts "</table>"
puts "<p> <hr><font color=blue><b>This information is only \
   filled out if you are a COMPANY member and are \
   submitting this for someone \
   else.</b></font><p><table><tr><td \
   width=50%>Do you want COMPANY to send the application \
   package, or do you want to handle the application \
   information and send the completed application to COMPANY\
   </td><td><table><tr><td>COMPANY should do it.</td><td>\
   <input name=doit value=COMPANY type=radio>\
   </td></tr><tr><td>I'll take care of it.</td><td><input \
   name=doit value=Member \
   type=radio></td></tr></table></tr>\
   <tr><td>My COMPANY ID is:</td><td><input \
   name=doit-id type=text></td></tr></table><hr>"
puts "<p>"
puts "To submit, press the <input TYPE=submit \
   VALUE=submit> button."
puts "</form>"
puts "<hr>"
puts "<font size=-2><address> Form generated by pro-
gram: &#169; \
   Copyright 1996, COMPANY, CITY/STATE .All Rights \
   Reserved.</address>"
puts "<address> Programming: &#169; Copyright 1996, \
   Infobahn Xpress, Los Alamitos, CA. All Rights \
   Reserved. </address> </font>"
##
##
## Form output completed.
##
##
exit
```

Once the data entry has completed (using the form that is shown in Figure 12.7) and the customer submits the form to the system using the submit button on the bottom of the page, the following actions will take place:

- The customer's personal data will be written to a record in an appropriate data file so that we will have the customer information. The record's key identifier will be the location that the customer selected

- The data file for the level of the customer's selected location is opened and the location's selected flag is updated. The date of processing is also appended to the record

Figure 12.7: *The data entry form (enter and sign in, please)*

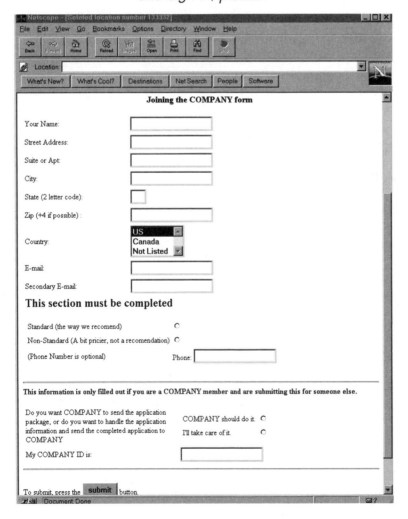

- The next higher level data file for that location will have three entries placed into it to represent the next three locations available in the structure (ex: 12312[1..3])
- If the next higher level data file above the location selection level has never been accessed before, the flag to turn the level on will be updated in the level.log file
- A confirmation mail message is sent to the person reserving the location (if an E-mail address is used) advising that the location has been selected

All this takes place in the CGI program called by the form, join.tcl, shown in Listing 12.4.

Listing 12.4: join.tcl

```
#!/usr/local/bin/tclsh
##
## join.tcl   - A procedure to add information to the
##               appropriate log files
##
##─────────────────────────────────────────
##
## expected values:
## name = name of individual (Required)
## street = street address (Required)
## apt = address second line (Optional)
## city = city (Required)
## st = state (Required)
## zip = zipcode (Required)
## cntry = country (US/Canada/other) (Required)
## email1 = main e-mail (Required)
## email2 = secondary e-mail (Optional)
## location = the location they selected (Required)
## mlm-phone = (Optional)
## ot = order type (a32 or p92) (Required)
##
## in order to support present members adding people
## to the downline we have added two additional
## items. doit is a yes/no value on who should send
## the application information, and doit-id is the
## way that the individual can assure that they
## remain the contact point if any questions arise.
##
##
## there are a number of files that are updated in
## this process
##
```

```
## files:
## /your/logdir/
## level.log  - contains the active levels and the
## status flag for the level: (0 = filled - 1 = open)
## [1..12].log - contains the state of each
##     location at that level
## States:
## 0 - Open, can be selected (must be open for this
##       procedure to be run, and to change it to
##       reserved (3) or in-process (2)
## 1 - Closed, This is an active FIC
## 2 - In-process, Forms out, waiting for them to join
## 3 - Reserved
## req.log - contains all unfullfilled location requests
##
## format of files:
## level.log:   level switch
## [1..12].log  location state <date of change>
## req.log       location <form-string> <date req>
##
## date format:  yymmdd
## form-string (broken into 2 lines for the text -
##            all on one line in reality):
## name~street~apt~city~st~zip~cntry~email1~email2~
##    location~mlm-phone~ot~~doit~doit-id
## -- any blank field will be filled in with unique
##      character string --
##
## Process:
## open the proper [1..12] log read until location
## found. If record is not state "open"(0) abort and
## error. If state is open(0) delete record by
## creating a state in-process(2) for that record
## and rewrite the file out. Once the file has been
## written out append the user record to the req.log
## file. send e-mail and update the level.log file.
##
##
## Error processing
##
proc outerr {code data} {
puts "<title>Error encountered</title><center><h1>Error \
    Encountered: $code</h1></center>"
puts "An error of type $code was encountered. This \
    means that the form was not completed and \
    processing has stopped. Here is what I, the \
    stupid computer, think caused the error:<p>"
switch $code {
  ID-BFD { puts "Input Data: Bad Field Data: [lindex $data \
            0]=[lindex $data 1]"}
  ID-MFD { puts "Input Data: Missing Field Data: \
```

```
                 $data is required"}
  UL-LNA { puts "Updating Location: Location Not \
      Available: Location taken on: [lindex $data 0]"}
}
exit
}
##
## start the processing
##
puts "Content-type: text/HTML\n"
puts "<title>Associate Location to Individual \
    Response Status</title>"
puts "<body bgcolor=ffffff>"
##
foreach envvar [lsort [array names env] ] {
 if {[regexp {^WWW_} $envvar]} {
  set varname [join [lrange [split [lindex [split \
      $envvar =] 0] _] 1 end ] _]
  if {$varname != ""} {
   set var($varname) $env(WWW_$varname)
  }
 }
}
##
## find out if they passed in the doit variables and
## if so adjust the final portion of the string to
## add those records to the database.
##
set recend "~~~"
if {[info exists var(doit)]} {
  set recend "~~$var(doit)~"
  if {[info exists var(doit-id)]} {
    set recend "~~$var(doit)~$var(doit-id)"
    if {[string length $var(doit-id)] < 1} {
      puts "<hr><b>Special note:</b> Next time you \
          enter one of these you may want to \
          include your ID number so we know who \
          added the person. Not that we are keeping \
          count, but if you say that you are taking \
          care of the form submission to us it does \
          help to know who you are. Thanks.<hr><p>"
    }
  }
}
##
## get datestamp
##
## In the cal.tcl program, and the add and delete
## items from that data file that work with that
## program we used the Tcl V7.4 method for computing
## and parsing dates.  In Tcl
```

```
## V7.5 there was the addition of the command
## "clock" that will do date and time stamp
## manipulation. If you are using Tcl V7.4 you will
## want to continue to use the methods that
## were shown in the cal.tcl program. If you are
## using Tcl V7.5 the method that is being used here
## should be used to replace the way that sortable
## dates were created. This single line of code will
## create a date in the format yymmdd using the
## system clock of the  computer the CGI is
## running on. If you are concerned about millennium
## processing, feel free to use 4 character dates
## with the format statement %Y%m%d
##
set dstamp [ clock format [clock seconds] -format %y%m%d  ]
##
## This section ensures that all the error checking
## is completed.
##
## let's make sure that a unset variable is either
## allowed to be unset or is set to the unique fill
## value (in this program we will be using the
## string tnibni for the unique fill value). If it
## is a required variable then call the error routine
##
## required:
## name~street~city~st~zip~cntry~email1~location~ot
##
## If we want we could force a phone entry. In this
## case we will include the code to do that even
## though there is no need to.
##
## If ot = mlm then mlm-phone is required
## name~street~apt~city~st~zip~cntry~em1~em2~loc~mlm-phone~ot
##
foreach vname "name street city st zip cntry email1 \
    location ot" {
  if {![info exists var($vname)]} {
    switch $vname {
      name { outerr ID-MFD {Your name} }
      street { outerr ID-MFD {Street} }
      city { outerr ID-MFD {City} }
      st { outerr ID-MFD {State} }
      zip { outerr ID-MFD {Zipcode} }
      email1 { outerr ID-MFD {E-mail} }
      ot { outerr ID-MFD {Order Type} }
    }
  } else {
    if {[string length $var($vname) ] < 1} {
    switch $vname {
      name { outerr ID-MFD {Your name} }
```

```
          street { outerr ID-MFD {Street} }
          city { outerr ID-MFD {City} }
          st { outerr ID-MFD {State} }
          zip { outerr ID-MFD {Zipcode} }
          email1 { outerr ID-MFD {E-mail} }
          ot { outerr ID-MFD {Order Type} }
        }
      }
  }
}
if {$var(ot) == "mlm"} {
  if {![info exists var(mlm-phone)]} {
    outerr ID-MFD "Order Type MLM changes the Phone \
        Number to - "
  }
  if {[string length $var(mlm-phone)] < 7} {
    outerr ID-MFD "Order Type MLM changes the Phone \
        Number to - "
  }
}
foreach vname "apt cntry email2 mlm-phone" {
  if {![info exists var($vname)]} {
    set var($vname) tnibni
  }
  if {[string length $var($vname)] < 1} {
    set var($vname) tnibni
  }
}
##
## all error checking has been completed. Process
## the data.
##
## Here we set the final output stream based on the
## data put in. This is the formatted data record.
##
set outstr "$var(name)~$var(street)~$var(apt)~\
    $var(city)~$var(st)~$var(zip)~\
    $var(cntry)~$var(email1)~$var(email2)~\
    $var(location)~$var(mlm-phone)~$var(ot)$recend"
##
## okay, what level?
##
set loc $var(location)
set lev [expr [string length $loc] -1]
##
## open the level file, load the database looking for the
## location and ensure it is open. If so change the
## state, add it to the element list, rewrite it
## back out sorted. If not, generate an error and exit
##
set f1 [open /thepathtothe/$lev.log r]
```

```
while {[gets $f1 val] >= 0} {
  if {[lindex $val 0] == $loc} {
    if {[lindex $val 1] != 0} {
      outerr UL-LNA [lindex $val 2]
    } else {
      set val "$loc 2 $dstamp"
      lappend oval $val
      break
    }
  } else {
    lappend oval $val
  }
}
while {[gets $f1 val] >= 0} {
  lappend oval $val
}
close $f1
set f1 [open /thepathtothe/$lev.log w]
foreach val [lsort $oval] {
puts $f1 $val
}
close $f1
##
## we have updated the old level file, now we have to
## create the new entries in the next level file.
## Increment the level and append the new records to
## the new level file
##
incr lev
##
## Tcl TIP - addition and subtraction are easy to do
## with the "incr" command. This command takes the
## value and by default adds one. You can also pass
## it the value to be incr'd…
##      example:
## % set knt 5
## 5
## % incr knt
## 6
## % incr knt -3
## 3
##
set f1 [open /thepathtothe/$lev.log a]
##
## Tcl TIP:  If you use a [set <variablename>]  it
## will return the value of the variable name if it
## is already set. This acts like an "echo" or a
## "puts" internally. This allows us to display the
## value and append a value to it. Another way of
## doing the indirection would have been to use the
## ${<variable>} method. Both methods work, and I
```

```
## have never heard a good reason for the using one
## method over another. Both methods allow for a
## case of double indirection.
##
puts $f1 "[set loc]1 0"
puts $f1 "[set loc]2 0"
puts $f1 "[set loc]3 0"
close $f1
##
## we have updated all the level files, we have
## validated all the user input, now update the file
## we store the user data entries in with the new
## record
##
set f1 [open /thepathtothe/req.log a]
puts $f1 "$loc $outstr $dstamp"
close $f1
##
## now, did we create entries on a new level? If so
## we have to update the level.log file.
##
set f1 [open /thepathtothe/level.log r]
while {[gets $f1 val] >= 0} {
  lappend lval $val
}
close $f1
lappend lval "$lev 0"
set f1 [open /thepathtothe/level.log w]
foreach val $lval {
puts $f1 $val
}
close $f1
##
## sort and eliminate duplicates from the level.log
## there are two options in sorting. Option 1 is to
## lsort the list and then do the write only if the
## value changes from the last write (as lsort has
## no unique qualifier to eliminate duplicates).
## Option 2 is to use the system services to do the
## sort and eliminate duplicates for you. Option 2
## is shown below. It should be noted that option 2
## is unix-centric. In addition, there is the slim
## chance that the level.log file might be over-
## written when it is in its temporary file mode.
## As level.log is never reducing the data in the
## log file, only expanding on it, there is little
## concern that the file would be overwritten.
##
exec sort -u /thepathtothe/level.log > \
    /thatpathtothe/level.tmp
exec mv /thatpathtothe/level.tmp \
```

```
        /thatpathtothe/level.log
##
## build the success message for the customer and
## let them know that we are done
##
puts "<center><h1>Congratulations!</h1></center> \
     Welcome to the start of what we all hope will be \
     a happy and a positive long term relationship. \
     Your Identifier is below. Please make sure that \
     you provide that on any and all correspondence \
     that you have with us as this is the number we \
     use to track your position. Your packet \
     of information should be in your hands soon."
puts "<p> Your Identifier number is:<br><center><font \
     color=green size=+5>$loc</font><p></center>The \
     input recorded is:<font size=+2 color=lime> \
     <center><br>Name and address:<br> \
     $var(name)<br>$var(street)<br></font>\
     (second address line not carried forward to this \
     screen)<font size=+2 color=lime><br>$var(city) \
     $var(st) $var(zip)<br>E-mail(1): \
     $var(email1)</font></center>"
##
## that completes the base processing of the
## program. If the individual has provided an e-mail
## address, we also want to be able to send them an
## e-mail acknowledgment.
##
## The following piece of code is used to force a
## message to be e-mailed out the person who sent
## this in... we have received the join request
## first set up our name for response purposes. Then
## clean up the e-mail address that they gave us to
## replace any nasty characters. Then make sure that
## the e-mail address is valid by making sure it has
## one @ sign. If it is process the message.
## Again we have chosen to use a unix-centric
## method. In this case we chose to have a file with
## the mail message in it and we are dumping that to
## the open e-mail pipe using an exec to the unix
## "cat" command. As usual, the other two options
## would be to have the file go through a tight
## read/write loop, or to include the message in the
## code. If we had included the message in the code
## then it would have been a good idea to also use
## that as an opportunity to personalize the e-mail
## with information that we have within the program
## already. This would allow the e-mail message to
## say "Dear $var(name), we know that you will be
## taking $var(city), $var(state) by storm in the
## near future... " - I refer to this as the
```

```
## "clearinghouse method" of responses as
## it appears to make you special when you receive
## it, even if it was yet another computer generated
## response.
##
proc sendout {a} {
  set msub "Autoprocessed e-mail from us to you "
  set frmname "our-email@domain.com (our company name)"
  regsub -all {\;|\[|\]|\||\<|\>} $a " * " trtonm
  if [regexp "@" $trtonm] {
    set f1 [open {|/usr/lib/sendmail -t} w]
    puts $f1 "From: $frmname"
    puts $f1 "To: $trtonm"
    puts $f1 "Subject: $msub"
    puts $f1 "[exec cat /location/ofthefile/thanks.txt]"
    close $f1
  }
  return
}
##
## send the e-mail and exit
##
sendout $var(email1)
exit
##
```

In the following figures the user has completed the form (Figure 12.8) and submitted it either successfully (Figure 12.9) or with an error message generated (Figure 12.10).

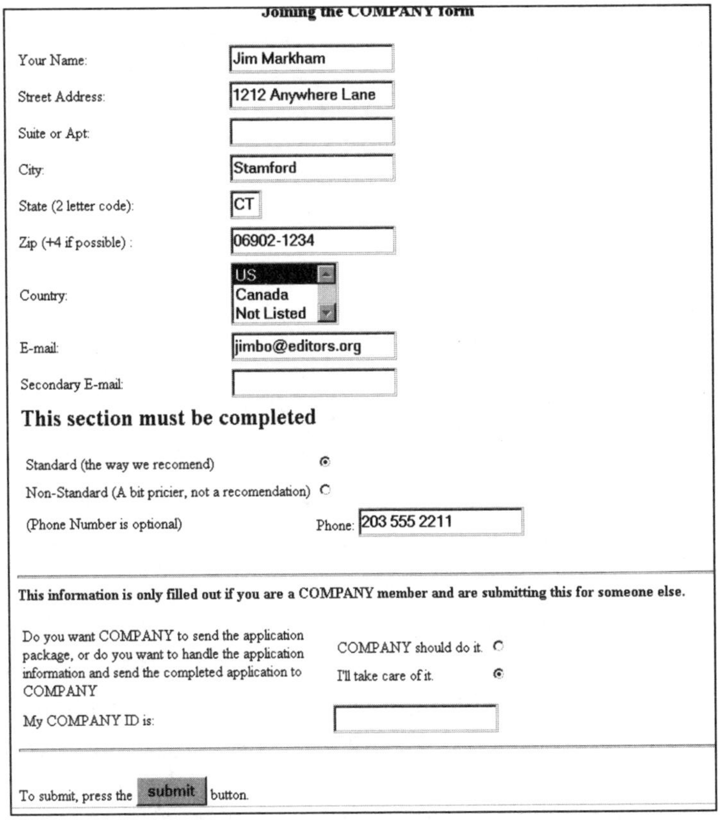

Joining the COMPANY form

Your Name:	Jim Markham
Street Address:	1212 Anywhere Lane
Suite or Apt:	
City:	Stamford
State (2 letter code):	CT
Zip (+4 if possible) :	06902-1234
Country:	US / Canada / Not Listed
E-mail:	jimbo@editors.org
Secondary E-mail:	

This section must be completed

Standard (the way we recomend)   ◉

Non-Standard (A bit pricier, not a recomendation) ○

(Phone Number is optional)   Phone: 203 555 2211

This information is only filled out if you are a COMPANY member and are submitting this for someone else.

Do you want COMPANY to send the application package, or do you want to handle the application information and send the completed application to COMPANY

COMPANY should do it. ○

I'll take care of it.   ◉

My COMPANY ID is:

To submit, press the **submit** button.

Figure 12.8: The completed form

Figure 12.9: The completed process

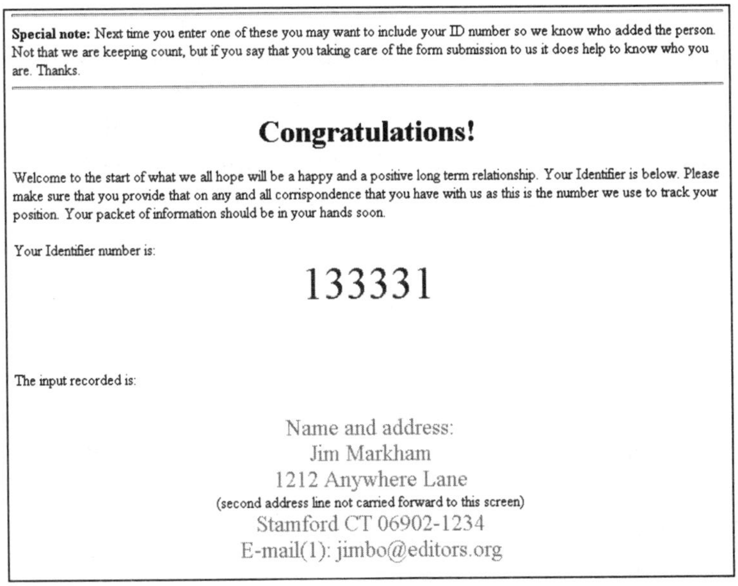

Special note: Next time you enter one of these you may want to include your ID number so we know who added the person. Not that we are keeping count, but if you say that you taking care of the form submission to us it does help to know who you are. Thanks.

Congratulations!

Welcome to the start of what we all hope will be a happy and a positive long term relationship. Your Identifier is below. Please make sure that you provide that on any and all corrispondence that you have with us as this is the number we use to track your position. Your packet of information should be in your hands soon.

Your Identifier number is:

133331

The input recorded is:

Name and address:
Jim Markham
1212 Anywhere Lane
(second address line not carried forward to this screen)
Stamford CT 06902-1234
E-mail(1): jimbo@editors.org

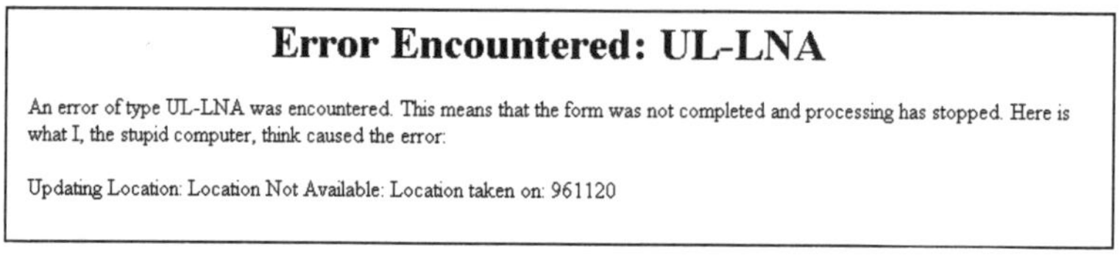

Error Encountered: UL-LNA

An error of type UL-LNA was encountered. This means that the form was not completed and processing has stopped. Here is what I, the stupid computer, think caused the error:

Updating Location: Location Not Available: Location taken on: 961120

Figure 12.10: *Sample error message*

Implementing the Network Marketing Handler in Perl

The implementation in Perl closely matches its Tcl cousin. There are four listings here as well, one for each one of the Tcl listings shown earlier.

Let's look at the levget.pl program shown in Listing 12.5 which shows the status of up to 21 levels in a table. You should never need more than 21 levels. The lifetime and structure of this network marketing handler will never last this long(as we pointed out, the number of people in the network marketing handler at 21 levels is rather high. We have six cells per row, two cells for each level with information for each level. The program starts a new row with every third level based on the value in the $rknt variable:

```
print "</tr><tr>" if (($rknt % 3) == 0);
```

The code uses three different subroutines to print the images for information on each level; i.e.. Hot, Cold or Closed. These routines, in turn, use another function, makeNumber, to create the image string based on the numbers passed to it. Using functions make the code less cluttered, since the main loop of the program simply calls these functions to display the underlying cells with regard to table implementation details.

Listing 12.5: levget.pl

```
#!/usr/loca/bin/perl
# File levget.pl
$|=1;
printf "Content-type: text/html\n\n";
```

```
# =======================================
# open the level log
# =======================================
$fpath="/pathtothe/datafiles";
# Debugged with:   $fpath="./level.log";
@levels = (); $lvlctr = 0;
open(FH,$fpath)||die;
while(<FH>){
    @levels[$lvlctr++] = $_;
}
close FH;

# =======================================
# For the "hot" image, display only once
# =======================================
print "<table bgcolor=pink border><tr>\n";
$hot = 1;
$rknt = 0;    # row counter

# =======================================
# Process a sorted list of levels
# =======================================
foreach $val (sort @levels) {
    ($thisLevel,$status) = split(' ',$val);
    # =======================================
    # Print only three levels at a time.
    # =======================================
    print "</tr><tr>" if (($rknt % 3) == 0);
if ($status == 1) {
    &printClosed($thisLevel);
    # print "<td>closed $thisLevel</td>";
    } else {
        if ($hot) {
    &printHotOpen($thisLevel,);
    # print "<td>hot $thisLevel</td>";
    $hot = 0;
    } else {
        &printColdOpen($thisLevel);
    # print "<td>cold $thisLevel</td>";
        }
    } # open
    $rknt++;        # track levels in file.
} # for loop

##
## print out the rest of the rows
while ($rknt < 21) {
    print "</tr><tr>" if (($rknt % 3) == 0);
    $rknt++;
    &printStop($rknt);
    # print "<td>Stop $rknt</td>";
```

```perl
}
print "</tr></table>";

# ===============================
# Create a number
# ===============================
sub makeNumber {
 my ($num) = @_;
 my $i;
 my $numstr = "";
 foreach $i (split("",$num)) {
     $numstr .= "<img src=\"/gif/nlib/$i.gif\">";
 }
 return $numstr;
}


# ===============================
# Print HOT link to CGI script
# ===============================
sub printHotOpen {
    my ($num) = @_;
    my $numimg = &makeNumber($num);
print << "HOTOPEN";
<td>Level: $numimg</td>
<td><a href="/cgi-bin/uncgi.cgi/levload.pl?lev=$num 0">
<img src="/gif/exit0a.gif" border=0></a>
<img src="/gif/fire.gif"></td>
HOTOPEN
}


# ===============================
# Print Cold link to CGI script
# ===============================
sub printColdOpen {
    my ($num) = @_;
    my $numimg = &makeNumber($num);
print << "COLDOPEN";
<td>Level: $numimg</td>
<td>
<a href="/cgi-bin/uncgi.cgi/levload.pl?lev=$num 0">
<img src="/gif/exit0a.gif" border=0></a> </td>
COLDOPEN
}


# ===============================
# Print STOP sign
# ===============================
sub printStop {
    my ($num) = @_;
    my $numimg = &makeNumber($num);
print << "STOP";
```

```
<td>Level:$numimg</td><a href="closed.html">
<td> <img src="/gif/traffc0c.gif" border=0></a></td>
STOP
}


# =================================
# Print Cashbag sign
# =================================
sub printClosed {
    my ($num) = @_;
        my $numimg = &makeNumber($num);
print << "CLOSED";
<td>Level:$numimg</td>
<td><a href="filled.html">
<img src="/gif/cashbag.gif" border=0></a></td>
CLOSED
}
```

Now let's look at the levload.pl function that is called to load a level with the <A> tags generated by levget.pl. The program (shown in Listing 12.6) uses an array to construct an array of digits as images for the lower levels. The makeNumber routine from levget.pl is used here as well to create the IMG tags. The level to display is derived from the QUERY_STRING or POST as in previous listings.

The current level determines the number of digits in the first item in each entry in the data file. The rest of the code simply creates the table and prints out the HTML tags for them.

Listing 12.6: levload.pl

```
#!/usr/local/bin/perl
#File: levload.pl
#
$|=1;
print "Content-type: text/html\n\n";

if ($ENV{'REQUEST_METHOD'} eq "POST") {
    read(STDIN,$buffer,$ENV{'CONTENT_LENGTH'});
} else {
    $buffer = $ENV{'QUERY_STRING'};
}

@pairs= split(/&/,$buffer);
foreach $pair (@pairs) {
    ($name,$value) = split(/=/,$pair);
```

```
$value =~ tr/+/ /;
$value =~ s/%([a-fA-F0-9][a-fA-F0-9])/pack("C",hex($1))/eg;
$contents{$name} = $value;
}


#
# Get the level from the incoming link
#
# if you want to use the environment variable for
# testing you can use: $level = $ENV{'lev'};
$level = $contents{'lev'};

# _____
# Post the page information
# _____
print << "FILEHEAD";
<HTML>
<HEAD>
<title>Level $level</title></head>
<body bgcolor=ffffff><center>
<h2>Almost There</h2></center>
At this point you can view the structure of
Level $level. You can also decide to select the
<img src="/gif/money.gif"> <b>open location</b>
image to join at that location. <p>If you see a
<img src="/gif/letter.gif"> image, it means that the
slot was selected by someone already, and that it is
<b>in-process</b>. When an in-process image becomes
a <img src="/gif/t_up.gif"> that means the person in
that location has sent the application back in,
they are <b>in the downline</b>, and the application
on the way to the parent company.  <p>In a few cases you
will see a <img src="/gif/dynamite2.gif">. These
<b>reserved</b> images mean that there have been
issues with the slot (like a person who sent in a
request to join... from Germany!) and no slots will
be created above it until the issues are settled.
<p>There is the slight possibility that someone
selected a <img src="/gif/money.gif"> for the same
slot you did at the same time you did. In those rare
cases the first to complete the form for the location
and submit it will be rewarded with the slot.
These are <b>very rare cases</b> and if it happens
you should return to this page and issue a browser
"reload" and then attempt the selection again.
<p><hr width=30%><font size=+2>NOTES:</font>
<ul><li>In order to select an item, put your pointer
over the image (generally the <img src="/gif/money.gif">
image) and select.
<li> Complete the form and submit it (completes the
joining
```

process). Please remember to use the submit at the
bottom of the form page

```
<li> Again, if you are told that the slot
is already taken, please return to this page
and use the reload button to refresh the page,
chances are you are using a cached page.
</ul> <p><hr width=30%>
FILEHEAD


$level = $contents{'lev'};

# =========================================
#    You must MODIFY THIS PATH
# =========================================
$fpath="./";

# =========================================
# Read info on each sub-level on this level
# =========================================
$rknt=0;        # loop counter
open(FH,$fpath . "$level.log");
while(<FH>){
$levels[$rknt++] = $_;
}
close FH;

# close another color scheme,.. please
print  "<table bgcolor=teal cellspacing=15> <tr>";
$tencnt=  0;   # table per row counter
$rowcnt=  0;   # row counter
$oparent= 0;   # old parent
$itmcnt=  0;   # loop count variable
$hot=0;

# =========================================
# Process each sub-level on this level
# =========================================
foreach $val (@levels) {

   # =========================================
   # Every 90th item generates a new table.

   # =========================================
if ($tencnt == 89) {
   $tencnt = 0;
   print "</tr></table><table bgcolor=teal
        cellspacing=15><tr>";
   } else {
     $tencnt += 3;
```

```
    }
# ============================================
# Extract level information
# ============================================
($thisLevel,$status,$code)  = split(' ',$val);
$slen = length($thisLevel) - 1;
$parent = substr($thisLevel,0,$slen);

  if ($itmcnt >= 3) {
    $itmcnt = 0;
    print "</tr><tr>";
  }
# ============================================
# Prints level if first time on this row.
# ============================================
  if ($oparent == 0) {
    print "<td>";
    $numimg = &makeNumber($parent);
  }

# ============================================
# Create image array.
# ============================================
  $img[$oparent] = &getimg($status,$parent,$oparent);
  $oparent++;
  if ($oparent >= 3) {
    $itmcnt++;
    # ============================================
    # Print information banner.
    # ============================================
    print
"<center>$numimg<br>$img[0]\n$img[1]\n$img[2]</center></td> ";
    $oparent = 0;
  }
}
print  "</tr></table></body></html>\n";
exit;

# ==================================
# Create a number from before
# ==================================
sub makeNumber {
 my ($num) = @_;
 my $i;
 my $numstr = "";
 foreach $i (split("",$num)) {
    $numstr .= "<img src=\"/gif/nlib/$i.gif\">";
 }
 return $numstr;
}
```

```
# ============================================
Returns an HTML link based on the value of
the incoming $val argument.


_____
val     state       image               link
_____
3       reserved    dynamite2.gif        res.html
0       open        money.gif            reqslot.pl
1       closed      t_up.gif             closed.html
2       in-process letter.gif           taken.html
# ============================================
sub getimg {
my ($val, $par, $tail) = @_;
my $retimg;
if ($val == 3) {
    $retimg = "<a href=\"/res.html\"><img
        src=\"/gif/dynamite2.gif\" alt=Reserved
        border=0></a>";
    } elsif ($val == 0) {
    $retimg = "<a href=\"/cgi-bin/uncgi.cgi/reqslot.pl?id=$par".
      "$tail\"><img src=\"/gif/money.gif\" alt=Open
        border=0></a>";
    } elsif ($val == 1) {
    $retimg = "<a href=\"/closed.html\"><img
        src=\"/gif/t_up.gif\" alt=Taken border=0></a>" ;
    } else {
    $retimg = "<a href=\"/taken.html\"><img
        src=\"/gif/letter.gif\" alt=In-Process
        border=0></a>";
    }
return $retimg;
}
```

The URLs to open slots point to the reqslot.pl applications which prints out the form for us. This reqslot.pl code is simple, since all it does is display the contents of an HTML form and uses the incoming value in "lev" to show where the user will be inserted. The code for the reqslot.pl program is shown in Listing 12.7.

Listing 12.7: reqslot.pl

```
#!/usr/local/bin/perl
# File: reqslot.pl
$| = 1;
printf "Content-type: text/html\n\n";
```

```perl
if ($ENV{'REQUEST_METHOD'} eq "POST") {
    read(STDIN,$buffer,$ENV{'CONTENT_LENGTH'});
} else {
    $buffer = $ENV{'QUERY_STRING'};
}

@pairs= split(/&/,$buffer);
foreach $pair (@pairs) {
    ($name,$value) = split(/=/,$pair);
    $value =~ tr/+/ /;
    $value =~ s/%([a-fA-F0-9][a-fA-F0-9])/pack("C",hex($1))/eg;
    $contents{$name} = $value;
    }

$id = $contents{'id'};
## =======================================================
## The only passed data that we care about is the
## slot ID.
## =======================================================
## Put the form up.
##
print << "PAGEINFO";
<html>
<head>
<title>Selected location number $id</title>
</head>

<body bgcolor=ffffff>
<center><h2>One last thing for you to do here</h2></center>
You have requested to join the COMPANY. <b>Welcome aboard</b>.
Below this text is a form that asks you the minimal
amount of information we need to get the information
you will need to join on its way to you.<p>
Please note that it is <b>very</b> minimal. We need
your name and mailing address so we can get the mail
to you. We ask for an e-mail address so we can let
you know when it was mailed, and when we expect it
back. We don't want your phone number (with one
exception), your age, your gender, religion, etc.
Like I said, we kept it minimal.
<p>
If you are already a COMPANY member, you can use
this form to add people to the downline. Make sure
that you complete the last section before submitting
the form. If you are submitting this for yourself,
please leave the last section blank.
<p><hr>
<center> <h3>Joining the COMPANY form</h3></center>
<FORM METHOD=POST ACTION="/jmi-bin/uncgi.cgi/join.pl">
<input type=hidden name=location value=$id>

<table>
```

```
<tr><td>Your Name:</td><td><input name=name
type=text></td></tr>
<tr><td>Street Address:</td><td><input name=street
type=text></td></tr>
<tr><td>Suite or Apt:</td><td><input name=apt
type=text></td></tr>
<tr><td>City:</td><td><input name=city
type=text></td></tr>
<tr><tputs "<tr><td>State (2 letter
code):</td><td><input name=st type=text
size=2></td></tr><tr><td>Zip (+4 if possible)
:</td><td><input name=zip type=text></td></tr>
<tr><td>Country:</td><td><select name=cntry size=3>
<option selected>US
<option>Canada
<option>Not Listed
</select>
</td></tr>
<tr><td>E-mail:</td><td><input name=email1
type=text></td></tr>
<tr><td>Secondary E-mail:</td><td><input name=email2
type=text></td></tr>
<tr><td colspan=2><h2>This section must be
completed</h2><table><tr><td>Standard (the way we
recommend)</td><td><input name=ot value=a32
type=radio selected></td></tr><tr><td>Non-Standard (A
bit pricier, not a recommendation)</td><td><input
name=ot value=p92 type=radio></td></tr><tr><td>(Phone
Number is optional) </td><td>Phone: <input
name=mlm-phone type=text></table></td></tr>
</table>
<p> <hr><font color=blue><b>This information is only
filled out if you are a COMPANY member and are
submitting this for someone
else.</b></font><p><table><tr><td width=50%>Do you
want COMPANY to send the application package, or do
you want to handle the application information and
send the completed application to
COMPANY</td><td><table><tr><td>COMPANY should do
it.</td><td><input name=doit value=COMPANY
type=radio></td></tr><tr><td>I'll take care of
it.</td><td><input name=doit value=Member
type=radio></td></tr></table></tr><tr><td>My COMPANY
ID is:</td><td><input name=doit-id
type=text></td></tr></table><hr>
<p>
To submit, press the <inPUT TYPE=submit VALUE=submit>
button.
</form>
<hr>
</body></html>
PAGEINFO
```

The reqslot.pl file, in turn, calls the join.pl source file. The code in the join.pl file (Listing 12.8) simply collects and validates the FORM information collected in the reqslot.pl file and writes it to disk. If there are any errors, the outerr function is called to display an error message back to the user and the entry is not processed. Items are written to disk only when all the entries are valid. The format of data on disk is in the same way as with the Tcl code.

Listing 12.8: join.pl

```perl
#!/usr/local/bin/perl
# File join.pl
#
$| = 1;
print "Content-type: text/html\n\n";
# =========================================
# Handling POST queries from the FORM.
# =========================================
# The following lines of code are used to collect
# data from the standard input. The length of the
# standard input is in the environment variable
# CONTENT_LENGTH.
#
if ($ENV{'REQUEST_METHOD'} eq "POST") {
    read(STDIN,$buffer,$ENV{'CONTENT_LENGTH'});
} else {
    $buffer = $ENV{'QUERY_STRING'};
}
@pairs= split(/&/,$buffer);
foreach $pair (@pairs) {
    my ($name,$value) = split(/=/,$pair);
    $value =~ tr/+/ /;
    $value =~ s/%([a-fA-F0-9][a-fA-F0-
9])/pack("C",hex($1))/eg;
    $contents{$name} = $value;
    }


# =================================================
## Comments verbatim from join.tcl file.
# =================================================
## expected values:
## name = name of individual (Required)
## street = street address (Required)
## apt = address second line (Optional)
## city = city (Required)
## st = state (Required)
## zip = zipcode (Required)
## cntry = country (US/Canada/other) (Required)
```

```
##  email1 = main e-mail (Required)
##  email2 = secondary email (Optional)
##  location = the location they selected (Required)
##  mlm-phone = (Optional)
##  ot = order type (a32 or p92) (Required)
#

#  ===================================================
##  Error handling subroutine
#  ===================================================

sub outerr {
    my ($code,$data) = @_;
print << "ERRMSG";
<html>
<title>Error encountered</title><center>
<h1>Error Encountered: $code</h1></center>
An error of type $code was encountered. This means
that the form was not completed and processing has
stopped. Here is what I, the stupid computer, think
caused the error:
ERRMSG

my ($item1,$item2) = split(' ',$data);
if ($code eq "ID-BFD") {
print "Input Data: Bad Field Data: $item1=$item2";
}
if ($code eq "ID-MFD") {
print "Input Data: Missing Field Data: $data is
required";
}
if ($code eq "UL_LNA") {
print "Updating Location: Location Not Available:
Location taken on: $item1";
}
print '\n</body></html>';
exit 0;
}
#  ===================================================
#  start the processing and reply with HTML text
#  ===================================================
print << "HTMLHEAD";
Content-type: text/HTML\n
<title>Associate Location to Individual Response
Status</title>
<body bgcolor=ffffff>
HTMLHEAD


#  ===================================================
#  process the do-it variable
#  ===================================================
```

```
$recend = "~~~";
if ($contents{'doit'} ne "") {
   $recend = "~~$contents{'doit'}";
      if ($contents{'doit-id'} ne "") {
         $recend = "~~$contents{'doit'}~$contents{'doit-id'}";
      if (length($contents{'doit-id'}) < 1) {
print << "REMIND";
<hr><b>Special note:</b> Next time you enter one
of these you may want to include your ID number so
we know who added the person. Not that we are
keeping count, but if you say that you taking care
of the form submission to us it does help to know
who you are. Thanks.<hr><p>
REMIND
      }
      }
}


# ==================================================
# Error checking section
# ==================================================
# The required fields are:
# name~street~city~st~zip~cntry~email1~location~ot
#
# If we want we could force a phone entry. In this
# case we will include the code to do that even
# though there is no need to.
#
# If ot = mlm then mlm-phone is required
# name~street~apt~city~st~zip~cntry~email1~email2~
# location~mlm-phone~ot
# ==================================================
# lists and constants used in this program
# ==================================================
$dstamp = `date +%y%m%d`;
$thanksfile = "./thanks.txt";
$levellog = "./level.log";
$pathtolog = "./";
$reqlog = "./req.log";
@vlist=("name", "street","city","st",
      "zip","cntry","email1","location","ot");
@vnames=("apt","cntry", "email2", "mlm-phone");


# ==================================================
# Check for, and bail out if any, empty fields
# ==================================================
foreach $vname (@vlist) {
   if ($contents{$vname} eq "" ) {
   &outerr("ID-MFD",$vname);
```

```
    }
}

# =================================================
# process special case of "mlm"
# =================================================
if ($contents{'ot'} eq "mlm") {
    if ($contents{'ot'} eq "" ) {
      &outerr("ID-MFD","Order Type MLM  changes the
        Phone Number to - ");
    }
    if (length($contents{'ot'}) < 7 ) {
      &outerr("ID-MFD","Order Type MLM  changes the
        Phone Number to - ");
    }
}
# =================================================
#            Set to default string
# =================================================
foreach $vname   (@vnames) {
    if ($contents{$vname} eq "" ) {
        $contents{$vname} = 'tnibni';
    }
}
# =================================================
# All error checking has been validated.
# =================================================

# =================================================
# Write the formatted data record.
# =================================================
$outstr = "$contents{'name'}~$contents{'street'}~
    $contents{'apt'}";
$outstr .= "~$contents{'city'}~$contents{'st'}~
    $contents{'zip'}";
$outstr .= "~$contents{'cntry'}~$contents{'email1'}~
    $contents{'email2'}~";
$outstr .= "$contents{'location'}~$contents
    {'mlm-phone'}~$contents{'ot'}$recend";
# =================================================
# okay, what level do we write this to?
# =================================================
$loc = $contents{'location'};
$lev = length($location) - 1;
# =================================================
# open the level file, load the database
# looking for the location and ensure it is open.
# =================================================
my @sorted = ();
my $sortCount = 0;
open(FL,$levellog);
```

```perl
while($input = <FL>) {
    my ($ilev,$icode,$imsg) = split(" ",$input);
    if ($ilev == $loc) {
        if ($icode != 0) {
          &outerr("UL-LNA",$imsg);
            } else {
        $sorted[$sortCount++] = $loc . " 2 " . $dstamp;
        }
    } else {
    $sorted[$sortCount++] = $input;
    }
}
close(FL);


# =================================================
# If so change the state, add it to the element
# list, rewrite it # back out sorted. If not,
# generate an error and exit
# =================================================
open(FL,">$levellog");
foreach (sort @sorted) {
    print FL $_;
}
close(FL);


# =================================================
# we have updated the old level file, now we have to
# create the new entries in the next level file.
# increment the level and append the new records to
# the new level file
# =================================================
$lev++;
open (FLEVEL,">>$pathtolog". $lev. "log");  # append
print FLEVEL "$loc" . "1 0\n";
print FLEVEL "$loc" . "2 0\n";
print FLEVEL "$loc" . "1 0\n";
close FLEVEL;
# =================================================
# we have updated all the level files, we have
# validated all the user input, now update the file
# we store the user data entries in with the new
# record
# =================================================
open (REQ,">>$reqlog");
print REQ "$loc $outstr $dstamp \n";
close REQ;
# =====================================================
# now, did we create entries on a new level? If so
# we have to update the level.log file.
# =====================================================
open(FL,">>$levellog");
```

```perl
print FL $val;
close FL;
# ========================================================
# sort and eliminate duplicates from the level.log
# Use the UNIX sort and mv routines to do this for us
# ========================================================
`sort -u $levellog ./tmp/t_sort`;
`mv ./tmp/t_sort $levellog`;
# ========================================================
# Give the user the message.
# build the success message for the customer and let
# them know that we are done.
# ========================================================
print << "MESSAGE";
<center><h1>Congratulations!</h1></center>
Welcome to the start of what we all hope will be a
happy and a positive long term relationship. Your
Identifier is below. Please make sure that you
provide that on any and all correspondence that you
have with us as this is the number we use to track
your position. Your packet of information should be
in your hands soon.
 <p> Your Identifier number
is:<br><center><font color=green
size=+5>$loc</font><p></center>
The input recorded is:<font size=+2 color=lime> <center><br>
Name and address:<br> $contents{'name'}<br>
$contents{'street'}<br>
</font>(second address line not carried forward to
this screen)
<font size=+2 color=lime><br>$contents{'city'}
$contents{'st'}
$contents{'zip'}<br>E-mail(1'}:
$contents{'email1'}</font></center>
MESSAGE

# ========================================================
# Give the user the message via email if necessary
# ========================================================
if ($contents{'email1'} ne "") {
    my $msub = "Autoprocessed e-mail from us to you ";
    my $frmname = 'our-email@domain.com (our company name)';
    my $a = $contents{'email1'};
    $a =~ s/\;|\[|\]|\||\<|\>//;
    open (MAIL, "|/usr/lib/sendmail -t");
    print MAIL "From: $frmname\n";
    print MAIL "To: $a\n";
    print MAIL "Subject: $msub\n";
    my $thanks=`cat $thanksfile`;
    print MAIL $thanks;
    close MAIL;
}
```

There you have them (four Perl listings that match their Tcl cousins' functionality to implement a network marketing handler.

Summary

This completes the chapter about developing an integrated application. In this application we used techniques that we covered in other chapters; namely, data files to generate tables, SSIs to generate tables from the data files, forms built on the fly, error processing and sending confirmation E-mail using sendmail, to create an integrated single application that performs a specific function.

The application chosen was one that allowed us to integrate the entire process using as many of the techniques already presented as possible. It is hoped that this chapter showed how to take portions of the programs we have used in this book to build entirely new applications.

The next few chapters will focus on building intranets, but it is important to remember that the only difference between an intranet and the Internet is the level of security concerns over data. And even then, those issues might not change all that much if you are not working with confidential employee data. The next chapter will continue to build display data with tables, but we will also touch on image maps and show how you can process image map data from within a CGI, as well as some detailed uses for regular expression processing as we search an employee white pages.

CHAPTER 13 INTRANETS: COMPANY WHITE PAGES

- Adding Data to Data Files Via Forms

- Performing Joins in Flat Data Files

- Creating Table-based Forms on the Fly

There are certain things that can be done on an intranet system that you would not attempt to do on the Internet. The key difference between an intranet and an Internet application lies in data *access* and *integrity*. Who has access to what data, and the value of that data to the enterprise.

In the first program we will look at, involving an intranet, we will be dissecting a complex phone book application that integrates data files from a number of sources. The user interface will be both via an image map and a search form. This will provide a total office directory, but more than that, by integrating this information into an in/out database we add greater value to the data. We also create an application that you most likely wouldn't want the world to have access to.

Included in this application is a form that allows portions of the data files to be updated. This form will be built on the fly when it is requested from data that resides in both the employee database as well as an administrative database.

The second Intranet application (provided in Chapter 14) allows disk space to be monitored on an HP system. This system keeps a historical record of every mounted disk on the system and uses a crontab to extract the data to a data file. Another program within the application is used to read the data and display tables to the users on request.

> **Note** The term **mung**, which means to change a value through adding, deleting or replacing portions of the normal value, is used quite a bit in this chapter. I first heard the term when I started getting into e-mail services. The phrase **mung the header** means that we are going to change some of the e-mail header data to hide a user's machine (now formally called **masquerading**) or to modify the return address. In this chapter, we will be munging the first and last name values of the data to create unique keys for other searches.

The Office Directory

This, the first of the two chapters on Intranet applications, will focus on a full featured office directory. The customer need is simple, they want to be able to access the data from either a map of the office (clicking on an office or an area of the map and finding out who or what that area is assigned to), or from a search form that allows first and last name searches. They also want to know specific information about the person when they click on that office or perform that search.

The employee information requested for a selection is the following:

- First and last name
- Phone/extension number
- Department
- E-mail

- Status (In/Out: if Out, then why?)
- Photo of the employee if available

In addition, there needs to be a way for an administrator to change the In/Out status of employees without having to manually edit the database by hand. The tool for doing this should also allow the administrator to see the phone book record of an employee, without having to access two applications at the same time.

In this case, the customer has asked for three programs in one. The first request is for a program that shows an image map and allows the user to get an area's description by clicking it or, if an *assigned* office, shows the same information that a phone book application returns on the user of that office. The second request is for a corporate phone book system that performs searches based on the user's first or last name. The final program is an administrative tool that permits update of *In/Out* database information. This tool should be a single entry form for all updating. It should also have links to the individual's information from that page (in the same format as the phone book system).

The first two programs in this application are actually the same piece of code with multiple paths. In other words, both programs exist in the same code. Here, we will refer to the first path (which handles image mapping) as *image map* and the second path (which handles name searching) as *search processor.*

Essentially, the customer would like information to be returned to a user when querying a database by either clicking on an office location within the image map or by entering the appropriate data within a search form. The returned data should be the same in both cases. The following is a simplified list of the data managed by the programs:

- First Name
- Last Name
- Phone/extension
- Department
- E-mail address
- In/Out Status
- Image of the individual

In addition, the image map should provide information about assigned rooms (not just offices and individuals). For instance, when a room is selected in the image map that is not an individuals office, the program must have the ability to state the purpose of the room selected. This shouldn't be necessary to hallways and such, only if the selection is an assigned room or space with a purpose, like a fire exit and stairwell.

Also an error message should be returned if an non-assigned location is selected (not one defined by the customer, but a default of the image map process).

Therefore, the requirements for the three programs are as follows:

Program 1: *Display selection from an Image Map*

- Allows any area to be selected
- Offices show all information about the employee assigned to that office including photo (if available), full name, department, phone extension, E-mail address, and In/Out status.
- The default In/Out status shall be In
- If the user is not in, then one of the codes/purposes from Table 13.1 will be used

Table 13.1: In/Out status

Code	Purpose	Explanation
V	Vacation	A prerequested vacation day
S	Sick	An unscheduled day out for personal illness
P	Personal	A day out for any other personal reason
C	Comp	A day off to compensate for pre-defined reasons
E	Education	A conference or educational reason for being out
T	Travel	Representing the business while traveling
J	Jury	Jury Duty. A right and a privilege
O	Offsite	Working, but not on the company premises
Out	Out without stated reason	Missing In Action

- Assigned space, but non-office, provides descriptive paragraphs of the space
- Unassigned space provides a standard error message and appropriate help text

Program 2: *Display a form (Search Processor)*

- The form allows a regular expression to be entered and searched on
- The form allows either first or last name searches
- The display of information from the search matches that of the room selection as in the image map program requirements above
- The display lists an error message if no match
- The match displays all possible matches based on the search criteria

Program 3: *Display a protected/hidden form (administrative tool)*

- The form is built by extracting the employee data from the data file
- The form uses the current In/Out state of the individual employee as the base state for that employee
- Any employee's state is changed by the form user
- Any employee record is accessed by clicking on the employee name field of the employee
- All changes to the form are submitted with a single submission
- All changes made to the state data file are echoed to the form user

HTML/Data File Design

Once again we will be using data files to maintain and control access to data. And yet once again, these programs could all be rewritten to make all the reads and writes from the data files to databases. In addition, in this chapter we are going to move away from straight CGI discussions to include a focus on an HTML feature, imagemaps. We will also discuss some readability issues in creating forms, imagemaps and table display output.

Program 1: ImageMap

This section will delve into an issue not discussed anywhere else in this text. Since imagemaps are not covered anywhere else in this chapter, it will be discussed here using the example from the requirements. Imagemaps and the map files have little to do with the HTTP standard, but they *do* have a great deal to do with the HTML, as they are defined in the 2.0, 3.0 and 3.2 standards. Because the customer requested an image map, there are a number of issues that come up. Imagemap *map* files must conform to the standard established by your the HTTPd server. In addition, there is the issue of whether you want to run the image map services in a client-based or a server-based model.

Originally a Netscapism, client side imagemaps allow the imagemap data to be passed to the client where the client will determine if an item was selected (based on the geometry of the selection/mouse-action) and where that selection should go based on the data in the selection. There is some overhead involved when loading that data to the client, especially if the client doesn't make use of that data.

Server side imagemaps leave all the selection information on the server. A user selection on the client will generate a GET request to the server passing in the X/Y coordinates for the selected location within the imagemap. The server will then query the imagemap map file for the image displayed to the user. Using the data from within this map file the server will send the new data to the browser. The disadvantage to this method is that it takes a connection to the server and requires the dislocation of the map file from the image placement.

Using the requirements stated above, the HTML is just a single image map that will be a picture/drawing of the office. A tool will be used to edit the image file to create the required map file. There are a number of tools available in the marketplace that permit imagemap map file creation. In addition you could create these files by hand using tools that provide the X/Y coordinates of points on the images you wish to map.

In creation of an office imagemap there is a need to establish a key piece of data that won't change. In many cases (and in our example here), there is an office number that won't generally move (facilities people like it that way). Therefore, you can usually use the office numbering scheme from facilities to assign a unique identifier to a location on the map. In the office that we will be modeling, the facilities people have also assigned a phone number. By assigning a phone number to an assigned office, rather than to an individual, we can create a simple key that links the disjoint data of office numbers and individuals together via the common reference of the phone number. In database terms, this link is referred to as a *join*.

The HTML to display an imagemap would look like this:

```
<title>Office Map - Glenbrook Campus</title>
<center><h1>My Company<br>Glenbrook Campus</h1></center>
To use this map, place the pointer over the office
you want information about and select it.
<p><hr><p>
<a href="/cgi-bin/imagemap/map/glencamp.map">
<img src="/gif/glen-camp.gif" ismap></a>
<p><hr><p>
[Standard copyright information goes here]
```

In this HTML, the program being called is /cgi-bin/imagemap (a program supplied with the NCSA HTTPd to support the use of imagemaps). The balance of the hyperlink is the path to the data file that supplies the map coordinates so that the pointer selection on items in the image map will work (referred to above as the "map" file). The image information also uses the ismap qualifier so it will return the X and Y coordinates of a mouse click when activated. That data will then be sent to the program /cgi-bin/imagemap along with the path information for the map database.

The map database that follows was written using the NCSA format. This format is designed to work with the /cgi-bin/imagemap executable that is provided by NCSA on the NCSA HTTPd server.

The following map file is a sample that was created using one of the more popular mapfile creation tools available in the public/shareware domain.

```
#$- This image map data file was created using a tool
#$- created by Todd C. Wilson called Map This
#$- This tool, which runs on PCs is highly
#$- recommended for use in developing the map files.
default /map/glen-def.html
# Office 30
rect /cgi-bin/uncgi/getpg.tcl?rm=30 0,10 44,56
# office 31
rect /cgi-bin/uncgi/getpg.tcl?rm=31 44,12 84,60
# Office 32
rect /cgi-bin/uncgi/getpg.tcl?rm=32 86,12 124,58
# Office 33
```

```
rect /cgi-bin/uncgi/getpg.tcl?rm=33 126,12 160,60
# Office 36a
poly /cgi-bin/uncgi/getpg.tcl?rm=36a 240,12 244,54
268,54 270,44 256,22 ( 256,12 242,10 240,12
```

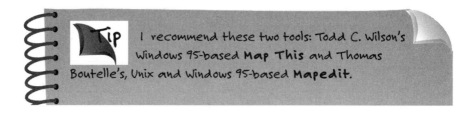

Tip I recommend these two tools: Todd C. Wilson's Windows 95-based **Map This** and Thomas Boutelle's, Unix and Windows 95-based **Mapedit**.

The format of the map file is:

- A # in the first column is a comment line
- The default file to show when something is clicked on is generally put in the first line
- Each item thereafter is a definition of a region that can be selected

There are four different region definitions. These are defined in Table 13.2.

Table 13.2: Region Definitions

Region	Definition
rect	The most common of all region definitions. In this case, a rectangle area is selected by identifying two opposing corner points.
Point	A single selectable point within the image map
circ	A circle is defined by the center point of the circle and either a radius or a single point on the circle's edge (this depends on which "format" your server uses).
poly	A polygon allows you to define the points that make up a line that will enclose a defined area. Generally that includes a start point at least one mid point and an end point. The system will create a virtual line from that end point to the start point. Try not to make a straight line; they don't generally encircle areas.

The format of the map data file can differ based on the server type. These two lines will produce exactly the same results, but the first one runs on NCSA's server and the second is used by CERNs.

```
rect /cgi-bin/uncgi/getpg.tcl?rm=32 86,12 124,58

rect (86,12) (124,58) /cgi-bin/uncgi/getpg.tcl?rm=32
```

Please note that the actions taken from within this file are to run a CGI procedure. That is what we will want to do when an office is selected. As the default item shows in our map data file, you could also choose to display a page.

In fact, the map file will allow any acceptable URI to be used for any valid recognized protocol. This permits the map data file to use the map to call a mailto: or an ftp: if that is the protocol you wish to use when an item is selected within the image map.

This has more to do with generic HTML issues than the specifics of this design. Therefore, it is important to be aware that there are changes in the HTML 3.2 specifications that will change how most people do this process. There are two factors effecting this. The first is the current support from both Microsoft and Netscape on the use of client-side imagemaps. The second is the ever-expanding need to see if a *fat client* and *fat server* can work together.

This poses an interesting question: If a user comes to a site where the images are turned off, why is the site still downloading imagemap information in between the <map name=mapname> and </map> tags? I don't have the answer to that, and that is part of the overhead that I discussed earlier when client-side imagemapping was first mentioned. If client-side imagemapping is to be used, the format to use for the image of the office layout, in a client-side map file is:

```
<title>Office Map - Glenbrook Campus</title>
<center><h1>My Company<br>Glenbrook Campus</h1></center>
To use this map, place the pointer over the office
you want information about and select it.
<p><hr><p>
<IMG SRC="/gif/glen-camp.gif " USEMAP="#mname">
<p><hr><p>
[Standard copyright information goes here]
<map name=mname>
<AREA SHAPE="RECT" COORDS="32, 86, 124, 58"
( HREF="/cgi-bin/uncgi/getpg.tcl?rm=32">
<—!continue until each area has been defined —>
```

```
<AREA SHAPE="RECT" COORDS="0, 0, 152, 242"
HREF="/map/glen-def.html">
</map>
```

> **Note** Client-side image maps only support the rect, poly and circle. Point is not supported. If no default is defined in a client-side imagemap, the default process is to do nothing and no special CGIs are required. If a default is to be used, define the default at the end rather than at the beginning, and define it as the entire image map. That way, if the click drops through all the possible selections, it will run the default.

In closing the image map issue, this type of processing will get even more complex as the HTTP specifications expand. The original HTTP 3.0 specification was dropped because it tried to do too many things for too many people, as stated in http://www.w3.org/pub/WWW/MarkUp/Wilbur/

WHAT HAPPENED TO HTML 3.0?

HTML 3.0 was a proposal for extending HTML published in March 1995. The Arena browser was a testbed implementation, and a few other experimental implementations have been developed (see: the Yahoo list of browsers, including UdiWWW, Emacs-W3, etc.).

However, the difference between HTML 2.0 and HTML 3.0 was so large that standardization and deployment of the whole proposal proved unwieldy. The HTML 3.0 draft has expired, and is not being maintained.

As it stands now, expect the introduction of the new 3.0 <fig> tag to make it into the next round of specifications. Once that happens, the client-side image maps will go away as more people use the <fig> capability. This will be done, not because there was anything wrong with the client-side implementation, but because the <fig> tag adds a tremendous amount of flexibility to what can and cannot be done with any figure, or portions of it.

And now back to the program we are working on . . .

Every office or room in this model is assigned a unique identifier. These identifiers are used to create linkages between multiple data files (the relational joins I mentioned before). In the book we work with the lowest common denominator, flat files. Consequently, the implementation is a bit different than a simple SQL statement to join two databases on a common field. Linkages between facilities room-IDs and the phone numbers, or key identifiers like a room-name if there is no phone associated to the room, are created and maintained in one data file. Linkages between the phone number and individuals are defined in another data file.

A search on the first data file will provide us with a linkage to the second data file across the phone number join, thereby providing the user data sought by the program. Also, if the item is an invalid room-ID, it must be a key identifier. That means that there is no employee linkage, but there should be an HTML file somewhere that can be pulled up and displayed to the user.

In Figure 13.1 there is a sample office (this image was provided by Andy Miller of Information Management Associates, Inc. Shelton, CT). This image is selectable. If a user were to select the area by the

Figure 13.1: *Image of the office map in Netscape Navigator*

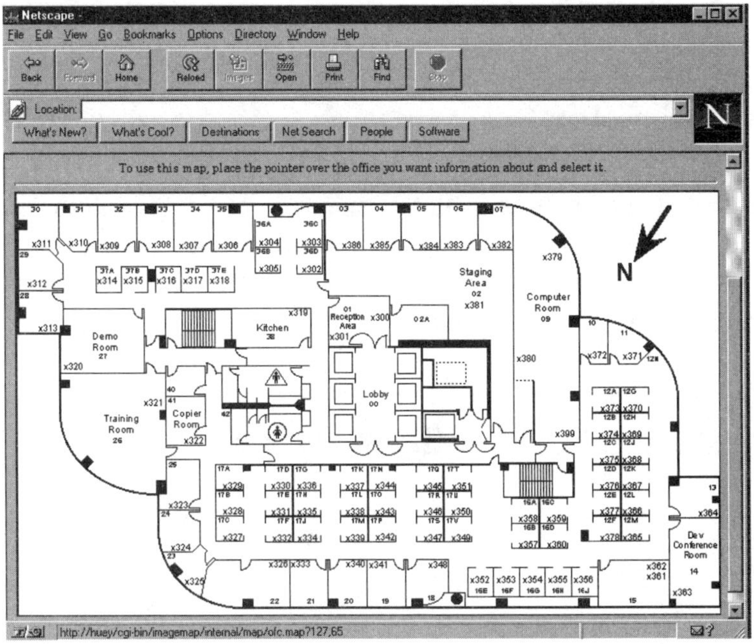

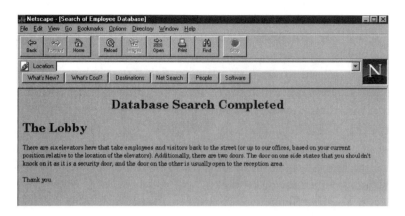

Figure 13.2: *Room description using Netscape Navigator*

elevators the text in Figure 13.2 would be displayed. While the area by the elevators is not a valid assigned location (much like fire stairwells and bathrooms aren't), these locations should display some valid information back to the user when they are selected. That is the reason why key identifiers are supported.

The way selection is determined is via the imagemap map data file. Within this file, as we have shown above, are the actions that each selection will take. In the case of both the assigned and the non-assigned area being selected, the selection of that portion of the image map calls the process that is used to obtain the user information passing in the room-ID or as in the example above, the key identifier from the selection.

Remember: the program that is called in the image map selection process is the *search processor* with an additional special section of code to go through to process the imagemap information. Let's take a look at the core of the program now.

Program 2: The Search Processor

Let's begin by recapping the three data files that have been defined thus far.

- A file for mapping the image map to actions taken upon selection (the imagemap map file)
- A file that contains unique room-IDs for every office, each of which has an assigned telephone extension (the *join* data file)
- A file that contains information on individuals (the *user* data file)

The search processor uses additional data files. To obtain e-mail addresses, we will use the data file maintained by Unix systems called *aliases*. Photographs can all be stored in a directory using a naming convention of lastname_first-initial.gif, which ensures that photo images file name will be unique in most circumstances. In a worst case scenario, this information could also be maintained in one of the data files.

If the company is too large (say, 5,000 employees at a single location), it may have a problem with the simple naming convention described above. In that case, the prudent thing to do would be for the company to assign a unique identifier to an employee when hired and use that identifier in the filename of the image.

> **Note** In some companies, that information is the social security number of the employee. If that is the case with your company, you might want to consider creating another system. The social security administration frowns on using that number for identification purposes. Additionally, many individuals dislike having that piece of information available to those who don't have a **need** to know.

Looking at each data file individually, there are some distinct formats that have to be supported and some simple ones we can create ourselves. The data files used in this process are shown in Table 13.3. The $dbpath is used to show that the files path is variable.

The fields for these files are shown in Tables 13.4 through 13.7.

Table 13.3: Files used by the display process

File	Description
$dbpath/rm2num.db	The data file that will provide facilities room-id to extension information
$dbpath/elist.db	The data file that provides employee information
/usr/lib/aliases	The file that will provide e-mail information
$dbpath/absent.db	The data file that provides the "out" information in the In/Out data field

Table 13.4: rm2num.db (field separator is a space)

room-id	The room number associated with the map file
phone-extension/key-id	The phone extension number or a special keyword identifier (ex: Copy for the copy room)

Table 13.5: elist.db (field separator is a tilde)

name	The employee's name in the format "last-name first-name"
extension/phone	An extension, voice mail, or phone number
department	The name of the employee's department.

Table 13.6: aliases (field separator is a space)

aliasname	The name that the employee is known by for e-mail (the alias)
email-address	The full e-mail specification for that alias

name	The employee's last-name and first-name compacted together into a single value
status-flag	A valid status flag for why the employee is in the Out column

Associations between the data files are:

rm2num.db - elist.db: The second field or rm2num and the second field of elist.db are common and associates the record in elist.db to the facilities room-id from rm2num

elist.db - aliases: Using standard naming conventions for e-mail addresses (in the example given we will use Last-nameFirst-initial), the first field of the elist.db can be split into its two portions (last-name first-name) and then be recombined into the e-mail standard. Then all aliases will be searched in the database and, if the key matches for the alias, the value before the "@" sign in the second field will be kept as a valid e-mail.

elist.db - absent.db: The absent.db format is a compression of the user's last-name and the first-name, and all lowercase. Again, the data from the first field in elist.db will be munged to match the format of the first field of the absent.db.

One last area of concern is the photo/images. As mentioned before, there could be a fourth field added to the elist.db file that contained a unique identifier for the employee. Then the image could be stored in a *image gallery* using the unique identifier for the image.

 **Note** An image gallery is a single location where image files can be stored. This allows the entire image gallery to be moved from one physical location to another using the Unix tar command on the entire directory, and allows a symbolic link to replace the directory in the path. This permits the image gallery to be located on a any mounted partition of the drive.

The other option, as used in the example, is to create a unique identifier. In this case, we have used the lastname_firstinitial.

This, too, can be munged from the data in the first field of the elist.db data file.

In terms of HTML design for the second program, use a very simple form. The form takes in data based on the first or last name of the user (selection by radio button, default = last name) and allows for complex searches of the database by supporting regular expressions (regex).

```
<TITLE>Corporate White Pages </TITLE>
<center> <h1>Corporate White Pages - Search
Processor" </h1> </center>
This page provides a way to search the Corporate
Employee database for an employee by either first or
last name.
<p>
To search enter a few characters of the name (for
instance "smi" for "smith"). All searches start at
the beginning of the first/last name (See Complex
Searching below to see how to change this behavior)
and all entries will be "wildcarded" by default.
Searches are <b>NOT</b> case sensitive.
<p><hr><p>
<FORM METHOD="POST" ACTION="/cgi-
bin/uncgi/getpg.tcl">
  Search by (<input name=sflflag type=radio value="last"
checked> Last <input name=sflfl
ag type=radio value="first"> First) Name: <input
name=sfield type=text>  [CL:  in printing, note
"sflflag" cannot be divided.
<p>
To submit, press this button: <inPUT TYPE="submit"
VALUE="Submit">
</form>
<p><hr><p>
<h2>Complex Searching</h2>
The search method being used is called <b>regex</b>
or regular expression. This is one of the two stan-
dard forms of doing searches in Unix (the other is
called "glob"). This method allows for complex
searching algorithms. It is not necessary to use
these, but they are available. One key thing that
you may want to do is "limit the wildcarding." That
can be accomplished by placing a "$" at the end of
the search string or. Special characters like this
within the search allow you to further define or
limit the search.
```

```
<p>
For instance, if a search is "smi" and you want to
get "smith," don't do anything. If the search is for
"smith" and you don't want to get "smithers," enter
the search as "smith$." Searches like this can get
real complex.
<p>
For a complex search, say all people with only two
character last names, you could use [a-z].$  - the
[a-z] construct tells the system that the name can
start with a character, and the "." after the "]"
says that you want an addition item that meets the
same criteria. As we stated before, the "$" says
that the search should not allow anything after the
two characters. If you wanted to, you could add an
additional "." for each additional character you
want added to the search. Obviously, to get a dump
of the database, just enter [a-z] without the "$".
<hr>
<-!  [Standard copyright information goes here] ->
```

The requirements for a response were a touch vague on format and style, but as you can see, there was a clear definition of three basic blocks of data:

1. Show the picture

2. Then the name, department, and phone information

3. And, finally, the e-mail and In/Out information

The In/Out data should put out the full text, not some cryptic flag or value. So, to meet this requirement, the response should break down into the field format shown in Figures 13.3 and 13.4.

Figure 13.3: *Basic alignment of the data return display*

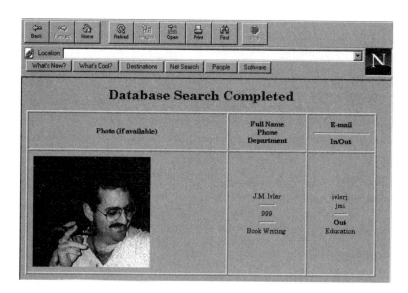

Figure 13.4: Screen snapshot of data return display

Program 3: Administrative Tool

This program will use the information from both the elist.db file (to obtain a complete list of all employees) and the absent.db file (to mark their current status). There is no HTML form to display because the form will be generated by the CGI script and uses the database to implement the size and format of the page.

In this case, the requirements are simple and, in their simplicity, will most likely be the undoing of successful software development. The customer wants an easy way of getting the information on who is in or out of the office into the system so it can be displayed when the users tools are used to obtain information on the office or employee. There is a requirement that this tool should be easy to use as it will most likely be used by administrative people, not programmers, to maintain a live data file.

As this data file is live, the form should be simple enough to use so that a user can locate an employee and just enter the employees in/out status in by the employees name. In addition, it would be great if the tool allowed a number of updates to be made to the form, and then processed them all at once.

Finally, we want to be able to allow someone the ability to access the employee record from the screen that they are on. They shouldn't have to swap back and forth between windows and screens just to validate the individuals record that they are working with.

To make this simple to use, the form will be generated with blocks of 10 users in a table, with each user getting one line in the table. The line will have the user's name and then a series of radio buttons with the "absent" code next to it. Since that code system isn't easy to use, between each block of 10 names there will be a simple table that associates the codes with the text values (a legend).

At the bottom of the form, there will be a single *submit* button. Once the data has been submitted, it will echo back any changes that were made to the data file so the user can confirm the results.

Tcl Design Issues, Programs 1 and 2: getpg.tcl

We have included both the image map program and the search processor program in one piece of code with split paths. This allows for code reuse and keeps the software that is common to both programs in a single file.

This program is going to look for only two environment variables from the uncgi process. In this case it's an either/or, as in if one is used the other will not be used. The variables that we want are going to be defined by the calling procedures. If the call is coming from the image map, it will return with an environment variable through uncgi that will be WWW_rm. If the variable is undefined, the call to the procedure must have come from a non-imagemap processor. In that case the variables WWW_sfield and WWW_sflflag will be returned.

This allows the CGI to make a quick decision on what path top follow within the code. First off, if the data returned shows that the selection is coming from the image map, we have to open the rm2num file and obtain the search key (the num) for that rm value. If we have a rm value, we also know that there should only be one record to locate with the value. (Assumption: there is only one phone per person—made when the phone was determined to be a unique key.) Additionally, if this is a map and the rm value returned a num that was a non-numeric, we know that we have an HTML file that should be output for the room as it wasn't an office. That check can be made with a regex that looks like this:

```
if { ![regexp {^[0-9]+$} $sfield] } {
}
```

This ensures that any value that doesn't start off with a digit as the first character of the field is not a valid extension (this will have to be within an if statement that only processes map type requests).

Additional design issues that are unique to this program deal with manipulating the key field. This field is the name field.

The name field is stored in a record from elist.db that looks like:

```
lastname firstname   ~ext        ~dept
```

And a possible record would look like:

```
Adams  Dilbert  ~911      ~ISDN
```

Now the data from this record will have to be manipulated to be the key search value for accessing the other data files. To access the aliases and absent.db data files, the name portion will have to be extracted into two chunks. To do this, the record will be parsed as follows:

```
set fname [string trim [lindex [lindex [split $inline ~] 0 ] 1 ] ]
set lname [string trim [lindex [lindex [split $inline ~] 0 ] 0 ] ]
set team [string trim [lindex [split $inline ~] 2 ] ]
set fphn [string trim [lindex [split $inline ~] 1 ] ]
```

(Assumption: the line read in from the elist.db data file is placed in the variable inline.)

At this point all the data from the record has been extracted to local variables. Name searches can now be performed on either the first or the last name. the program can also do searches against the fphn value if this record was pulled to see if there was a match on the extension/phone for the image map check. In fact, using this method we could, at a later time, even allow checks to be made against the "department" value that we stored in the variable team.

The string trim was used to ensure that that data contained within the variable has no extra white space before or after it. At this point the variables lname and fname can be munged together to support key access to the aliases and to the absent.db data files.

The aliases file uses the format of (in the case of the record example shown before):

```
dilberta: adamsd@techno-drens.com
```

The alias:

```
[string match [string tolower $lname][string range [string
( tolower $fname] 0 0 ]
```

will be checked to see if it matches:

```
[lindex $inlin 0]
```

where inlin is the record from the aliases file. If there is a match, the
e-mail values can be set to:

```
[lindex [split [lindex $inlin 0] : ] 0 ]
```

(or dilberta) and a second e-mail address would be the one:

```
[lindex [split [lindex $inlin 1] @ ] 0 ]
```

(or adamsd).

If this fails to catch the alias, there is no known e-mail address for
the person.

In much the same way, the absent.db uses the two names merged
as a way to ensure that the values will be unique. The following Tcl
code will create the proper key to access the file:

```
set outname [string tolower $lname ][string tolower $fname]
```

Or, if you wanted to be obtuse, that could be extracted in a single
step from the original line read in from the elist.db file as:

```
set outname [string tolower [string trim [lindex [lindex \
[split $inline ~] 0 ] 0 ] ] ][string tolower [string trim \
[lindex [lindex [split $inline ~] 0 ] 1 ] ] ]
```

In the cases above, the sample record would have generated the
unique key adamsdilbert.

Based on this series of design criteria, we can establish a basic
program that will perform initial process functioning based on
whether a variable is set. Additionally, the various ways that the first
field will have to be munged to make this a search field have been
clearly outlined.

It should be noted that the unique key used for the e-mail is not a
very good one. What happens when Sally Smith and Sally Supervisor
both have the same e-mail address (sallys) or Stan Fixitman and Stan
Fluidynamics both work at the company (stanf).

As you can see, the headache of every postmaster at every company is that there is no way, besides using a unique ID (back to the employee number, or worse yet the social security number) that no one will understand or remember to ensure unique E-mail addresses.

When you use unique identifiers the IDs are generally very cryptic ("Hi, my e-mail address is: 999886767@thebigplace.com") and generally fail to be useful over a long time, unless the people you deal with have aliasing in their mail system. These methods are not the best way to support a decent e-mail naming convention.

That is one reason why a number of companies are going to the format lastname.firstname@domain.com, although this doesn't work well when you have common names like "John Jones." There is one solution. Use unique identifiers as the alias names, and not the e-mail names. In this case, you would have an alias file that has your employee number in it. That could be followed by any number of valid e-mail addresses or other aliases for that employee.

Unfortunately, this is not the time nor the place to address that level of problem. You should remember that a corporate e-mail policy should take into account the fact that names are not unique, and that random numbers are not memorable. One option that works well is to use employee first name and then a four digit number. If you think you will end up with more than 9,999 people named "Joe," use a five-digit number. While a lot of people (like me, with unique names) would end up with names like jm0001, people like "john" or "fred" would also end up with unique IDs for corporate e-mail.

Program 3: The In/Out Processor (Administrator Tool)

To do this correctly, there are two actual programs that will be run. The first is a program that creates the form, and the second is one that processes it. Overall, the design aspects of both are simple. The form creation program will go through the elist.db file loading up each name into the four variables listed in Table 13.8.

Once the rotation through the elist.db has been completed, the program closes the file and opens the absent.db file. Each record is read in and parsed into two fields. The first is the `keyname` which matches `value`. The second is the code flag which is inserted into the `recode(value)`. The `inout(value)` flag is also set when a value is found in the absent.db data file.

value	compound lowercase lastname + lowercase firstname
inout(value)	the in/out flag - set to a null when employee loaded
uname(value)	Lastname <space> Firstname
lname(value)	Lastname

Then the program builds the table header and loops through the data building 10 row tables with the appropriate table header above each row.

The rows will be in the format of a series of radio buttons, starting with the default *In* button in one cell. It will then be followed by a series of buttons where the absent code value (as defined in the table header) comes first, followed by its associated radio button.

Finally, in the third cell, is the individual's full name. This contains a hyperlink from the name to a call of Program 2, the search processor, with the keyword being the full last name of the individual for the row.

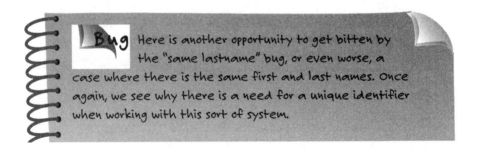

Bug Here is another opportunity to get bitten by the "same lastname" bug, or even worse, a case where there is the same first and last names. Once again, we see why there is a need for a unique identifier when working with this sort of system.

Once all the rows have been printed, a form submit button is placed on the bottom of the form.

That completes the design for creating the form. The key issues raised in the In/Out portion of the design again relates to unique keys and names. There really is little in the way of being able to guarantee a unique identifier unless the enterprise gives each person his/her own sequential number and never goes back to a prior one. It should be noted that many large companies do just that. In those cases, it's possible to leave the firm and return 10 years later and get your original employee ID number.

This software was originally designed for a company of less than 200 employees. Therefore, there was no unique name problem (and the possibility of one was fairly low) with the methods being used here. In a large work environment, the proper unique key would most likely be provided by the Human Resources or the Accounting department and the code would have to be modified to use those unique keys. Compared to creating this form, the program that updates the data file is simple.

> **Tip** There is one precaution to be taken. Since we are working with data files, and the records and the file were not locked, there is the possibility that the information in the data file may have changed between the time we took in the initial data and the time we were ready to update it. In order to avoid writing bad data to the file (overwriting data that was changed) we will write to a temporary file and then re-read the absent.db before we do a rewrite of the data file.

Here a temporary file is created and the program processes each and every record in the form to that file. Once these records are put into a temporary file, the program opens the old absent.db data file and reads in all the records. Then it processes the new temporary file one record at a time to see if there is a matching record and, if so, did it change. It also determines whether there are any new entries. If there are, it will add them to the absent.db data file.

Finally, it completes the updating of the data file and announces to the user if and what changes were made. If there were changes, it creates a new absent.db data file.

Presenting the Tcl Code

The following listings detail the processes described earlier. The Listing 13.1 will process the imagemap and search processor. The Listings 13.2 and 13.3 detail how to manipulate the data in the absent.db using the administration tool.

```tcl
#!/usr/local/bin/tclsh
##
## getpg.tcl
##
## put out the standard headerline along with
## the title and h1 header
##
##
puts "Content-type: text/html\n\n"
puts "<title>Search of Employee Database</title>\
     <center><h1>Database Search Completed\
     </h1></center>"
##
## define some file locations - you will want to
## change these to meet your needs
##
set df1 "/usr/local/.df"
set df-map "/usr/local/.map"
set db-elist "/usr/local/.dbe"
##
## get the variables
##
if { [info exists env(WWW_rm) ] } {
 set ref $env(WWW_rm)
 set stype map
} else {
 set sfield $env(WWW_sfield)
 if { [info exists env(WWW_sflflag) ] } {
  set sflflag $env(WWW_sflflag)
 } else {
  set sflflag last
 }
 set stype form
}
##
## process a map variable properly
##
##
if { $stype == "map"  } {
 set f1 [open $df1/rm2num.db r]
 set fphn ""
 while {![eof $f1]} {
  gets $f1 inline
  if { $ref == [string trim [lindex $inline 0] ] } {
   set sfield [lindex $inline 1]
   break
  }
 }
close $f1
```

```
}
##
## set the sfield properly if it is null
##
if {$sfield == ""} {
 set sfield None
}
##
## if the type was map, and it is not a valid
## room/phone - dump the proper file
##
if { $stype == "map" } {
 if { ![regexp {^[0-9]+$} $sfield] } {
  puts [exec cat $df-map/$sfield]
##
## Transportability note:
## If you are running this software on a PC or
## Mac the above exec will fail. In that case
## you should use a read/write routine like the
## one used in the calendar program
##
exit
 }
}
##
## set initial variable values
##
set lname ""
set hit1 1
##
## open the elist and start the search loop
##
set f1 [open $db-elist/elist.db r]
while { ![eof $f1] } {
 set inline " "
 gets $f1 inline
 set hit 0
##
## on a map - do the join on the phone number
##
 if { $stype == "map" } {
  if { [string match $sfield [string trim [lindex \
        [ split $inline ~ ] 1 ] ] ] } {
   set hit 1
  }
 } else {
##
## if a last name search - look at the last name field
##
  if { $sflflag == "last" } {
   if { [regexp -nocase ^$sfield [string trim \
```

```
                    [lindex [lindex [split $inline ~] 0 ] 0 ] \
                ] ] } {
        set hit 1
       }
    } else {
##
## if a first name search - look at the first name field
##
      if { [regexp -nocase ^$sfield [string trim \
            [lindex [lindex [split $inline ~] 0 ] 1 ] \
                ] ] } {
        set hit 1
       }
     }
   }
##
## we have a hit! prep it for display.
##
  if { $hit } {
##
## we have a record, if it is a first put out
## the header bar
##
    if { $hit1 } {
      puts "<table border cellpadding=10 width=100%>"\
            <tr><th>Photo (If available)</th><th>Full" \
            Name<br>Phone<br>Department</th><th>"\
            E-mail<hr>In/Out</th></tr>"
      set hit1 0
    }
##
## record found, split up the line to its
## proper fields
##
    set fname [string trim [lindex [lindex \
                [split $inline ~] 0 ] 1 ] ]
    set lname [string trim [lindex [lindex \
                [split $inline ~] 0 ] 0 ] ]
    set team [string trim [lindex \
                [split $inline ~] 2 ] ]
    set fphn [string trim [lindex \
                [split $inline ~] 1 ] ]
##
## search for the alias/email data
##
    set f2 [open /usr/lib/aliases r]
    set outname [string tolower [string trim \
                [lindex [lindex [split $inline ~] \
                0 ] 0 ] ][string tolower \
                [string trim [lindex [lindex \
                [split $inline ~] 0 ] 1 ] ] ]
```

```
    set email "None Available"
   while { ![eof $f2] } {
    gets $f2 inlin
    if { [string match [string tolower $lname] \
           [string range [string tolower $fname] \
            0 0 ]: [lindex $inlin 0] ] } {
    set email "[lindex [split [lindex $inlin 0] : \
               ] 0 ] <br> [lindex [split [lindex \
               $inlin 1] @ ] 0 ]"
    break
    }
    }
##
## we have completed the email search
##
    close $f2
##
## in/out search
##
   set f2 [open $db-elist/absent.db r]
   set inout "In"
   while { ![eof $f2] } {
    gets $f2 inlin
##
## we have a match. process it for code value to proper
## value translation
##
    if { [string match $outname [string trim \
           [lindex [split $inlin ~] 0 ] ] ] } {
    switch -regexp [lindex [split $inlin ~] 1 ] {
     V {set inout "<b>Out</b><br>Vacation" }
     E {set inout "<b>Out</b><br>Education" }
     S {set inout "<b>Out</b><br>Sick" }
     O {set inout "<b>Out</b><br>Offsite" }
     P {set inout "<b>Out</b><br>Personal" }
     C {set inout "<b>Out</b><br>Comp" }
     J {set inout "<b>Out</b><br>Jury" }
     T {set inout "<b>Out</b><br>Travel" }
     default {set inout "<b>Out</b>" }
    }
   }
   }
##
## search for and load up the data to display
## the image
##
   set img "<img src=\"/usr/local/.img/dummy.gif\">"
   if {[file exists /usr/local/.img/[string \
       tolower $lname]_[string range [string \
        tolower $fname] 0 0 ].gif ] } {
    set img  "<img src=\"/usr/local/.img/[string \
```

```
                tolower $lname]_[string range \
                [string tolower $fname] 0 0 ].gif\">"
   }
##
## display the three fields
##
##
   puts "<tr><td valign=center>$img</td>\
        <td align=center>$fname $lname\
        <hr width=25%>$fphn<hr width=25%>$team\
        </td><td align=center>$email<hr width=25%>\
        $inout</td></tr>"
   }
}
##
## it isn't found as a searched name or is an
## empty room...
##
if {$lname == ""} {
 puts [exec cat $df-map/None]
} else {
 puts "</table>"
}
##
## put out any footer data
##
 puts "<h2>Notes:</h2> E-mail allows for any \
        name shown to be used as \
        <i>name</i>@company.com . <p> The \
        In/Out field is used to indicate that the \
        person has advised the Administration that \
        they are not available (thereby having an \
        <b>Out</b> notation)."
}
exit
```

Listing 13.2 creates the form that will be used by the administration people to update the in/out data file. Listing 13.3 processes the data that is generated when the form is submitted.

Listing 13.2: inout.tcl

```
#!/usr/local/bin/tclsh
##
## inout.tcl
##
## Procedure to build employee in/out form
##
```

```
puts "Content-type: text/html\n\n"
puts "<title>In/Out Database Update</title>\
     <center><h1>In/Out Database \
     Update</h1></center>"
##
## load the employee names
## value = compound lowercase lastname +
##            lowercase firstname
## inout(value) = the in/out flag -
##            set to a null when employee loaded
## uname(value) = Lastname <space> Firstname
## lname(value) = Lastname
##
set f1 [open /pathtofile/elist.db r]
##
## while not end of file get every
##  line and process it
##
while { ![eof $f1] } {
 gets $f1 inline
 if { [string trim $inline] != ""} {
  set arrval [string tolower [string trim \
     [lindex [lindex [split $inline ~] 0 ] \
     0 ] ] ][string tolower [string trim \
     [lindex [lindex [split $inline ~] 0 ] \
     1 ] ] ]
  set inout($arrval) off
  set uname($arrval) "[string trim [lindex \
     [lindex [split $inline ~] 0 ] 0 ] \
     ] [string trim [lindex [lindex \
     [split $inline ~] 0 ] 1 ] ]"
  set lname($arrval) "[string trim [lindex \
     [lindex [split $inline ~] 0 ] 0 ] ]"
}
}
##
## close the file
##
close $f1
##
## Load the absent database
## inout(value) = on if in the database
## recode(value) = the reason why they are out
##
set f2 [open /pathtofile/absent.db r]
while { ![eof $f2] } {
 gets $f2 inlin
 set inout([lindex [split $inlin ~] 0 ]) on
 set recode([lindex [split $inlin ~] 0 ]) \
     [lindex [split $inlin ~] 1 ]
}
```

```
close $f2
##
## database loaded
## output form header and the "out codes" table
##
puts "<hr><p>If the person is in, select the IN \
      button, otherwise, select the OUT button (or \
      the appropriate code in the out button field). \
      Remember, you have to commit these changes by \
      pressing the commit button on the bottom of \
      the  page.<p><hr>"
puts "<p><h2>Out Codes</h2><table \
      border cellpadding=4><tr><th>V</th><th>S\
      </th><th>P</th><th>C</th><th>E</th><th>T\
      </th><th>J</th><th>O</th><th>Out</th></tr>\
      <td>Vacation</td><td>Sick</td><td>Personal\
      </td><td>Comp</td><td>Education</td><td>\
      Travel</td><td>Jury</td><td>Offsite</td>\
      <td>Out without reason stated</td>\
      </tr></table><p>"
##
## put the form line
## for every person set the checked value (used in
## the "out" portion of the table) to a null value.
## Once we have put out a table of 10 names, put
## another "out codes" table.
##
## — set checked as required for each line, set the
## name as a hypertext link to the CGI program to
## create the database search output.
##
## Oh yes, remember that this is a form ;-)
##
puts "<form method=\"POST\" action=\"/\
       cgi-bin/uncgi/admin/ioupdt.tcl\">"
set knt 0
puts "<table border cellpadding=6>"
foreach arritm [lsort [array names uname] ] {
 foreach cval {V S P C E T J O out} {
  set chk($cval) ""
 }
 if {$knt == 10} {
  set knt 0
  puts "</table><p><table border \
      cellpadding=4><caption>Out Codes</caption>\
      <tr><th>V</th><th>S</th><th>P</th>\
      <th>C</th><th>E</th><th>T</th><th>J</th>\
      <th>O</th><th>Out</th></tr><td>Vacation\
      </td><td>Sick</td><td>Personal</td><td>\
      Comp</td><td>Education</td><td>Travel</td>\
      <td>Jury</td><td>Offsite</td><td>Out \
```

```tcl
      without reason stated</td></tr>\
      </table><p><table border cellpadding=6>"
  } else {
    incr knt
  }
## this will display the information for a person
## who is in
##
  if {$inout($arritm) == "off"} {
   set outs "<tr><td>In <input type=radio name=$arritm\
      value=\"off\" checked></td><td> V \
      <input type=radio name=$arritm \
      value=\"V\"> S <input type=radio \
      name=$arritm value=\"S\"> P <input \
      type=radio name=$arritm value=\"P\"> \
      C <input type=radio name=$arritm \
      value-\"C\"> E <input type=radio \
      name=$arritm value=\"E\"> T <input \
      type=radio name=$arritm value=\"T\"> J \
      <input type=radio name=$arritm value=\"J\"> \
      O <input type=radio name=$arritm value=\"O\"> \
      Out <input type=radio name=$arritm \
      value=\"out\">    </td><td>
    <a href=\"/cgi-bin/uncgi/getpg.tcl\
        ?sfield=$lname($arritm)\"> $uname($arritm)\
        </a> </td></tr>"
} else {
##
## process the person who is out
##
  set code $recode($arritm)
  if {$code == ""} {
  set code "out"
  }
  set chk($code) "checked"
set outs "<tr><td>In <input type=radio name=$arritm \
    value=\"off\"></td><td> V <input type=radio \
    name=$arritm value=\"V\" $chk(V)> S <input \
    type=radio name=$arritm value=\"S\" $chk(S)> \
    P <input type=radio name=$arritm value=\"P\" \
    $chk(P)> C <input type=radio name=$arritm \
    value=\"C\" $chk(C)> E <input type=radio \
    name=$arritm value=\"E\" $chk(E)> T <input \
    type=radio name=$arritm value=\"T\" $chk(T)> \
    J <input type=radio name=$arritm value=\"J\" \
    $chk(J)> O <input type=radio name=$arritm \
    value=\"O\" $chk(O)> Out <input type=radio \
    name=$arritm value=\"out\"  $chk(out)>  \
    </td><td> <a href=\"/cgi-bin/uncgi/getpg.tcl\
    ?sfield=$lname($arritm)\">\
    $uname($arritm)</a> </td></tr>"
```

```
  }
  puts "$outs"
}
##
## We have finished outputting all the tables...
## finish up by closing the form
##
puts "</table>"
puts "<p><hr><p> You must use the <b>commit</b>\
     button to make the changes.<p><center><input \
     type=submit value=\"COMMIT\"></form>"
```

Listing 13.3: ioupdt.tcl

```
#!/usr/local/bin/tclsh
##
## ioupdt.tcl
##
## This program will update the in/out data file
##
## standard header info out to stdout
##
puts "Content-type: text/html\n\n"
puts "<title>In/Out Database</title> <center>\
      <h1>In/Out Database Update Completed\
      </h1></center>"
set hit 0
##
## to make it easy to locate or relocate the files we
## use the two fdir's below. please change them to
## match your systems needs we recommend that you use
## a hidden directory(. prefixed) for the permanent
## file.
##
set fdir1 "/tmp/db"
set fdir2 "/usr/.dbloc/priv/"
set f1 [open $fdir1/newabsent.db w]
##
## get the array names
##
foreach itm [lsort [array names env] ] {
 if {[regexp ^WWW_ $itm]} {
if {$env($itm) != "off"} {
   set out([lindex [split $itm _ ] 1 ]) $env($itm)
  }
 }
}
##
```

```tcl
## open up the second database
##
set f2 [open $fdir/absent.db r]
while { ![eof $f2] } {
 gets $f2 inlin
 set recode( [lindex [split $inlin ~] 0 ] ) \
              [lindex [split $inlin ~] 1 ]
}
##
## load everything in and close it
##
close $f2
##
## now sort it and process the items resetting them
## as necessary and writing them out to
## the temp file. Make sure that you also write out
## any changes to standard output.
##
foreach itm [lsort [array names out] ] {
 puts $f1 "$itm~$out($itm)"
 if {[lsearch [array names recode] $itm] >= 0} {
  if {$recode($itm) != $out($itm)} {
   set hit 1
   puts "<br><i>Changed</i>: $itm from\
        <b>$recode($itm)</b> to <b>$out($itm)</b>"
  }
 } else {
  set hit 1
  puts "<br><b>ADDED</b>: $itm = $out($itm)"
 }
}
foreach itm [lsort [array names recode] ] {
 if { [string trim $itm] != ""} {
  if {[lsearch [array names out] $itm] < 0} {
   set hit 1
   puts "<br><b>Removed</b>: $itm"
  }
 }
}
##
## temp database update completed - user has been
## notified of all changes if any were made
##
close $f1
if {$hit == 0} {
 puts "No updates made to the database."
}
##
## let's replace the absent.db
##
exec mv $fdir1/newabsent.db $fdir2/absent.db
##
exit
```

Perl Design and Code

The Perl code that follows takes steps which are very similar to the Tcl code. The modifications you have to make to this code are in the start of the file where you have to set the following variables to point to the correct paths and set permissions to be able to read these files. The defaults in the Perl code are set to:

```
$rm2num = "./rm2num.db";
$elistdb = "./elist.db";
$aliases = "./aliases";
$absent  = "./absent.db";
```

Now on to the code. First we check if a room is selected and if so, we will search the data files given the room number and ignore the last/first name fields. However, if the $rm field is empty, then we have to check the sflflag flag to see if we are using the last name or the first name. The type of search is set in the stype flag as shown here:

```
$rm = $contents{'rm'};
$rm = "";
$sfield = $contents{'sfield'};
$sflflag = $contents{'sflflag'};
$sflflag = "last";
$sfield = "I";
$stype = ($rm) ? "map" : "name";
```

If we are searching by rooms, we have to figure out the extension given the name of the room. This means matching extension to the room number in the num2db file. The following code shows how to look up the room numbers in the rm2num file and stop if there is not any match. If there is a match, we will move on to search for it.

```
open(ROOMS,$rm2num) || die "<B>Cant open $num2db</B>";
while(<ROOMS>) {
($room,$extension) = split(/ /,$_);
$extension =~ s/\n//; # dont chop it!
if ($room eq $rm) {
  $found = 1;  # flag yourself for later
  $sfield = $extension;
  last;  # bail out of loop.\
  }
}
close ROOMS; # done with file
if ($found)        {
&findIt($sfield,"byroom");
} else {
```

```
print "<B>Cant find $rm</B></body></html>";
exit(0);
}
```

If it cannot find the room with an extension then there is no point looking further since this room is not in our data files. The script then exits with an error message. If the room is found then we call the printing function called findit(). The same findltr() function is called with different parameters when we are searching for last or first names.

```
if ($sflflag eq "last") {
&findIt($sfield,"last");
} else {
&findIt($sfield,"first");
}
```

The findIt() function will print out all the necessary HTML, however, if no match is found, the program stops with an error message. Since we don't know when that will happen, the findIt() function does not close out the HTML file and so it is necessary to close out the HTML output with the following function call later:

```
&closeHTML();
```

The findIt function looks up the employee list file and matches extensions of employees with the extensions assigned to a room or based on the input parameter by matching a first or last name. All employee names are matched in the loop and the first match terminates the loop.

```
if ($match eq "byroom") {
$useThis = $ext;
} elsif ($match eq "first") {
$useThis = $fname;
} else {
$useThis = $lname;
}
```

Each table entry is then printed only if the incoming string is matched correctly with the string we have to compare with:

```
if ($useThis =~ /$incoming/) {
&printTableEntry($lname,$fname,$ext,$dept);
```

The printTableEntry function simply collects the information from the elist.db and aliases file to print out the relevant employee information. If there are any GIF images, then appropriate image is used otherwise a dummy GIF file is used.

The bulk of the work in this function is done for putting strings of the first and last names together to come up the email address. Here's an example of how the E-mail addresses are made by concatenating the last name to the first letter of the first name. (You might want to use a different scheme.) Here's the snippet of code where the work is done:

```perl
$findstr = substr($fname,0,1) . $lname;
$findstr .= "|" . $lname;
$findstr = lc $findstr;
$foundemail="None";
```

The lc function returns a string with only lower case characters. The substr function returns a substring starting at the offset (second parameter, starts from 0) up to the length in the third parameter. (The third parameter may zero to get all the characters up to the end of the string.)

The code for this complete program is shown in Listing 13.4.

Listing 13.4 pdisplay.pl

```perl
#!/usr/local/bin/perl
# ==============================================
#                    PROGRAM 1.
# ==============================================
# Handling POST and GET queries from the FORM.
# ==============================================
$| = 1;
print "Content-type: text/html\n\n";
print "<HTML><TITLE>Database Search</TITLE><BODY>\n";
print "<H1>Database Search</h1>\n";
if ($ENV{'REQUEST_METHOD'} eq "POST") {
    read(STDIN,$buffer,$ENV{'CONTENT_LENGTH'});
} else {
    $buffer = $ENV{'QUERY_STRING'};
}
# ==============================================
# The @contents array will hold form input
# ==============================================
@pairs= split(/&/,$buffer);
foreach $pair (@pairs) {
    ($name,$value) = split(/=/,$pair);
```

```
    $value =~ tr/+/ /;
    $value =~ s/%([a-fA-F0-9][a-fA-F0-
9])/pack("C",hex($1))/eg;
    $contents{$name} = $value;
    }
# ============================================
# Define file locations.
# ============================================
$rm2num = "./rm2num.db";
$elistdb = "./elist.db";
$aliases = "./aliases";
$absent  = "./absent.db";
$tableHeader = 0;
# ============================================
# Get the room number or field type.
# $rm is set to nothing if we search by name
# in which case sfield is either "first"
# or "last"
# ============================================
$rm = $contents{'rm'};
$rm = "";
$sfield = $contents{'sfield'};
$sflflag = $contents{'sflflag'};
$sflflag = "last";
$sfield = "I";
$stype = ($rm) ? "map" : "name";
$found = 0;
if ($stype eq "map") {
   open(ROOMS,$rm2num)|| die "<B>Cant open $num2db</B>";
   while(<ROOMS>) {
   ($room,$extension) = split(/ /,$_);
   $extension =~ s/\n//; # dont chop it!
   # print $room,$extension, "\n";
# ============================================
# Compare room numbers
# ============================================
   if ($room eq $rm) {
     $found = 1;
     $sfield = $extension;
     last;
     }
   } #  while loop
   close ROOMS;
# ============================================
# Search by room
# ============================================
   if ($found)        {
   &findIt($sfield,"byroom");
   } else {
   die "<B>Cant find $rm</B></body></html>";
   }
```

```
} else {
# ==========================================
# Search by either first name or last name
# ==========================================
    if ($sflflag eq "last") {
    &findIt($sfield,"last");
    } else {
    &findIt($sfield,"first");
    }
}
&closeHTML();
exit(0);

# ==========================================
# Get the name of employee from room name/ext.
# ==========================================
sub findIt() {
    my ($incoming,$match) = @_;
    my ($fullname,$ename,$ext,$dept,$useThis);
    my ($fname,$lname);
    # print "Looking for [$incoming] via [$match]
\n";
    open(ELIST,$elistdb)|| die "<B>Cant open $elist-
db</B>";
    $fullname = "";
    while(<ELIST>) {
    ($ename,$ext,$dept) = split('~',$_);
    $dept =~ s/\n//;
    $ext =~ s/ //g; # remove spaces in extension.
    ($lname,$fname) = split(' ',$ename);
    if ($match eq "byroom") {
    $useThis = $ext;
    } elsif ($match eq "first") {
    $useThis = $fname; # on first name
    } else {
    $useThis = $lname; # on last name
    }
    #
    # check if match found!
    #
    if ($useThis =~ /$incoming/) {
    &printTableEntry($lname,$fname,$ext,$dept);
    }
    }
    close ELIST;
    &closeTable();
}
# ===================================================
# print one item entry for table. Print header
# just once.
# ===================================================
```

```perl
sub printTableEntry() {
    my ($lname,$fname,$extension,$dept) = @_;
    my ($email,$alias,$findstr,$foundemail);
    my ($img,$imgstr,$fullname);
    my ($inout,$status,$bloke,$keyword);
    if ($tableHeader == 0) {
    print         << "TABLEHEAD";
<TABLE border cellpadding=10 width=100%>
<TR>
<TH>Photo(if available)</TH>
<TH>Full Name </TH>
<TH>Phone </TH>
<TH>Department</TH>
<TH>email Address</TH>
<TH>Status</TH>
</tr>
TABLEHEAD
    $tableHeader = 1;
    }
    $findstr = substr($fname,0,1) . $lname;
    $findstr .= "|" . $lname;
    $findstr = lc $findstr;
    $foundemail="None";
open(FA,$aliases) || die "</table>NO
ALIASES!!</body></html>";
    while(<FA>) {
      ($alias,$email)= split(':',$_);
      if ($alias =~ /$findstr/) {
        $foundemail = $email;
        last;
      }
    }
    close(FA);

    $img = "<IMG SRC=\"dummy.gif\">";
    $imgstr = "./" . $lname . "_" . $fname . ".gif";
    if (-e $imgstr) {
    $img = "<IMG SRC=\"" . $imgstr . "\">";
    }

    $inout = $lname . $fname;
    $inout =~ s/ //g; # remove any spaces
    $inout = lc $inout;
    open(FA,$absent);
    while(<FA>) {
      ($bloke,$status)= split('~',$_);
      $status =~ s/\n//;
      if ($bloke =~ /$inout/) {
        $keyword = $status;
        last;
      }
```

```
        }
close(FA);
$inout = "In";
$keyword = substr($keyword,0,1);
if ($keyword eq "V") { $inout =
"<b>Out</b><br>Vacation";
} elsif ($keyword eq "E") { $inout =
"<b>Out</b><br>Education";
} elsif ($keyword eq "S") { $inout =
"<b>Out</b><br>Sick";
} elsif ($keyword eq "O") { $inout =
"<b>Out</b><br>Offsite";
} elsif ($keyword eq "P") { $inout =
"<b>Out</b><br>Personal";
} elsif ($keyword eq "C") { $inout =
"<b>Out</b><br>Comp";
} elsif ($keyword eq "J") { $inout =
"<b>Out</b><br>Jury";
} elsif ($keyword eq "T") { $inout =
"<b>Out</b><br>Travel";
} else { $inout = "<b>Out</b><br>No reason!"; }

    $fullname = $lname . "," . $fname;

#=================================================
# Close out the table entry with collected data.
#=================================================
print << "TABLEENTRY";
<TR>
<TD>$img</TD>
<TD>$lname,$fname</TD>
<TD>$extension</TD>
<TD>$dept</TD>
<TD>$email</TD>
<TD>$inout</TD>
</tr>
TABLEENTRY

}

#=================================================
# close the table after last entry
#=================================================
sub closeTable() {
print "</table>" if $tableHeader;
}
sub closeHTML() {
print "</body></html>" if $tableHeader;
}
```

Now for the administrative tool that is composed of two programs. The first program lists the status of all the employees listed in the absent.db file. The person using this tool can then set the status of each listed employee and the submit the information to another program which updates the absent.db file.

Let's look at the code that generates the tool for displaying the current status of each employee based on information in the absent.db file. The first thing to do after printing the HTML header is to collect the user information in the elist.db file and initialize all status indicators to "off." The list of employees is kept in an associative array called %employees and each item in this array is indexed by a key created by concatenating the first and last names together.

```
while ($input=<FH>) {
    ($fullname,$ext,$dept) = split('~',$input);
    $fullname =~ s/\s+/ /g; # remove one or more spaces
    ($lname,$fname) = split(' ',$fullname);
    $ename = lc($lname . $fname);
    $input .= "~off";
    $employees{$ename} = $input;
}
close FH;
```

Once this list has been created, we can use its items as fields, each of which is delimited with a tilde (~). The item to take care of is to replace all "off" codes with any codes present in the absent.db file. This is done in the following section of code:

```
open(FH,$absentee)||die"<h1>absent:$!</h1></body><html>";
while ($input=<FH>) {
    ($rname,$code) = split('~',$input);
    if ($employees{$rname} ne "") {
      $code = substr($code,0,1);
      $employees{$rname} =~  s/off/$code/;
    }
}
close FH;
```

Since the codes have to be only one character long, they are clipped with the substr function to remove spaces, new lines, etc. Now it's a matter of cycling through this list of employees and print out the codes as table entries. We use a subroutine to print out the codes using the codes listed in the @codes array. Values for radio buttons are set to checked or nothing based on the code for each employee and if it matches items in the list present in @codes. Listing 13.5 is the code to handle the display portion.

Listing 13.5 padmin.pl

```perl
#!/usr/local/bin/perl
#
$|=1;

print << "HTMLHEAD";
<html>
<head>
<title>In/Out Database Update</title>
<center><h1>In/Out Database Update</h1></center>
</head><body>
HTMLHEAD

# MODIFY THESE FILE LOCATIONS FOR YOUR OWN USE!!
$elist = "/your/path/here/elist.db";
$absentee = "/your/path/here/absent.db";

#

# Look up employees
#
%employees = {};
open(FH,$elist)||die"<h1>elist: $!</h1></body><html>";
while ($input=<FH>) {
    ($fullname,$ext,$dept) = split('~',$input);
    $fullname =~ s/\s+/ /g; # remove one or more spaces
    ($lname,$fname) = split(' ',$fullname);
    $ename = lc($lname . $fname);
    $input .= "~off";
    $employees{$ename} = $input;
}
close FH;

#
# Check absentee list
#
open(FH,$absentee)||die"<h1>absent:$!</h1></body><html>";
while ($input=<FH>) {
    ($rname,$code) = split('~',$input);
    if ($employees{$rname} ne "") {
      $code = substr($code,0,1);
      $employees{$rname} =~ s/off/$code/;
    }
}
close FH;

# define vacation codes
@codes = ('V','S','P','C','E','T','J','O',"out");

#  ====================================================
```

```perl
#    output form header and the "out codes" table
#    ======================================================
print << "OUTCODES";
<hr><p>If the person is in, select the IN button,
otherwise, select the OUT button (or the appropriate
code in the out button field). Remember,
you have to commit these changes by pressing
the commit button on the bottom of the page.<p><hr>
<p><h2>Out Codes</h2><table border cellpadding=4>
<tr><th>V</th><th>S</th><th>P</th><th>C</th>
<th>E</th><th>T</th><th>J</th><th>O</th><th>Out</th>
</tr><td>Vacation</td><td>Sick</td><td>Personal</td>
<td>Comp</td><td>Education</td><td>Travel</td><td>Jury</td>
<td>Offsite</td><td>Out without reason
stated</td></tr></table><p>
<form method="POST" action="/cgi-bin/test-cgi.pl">
<table border cellpadding=6>
OUTCODES


#    ======================================================
#    for every person set the checked value (used in
#    the "out" portion of the table) to a null value.
#    Once we have put out a table of 10 names, put
#    another "out codes" table.
#    ======================================================
#    — set checked as required for each line, set the
#    name as a hypertext link to the CGI program to
#    create the database search output.
#    ======================================================
$knt = 1;

foreach $emp (sort keys %employees) {
    &printCodes() if (($knt % 10) == 0);
    $knt++;
    ($fullname,$ext,$dept,$record)   =
split('~',$employees{$emp});
    ($lname,$fname) = split(' ',$fullname);

    if ($record =~ /off/) {
    print "<tr><td>In<input type=radio name=$emp
      value=\"off\" checked></td><td>";
    foreach $i (@codes) {
    print "$i <input type=radio name=$emp value=$i>\n";
      }

    }else{
    print "<tr><td>In<input type=radio name=$emp
      value=\"off\"></td><td>";
    foreach $i (@codes) {
      $chk{$i} = "";
      $chk{$i} = "checked" if ($record eq $i);
```

```
      }
    foreach $i (@codes) {
      print "$i <input type=radio name=$emp
        value=\"$i\" $chk{$i}>\n";
      }
    }
($fullname) = split('~',$employees{$emp});
print "</td><td><a href=\"/cgi-bin/
    io2.pl?sfield=$lname\">$fullname</a></td></tr>";
} # foreach loop

print "</table><p><hr><p> You must use the
    <b>commit</b> button to ";
print "make the changes.<p><center><input type=submit
    value=\"COMMIT\"></form>";
print "\n\n";

#    Print out the codes in a table
sub printCodes() {
print "<P> Print Codes ";
print << "TABLEITEM";
</table><p><table border cellpadding=4>
<caption>Out Codes</caption>
<tr>
<th>V</th><th>S</th><th>P</th>
<th>C</th><th>E</th><th>T</th>
<th>J</th><th>O</th><th>Out</th>
</tr>
<td>Vacation</td><td>Sick</td><td>Personal</td>
<td>Comp</td><td>Education</td> <td>Travel</td>
<td>Jury</td><td>Offsite</td>
<td>Out without reason stated</td>
</tr></table>
<p><table border cellpadding=6>
TABLEITEM
}
```

Finally, we come to the program that manages the absent.db file. When this program is called it's input is a list of variables of employee names listed in the elist.db file. Each variable has a value based on the radio buttons the radio buttons set up in the previous program.

The absent.db file is modified in the following fashion: First, if the employee is listed in the file, then their status is changed if the value of their named variable is not "off.. Second, the value is "off" and that employee was listed in the data file then that entry for the employee in the file is deleted. (This is printed out as a "delete" message.) Finally, if there is an employee whose status is not "off" and is also not listed in data file, the employee and their status is added to the file. Since more than one type of program may be working with this data file, any employees not specifically targeted by the input are not removed from the absent.db file.

Now for the code. Basically, what we do is keep a copy of the absent.db file in memory as an associative array indexed by the name of the individual. All modifications to this array can be easily made without going to the disk. Once the modifications are made, we can simply overwrite the absent.db file on disk. You can safely load the absent.db file in memory but should avoid using extremely long elist and absent files since this may affect performance a bit.

Listing 13.6 is the code for updating the absent.db file.

Listing 13.6 pupdate.pl

```perl
#!/usr/local/bin/perl
#
$| = 1;
print << "HTMLHEAD";
Content-type: text/html

<HTML><HEAD><title>In/Out Database</title>
<center><h1>In/Out Database Update Completed</h1>
</center>
</HEAD>
<BODY>
HTMLHEAD


# =========================================================
#                 Handling POST queries from the FORM.
# =========================================================
# This following lines of code are used to collect
data from the
# standard input. The length of the standard input
is in the
# environment variable CONTENT_LENGTH.
# =========================================================
#

if ($ENV{'REQUEST_METHOD'} eq "POST") {
    read(STDIN,$buffer,$ENV{'CONTENT_LENGTH'});
} else {
    $buffer = $ENV{'QUERY_STRING'};
}
```

```perl
@pairs= split(/&/,$buffer);
foreach $pair (@pairs) {
    ($name,$value) = split(/=/,$pair);
    $value =~ tr/+/ /;
    $value =~ s/%([a-fA-F0-9][a-fA-F0-9])/pack("C",hex($1))/eg;
    $contents{$name} = $value;
    }


#
## MODIFY THIS LOCATION for your own use!!!
#$absentee = "./absent.db";

$hit = 0;      # count the number of hits (if you want)
%original={}; # old status here

# =================================
# read old status
# =================================
open(FH,$absentee)||die"<h1>$!</h1></body></html>";
while($input=<FH>) {
    chop($input);
    ($ename,$code)=split('~',$input);
    $original{$ename} = substr($code,0,1);
    print "<BR> $ename~$original{$ename}\n";
}
close FH;


# =================================
# Copy old status to anew
# =================================
%absent=%original;
for $i (sort keys %contents) {
    if ($contents{$i} ne "off") {
      if ($original{$i} ne "") {
    print "<br><i>Changed</i>: $i; # 2 long 2 print
    print " from <b>$original{$i}</b>to<b>$contents{$i}</b>";
        $absent{$i} = $contents{$i};
        $hit++; # changed
      } else {
      print "<br><i>Added</i>: <b>$i</b>";
        $absent{$i} = $contents{$i};
      }
    } else {   # Remove employees who have returned.
      if ($original{$i} ne "") {
      print "<br><i>Removed</i>: <b>$i</b>";
      delete $absent{$i};
      }
    }
}
# =================================
```

```
# Close HTML output
# =================================
print "</body></html>";

# =================================
# Overwrite the file on disk
# =================================
open(FH,">$absentee")||die"<h1>$!</h1></body></html>"
;
foreach $i (sort keys %absent) {
    print "$i~$absent{$i}\n";
}
close FH;
```

Summary

Much like Chapter 12, we have an integrated application. The environment differs in that here we are no longer providing data to the world, but to internal users. In this way there are some application changes, as you have seen, and possibly some different security concerns (access to personnel data versus hackers attempting to disrupt systems and service delivery).

In this chapter we used forms to update and maintain control over data that was in a secured/non-public data file (the In/Out database), we integrated the procedures to system data files (the aliases data file used by e-mail), data access by users was supported through a graphical and non-graphical interface, with a high level of code reuse.

As a security issue, access to the forms used for updating the In/Out status could have been in protected directories requiring a password to access them (using .htaccess).

In the next chapter we will look at how systems management activities can be enhanced by using the Web browser as a tool in viewing information about the system status. Again we will build on many of the methods and techniques that were used here, and in prior chapters, as we face a totally different application.

CHAPTER 14
INTRANETS: SYSTEMS MANAGEMENT

- Using crontabs to Create Data Files

- Reducing Data from crontab Generated Data Files

- Creating Tables from Reduced Data

Chapter 13 touched on one intranet application that leveraged some flat file databases to create a *White Pages* application. Now we will use crontabs to obtain information about disk usage on a system. This information is stored in a data file on a disk that is accessible by the HTTPd server and can be displayed within a browser.

Maintaining Different Hardware Platforms

Recently, a request came to me from a systems manager in charge of maintaining a series of different networked file servers. He wanted to

443

get all the latest disk information from any single file server, along with an historical perspective, from a single location using a browser.

The systems manager wanted the capability to bring up a disk status history for a single platform and have it present hourly statistics based on the hour that the disk is on that system, and on the percentage of disk used. The system manager's environment crosses a number of HP platforms running HP-UX V9 and V10.

The network in place allows for a single disk to be shared by all platforms. This disk will be mounted on all HP machines and on the machine to be used as the HTTPd server. When any of the file servers being monitored starts to have its disk space fill up the following visual clues should appear within an HTML page generated from the data within the data files stored on the shared disk:

- Note: green @ 90%
- Caution: yellow @ 95%
- Warning: red @ 97%
- Error: red flashing @ = 100%
- BAD ERROR: white flashing @ > 100

To meet these needs, two programs are required. A brief description of each is listed in Table 14.1.

Table 14.1: Maintaining a multiplatform system

Program 1 Capabilities	Program 2 Capabilities
Find all disks on the system	Access a file of disk results for a system
Determine amount of free space on each disk	Display a daily table of the disk information for each day of data in the file
Record results in a file that is accessible by the server	Properly associate visual indicators as required

Program 1: Gathering Data

In this case, there is no need to perform HTML design as this program will be run as a cron job to create the data file. A cron is what many people think of as batch processing. The crontab entries allow the system to run processes in an automated fashion based on the information within the crontab. The information provided tells the system who is running the cron, the time, dates and frequency of the task, and the actual task that is to be run. For more information on cron, crontab and at (another Unix command that allows detached spool like tasks), please see any Unix manual, or the man pages provided on a Unix system.

This section deals directly and specifically with Unix platforms; the HP platform running HP-UX V9.0 and V10.01 to be exact. This particular program is not highly transportable as it has been refined for the user-specified platform. While the program is HP-UX specific, the methods used for data extraction in Program 1 and for data display in Program 2 are very transportable.

Transition Tip In the introduction I pointed out that Tcl and Perl both run on Wintel and MacOS based platforms, and that most of the code could be transported from Unix to these platforms with no problem. In this case, rather than state over and over again when the application isn't transportable I will state that the entire application in this chapter is not transportable, although the concepts, methods and techniques used for the CGI are.

The first program is designed to obtain the disk data, with some interesting requirements. Some disks will not be on the system at all times. In this case, the information is based on the disk hour (the number of hours that the disk is on the system), not the system hour (the actual clock time that the disk is on the system). This governs how the data is displayed and defines how it will be recorded. Whenever a new disk is added, the addition of that disk will cause a new record to be written to the data file for that disk. The system will use a *single data file* and maintain each hour as a single record, but the hour will not be utilized when displaying the data, only the fact that a disk was mounted for an hour will be noted.

Since the actual hour is recorded, it would require very little work to modify the display CGI to properly associate the actual clock hours that the disk was mounted to the display. This requirement shows that the time period for which the disk usage is displayed is not as important as the information concerning how full a disk was over any one hour period. In this case the information important to the system manager was not the hour (the real time that the disk was on-line) but the ability to know how much space was being used on the disk or partition during that hour the partition was mounted on the file server.

Note An alternative to this is to note the individual disks mounted on a system in one data file (updating as new disks are added and removed). The disk information is then stored in a separate data file with date-time stamps and disk usage information. This method provides the capability of viewing the mounted disks in clocktime not just the hours that they were mounted. In this way the customer is able to note what hour of the day the partition is mounted and the space utilization for that hour of that day.

Using the single data file method generates a single data line for each hour. Because we care about the disks and partition on a system rather than their individual use (clock times), this method provides all the data needed and does it with only one file open.

The data is gathered and entered hourly into the data file using a standard format of:

```
Datestamp <space> rootdirectory % + /directory % + /directory % +
```

Here the time-date stamp is the date in the following format (note: this is standard HP-UX format for the display of the date command):

```
day-of-week mo day-num hh:mm:ss TZ yr
```

The first entry is the root directory and the percentage used: / xx%.

A + sign is used to separate directories. Each directory starts with a / before the name and a + sign where the string ends. For example:

```
Fri Sep 20 06:00:01 PDT 1996 / 68% + /usr2 94% + /usr 90% +
⇒   /users 80% +
```

Remote mounts should be ignored since the disk is not actually residing on the machine in question.

Designing a crontab

This program, designed to be run as a crontab, generates information on the percentage used by individual disks on the system. Tcl and Perl require different approaches, but net the same results.

Requirements and Data Analysis

Since the requirements stipulate that the machine being used is an HP running HP-UX, the bdf command is available. This command generates percentage information as part of its output (unlike the df command in BSD Unix). The formats of the two outputs are shown in Table 14.2.

The first line of the output from a bdf command must be stripped as it is non-data. The fastest and easiest way to do this is to not store data on any information that starts with a character a-z in the first position of a line (note that all file systems start with a /). This also eliminates all disks mounted from other systems as they start with the mount point (host.domain.com:/diskname) not the disk name.

To get the date-time information for datestamping the output line, the system time will be used by capturing the output from the date command (which on HP-UX V10.01 matches the format declared in the database design section).

Listing 14.1 provides the Tcl code for the crontab that is used to gather the data and reduce it to what is in the data file.

Listing 14.1: getdata.tcl

```
#!/usr/local/bin/tclsh
##
## getdata.tcl
```

Table 14.2: Sample output from bdf/df command

Output	File system	kbytes Total	kbytes Used	kbytes Available	kbytes % Used	Mounted On
bdf output from HP-UX V10.10	/dev/vgroot/root	499194	279067	170207	62%	/
	/dev/vgroot/usr	40375	588568	698826	94%	/usr
	/dev/vg01/lvol2	48589	35095	8635	80%	/users
	/dev/vg01/lvol1	125325	81314	31478	72%	/tmp

Output	File system	Blocks Total	i-nodes		kbytes % Used	Mounted On
df output from HP-UX V10.10	(/dev/vg01/lvol1):	66756	10343		NA	/tmp
	(/dev/vg01/lvol2):	17370	2685		NA	/users
	(/dev/vgroot/usr):	82750	118785		NA	/usr
	(/dev/vgroot/root):	320414	71578		NA	/

```
##
## this procedure is run as a crontab and is
## used to generate the data file for the disk
## space usage tables
##
## Make sure we have the right system (and run the
## correct command based on system type)
##
if {[regexp {HP-UX} [exec uname -a ] ]} {
  set ofil /xmount/disklog.data
  set datastrm [exec bdf]
} else {
  set datastrm [exec df]
}
##
## use the system date - we are using the [exec date]
## feature again, rather than clock. Since
## portability is not an issue in this code this is
## not a major issue.
##
set tmstr [exec date]
##
## for each line read in the bdf
## make sure it's a valid line to parse
## parse the data
##
foreach lin [split $datastrm \n] {
  if {![regexp -nocase {^[a-z]} $lin ]} {
    lappend olin [lindex $lin 5] [lindex $lin 4] +
  }
}
##
## open a file and put the parsed data into it
##
set f1 [open $ofil a+]
puts $f1 "$tmstr $olin"
close $f1
##
## file closed - fini
##
exit
```

Gathering the Data in Perl

In the Perl world, data is stored on disk by collecting the output from the df command in the array of lines called @input. The $result variable contains the entire output from the df command including all carriage returns and headers:

```
$result=`df`;                    # exec the df command
```

The @input array contains the items of the $result variable after splitting on \n:

```
@input = split(/\n/,$result);  # split lines into array
shift @input;                    # remove first item
```

The first line of the @input array is removed with the shift command. Basically, the shift command forces all the elements of a given list to the left. The first item of an array is removed and all the rest of the items move up a notch.

The $olin variable is used to construct the output string. Only the name and percentage- used variables from each line in @input are extracted to form an entry in the $olin string. The foreach loop traverses the @input array and assigns each string to the default variable, $, which in turn is split up based on spaces between words.

```
($dev,$size,$used,$avail,$perc,$name) = split(' ',$_);
$olin .= " $name    $perc +";
```

The log file is then opened and appended with the results in the $olin string. The initial program is shown in Listing 14.2.

Listing 14.2: A program to append to log file

```
#!/usr/local/bin/perl
# ─────────────────────────
#   Equivalent perl script that can be called from cron
#   to append to the data file.
# ─────────────────────────
$filename = "/xmount/disklog.data";
$olin = `date`;                  # get date
chop $olin;                      # remove cr/lf
$result=`df`;                    # exec the df command
@input = split(/\n/,$result);  # split lines into array
shift @input;                    # remove the first line
foreach (@input) {
    ($dev,$size,$used,$avail,$perc,$name) = split('
',$_);
    $olin .= " $name    $perc +";
}
# ─────────────────────────
# Append to log file
# ─────────────────────────
```

```
$lines[0] = olin;
open(OF,">" . $filename) || die "Cannot Open  $!\n ";
print OF $olin . "\n";
close OF;
```

Transition Tip There is one catch with this design. If there is no other cron script that wakes up every 24 hours and deletes the log file, there will be an infinitely long log file. The Perl code, differing from Tcl implemented the **round-robin** technique that allows only 24 lines in the log file at one time, but it may be easier to write a cron entry to delete the file just after midnight so that all the hours match up.

The Tcl code assumes that there is a historical need for data on the disks and doesn't perform any cleanup. The way that you would be able to maintain the history and clean the log would require two separate Unix grep commands and one mv command. The lines for that are:

```
grep -v "MMM dd" /pathto/logfile.db > backuplog.db
grep "MMM dd" /pathto/logfile.db > templogfil.db
mv temploffil.db /pathto/logfile.db
```

"MMM dd" is the date in the format of the month and the day inside quotes, like: "Dec 7", or "Nov 29" (note that single digit days are space-filled before the number).

To check the usage for the last 24 hours regardless of day, append entries to the front of the log file. Each subsequent entry will then be *that number of hours ago*. For example, the fifth entry will show usage five hours ago, the sixth will show usage six hours ago and so on.

To do this, first create an array called @lines and assign the first value to the $olin string:

```
$ctr = 1;
$lines[0] = olin;
```

Then, read the rest of the file into the @lines buffer. If the log file does not exist, it will not be opened. The -e test on the filename will return true if the file exists, like this:

```
if (-e $filename) {
    open(OF,"<" .$filename) || die "Cannot open $! for reading";
    while ($lines[$ctr] = <OF>) {
      $ctr++;
      }
    close(OF);
    }
```

The number of lines in the @lines is then limited to just 24 with the assignment of $ctr to 24.

```
if ($ctr > 24) { $ctr = 24; }
```

Append the rest of the file with the previous entries in the log file with the for loop limiting the number of lines written to 24.

```
open(OF,$filename) || die "Cannot Open  $!\n ";

for($i=0;$i<$ctr;$i++) {
    print OF $lines[$i] . "\n";
    }
close OF;
```

The complete Perl code to implement this round-robin technique is shown in Listing 14.3.

Listing 14.3: Appending the file with round-robin technique

```
#!/usr/local/bin/perl
# ─────────────────────────
#  Equivalent perl script that can be called from cron
#  to append to the data file.
# ─────────────────────────
$filename = "/xmount/disklog.data";
$olin = `date`;                    # get date
chop $olin;                        # remove cr/lf
$result=`df`;                      # exec the df command
@input = split(/\n/,$result);      # split lines into array
shift @input;                      # remove the first line
foreach (@input) {
    ($dev,$size,$used,$avail,$perc,$name) = split(' ',$_);
    $olin .= " $name  $perc +";
}
# ─────────────────────────
# Add the line to the end of the log file.
```

```
# _____
$ctr = 1;
$lines[0] = olin;


# _____
# Read the rest of the file into the $lines buffer.
# _____
if (-e $filename) {
    open(OF,"<" .$filename) || die "Cannot open $!";
    while ($lines[$ctr] = <OF>) {
        $ctr++;
        }
    close(OF);
    }
if ($ctr > 24) { $ctr = 24; } # just in case.
# _____
# Append to log file with the latest line in the front
# and allow only up to 24 lines in the file.
# Remove the counter if you want the file to grow
# ad infinitum and thus keep a history...
# _____
open(OF,$filename) || die "Cannot Open  $!\n ";

for($i=0;$i<$ctr;$i++) {
    print OF $lines[$i] . "\n";
    }
close OF;
```

Program 2: Data Display

This program will be run as either an SSI or from within a form. In either case it has to display the data in a simple to read format.

The format will be a table with a date above it. This table is created by diskstat.tcl and the HTML will be documented there. The first column of the table contains the name of the disk being reported on, while the top row contains the hour number in military count (0-23). If there is more than one date in the file (if we are keeping historical data on-line and available) then each day will have it's own table.

Each row represents a mounted disk and has columns that will contain 0-23 percentage values. These values stipulate how much disk space was available for that hour number that the disk was on line. In most cases this is a one-to-one relationship between the disk on-line time and the actual clock time. In cases where disks are mounted for a short time and then dismounted, it will be for the total number of hours that the disk was mounted.

Extracting Data into Tables

diskstat.tcl extracts the data from the data file generated by the program above. The data is extracted and placed into tables that have a set format. Each table is preceded by the date that is in the file for that series of records. When the date changes from the information in the file (we move from one day to another) the table is completed and will be closed, and a new table is created for the next day. In Figure 14.1, the maximum number of columns is set to 24hour columns (numbered 0-23) and is preceded by a *disk* column that contains the name of the partition. The total number of rows is established by the number of partitions that the data file states are being recorded.

If-then-else logic is used to modify the fonts for those items loaded into the table if they fall within the boundaries for visual identifiers established by the customer.

- Note: green @ 90%
- Caution: yellow @ 95%
- Warning: red @ 97%
- Error: red flashing @ = 100% (Note about Figure 14.1: Since the text actually blinks, the only ways to indicate this were either to supply two screen shots, or supply one with the 100% in blink-out mode. I chose the latter.)
- BAD ERROR: white flashing @ > 100

Displaying Disk Using diskstat.tcl

This program will be called by either a form or as an SSI. In either case, it will read the data file and extract all the current disk data. The data is displayed in a series of daily tables with each partition of the disk clearly delineated and monitored. Columns are marked for hours, starting at 0 and going to 23. Usage will be indicated by the percentage used value inserted in the proper place within the matrix.

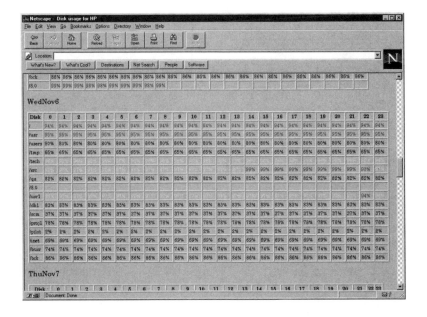

Figure 14.1: A badly beaten system in need of new disk space

As was mentioned earlier in the chapter, this data file can grow quite large. One option is to extract monthly data and store the old data files by month in a compressed format (see Listing 14.4). A simple shell script to perform that would use the three Unix commands in the Transition Tip within a file. That file would be run as a monthly crontab. Compression could be accomplished with the addition of one line to compress the backup data file using the compression method of your choice.

Listing 14.4: diskstat.tcl

```
#!/usr/local/bin/tclsh
##
## diskstat.tcl
##
## The following procedure can be uncommented to
## replace the "if-then-else" structure used to
## set the colors of values over 90 in the display
## In this procedure, a regular expression is used
## along with the switch statement that allows for
## the color identifier to be set based on the value
## passed in. This procedure will set the proper
```

```
## font value for the display
##
## proc colr {val pval} {
##    switch -regexp $val {
##      ^9[1-4] {return   \
##          <font color="green">$pval</font>}
##      ^9[5-6] {return \
##          <font color="yellow">$pval</font>}
##      ^9[7-9]  {return \
##          <font color="reg">$pval</font>}
##      ^100 {return "<blink> \
##          <font color="red">$pval</font></blink>}
##       default {return <blink> \
##          <font color="white">$pval</font></blink>}
##    }
##  }
##
## open the data file and initialize variables
##
set f1 [open /xmount/disklog.data r]
set dev ""
set valulst ""
##
## The big loop… process all the data in the file
## - get a line of data, parse it, see if we have the
##   partition already defined, if not, add it to the
##   list of partitions.
##
while {[gets $f1 inline] > 0} {
  set valu [lindex $inline 0] \
    [lindex $inline 1][lindex $inline 2]
  if {[regexp -nocase {^[a-z]} $valu]} {
    if {[lsearch $valulst $valu] < 0 } {
      lappend valulst $valu
    }
    set wstr [string range $inline \
      [string first {/} $inline] end]
##
## split the data record and then for each value in
## the data record do…
##
    foreach lwstr [split $wstr {+}] {
      set lwstr [string trim $lwstr]
## If not end of record
      if {[string range [lindex $lwstr 0] 0 0] \
        == "/"} {
        set aval [lindex $lwstr 1]
        regsub {\%} $aval "" bval
##      Uncomment this section to use the procedure
##      described above for color assignment
##        if {$bval > 90%}
```

```
##           set aval [colr $bval $aval]
## end of replace code
## remove all the code between this point and the
## comment card that looks like ##@@@@@
        set filv $aval
        if {$bval > 90} {
           set aval "<font color=green>$filv</font>"
        }
        if {$bval > 95} {
           set aval "<font color=yellow>$filv</font>"
        }
        if {$bval > 97} {
           set aval "<font color=red>$filv</font>"
        }
        if {$bval == 100} {
           set aval "<blink><font
color=red>$filv</font></blink>"
        }
        if {$bval > 100} {
           set aval "<blink><font
color=white>$filv</font></blink>"
        }
##@@@@@
## removal of the above code, and uncommenting
## the procedure and the if, will replace the
## complex if statements with a smaller and
## cleaner way of setting the formats and flags.
##
        lappend $valu-[lindex $lwstr 0]
"<td>$aval</td>"
        if {[lsearch $dev [lindex $lwstr 0]] < 0 }
{
           lappend dev [lindex $lwstr 0]
        }
     }
   }
 }
}
close $f1
##
## Completed obtaining input, now let's display
##
puts "Content-type: text/html\n\n"
puts " <title>Disk usage for host</title> This
page"\
   "shows the disk usage on a day by day" \
   "basis.<p>This usage is tracked from the data"\
   "generated by a crontab that runs hourly on"\
   " the effected computer system."
foreach v $valulst {
  puts "<h2>$v</h2>"
```

```
puts "<table border=1>"
puts"<tr><th>Disk</th><th>0</th><th>1</th>"\
  "<th>2</th><th>3</th><th>4</th><th>5</th><th>6"\
  "</th><th>7</th><th>8</th><th>9</th><th>10</th>"\
  "<th>11</th><th>12</th><th>13</th><th>14</th>"\
  "<th>15</th><th>16</th><th>17</th><th>18</th>"\
  "<th>19</th><th>20</th><th>21</th><th>22</th>"\
  "<th>23</th></tr>"
foreach d $dev {
  if {[info exists $v-$d]} {
##
## this regsub cleans up curley braces in lists
##
    regsub -all {\{|\}} [eval set $v-$d] "" bval
    puts "<tr><td>$d</td> $bval</tr>"
  }
}
puts "</table>"
}
exit
```

Processing the Display using Perl

Basically, what we are doing is taking one line from each file and creating an HTML table with the input data. This program, disklog.pl, uses the variables listed in Table 14.3 for processing.

Table 14.3 disklog.pl variables

Variable	Description
$wday	current day of the week
$mon	current month in ASCII
$mday	current day of month
$tod	current time of day as HH:MM:SS
$tz	current time zone
$hr,$min,$sec	current time of day
$year	current year
$info	current output line
@names	list of directory names
%usage	individual usage string for a directory
$numdisk	counter of number of directories

When the script is invoked, it prints the standard header back to the browser just as in any other CGI script. The Perl program also creates the 25 columns for the hour number and the name of the directory.

```
print << "HTMLHEAD";
<HTML><HEAD><TITLE>Disk Stats</TITLE></HEAD><BODY>\n
<H1> Modify your own header here!</H1>
<TABLE BORDER>
<TR><TH>Disk</TH>
HTMLHEAD
for ($i=0;$i<24;$i++) { printf "<TH>%d</TH>",$i; }
print "</TR>";
```

The program opens the input file and reads every line. There should never be more than 24 lines in this file since it's currently updated only once per hour throughout the day. Each line is read into the $input buffer within the while loop:

```
open(FB,"./disklog.dat.r") || die "Cannot open $!\n";
while($input=<FB>){
```

The first order of business is to remove the {} braces in the mounted directories. Note how the curly braces are escaped with backslashes to allow the regular expression parser in Perl to use the curly braces literally.

```
$input =~ s/\{\}//; # remove {} from input
```

Extract the weekday, month, day of the month, time and time zone from the input line. These are separated by spaces. The time value is separated by colons.

```
($wday,$mon,$mday,$tod,$tz) = split(' ',$input);
($hr,$min,$sec) = split(':',$tod);
```

The end of the time zone is where the data begins for the display. Each entry of data is separated by plus + signs. Carve off the substring from the first / character to the end of the string into the $info string.

```
$index = index($input,'/');
$info =  substr($input,$index);
```

The individual information for the disks and percent usage is extracted into the @disks array.

```
@disks = split(/\+/,$info);
```

Process each item in the @disks array one item at a time. The name and percentage in each item are separated by spaces. Empty names are discarded.

```
($name,$perc) = split(' ',$i);
if ($name ne "") { ...process non-empty strings .. }
```

Now create strings based on the percentage used. The value of $hash is set to the cell value to show for the table based on the value of the percentage for the disk name.

```
$hash = sprintf "<td>%d%%</td>",$perc;
if ($perc > 90) {
$hash = sprintf "<td><font
color=green>%d%%</font></td>",$perc; }
    if ($perc > 95) {
    $hash - sprintf "<td><font
color=yellow>%d%%</font></td>",$perc; }
    if ($perc > 97) {
    $hash = sprintf
"<td><fontcolor=red>%d%%</font></td>",$perc; }
    if ($perc == 100) {
    $hash = sprintf "<td><font
color=red><blink>%d%%</blink></font></td>",$perc; }
    if ($perc > 100) {
    $hash = sprintf "<td><font
color=white><blink>%d%%</blink></font></td>",$perc; }
    $usage{$name} .= $hash;
```

The file is closed after all the records have been read. Now it's simply a matter of creating the table entries for the output.

```
while(($key,$value) =  each(%usage)) {
    printf "<TR><TD>%s</TD>%s</TR>", $key, $value;
}
```

There is an extra @names array in the program. This array stores the names of the disks being monitored. To display the entries sorted by name of the disk, use the following code:

```
foreach $i (sort keys %usage) {
    printf "<TR><TD>%s</TD>%s</TR>", $i, $usage{$i};
}
```

By traversing through the foreach loop, the $i variable is assigned the value of the sorted names array. Remember that the %usage array is indexed by the name of each disk. The @names array must be sorted and then each entry for the corresponding item in the %usage array must be printed out.

To close the table and the HTML file, follow the code shown in Listing 14.5.

Listing 14.5: Disklog.pl

```perl
#!/usr/local/bin/perl
# ────────────────────────────
# The program displays a 25 column wide table based
# on the input from the disk usage output from a
# cron command. The input file is created periodically,
# once per hour.
# ────────────────────────────
# These are the local variables used in the program
# ────────────────────────────
# $wday = week day
# $mon  = month in ASCII
# $mday = day of month
# $tod  = time of day as HH:MM:SS
# $tz   = time zone
# $hr,$min,$sec = of time of day
# $year = year
# $info = to show data for
# @names = names of disks to monitor
# %usage = indexed by disk name with percentage per item.
# numdisks = number of disks
# ────────────────────────────


# ────────────────────────────
# Initialize all variables and arrays.
# ────────────────────────────
@names = ();
%usage = {};
$numdisk = 0;
# ────────────────────────────
# Reply to browser
# ────────────────────────────
$| = 1;
print "Content-type: text/html\n\n";
# ────────────────────────────
# Send HTML page
# ────────────────────────────
print << "HTMLHEAD";
<HTML><HEAD><TITLE>Disk Stats</TITLE></HEAD><BODY>
<H1> Table </H1>
<TABLE BORDER>
```

```
<TR><TH>Disk</TH>
HTMLHEAD
for ($i=0;$i<24;$i++) { printf "<TH>%d</TH>",$i; }
print "</TR>";
# ————————————————
# Process all input
# ————————————————
open(FB,"./disklog.dat.r") || die "Cannot open $!\n";
while($input=<FB>){
    $input =~ s/\{\}//; # remove {} from input
    ($wday,$mon,$mday,$tod,$tz) = split(' ',$input);
    ($hr,$min,$sec) = split(':',$tod); # get time
    $index = index($input,'/');  # find first directory
    $info =  substr($input,$index); # get rest of data
# ————————————————
# Process each disk's input
# ————————————————
    @disks = split(/\+/,$info);
    foreach $i (@disks) {
    ($name,$perc) = split(' ',$i);
    if ($name ne "") {
     $hash = sprintf "<td>%d%%</td>",$perc;

     if ($perc > 100) {
      $hash = sprintf "<td><font
color=white><blink>%d%%</blink></font></td>",$perc;
      }
     if ($perc == 100) {
      $hash = sprintf "<td><font
color=red><blink>%d%%</blink></font></td>",$perc;
      }
     if ($perc > 97) {
      $hash = sprintf "<td><font
color=red>%d%%</font></td>",$perc; }
     if ($perc > 95) {
      $hash = sprintf "<td><font
color=yellow>%d%%</font></td>",$perc; }
     if ($perc > 90) {
      $hash = sprintf "<td><font
color=green>%d%%</font></td>",$perc; }
# ————————————————
# Assign output string
# ————————————————
     $usage{$name} .= $hash;
     $names($name) = $hash;  # store away just in case.
     } # if non-empty name
    }
    print "\n";
}
close(FB);
```

```
# _____
# Print table entries in the order they are created.
# _____
while(($key,$value) = each(%usage)) {
    printf "<TR><TD>%s</TD>%s</TR>", $key, $value;
}

# _____
# Uncomment these lines to sort by directory name
# _____
# foreach $i (sort keys %usage) {
#    printf "<TR><TD>%s</TD>%s</TR>", $i, $usage{$i};
# }
print "</TABLE>\n";
print "</BODY></HTML>";
```

Summary

This program, although simple in its purpose, provides a clear method of seeing what the status of the disks were for the system manager. The program's ability to maintain accurate historical data permits the systems manager to see where disk space is being used. This allows systems management to proactively act on disk cleanup and, when required, order a new hard drive prior to a crisis ensuing.

As was pointed out, there are areas of concern when it comes to the space requirements for the data that is used to generate the display. This program, as it is now designed, doesn't really take that issue into consideration as it was not a requirement of the initial customer for whom it was designed.

Here, the best option is to have a second crontab running at the very beginning of each month that does a compress and backup of the old data (for the last month), but leaves the information attainable for historical purposes.

Sometimes the most simple of tasks is the one that can bring the greatest overall savings.

On that note we will close this section. We have covered a large number of applications, and have looked at many different ways of leveraging CGI's to work for you. The next section will discuss some of the management issues with Webservers and CGI development.

PART THREE

Advanced Discussions: Server Issues

?

—1862 cable by Victor Hugo to his publisher

!

—The response

Part 3 details server issues. We will discuss how to work with the NCSA HTTPd sever to allow CGIs to work best in your environment. We will talk about Server Side Include issues, security issues (and .htaccess), and server set up issues.

We will also take time to explore what a server tells you about your site and how to make that information useful. The following chapters are much like the quote at the top of this page; taken out of context they don't mean all that much.

Once the full story of the quote is known, it all becomes clear. Victor Hugo's cable of "?" was in response to his agents claim that sales of his book Les Miserables were very high in France. The agent's response of "!" was his way of saying that the figures were correct.

In much the same way the log files that are maintained by the HTTPd processor are filled with gems of information if you just understand the shorthand in which they are written, and how they can help you. It is hoped that Chapters 15 and 16 will help you mine these gems.

As for Chapter 17, it was supposed to be a short few closing pages and thoughts. Nothing ever comes out like you plan. We hope you enjoy what we put there instead.

Chapter 15 **Systems Management of the Web and CGIs**

Chapter 16 **Web Management Issues: Server Setup and Log Files**

Chapter 17 **Pontificating**

CHAPTER 15

SYSTEMS MANAGEMENT OF THE WEB AND CGIs

- Basic Security
- .htaccess
- The cgi-bin

This chapter focuses on some of the key aspects of making an Intranet or Internet World Wide Web work. It's not as easy as throwing a server on the system and walking away. This section will detail some of the more gruesome aspects of Web and CGI management, as well as some of the thoughts you should have before even getting involved with a Web-based project.

Why are we going into this now? Why didn't we start with this type of information? As explained in the Introduction to this section and the book, we wanted to cover the basics first, then to get into the code as quickly as we could and then to wrap up with some information we felt was important, but wasn't code related.

There are any number of books available that will provide you with the basics of Web server management. Our hope is provide you with some insight on how this effects CGIs and CGI development. We will focus on issues of control over content, development and access. We will discuss the benefits of firewall location in regarding firewalls, and how you can run both an intranet and Internet access machine.

Finally, this chapter will focus on some concerns about the cgi-bin area that you should consider when initially starting up a Web server.

Security Issues

In Chapter 2, we discussed some of the issues revolving around security and the need to protect your services from the bad guys on the Internet. We discussed security models, and focused on the firewall and how it protected the internal machines. Finally, we focused on the concept of having your Web server as a machine in the DMZ where it could be sacrificed.

As pointed out before, we don't believe that a machine, and the data on it, is a commodity to be sacrificed to the evil hackers on the hope that once they compromise that platform they will leave the rest of your site alone. We don't think that will work, and it provides you with a false sense of security. Also, your Web server and the data that it serves is going to be part of your public persona. It is a portion of your image that you show electronically. It is part of who you are. Would you let people spray paint your billboards on the hope that they wouldn't break into your offices and steal furniture? We know we wouldn't, so why should we treat our electronic storefront any different than we do our image elsewhere.

An additional issue is that the sacrifice model assumes that you won't want to communicate with the internal machines, like reading data from the databases you maintain there. If you are going to allow the machine to be compromised, you certainly don't want to allow any holes where someone who has compromised that machine can attack your internal services from that external machine.

So, we certainly aren't going to put our Web server in the DMZ to be handed over to the evil net persona's. That means that we will be putting it on the internal portion of our systems, somewhere behind the firewall, protected. To best accomplish this, a rule should be made on the firewall that will allow for the HTTP method to be transparently permitted to the Web server. If the Web server is also being used to service FTP requests (as the ftpserver) the firewall should also permit FTP services to access the machine through the firewall.

All other services to that machine (the Web server/ftpserver) across the firewall should be denied.

Using this method, we have taken over control and security of the overall server system. Now we can use features of the operating system, as discussed in Chapters 2 and 3. In addition, by using products like wu-ftp, we can add further levels of security to the FTP services.

What of the HTTPd services? Can we secure them? In some way these services can be secured. Using protocols like the Secure Sockets Layer (SSL) or SHTTP (Secure HTTP), we can add a layer of common security protocols across the service. These will add various levels of security using encryption technology. These are mostly useful for transactions where there is the risk of violating the data in transit (like a financial transaction) rather than securing the actual application and the server.

So what can you do to secure the site?

There are any number of ways to define security. If you want to, you can:

- Scoop out much of the /etc/services file
- Move certain programs from their normal location to a secondary one. For example, you could move the rm command to /bin/tcmd/nuse (this would require the creation of the tcmd and nuse directories).
- Attempt to confuse a would-be intruder by renaming the common utilities rm to away. Then you could set the actual rm command to /bin/false, or to a procedure that logs the usage.
- Use a procedure, like super. A program from the public domain that wraps all access to commands in a shell that logs command usage.

super it is also designed to permit and deny access to certain commands based on user and group. Generally super is used to allow normal users access to commands as root, but, with a few minor changes to the source code, it can be modified to allow any command access to be recorded and not only be used for root access.

As you can see, there are any number of ways to secure the HTTP server on the site so that it is not possible to leverage that machine to make attacks on either internal or external hosts. While this book isn't a primer on security, there are a number of books referenced in the resources list in the appendix which detail security issues.

As to why you would go through all this trouble, one of the key reasons is to permit you to maintain a secure channel between the HTTP server and the internal machines that may be used to store and to maintain data.

There are also, in most HTTP servers, additional configuration controls and commands that permit finer granularity of access control to pages and to data that reside on the HTTP server. This can generally be done from within the configuration files (discussed in the next chapter) or from the .htaccess files. The .htaccess files use the same directory limitations that are available from within the configuration files, but are done in a way that permits direct access to configuration by the person maintaining the directory and doesn't require server restart to upgrade or to modify the security of the directory. Hammer and others in the re-engineering profession refer to this type of file as empowering, since control for security of the data within the sphere of control for that directory belongs to the person who accepts responsibility for that directory.

.htaccess

The .htaccess file provides the ability for information protection on the HTTP server. That means that access control via the HTTP protocols are controlled on all the page information and data within a directory. This protection is generally done by a user name and a password schema. What does that mean for you? It means that you can provide limited access to the pages under a directory structure by allowing only certain people and certain actions within the directory structure.

This requires the use of two files. The first is the .htaccess file that lives in the directory where the access will be granted/limited. The second is the .htpasswd file which can live in any location within the server. The full Unix pathname is required to define the file and its location.

Here is an example of the contents of the .htaccess file. Don't worry, each and every part of it is explained in Table 15.1

```
AuthUserFile /secdir/.htpasswd
AuthGroupFile /dev/null
AuthName ByPassword
AuthType Basic
<Limit GET>
require user zippy
</Limit>
```

As you can see, the file has some interesting capabilities. Using this file, we can allow or disallow access from domains, from individual groups of users, or from the individual user. Let's take a closer look at how we would accomplish each of these.

Table 15.1: Directives within the .htaccess file

Directive	Description
AuthUserFile	The location and name of the file where the password information will reside.
AuthGroupFile	The location and name of the file where the groups and group members are defined. Use /dev/null if there is no AuthGroupFile being used.
AuthName	When prompted for the password, this is the title of the prompt. It is also used to store the password authorization so the user won't be prompted for the password if they return to this location in this session. Try to use something descriptive, yet not common.

Table 15.1 (cont.): Directives within the .htaccess file

Directive	Description
AuthType	In most cases. this would be "Basic." Some browsers and servers will support other types of authorization. Options include; PEM, PGP, KerberosV4, KerberosV5, and Digest.
<Limit ...>	Starts the list of limitations. Limitations can be on "GET", "POST", and "PUT", either individually or as a group.
order deny,allow	This allows a directory to allow or disallow its access based on from where the person trying to gain access (the IP address or its associated domain name).
deny from	The domain name to be denied (keyword all).
allow from	The domain name to be allowed (keyword all).
require	Used to ensure that one of the three, if not all three, of these criteria are met prior to allowing access: Keywords: user (that the user's name is valid in the database), Group (only users of a certain group can access the directory), valid-user (only a user with the proper user name password combination is allowed access).
satisfy	Allows the file to state that any match criteria is acceptable. Keywords: any/all (all is the default).
</Limit>	End of limitations.

Allowing and Disallowing Domains with .htaccess

In this case, we have no need for the password and the group files. In addition, we will be using the basic method. So our .htaccess file would start with:

```
AuthUserFile /dev/null
AuthGroupFile /dev/null
```

```
AuthName AllowLocalAccess
AuthType Basic
```

Note that we have set the password and the group files to /dev/null. This has been done to ensure that there is no chance of picking up some stray and unnecessary file.

```
<Limit GET POST>
order deny,allow
deny from all
allow from .localdomain.com
</Limit>
```

Here we have limited access to the directory by stating that the user can only do GETs and POSTs if the domain that they are in is permitting that. The first thing we do is deny everyone access to do GET and POST; this is the default state. We use the keyword all to make the default cover anyone we don't wish to have access. Then, we open up access with the allow directive to those domains to which we want to allow access. Note that we prefix the domain with a ".". That means that any subdomain within that domain can access the directory.

The allow and deny directives are permitted to have multiple hosts on the allow and deny lines. The following line in the file above would have allowed people from .localdomain.com and .otherlocal.com to access the private directory. Supported formats for the location name are in Table 15.2

```
allow from .localdomain.com .otherlocal.com
```

Table 15.2: Allow and deny (acceptable formats for location

Item	Format
a domain name	.localdomain.com
a host name	badkid.localdomain.com (note that there is no preceeding ".")
a full IP address	192.168.1.100
a partial IP address	192.168.1. (note that it must end in a ".")
all	The keyword for every host in the world.

You can further enhance the limitations by using the following directive:

```
require user ivler
require group authors
require valid-user husain
```

The require directive states that, if the person is permitted by the allow directive, they still have to be in the permitted users file (.htpasswd) if the keyword is *user*. This also means that the "user" must be in the group file if the keyword is *group*. And, if the keyword is valid-user, the users must enter their name and password to validate that they are permitted into the directory.

By default, the user must satisfy all the given directives. The file can contain the directive satisfy. The satisfy directive is used to allow any (a keyword) require directive to be satisfied and then all directives will be satisfied. Again, the default is the keyword *all*, so it is not required. This is used to open the security up a tad, rather than keeping it tightly closed.

Allowing and Disallowing Users with .htaccess

How do we permit or deny access to the directory by user name? This was touched on a bit above when we used the require directive. To allow or to deny users, you must have a file that is used to hold user names and passwords. This file is not the same as that used to store account passwords (/etc/passwd). This means that you don't have to create accounts for users to provide security on Web access to a directory.

The path to the file that contains the user names and passwords is defined in the AuthUserFile directive. The path name *must* be the full Unix pathname to the file. We could do the following if we were protecting a directory called /usr/name/inprogress/:

```
mkdir /usr/name/inprogress/.data
./htpasswd -c /usr/name/inprogress/.data/.htpasswd username
```

The first command will make a hidden directory; the second will run a program called htpasswd (the code, htpasswd.c is provided in an NCSA HTTPd distribution). That program will create (the -c option) the file /usr/name/inprogress/.data/.htpasswd and load the user name username to the file. It will then prompt a password from that user, and a confirmation. That will look like:

```
./htpasswd -c /usr/name/inprogress/.data/.htpasswd username
Adding password for username.
New password:
Re-type new password:
```

To add additional user names and passwords, you can simply use the htpasswd program without the -c option.

Can this process be automated? Can it be run from a user interactive Web page? Yes. The CGI script will need to do two things. First, it will have to be able to open and write to the .htaccess file if the person is adding a new entry (name). Then, it will have to be able to run the htpasswd program against the correct .htpasswd file (for additions or for updates). Neither of these is impossible and can be easily performed in Tcl, Perl and even in shell. Some of the gotcha's to look out for are disallowing duplicate user names, making sure that users are aware that the password information is passed in the open and should not match any other password information that they have online and, most importantly, not allowing for one user to change the password of another.

Allowing and Disallowing Groups with .htaccess

Grouping is a concept that allows a number of users to be established as part of a group. This allows a directory to be secured with a group access which lowers the amount of overhead for the person maintaining access.

Let's use the example above, where we want to add a new person to the area. There are two ways this can be done. The first, as outlined above, required that the .htaccess file be opened up and then the user added to that file. Then we had to create the user entry in the .htpasswd file.

In actuality, the last thing you want to be doing is opening and closing, writing and rewriting the .htaccess file. Sure, it can be done, but we can drive cars off cliffs and we don't do that just because it can be done. If there is an easier route, why not take it. That easier route is the group access file.

In this case, we provide group access to the directory by changing the .htaccess file as follows:

```
AuthUserFile /pathto/passwdfile/.htpasswd
AuthGroupFile /pathto/groupfile/.htgroup
AuthName grouptest
AuthType Basic
<limit GET POST PUT>
require group the-group
</limit>
```

In the file .htgroup, you would have a record that looked like:

```
the-group: user1 user2 user3 user4
```

where user1,user2, user3, and user4 were users who had entries in the .htpasswd file.

Now, we can see a system where each month you add a new month-group to the .htaccess file in the require line. Then, if a user wants to be added, they could be added to the latest month-group in the .htgroup file and have an entry added in the .htpasswd file.

Using this method, we are not having to access and update the .htaccess file at all, and it provides a clean and clear method of adding new people to the access list. Also, using month-groups like the example method keeps the groups nicely compacted into a scheme that can be used to require people to re-access themselves to the system if you so choose. Another common grouping method is by first character and, since both Tcl and Perl have strong sort capabilities, this is also fairly easy to implement.

Intranets and Internet: Some Differences and Considerations

Throughout this book, we have attempted to show some of the differences between intranets and Internets. One of the key aspects that we always return to deals with security. On intranets, there are usually documents and information that you don't want to share with the outside world. For instance, it wouldn't be very acceptable if someone from the outside world obtained access to your intranet white pages programs, especially if that someone was a competitor, or worse yet, a headhunter.

To ensure that Internets and Intranets don't co-mingle, it is important to provide unique platforms for each. If that cannot be done, try some of the following ideas.

1. Place the two servers onto different ports. The default server port is 80; some common ones besides 80 are 8080, 8088 and 8008. If you place your intranet server on any port over 1024, such as port 3100 (the suite number of the floor you are on) or 6200 (the last four digits of a phone number) or even an address like 62030 (as in 62030 Westbrook Lane), it is still a legitimate location for the server and its just very well hidden from access. The key to using a secondary port for the intranet server is to make it memorable to the inner office, but make it harder for someone else to understand.

2. Use the controls, as explained before in the .htaccess file, to limit access to the intranet server from the access.conf file (discussed in detail in the next chapter). While we will be discussing the access.conf file in the next chapter, one of the many things that it permits is control over what users are permitted to access what directories and what users are not. These same levels of control can be leveraged using .htaccess files at the directory level. If you have a proxy server providing access to the external Web, you must ensure that the server doesn't state that access is coming in from the internal domain. You should arrange for the proxy server to be on a separate subnet within the domain and use IP filtering. It is possible to spoof IPs and this could lead to a possible vulnerability.

3. Use an .htaccess or access.conf to control access to the cgi-bin. In this way, an intruder could get to static areas, but all activities that require access to the databases or to the CGI programs that access internal databases would be limited

4. In much the same way, you could use multiple cgi-bin areas to control who has access to what cgi-bin. In that case the standard cgi-bin area would be open, but you would use .htaccess and access.conf to limit the ability of a person to access the special cgi-bin areas.

While all four of these methods attempt to provide some level of security and control over database, program, and intranet access, these all leave open certain vulnerabilities on the machine that is acting as your dual HTTP server.

If the HTTP server is attacked, there is the possibility that the person penetrating could violate the integrity of the system. This means that they could get access to the computer and cause the computer to issue commands that would effect the disk. In this case, you would want to ensure that the machine had a very limited number of accounts and that the disks were partitioned in such a way that anyone able to violate the system would be unable to write over any partition of which they were not the owner (there is also an excellent program called tripwire that can be used to ensure file and system integrity).

This would require that each of the HTTP servers on the machine was created with a different user and group ID. In addition, these IDs should be established as non-loginable. There should be a matching set of IDs in the /etc/passwd file that permits a login to the User ID (UID) and the Group ID (GID), but under a different name so the maintainers of the HTTP servers don't work on the machine as root.

We want to focus for a moment on one other aspect that you should consider before you co-locate the external and internal HTTP servers. In the first section, when we discussed Internet security, we focused on any number of techniques to limit access from the external world to your internal services. Every time you need to cross a protocol and a port with a service, you are opening a possible channel that could be used by an intruder. One way of hiding these services and accesses to other machines is to remove the services from the /etc/service and /etc/inetd files. Establish the services on alternative ports, much like we are doing by running the HTTP server at a nontraditional port.

In performing the basic security functions above, you can create a virtual HTTP server that can be used for Intranets, but can co-locate with the external server. While this is not a recommended method of establishing services, it does permit a small business the opportunity to lower the hardware costs and to provide both Intranet and Internet services at a reasonable cost, and with some level of security protecting the overall services, functionality and proprietary aspects of the Intranet from Internet access. Again, I cannot overstate that security through smoke-and-mirrors is not security in any real sense of the word. It will make it harder for the average hack to get in, but anyone who wants to come in will be able to bypass it sooner or later with enough time, energy and interest.

The answer, as always, to security questions on the Net is to secure with the proper levels of security for the value of the data that you would lose if it was not secured. If an individuals banking information were to be made public because someone was able to break into a bank, even to view it, then they would be most upset. We expect that data to be held most secure (yet, this is the same data that we entrust to the post office to deliver to us once a month with only a small white envelope protecting it from being breached). A bank, being aware that our perceived needs (note, not our actual needs) cannot allow them to be seen as a breach of our account information, needs high levels of security to ensure that those needs and perceptions are met.

Concerns About What You Got

One of the better aspects of the world of CGI development is that it is so easy to create an active environment using CGIs. This, like all things in life, has its strength as well as it's weaknesses. In fact, some of the programs that you are provided with right out of the box when you install a server can act as some of the greatest problems for you.

Programs that are generally delivered with a server include Perl, C, Tcl and shell scripts that require no input, or use standard input. Since these programs are so readily available, there is always the possibility that someone may attempt to access these CGI scripts from within your cgi-bin area. This could be considered a glaring security hole, unless you wanted them to get access to a finger gateway on your host.

In addition, programs like the finger gateway, the various test programs that dump all the environment variables, and others also could pose a threat to your system's integrity.

To avoid these issues, start with a clean cgi-bin directory on your HTTP server. Take all the programs that are provided when you first start and move them to a directory that is hidden and is set with execute only access. Set all the files as execute access only as well. Then, if you need to use one of these programs, create a symbolic link from the cgi-bin area to the proper filename in the proper directory. Make sure the link name is esoteric to ensure that someone doing a view source on the HTML wouldn't be able to see where the link is, or what the CGI is supposed to be doing.

It is important that you consider all aspects of your system when working with it. If there is the possibility that someone can get into your system and breach it, they will. It may happen as part of an oversight on your part and pure dumb luck on theirs. There could have been no malicious intent. But remember, we are talking about your electronic presence.

Directory Listings

Way back in Chapter 2 we mentioned that we would talk about default files and directory listings as security issues. While these values are set in the configuration files, they are mentioned here because they are security issues as well.

In the configuration files discussed in the next chapter we will talk about establishing a default file. That is the file that the system will return if a URL comes in without a file defined. For example, if your system was called companya.com and there was a request to your system for a HTTP service that looked like http://www.companya.com/ the system should return some file. The file that this returns is called the default file. When the server sees the URL above the server checks to see what the default file is supposed to be and it will return that file to the user.

In most systems the default file is called index.html . This file name can be changed in the configuration file. It also can be a list of file names, and it will return the first name on the list. This allows the default file to be a Server Side Include file (index.shtml) or a series of possible files {index.shtml index.html main.html README badlocation.html}. In this series it would start looking to return the first file in the series, and would continue until it hit the last file. If no default file is found it will then try to index the directory if permitted.

This is where things get scary security-wise. In some cases it might be useful to allow someone to get a directory listing. If you are using the directory to allow people to access it like an FTP archive, then it's nice to let the system take over the listing tasks. What about having listing on and not having a default file in the directory, like an image library? Do you really want your image library to become a place where people from all over the net can drop by and take images?

As we have said, a directory listing can be a very useful tool (it is useful when you are doing development and want to be able to just jump around the directory loading files), but it is also something that is open to potential security abuses. The easiest way to ensure that the directory listing services are not abused is to make sure the last file-name in your default list is something like badlocation.html. Then, make sure that every directory has a file in it called badlocation.html that links to a single file. This file should indicate to the user that he or she has come to a location that they could not have reached by following the links on the site. (They should be aware that the owner of the site would prefer that they follow the links that you provide.)

Summary

In this section, we covered some of the key aspects dealing with security of the HTTP server. We discussed where it should live and looked at methods for securing it on the machine. We also covered issues dealing with securing access to information that is on the HTTP server through the .htaccess file. Finally, we covered the need to secure the CGI area (cgi-bin) from the software that gets run, and the need to use default files.

All this information is a precursor to the next chapter where we will cover some of the initialization issues dealing with the server and log file analysis. Specifically, we will be looking at how the initialization files secure the HTTP server, how they define the environment in both the CGI and HTTP sense, and how they can be tuned to meet your needs. Then, we will look at all four log files that are kept by most standard (NCSA type) servers. We will look at what is recorded and how that information can be used. We will even look at what Web analysis is and why you want to do it for your environment.

CHAPTER 16

WEB MANAGEMENT ISSUES: SERVER SETUP AND LOG FILES

- Understanding and Using the Configuration File

- Understanding the Log Files

- Debugging Using the Log Files

This chapter will focus on how the initial setup of the server can affect your ability to use CGIs, SSIs, and other enhanced features available via configuration files. There is an assumption that you have access to these files, or that you can request changes so you can use these features.

After a look at how we set up the server, we will look at what the server tells us. This information is recorded in the log files that the server keeps on the transactions that are processed through the server.

We will look at some very simple Unix commands that you can use to get a view of the data in your log files, but we will not be providing any real software to do log file analysis. One of the main reasons for that is one of the basic philosophies of the book. Why recreate the wheel?

483

In the book, we didn't do a guestbook because there are over 20 great guestbooks already out there in Perl, Tcl, C and every other language known to CGI. In much the same way, this text will not provide a log analysis tool because there are so many out there that it would be an effort in futility. What we will do is explain the log files, their formats, and how the information in them can be used.

As for who has the best analysis tool and why, this text won't even get into that. We have used MK_Stats from Matt Kruse, W3Perl from Laurent Domisse, getsats from Kevin Hughes, Analog by Stephen Turner and even Thomas Boutelle's wusage program to perform log file analysis. These programs all have their strengths and their weaknesses, and also represent less than 10 percent of all that's available. We will provide a reference page in the appendix that will point you to all these programs and many more, but we won't be recreating that very well-built wheel here.

So let's start by looking at what we can do to the configuration files and how we manage the server.

.conf Files

The configuration (.conf) files used by the HTTP daemon are simple in their set up. They are also well-defined in any number of man pages and server texts. What we will be going through in this section will deal with how the files are set up and special features of which you should be aware.

We will be looking at the NCSA HTTPd 1.5 configuration files within this text. Now, if you are using a Netscape Enterprise Sever or the IIS from Microsoft, chances are you will never see these server configuration files. On the other hand, if you use Apache, some of this material might look really familiar from the Web page at www.apache.org/info.html:

> The Apache group was formed around a number of people who provided patch files that had been written for NCSA httpd 1.3. The result after combining them was A PAtCHy server.

There are three basic configuration files (excluding mime.types which is a required file for the system to function). These files control all the server, document and security configuration of the server and are used at server initialization (when the server starts up).

As each one of these could generate a chapter in itself (as an example, the server configuration file, http.conf, contains over 32 directives and sub-directives to manipulate the configuration of the server), we won't be covering all the varied details of each of the configuration files. What we will be doing is looking at how configuration effects CGI access and control as well as SSI issues.

Server Configuration and CGI

The directives in Table 16.1 are located in the server configuration file. This table lists server directives that should be understood for how they work with the CGI or logging system. Again, these server configuration files are NCSA HTTPd specific, but there is a very high probability that the server you use has a file similar to this with similar directives.

Table 16.1: Server Directives

Directive	Use	Description
ServerRoot	ServerRoot /path/tofiles/	Declares the path for the server's files. This allows all server configuration files and locations to be made relative to that root, rather than requiring an explicit and complete path name for each file or location. The helps the administrator perform server maintenance as it allows the server to be moved from one disk location to another (say you decide you need more space and need to move the server to a larger disk partition) without having to worry about changing a large number of path references.
AccessConfig	AccessConfig filename	Tells the location of the access configuration file (default: conf/

Table 16.1 (continued): Server Directives

Directive	Use	Description
		access.conf. The filename can be the complete path or a path relative to ServerRoot.
ResourceConfig	ResourceConfig filename	Tells the location of the resource configuration file (default: conf/srm.conf). The filename can be a complete path or a path relative to ServerRoot.
TypesConfig	TypesConfig filename	Tells the location of the mime.types file. The filename can be a complete path or a relative path to Server-Root.
KeepAlive	KeepAlive state	State can be either ON or OFF. KeepAlive allows the server to keep the connection between the server and the client open if the client understands KeepAlive. This permits requests for additional items that are embedded in the original request to be obtained over this stated connection. In this way, an HTML file that contained three images using KeepAlive would be able to serve the document and its images to the client in a single instance rather than having to go through the start-up time for each requested item.
MaxKeep-AliveRequests	MaxKeep-AliveRequests #	The maximum number of requests that the KeepAlive will service. Default is 5 and use of MaxKeep-AliveRequests 0 will allow it to stay open until KeepAliveTimeout has been reached.
KeepAlive-Timeout	KeepAlive-Timeout #	The number of seconds before the connection is timed out. Default is 10.

Table 16.2 also contains directives that are in the server configuration file. These directives control the log files.

Table 16.2 Log file Server Directives

Directive	Use	Description
ErrorLog	ErrorLog filename	The name of the error log file. The default filename is logs/error_log and is a relative path from the ServerRoot. Setting ErrorLog /dev/null effectively turns off all error logging.
TransferLog	TransferLog filename	The name of the transfer or access log. Officially called the transfer log, this log file is also referred to as the access log, as the default filename for the log file is logs/access_log.
AgentLog	AgentLog filename	The name of the log that captures the agent information from the client. The default is logs/agent_log
RefererLog	RefererLog filename	The name of the log that captures the referrer information from the client. The default is logs/referrer_log.
RefererIgnore	RefererIgnore string	Many times there is a desire to ignore certain information from the referrer. That is especially true when you don't want to see all the information about pages on your system that reference other pages. In this instance, you can tell the server to ignore all headers that have in it the string you declare. You can declare as many strings as you want and they will not be logged.

Resource Configuration

This file is generally called the srm.conf file. I have always thought of *srm* as yet another three-letter acronym. In my case, I took it to mean Server Resource Manager file.

This file defines the directory root and directory indexing options (see the discussion on security in Chapter 16. It also allows you to add new types and to control what error document is delivered to the user when an error status is recorded. As usual, some of these features and functions have an effect on you while working with CGIs. Table 16.3 lists the ones in which you should be most aware.

Table 16.3: Noteworthy Resource Directives

Directive	Use	Description
AccessFile-Name	AccessFile-Name filename	For those of you who want to obscure the security a bit more, you can use this directive to set the access filename from .htaccess to another name, like .htacces2.
DirectoryIndex	DirectoryIndex filename	At the end of the Chapter 15 (and in Chapter 2) we talked about directory indexing and default file names. This is the value that you set to establish the default filenames to be sought. As of NCSA HTTPd 1.5 you have been allowed to use a list of filenames and it will return the leftmost one it finds.
AddType	AddType type/ sub-type extension	Used to override the mime.types file's default configurations. In this case, a new type of file can be defined, along with the extension for that file. When a header is sent, it is sent with mime type information which allows it to be changed based on the file extension. For example, when we build the header and put out the type as Content-type: text/html\n\n we are doing the task normally done by the server when it sees the extension of the filename.
ErrorDocument	ErrorDocument type file	The description of how to use this follows.

Yes, you can have an error generate a document other than the error message on the gray screen. This can be done by using HTML files in the DocumentRoot directory, or in a named sub-directory. That's the good news. The better news is that the document you return can be a CGI script.

For instance, if we have a person who generates a status 400 error, we could be real nice and try to help them. We could have a CGI that verifies that the name of the path was correct and, if not, was it close? If it was close, does the file they want exist within the path? If the file exists, why not let them know that the one they asked for wasn't found, but give them a link to the one that looks like what they may have actually wanted.

Would such a program be right all the time? Nope. But it would be right enough of the time to make people aware that you do this at your site and this is a very nice feature to implement.

When you use a CGI script for error messaging, there are three additional environment variables that are provided. These are detailed in Table 16.4.

Table 16.4: Additional Environment Variables Used by ErrorDocument

Variable	Description
REDIRECT_REQUEST	The request as originally sent exactly to the NCSA HTTPd server.
REDIRECT_URL	The requested URI that generated the error.
REDIRECT_STATUS	The status number and message that NCSA HTTPd would have sent to the client had it not been circumvented by the srm configuration.

Access Configuration: Security One Last Time

In Chapter 15, we talked about the conf files being able to do some security set up. We also talked about using the .htaccess file to provide levels of access control. Here we will use the configuration file to show how we can define Global Access Control or per-directory access control. The access.conf file maintains the access information for each and every directory that you choose to list. It also contains access information for the default security model that you will have on the directory. Table 16.5 lists the access configuration file directives and how they work.

Table 16.5: Access Directives

Directive	Use	Description
Directory	<Directory dir>	Where dir is the absolute pathname of the directory being defined/protected.
	</Directory>	There is a closing directive to this </Directory> once completed. All the directives within this table can be used between the opening and closing of the Directory directive.
Options		See the detailed text and Table 16.6 below.
AllowOverride	AllowOverride type	Where type is one of any of the following: *None:* No Access Configuration Files are permitted *All:* Access Configuration Files are unrestricted in this directory *Options:* Allows use of the options directive (see below) *FileInfo:* Allows use of the AddType and AddEncoding directives *AuthConfig:* Allows the use of the directives permitting authorization configuration (items in this table that begin with "Auth") *Limit:* Allows the use of the <limit> directive and all the subdirectives *Redirect:* Allows the use of the Redirect directive (Redirect is an srm.conf directive and allows for entire virtual directories to be created and then redirected at the server level to physical disk locations)

Table 16.5 (continued): Access Directives **491**

Directive	Use	Description
AuthName	AuthName nameval	The name of the secure area. I have heard this referred to as the domain (to be confused with DNS domains) and realm, as in the lands one has control over. I guess I find neither satisfactory. This is the name for the secure space you are defining.
AuthType	AuthType type	Currently the only valid type is basic.
AuthUserFile	AuthUserFile filename	The full absolute path to the user authorization file (created with the .htpasswd program) for the directory.
AuthGroupFile	AuthGroupFile filename	The full absolute path to the group filename for the directory.
Limit	<limit> </limit>	Used to enclose the limitation directives below.
order	order x	Where x is either:
		allow,deny deny,allow mutual-failure
		This specifies the way all limit directives are evaluated. It allows you to clearly state who is allowed, and anything not allowed is denied (first option). The reverse can also be stated (second option) and then a third option that says that anything not either explicitly allowed or denied is denied by default.
Deny	deny name	Used to deny access to a directory. The following forms are allowable:
		The keyword all
		The IP address or complete domain name

Table 16.5 (continued): Access Directives

Directive	Use	Description
		A single host name or the single IP address of a host
		A partial IP address (10.1.10. would match all addresses in that class C domain). If the trailing dot is omitted and the address is 10.1.10 it would close off both the 10.1.10.* class C and the 10.1.10[0-9]. Class Cs - the dot is very important)
allow	allow name	Used to allow access to a directory. The same forms are supported for allow as for deny. In both the allow and deny directives, the default is keyword all.
Require	require entity [1-n]	Requires authentication for the entity where the entity is:

user
group
valid-user

Where user allows only named users, group only allows people within named groups (from the AuthGroupFile) and valid-user allows any user defined in the AuthUserFile. |
| Referer | referer URL | Where the URL is the a complete or partial URL/path of the documents that must be accessed prior to accessing the ones within this directory. |
| Satisfy | satisfy all\|any | When require is used with allow, this directive makes it an or (any) and and (all) condition before access can be granted. The default is all the and |

Table 16.5 (continued): Access Directives

493

Directive	Use	Description
		condition. In this condition, both the allow and the require must be satisfied before access is permitted.
OnDeny	OnDeny URL	Where URL is the path to the redirect for access denied.

While most of Table 16.5 makes perfect, clear sense, there are some rather powerful commands that are hardly ever utilized and are aren't really pushed to the limits of what they can do. The referer directive within the <limit> block is a great example of this.

In many cases, you will want to pre-qualify access to an area. For instance, we want to limit people coming to view the latest information on a product until we have put them through an anticipation process of two or three screens (sort of like waiting on line at Disneyland). We can use the referer directive to ensure that they cannot jump directly to the location, but have to come in through the path that was laid out for them. You can use this same methodology to force people to respond to a form before allowing access, yet not requiring them to enter a user name password to get to the directories that you want them to have to pass through.

The Options Directive

This is the core of allowing CGI access to a directory. This directive tells a directory what it can and can not do. Table 16.6 lists all the options available when configuring the options directive;

Table 16.6: The Options Directive

Subdirective	Description
None	All features for the directory are disabled.
All	All features for the directory are enabled

Table 16.6 (continued): The Options Directive

Subdirective	Description
FollowSymLinks	If symbolic links are used within the directory, the server will follow them.
SymLinksIfOwnerMatch	A tad more restrictive, symbolic links will only be followed if the target file/directory is owned by the same UID as the link that was pointing to it.
ExecCGI	This is it! Once this command has been issued the directory is permitted to run CGI scripts.
Includes	Yet another one! This is required if Server Side Include files are permitted to be run from this directory.
Indexes	Allows the server to generate server side indexing in the directory.
IncludesNoExec	They can use Server Side Include directives with the exception of the exec directive from within this directory.

As important as this section is, we can't just let this pass without providing a few samples of some <Directory> directives. Table 16.7 lists them.

Table 16.7: Sample <directory> directives

Directive	Description
<Directory /u1/www>	Start
Options All	Set all options on
<Limit GET POST PUT>	Start limits
order allow,deny	Allow first, then deny
allow from all	Allow all access
</Limit>	End limits
</Directory>	End

Table 16.7 (continued): Sample <directory> directives

495

Directive	Description
<Directory /u1/www/docs/priv>	Start
AuthType Basic	Use Basic Authorization
Authname Work Only	Realm: Work Only
AuthUserFile /u1/sec/docs/priv/.htpasswd	Use an .htpasswd file in another mirror directory
<Limit GET POST PUT>	Start limits
order deny,allow	Deny then allow
deny from all	Deny everyone
allow from .myco.com	Allow from this domain only
require valid-user	Require that the user be in the .htpasswd file
</Limit>	End limits
</Directory>	End
<Directory /u1/www/docs/noofc>	Start
<Limit GET POST PUT>	Start limits
order allow,deny	Allow everyone, then deny
allow from all	Allow the world
deny from .myco.com	Deny from the domain
</Limit>	End limits
</Directory>	End
<Directory /u1/www/docs/frnds>	Start
AuthName My Friends	Realm: My Friends
AuthGroupFile /u1/sec/docs/frnds/.htgroup	Use a group file in another mirror directory
<Limit GET POST PUT>	Start limits
require group	Require a groupmember
</Limit>	End limits
</Directory>	End

There are many more options other than the few examples shown here. The best way to discover what works and what doesn't is to explore. Remember that this is one of the key pieces of security that is provided as part of the server. It isn't the best security in the world, but it has a great deal of ability if you leverage it.

The Log Files

Before we get into the files, let's talk about where they are configured and how they can be configured. In the http.conf file, there is a section that is dedicated to the log files. This section supports the directives in Table 16.2

Common Log Format and Extended Common Log Format

Common Log Format (CLF) is the way that logs were originally kept way back in the dark ages of NCSA HTTP 1.3. Then, as time progressed, Webmasters asked for additional log file information. The initial log files recorded transfers in the "transfer log" (now also known by almost all as the access log based on the default name it has of access_log). The log information was minimal, it was about who transferred what, when, where, how much, and status. For most of us, this was great. The information was in a format pretty close to what many of us knew from working with E-mail systems and their log entries.

Over time, the need for more information created some additional log files. The first (also in 1.3) was the error log. In this case, we wanted all standard error messages generated by the server to be logged in a single place where we could find them. This proved to be very useful for those who debug CGI scripts, and as a CGI developer you tended to be running the CGI and then immediately tail-ing the log file to see if the CGI worked in runtime.

After the error log, there was a need to know what browser was coming into the site. This information also proved useful to the CGI developer as it allowed the developer to use the best possible HTTP extensions for the most popular browsers that were accessing the site.

The last log file that we have is the referrer log. This log file told us from where people were coming. In this way we could see where people were when they accessed our pages, we could track from which pages people accessed us. This also allowed us to write utilities that backtracked those links to see if the person had a link to our work.

Unfortunately, these four files proved to be disconnected enough that sometimes getting useful data from them was more than difficult. In response to that, an effort was made in the release of NCSA

HTTPd 1.5 to support a new, joined log format called Extended Common Log Format (ECLF).

This log format is optional and is turned on by setting it on within the configuration file. When this option is set to on, the following changes take place:

- The referrer log is not used
- The agent log is not used
- The access log has the referrer and the agent information added as the last two fields of the record

This information, in this format, has some real benefits in terms of being able to understand where people come from and what they access. It tightens the relationship between the access data and the referrer and the agent data, permitting a better level of reporting.

Unfortunately, this ECLF is just that, another extension. Many analysis programs do not recognize the extended format and, therefore, will not properly parse the extended data or make use of the features.

Getting Useful Information, or What's In Them There Files?

Each and every log file contains data that can be of some use, even if you don't have an analysis tool. By using some simple Unix command, we can generate information that can be of use to us when we need to have it.

The next couple of pages will explore the log files and their formats and, also, provide information on how to make the data in the log file useful to you. It should be noted that the examples being used are very Unix-centric.

Transfer/Access Log

The transfer/access log will contain records of who accessed the system, when they accessed it, what they wanted, if they got it and how much was sent. If the log is using ECLF, the record will also contain two optional fields: the referrer and the agent. Table 16.8 details all the fields that make up the log record. The record format is:

```
host rfc931-info authuser date URI status size <referrer agent>
```

Table 16.8: The Structure of the Transfer Record

Record Item	Description
host	DNS resolved name or IP of the client
rfc931-info	Any information returned by identd from this client (default is a "-")
authuser	Set when user authorization has taken place (user has entered an authorized/protected directory on the server, the default is a "-")
date	The date in the format: [DD/Mon/YYYY: hh:mm:ss] (brackets included)
URI	The URI request sent to the server. (Security note: That means the entire URI request. In the case of a GET, as we discussed earlier, that includes all the information that was passed in with the GET request)
status	The status code for the completion of the server's action on the request (Table 16.9 contains status code values)
size	The number of bytes transferred (excluding some header information)
referrer	OPTIONAL: Requires ECLF. This file lists the name of the page the user was on prior to issuing the command. The value of having this data is to know how people move around the site. With authuser set, we could trace the way a user transverses the site which provides insight to site design and enhancements.
agent	OPTIONAL: Requires ECLF. This field will list the agent information about the visitor. In most cases, this isn't of extreme value as an associated record to this log. The exception is when a visit come from a search engine or a site indexer. In these instances, the value in this field can indicate that it was an autonomous agent or robot that was at the site.

The transfer log is the mother of all log files. Within this log file are all the raw materials you need to determine how well your site is doing, where people are going, what people are interested in and how well your site functions overall. The information within the log file is like a river flowing from a gold mine and all you need are the right tools to strike it rich. Or you could be panning the muddy waters for ages and never really get a strike.

I won't go into all the tools that are available; a list of resources has been provided in the appendix and there will be even more on the Web site for this text. However, we will go into a few Unix commands you can issue that will help you get fast statistics.

First and foremost we can get a daily count by using a simple command like:

```
$ grep "dd/Mon" access_log | wc -l
```

where dd/Mon is the month and day in the format the log file expects (for example, 07/Dec). This will give a count of the number of accesses that were recorded. This isn't truly an accurate reflection of access to your site, as you really don't want to count the images (and they do show up in the log file). So we can call the above a "traffic count" as that is what it reflects. To get page access counts, we have to remove images (and other nonpage files, like sounds, etc). A command like the one below will give a count of all accesses on a date that were not image files (assuming we use .gif and .jpg as image file extensions):

```
$ grep "dd/Mon" access_log | grep -v ".jpg" | grep -v ".gif"
⇒ | wc -l
```

or a shorter form (where we use the regular expressions within the grep command):

```
$ grep "dd/Mon" access_log | grep -v ".jpg\|.gif" | wc -l
```

This command is much better at reflecting the number of pages served. But you may also want to go so far as to remove all pages that were accessed from your site, assuming you want to look at traffic from external sources. To do that, the grep is modified yet again (if your site is wwinfo.com, for example):

```
$ grep "dd/Mon" access_log | grep -v ".jpg\|.gif\|wwinfo.com"
⇒ | wc -l
```

As you can see, we can keep on working with the exclusion capabilities of the grep command to get the data we want in as fine a level of detail as we need. If we wanted, we could save that data to a file for additional processing using the redirection capabilities of most Unix shell's and replace the | wc -l with > filename.new.

This log file can also be mined for information on what images people are loading and what images they are stopping before the data completes. A line in the log file like:

```
152.123.194.4 - - [04/Dec/1996:10:06:05 -0800] "GET
⇒  /fifree/gif/t_up.gif HTTP/1.0" 304 0
```

says that on December 4th the person at 152.123.194.4 stopped a request of the image t_up.gif (note the 304 status code). If we see a large number of people stopping images, or pages, we can review the pages and see if the content is correct, or if the images are too large and their loading is too slow.

Here is one message you never want to see:

```
ikra.com - - [05/Dec/1996:11:13:03 -0800] "GET
⇒  /fifree/tree/ficftart.shtml HTTP/1.0" 404 0
```

In this case, we can see that a user at ikra.com came to the site and attempted to go to a page ficftart.shtml there. The 404 status says that the page was not found (Table 16.9 lists additional status codes). It is fortunate that it was not, as this instance is a typographical error by the user and the page did exist under its proper name ficstart.shtml. This is a good way to see if there are dead links at your site, or links to pages that are not properly formed.

Table 16.9: NCSA HTTPd status codes

Code	Meaning
302	REDIRECT
400	BAD_REQUEST
401	AUTH_REQUIRED
403	FORBIDDEN
404	NOT_FOUND
500	SERVER_ERROR
501	NOT_IMPLEMENTED

If the site is using ECLF, there is a really nice piece of information that can be extracted. That information has to do with understanding how agents and indexers work against the site. In this case, we'll discuss one of the agents that most public sites like to have visit, scooter (Digital Equipment Corporation's autonomous agent that is used to index the World Wide Web for the Alta Vista search engine). The agent can come to your site by many means; the most common are that someone else has a link to a page on his/her site, and scooter was indexing that site and got your page, or someone asked scooter to drop by and index the site.

If ECLF is turned on, a check to see if scooter was there for a visit and to ascertain what scooter did is formatted as:

```
$ grep Scooter/1.0 access_log
```

This will display a series of records that can then be saved in a log file for later use or, if all you want to know is the records hit and what order, the command below will only display the file accessed.

```
$ grep Scooter/1.0 access_log | cut -f 2 -d \" | cut -f 2 -d " "
```

Agent Log

Since we closed discussion of the transfer log with how little use the agent information generally is in that log, let's look at the agent log as if it was separate (not in the ECLF). This log file records the name of the client that was used to access the server. A dump of some log file records looks like:

```
Mozilla/2.0 (Compatible; AOL-IWENG 3.0; Win16)
Mozilla/2.0 (compatible; MSIE 3.01; Windows 95)
Mozilla/2.0 (compatible; MSIE 3.01; Windows 95)
Mozilla/2.0 (compatible; MSIE 3.01; Windows 95)
Mozilla/3.01Gold (Win95; I)
Mozilla/3.0 (Win95; I)
Mozilla/3.0C-AOL (Win95; I; 16bit) via proxy gateway
    CERN-HTTPD/3.0 libwww/2.17
Mozilla/2.0 (compatible; MSIE 3.01; Windows 95)
Mozilla/2.02E (Win16; I)
Mozilla/2.02E (Win16; I)
Mozilla/3.01 (Macintosh; I; PPC)
Mozilla/3.01 (Macintosh; I; PPC)
Mozilla/2.0 (compatible; MSIE 3.01; Windows 95)
Mozilla/3.0 (Win95; I)
ArchitextSpider
```

```
Scooter/1.0 scooter@pa.dec.com
InfoSeek Sidewinder/0.9
```

This information tells us the browser information or, in the case of the last three entries, the agent (in this case, search and indexing agents) that accessed the server at the site. The following Unix line can be modified to get a feel for which browsers are accessing the site and can be used to help decide what extensions should, or should not, be supported.

```
$ grep "Mozilla/3" agent_log | grep -v "MSIE" | wc -1
```

That line will let us know what browsers came in meeting the Mozilla 3.* standard, but were not Microsoft's Internet Explorer. To find out how many were Internet Explorer, we would just eliminate the -v from the second grep.

It is interesting to often view and review these logs. The command

```
$ grep -v "Moz" agent_log | wc -1
```

will give you a count of the number of nonMozilla accesses the server had. Mozilla was the name originally given to Netscape's browser (as in a sly reference to Godzilla, Mozilla was the killer application for the Net. Some of you might even remember the old Mozilla animated Netscape logo, before the star field and the big "N").

Non-Mozilla agents can be browsers (like NETCOMplete/3.0), but, in most cases, these are agents that have wandered to your site. The charm is that every once in a while you will find a header that indicates that someone came to your site with a development version of a browser (like Microsoft Internet Explorer/4.40.308 (Windows 95) when the current implementation of Internet Explorer is 3.01) or with a browser that you thought had all but disappeared (like Lynx/2.5FM libwww-FM/2.14(Lynx is a nongraphical browser used by people still on VT100 or stuck in terminal emulation windows).

As to how this helps you, if you know what the most popular browsers coming to the site are, you can determine whether you can move to an extension. A good example of that is determining when you want to move to the use of frames in your site's design. Based on the browsers that are accessing the site, and the number of browsers that support the use of frames verses the ones that don't, you can make a decision to become frames active or not.

Again, this is useful for determining extensions, but it has no use for determining things like plug-in capabilities. While we think plug-ins were a great concept, they will only be truly viable when the developer doesn't have to concern themselves with what is placed on the site and if the user has the ability to use the information in that presentation format.

Referrer Log

While it's nice to know who came to visit and where they came from, it also helps a site if we know when they came from off site, and where they were when they came from there to us. The best of both worlds occurs when you are using the ECLF and these pieces of information are tied together in a cohesive unit. But, even when this information is separate, it still can provide some interesting gems of wisdom.

The format of the log entry is:

```
http://www.wwsite.com/ -> /gif/smiley.gif
```

This shows that there was a request on the index page of www.wwsite.com to the URL /gif/smiley.gif or a gif format image of, we can assume, a smiley face. While that's nice, what we really want to know is where were people when they came to the site from external pages, and we don't really care about what images they loaded. To get this information, we would eliminate the www.wwsite.com references and all .gif references using a grep with the -v option

```
$ grep -v "www.wwsite.com\|.gif" referer_log
```

```
http://www.web.com/pleasant/kyle/flyer.html -> /fifree/
http://members.com/palefacepp/freedom/freedom.html -> /fifree/
http://members.com/palefacepp/freedom/freedom.html -> /fifree/
http://www.angel.com/in/IPHN/Income.html -> /fifree/
http://av.yahoo.com/bin/search?p=plopit&b=21&d=a&hc=0
    &hs=0 -> /fifree/
http://members.com/palefacepp/freedom/freedom.html -> /fifree/
http://www.net-quest.com/~ivler/mc/mc.html -> /fifree/
http://altavista.digital.com/cgi-bin/query?pg=q&what
    =web&fmt=.&q=plopit -> /fifree/index.shtml
```

As this sample shows, the index file at the site in the /fifree/ directory has been referenced by a large number of other locations.

Included in those references are two searched, one from Yahoo and another from Alta Vista. In fact, we can see that the search strings used at both sites was the word "plopit" and that it came up on the first page at Alta Vista, but on the third page at Yahoo.

In addition, we can see that a large number of visitors have come from members.com.

How does this information benefit us? We can start by looking at how we got indexed in the search engines. There is usually a way to increase your standing and location in the search engine, if you understand what the rules were that weighted your page in the search. By looking at other pages that show up when you search for "plopit" you can see what, if any, differences there are in the methods that were used in the pages.

Look at the other page's source. Are they using meta tags? How? All this information is of value. If a search engine says it had 1000 hits on a term, and it returned to you a list of the first 10 of 200, just how far are you going to sift before you say you have seen enough? That's what your customer is going to think. The idea is to get the most prominent display for your site in a search engine. You want to be in the one-one position, the first listing on the first page.

Now that we have covered the search engines, let's go look at members.com. Here is a site that has a reference to you. If you don't know about the reference, you had best go look at it. Why? Because you may think, "great, a reference" but remember, everyone out there is able to become a publisher overnight on the Net. That means that this reference could be on a page that starts with <title>Never Do Business With These Companies</title>. Not a page on which you want to be listed and not a page from which you want to see a large number of hits.

In addition, some people have been known to use postings to Usenet newsgroups to generate floods of requests to servers of companies or people who they do not like. This is known as a denial of service attack against your site, and it could be very damaging. One way to see if it is happening is to look and ascertain if a large number of entries look like:

```
news:32A41BA4.2636@rrnet.com -> /fifree/
```

This means that someone was using the browser to read newsgroups and that there's a high probability that there was a URL reference in this article to your site. Does that mean it's good or bad? One way to tell is to go to dejanews.com and see if you can locate the article there. Another place to check is Alta Vista's Usenet search. If you're lucky, you'll see the posting in the proper place and a great letter about the site. If you're not lucky, you could see anything from a disgruntled person to a person who wanted to disrupt your site by saying that there were tons of free stuff there... or some such poppycock.

We started the discussion on how this information is better left in the transfer log using ECLF and the focus had been on the "how" they got to the page. As you may have noticed, we have been able to use the information provided for much more than that. Many people stop using the logs once they have generated the statistics provided by many of these Log Analysis programs. Those programs only scratch the surface of the information that can be garnered from the log files that HTTPd maintains.

If you thought that the error log was only for errors, get ready for yet another surprise.

Error Log

The error log will record all instances of the following:

- Server startup
- Server restart
- Server halt
- Debugging dumps from USR1 signals
- Messages to standard error from within scripts
- Malformed script headers
- Client timeouts
- Segmentation faults and bus errors from the server
- .htaccess security violations (on the part of the .htaccess file)
- .htaccess security failures (user authentication errors)
- errors (file doesn't exist)
- Sever resource limit errors

In each and every way, all these incidents are worthy of being logged, but the power of the error log is in its ability to be used as a debugging tool. That will be covered at the very end of this chapter. As for making use of the information within the log file, knowing how we feel about security, you know that there are lots of gems to be found here.

Some bothersome lines are error log entries like:

```
invalid command name "}"
puts: stdout: broken pipe
couldn't open "/user/wwinfo/logs/4 0.log": no such
    file or directory
```

In the first, case we had a Tcl error in a script that generated an invalid command. This could happen because a value was evaluated improperly. This is a problem within the code, but since the code being run isn't announcing who it is, it is hard to track down.

The second case could have happened for any number of reasons. In general, you will see this command following a line that looks like:

```
[Mon Dec  9 13:47:56 1996] httpd: send aborted for
    dialup040.telenet.net, URL: /bin/getidx.tcl
```

That means that the person at the site dialup40.telenet.net used the stop button on the browser before the CGI program completed. That caused the CGI program to throw an error, and that is the broken pipe message received.

In that last case, there was a problem in the way the file had been requested. In this case, we can see that the file requested was "4 0.log" and that is an invalid filename with the space in it that way.

While not the best run-time debugging tool, it's not bad. There is a way to make it better.

Debugging CGI: Is It Really This Easy?

The error log file can be used to capture output to standard error or, in the instance of run-time CGI errors, the *error log*. This log file makes debugging CGI code in runtime possible.

In Chapter 4, when we had discussed some of the advantages of using uncgi and environment variables for the entry of the values passed in from the server, we looked at how to use standard output to validate the code while in test. It was a messy way to validate and it really couldn't be used when the routines started to run. So, how do you perform run-time debugging?

In much the same way we did before with standard output. But, instead of using standard output, we will now use the ability to write to standard error using the Tcl command puts stderr "error string". When the server is fed this string from the CGI, it will record the message in the error log. This allows us to use the error log as a run-time debugging tool. It is not recommended that this process be used for production software, since each error message will increase server overhead and also decrease your available disk space.

One key feature, and this explains why we tend to lean to interpretive languages for Web services, is that you can add a debugging line to production code with almost no impact on the performance of the code on the server. There is no need to recompile the code, to make sure the executable is linked to all the proper libraries, to ensure permissions are properly set on the binary executable. Using standard error from Tcl or Perl is a fast and simple method of ensuring that problems can be addressed and dealt with quickly.

Let's look at the three error messages listed just discussed:

```
invalid command name "}"
puts: stdout: broken pipe
couldn't open "/user/wwinfo/logs/4 0.log": no such
    file or directory
```

To find out which CGI is generating the }, we could add a line at the beginning of 5 of the 20 routines we have at the site. The line would generate the name of the routine to be written to the error log. If we see the same } error showing up time and time again after the name of a single routine, we can take that routine off line and test it, locate the error, and fix it.

In the second case, there isn't a great deal we can do. People will always be aborting, and pipes will always be broken.

In the third case, we know what routines use file opens to that data file. The question is, why is that error being generated on some very few opens and not on all of them. It most likely has more to do with the input stream than with the actual open. In this case, the answer is to echo back the input stream to standard error and see how it differs from the successful file open.

In both the first and the last example, we are able to use the error log as a runtime analysis tool.

Build It or Buy It?

Earlier we talked a bit about some of the neat analyzers available. Most of these are shareware, and some are really good enough to be pay-for products. It is fair to say that commercial vendors of Web tools and HTTP servers are going to move to a model that includes a full log analysis suite within the server's administrator program, many already have. These are special programs that are used to administrate commercial servers using HTML pages, Java applications and CGI scripts.

As more of these commercial vendors move to remote Web-based server administration, it will be only a matter of time before those that work in the freeware, shareware and postcardware areas develop administrators for NCSA, Apache and all the other HTTP servers that come from noncommercial sources. This will make it even harder to create a value-added product that meets the needs of log analysis. In the end, we see the server manufacturers leading the way to a standard method of ensuring proper log file analysis that will meet the needs of the high-end market. The low end will continue to support the freeware and low-end shareware distributions.

In many cases, we find that building a simple, small analysis tool to analyze some small portion of the log space is fine. However, for any real tracking or trend analysis or deep statistical analysis, tools like the ones previously mentioned in the discussion on the log files are more than effective in meeting your needs.

Additionally, today there are a number of companies that are allowing use of their analytical tools to import the log files in CLF and they then use their existing analysis toolsets to leverage the data and provide graphical analysis and trending.

So, do you build it or do you buy it? In most cases, we would say build what you need for fast access to information. Many of the commands that have been provided here are used on a daily basis when a Webmaster or a CGI developer provides support. For broad brush analysis, many of the less costly tools will meet most of the users' needs.

Summary

In this chapter, we covered basic configuration issues that dealt with CGI operation including SSIs, security and CGI debugging. With that, we finished the meat of the book. By now you should have more than a passing understanding of how CGIs work, the model of the HTTP protocol, how the server works, and, by using the information in the second section, you should have some functional CGIs up and running.

There are thousands of uses for CGIs and we haven't been able to touch on even a fraction of them. What you should have at this point is a firm understanding of the power that they offer for creating better Web sites, and how you can harness that power using any language you want.

In the next chapter, the final chapter, we will be talking about the future of CGIs, HTTP and the Web in general.

It was bound to happen. As we were finishing off Chapter 17, and most of this book had gone to production, Hans van Oostrom (hans@anest4.anest.ufl.edu), a user on the net, posted the following request:

> I want to be able to generate a What's New page automatically on my server. I would like a program that will run (timed with cron) on my server and traverses through a directory tree and looks at the dates of all the .html files. If a file is less than 7 days old I would like a link to the page to appear in a html file, maybe with the first couple of lines of the file. I can write this myself, but I am sure someone has already done this. Does anyone know where I can find something like this?

While I'm sure Hans had something different in mind than what we created and have added to this text in Chapter 17, his desire has been more then met with this additional piece of code. So, instead of some dry wrap-up of what we hope you got from this text, there is yet one more piece of code coming your way. The good part is, it even shows you how to use cookies in a nice way.

CHAPTER 17 PONTIFICATING

- What Did We Cover?
- What is the Future?
- What's New?

Think of this chapter as an introduction to a sequel. Here we will recap what we wanted you to get from the book, talk about some things that didn't fit anywhere else in the book, and look at what's new.

Where We Have Been

The book was intended to be used as a tool to help you understand how the Web works, how CGIs work, and how to build applications that work. All the applications in the text were built for real operations. These were used by a number of Alpha and Beta test sites, and many are still in operation.

511

We wanted to prove that the programming language isn't an issue, but that CGI development is simply part of the overall client-server software development framework. We wanted to solve problems and explain how and why we used a certain approach. The intention was for you, the reader, to focus on how things get accomplished, not just the language or the tools used. Therefore, we avoided promoting one language over another.

While we tried to remain neutral in discussing commercial products and companies, it is clear that we do have a bias for open standards and open systems. That was obvious in our selection of Perl and of Tcl as the programming languages rather than proprietary languages like Visual Basic.

There was also a great deal going on in the world of the Internet simultaneous to the writing of this book. When we started, ActiveX was a proprietary technology of Microsoft and, when we ended, the Open Systems Group had offered to take it on as a Standards body. When we started, Java was still more light than heat and, when we ended, the 100 percent Pure Java initiative was taking off and Java had matured with a new release of the product. On the browser side, we started this when Netscape and Microsoft had not yet released their 3.0 products. At the time this book was completed, there were Netscape 4.0 and Microsoft 4.0 entries in the log files at the sites we used for Chapter 16.

To show how much the world has changed during the writing of this book, it was started when no one was thinking about the Web on TV. The closest conversation you would hear about that generally revolved around cable modems. As we came to a close, the log files contained entries like:

```
proxy-9.isp.alma.webtv.net - - [<date>] "GET /
    HTTP/1.0" 200 9839
```

Not only does Web-TV exist, but people are actually using it!

What amazes us is that despite all the changes that have taken place (from Sun's Java to Netscape's Communicator with Collabra), people are still out there trying to solve the same client-server issues this year that they were attempting to solve last year. There continues to be people using CGIs to plug away at making Web sites more active, reactive and proactive. And they're still plugging away with Tcl, Perl, C, and even COBOL.

The Future of CGI, Tcl, and Perl

As book authors, we are not wizards with crystal balls; we leave those tasks to people who write magazine editorials that can be forgotten in a year. That qualified, we can see that Sun Microsystems owns some very strong technologies. They have Java as a cross-platform development language, they have a plug-in that can run an X-window within the browser, and they have a scripting language that will be able to play with both the display and the higher level code. All these bode well for the developer in both the CGI and API worlds, the client and the server worlds, and the Intranet and Internet worlds.

One of the things we didn't get into in this book is client security. That means that the client runs in a *sandbox* or an area of the system that is roped off and isn't allowed to play with other parts of the system. This provides levels of security to protect the client system from having something harmful mistakenly downloaded to it.

Safe-Tcl, a portion of Tcl that is used in the Tcl/Tk plug-in, has already incorporated the concept of the sandbox into the browser extension. Java, too, works within the sandbox model. At the time of this writing, there were also methods of electronic signature and authentication being discussed as ways to ensure nondestructive behavior in client-side embedded applications.

There will always be people building CGI applications on a one-to-one level, but as Object Technology and the Internet Object Broker (IIOP, Internet Inter-ORB Protocol; see Object Management Group (OMG) Web-site at http://www.omg.org/ for the latest information) become part of the mainstay, we will see more people moving to pre-packaged technologies. As fast as the world moves, though, there will always be a need for the people building the pages to be able to put their abilities to work and make the pages they own or build active. And that means CGIs.

On the coding front, more people will be moving to the use of Java as the CGI language of choice. For Tcl programmers, this could be a good thing. Consider that Tcl is a easy-to-use, easy-to-learn scripting language that offers very powerful capabilities for list and string processing. Also, it has a high degree of extensibility and works and plays well within the TCP/IP playground. Add to that the fact that it is currently a part of the Sun Microsystems product family and you can start to see a glimmer of hope in each Tcl programmer's eye.

That isn't to knock Perl.

According to Perl coders, one key strength to the language has been its ability to be compiled (and thereby run faster than Tcl). The same can also be said about the latest release of Tcl (version 8.0, a beta of which is on the CD). That makes Perl's strongest reasons for being used in the future is its large user base and the high amount of current, state-of-the-art software written in it.

There is a great deal to be said for both of those statements. Perl is here to stay, but we don't feel that it will remain the dominant language for CGI coding. Over time, a large number of the Perl and Tcl functions will be taken over by Java applications that plug into the server via APIs.

But those days are still far away . . . in Internet time.

So, What's New?

As we stated in the summary of Chapter 16, there was a unique request put out in the CGI Usenet newsgroup just as we were finishing the book. Because the code has some real beneficial applications, we wrote a program to meet the needs of the requester and posted it to the newsgroup. It was then that we realized this particular piece of software would be great in the book. Unfortunately, Part 2 of this book (the code-filled chapters) was already completed.

So we figured that we would end the book by telling you what's new and then providing you with the code to help answer that question when users come to your site. Sure, it's a stretch, but we really wanted to give you just one more piece of code, and we got the editors to allow it (just this once).

So here is *What's New*! It's a program that really tells visitors what has changed since they last visited your site.

Requirements for What's New

You've no doubt seen a *What's New* page before. It's the page most often ignored at a site. Usually it is static and updated by hand, and the chance that it will actually tell us what's new at the site is negligible, at best.

That said and done, what if *What's New* were to actually provide information that was actually useful to a visitor. What if you could tell when someone last visited a site and, based on that information, tell them what files have changed or have been added and then provide a link to that file, based on its title?

The requirements for a piece of code like that are:

- Know when a user last visited a site
- If unknown, display a default *What's New* page and tag the user to know when they come again
- If the user has been here before, find out when and then list all the site's files that have changed. The listing should be by date, with the newest listed first. The listing should be the file's title hyperlinked to the actual file
- When a user visits the What's New page, the user should have a new visit date created and associated to them

To make this a fast search for the visitor, the site should be indexed nightly. That will require that a crontab procedure be created to index the site. It is important to remember that we want any agent we build to have the smarts to know that a directory shouldn't be indexed. That information should be placed in the directory or in a known file.

In the case of agents coming in off the Internet (like Alta Vista's scooter), there is a standard file called robots.txt for which it looks. This file has a defined format that the visiting agent expects to see and can understand. It's the way you can communicate with agents coming to your site (robots.txt is defined in Appendix A). What we want is a way to communicate that to our agent. In this case, since the agent transverses the tree structure, we will use a hidden file within the tree structure to deny access to it for the agent.

If the agent sees the hidden file when it goes to a directory structure, the structure, and everything under it, will *not* be searched or accessed. In this way, you can keep private structures private, or work areas clear of indexing.

So, we have two separate pieces of software to create. The first is the indexing agent, the second is the *What's New* display program.

The Indexing Agent

What we want to be able to do is recurse from a single given root through a directory tree structure. The most effective way to create this software is to use a recursive procedure that calls itself as it runs through the tree. In this way, we can create a very small agent that can do a very large task.

Here is what the agent will have to do:

1. Open a file for write access (the resulting index from the process).
2. Go to the root of the tree and select the first file or directory.
3. Verify that the directory can be searched and indexed.
4. If indexable, then continue.
5. If a directory, call yourself, passing in the name of the directory being searched as the root.
6. If a file, obtain the last modified date and the title, if there is one (see step 7), and write it to the index along with the URL for the file.
7. Follow this rule for title searching:

    The title must be in the first 10 lines of the file.

    The title must be on one line starting with <title> and ending with </title>.

    Nothing else should be on the title line.

8. Continue this transversal of the tree until each file has been recorded.

To begin this process we have to determine what information will be needed by the recursive procedure to do its job.

It will need to know what it thinks is the head of the tree is (where the root of the search will start), and it needs to be able to make a URL from the file (replace the DocumentRoot of the file specification with the URL information). So it also needs to know what the DocumentRoot of the structure is, and what the URL is for that DocumentRoot. In addition, it should also know the fileid of the open file to which it is supposed to write.

There is also the possibility that the person running the agent may only want HTML files, or.txt files. We have to provide a way of limiting what gets indexed by only allowing what the user wants to index.

This means that we will be passing five items to the recursive procedure. These are:

- The current root being searched
- The real DocumentRoot
- The limiting search-value
- The fileid of the open file
- The URL to replace the real DocumentRoot with when we create the URL link for the file

So the call to the recursive procedure would initially look like:

```
bldit /the/pathto/search/DocumentRoot \
      /the/pathto/DocumentRoot *htm* \
      $fhandl http://www.myurl.com
```

and the procedure would start with

```
proc bldit {root rmrt sval fhandl url} {
```

To check to see if the file exists to *not* index the directory, we would have to next do a file check.

```
if {[glob -nocomplain $root/.noindx] != ""} {
  return
}
```

In this case, we look for the file .noindx in the current directory and, if it is found, we exit the procedure.

If the file telling our agent to not index is missing, we can continue to index the directory. In this case, we would start a search of the directory, again using the glob command and, if the file we found was another directory, we would then recurse by calling this procedure again.

```
foreach fil [glob -nocomplain $root/*] {
  if {[file isdirectory $fil]} {
    bldit $fil $rmrt $sval $fhandl $url
```

In doing this, we start by using a foreach to check every file in the directory, and then we do a check on the individual file. If the file is a directory, we call the bldit procedure, passing it all the same values it had before, but with a new root to be checked.

When these procedures unwind, they will unwind back into the foreach loop, so they will continue to recurse the directory tree that they were originally in before they started transversing the branch from which they are returning.

If the file is not a directory, but is a file, we have to ensure that it matches its established rules. We have two options here. The first is to use a glob string match; the second is to use regular expressions.

```
if { [string match $sval $fil] } {
```

or

```
if { [regexp $sval $fil] } {
```

If we have a match, then replace the DocumentRoot with the URL.

```
regsub -all $rmrt $fil $url ofil
```

Get the date last modified from the document, and store it in a millennium friendly format (YYYYMMDD).

```
set a [catch [set dt [clock format [file mtime $fil] \
    -format %Y%m%d] ] ]
```

Once that is done, seek out the document's title from the title line and parse it out.

```
set knt 0
set f1 [open $fil r]
while {$knt < 10} {
  incr knt
  gets $f1 lin
  if {[regexp -nocase {title\>} $lin] != 1} {
    set ftit "No Document Title"
  } else {
    regsub -nocase -all — {\<title\>|\<\/title\>} \
        $lin "" ftit
  break
  }
}
close $f1
```

Once the title has been obtained, write the line out to the file and exit the procedure.

```
puts $fhandl "$dt~$ofil~$ftit"
```

As a coding style comment, we could have used a different regexp in the file read loop. To ensure that we had both a <title> and a </title> the loop could also be written as:

```
set knt 0
set ftit "No Document Title"
while {$knt < 10} {
  incr knt
  gets $f1 lin
  if {[regexp -nocase {title\>} $lin] == 2} {
    regsub -nocase -all — {\<title\>|\<\/title\>} \
        $lin "" ftit
  break
  }
}
close $f1
```

This sets the default line once, and then requires that both the <title> and the </title> be present (it requires the return value be a 2). In the first one, we would even be able to parse the title if the </title> had been placed on a second line. With a small amount of additional logic, this routine would be able to handle the parsing of:

```
<title>
title text
</title>
```

This, although not a requirement, would be a nice addition to the logic. There is one minor nit of which you should be aware. Files that come from an MS-DOS file system and are stored on a Unix file system have ^M (carriage return) values at the end of each line. The Unix file system (and the code) will read these as new lines. We highly recommend that files stored on Unix file systems have the following Unix command run against them to eliminate the carriage returns:

```
tr -d "\015" < infile > outfile
```

The code in Listing 17.1 will act as the agent for gathering the index data file.

Listing 17.1: agent-wn.tcl

```
#!/usr/local/bin/tclsh
##
## agent-wn.tcl
##
## This robot/agent is a recursive procedure that
## will transverse a given root creating a data file
## of all items in there with the last modified date
```

```tcl
## and the name of the item (as a URL) as well as
## any "title" that would have been on the first 10
## lines of the item
##
proc bldit {root rmrt sval fhandl url} {
##
## see if the user wants this directory excluded -
## the key file is called .noindx . If it exists then
## break
##
if {[glob -nocomplain $root/.noindx] != ""} {
  return
}
foreach fil [glob -nocomplain $root/*] {
  if {[file isdirectory $fil]} {
    bldit $fil $rmrt $sval $fhandl $url
  }else {
    if { [regexp $sval $fil] } {
##
## - substitute the url for the root directory
##
      regsub -all $rmrt $fil $url ofil
##
## - get the last modified date in millennium format
## YYYYMMDD
##
      set a [catch [set dt [clock format [file mtime $fil] \
          -format %Y%m%d] ] ]
##
## look for a doc title in the first $knt lines - I
## wouldn't check more than the first 10 lines...
##
      set knt 0
      set f1 [open $fil r]
      while {$knt < 10} {
        incr knt
        gets $f1 lin
        if {[regexp -nocase {title\>} $lin] != 1} {
          set ftit "No Document Title"
        } else {
          regsub -nocase -all — {\<title\>|\<\/title\>} \
              $lin "" ftit
          break
        }
      }
      close $f1
##
## - write to the data file
##
      puts $fhandl "$dt~$ofil~$ftit"
    }
```

```
      }
    }
  }
##
## the main routine.
##
## call the procedure.
## Parameter    Value
##    0         Procedure name
##    1         The specified root
##    2         The DocumentRoot to be replaced by
##                 the URL
##    3         Valid extensions that follow "string
##                 match" criteria (glob) or regexp
##                 (as we use)
##    4         A file handle (the value given to the
##                 open file)
##    5         The URL to replace item 2
##
##
## NOTE: If you are going to index a public_html
## directory (the default for user directories) you
## may want to make sure that the regexp is a bit
## clearer, or the one below will list everything in
## the directory structure.
##
set fhandl [open test1.dat w]
bldit /the/pathto/document-root \
    /the/pathto/be/eplacedwith/theurl \
    htm \
    $fhandl \
    http://www.myurl.com
close $fhandl
##
## Fini!
##
exit
```

A sample of the data file that this would generate is:

```
19960325~http://mycompany.com/idxsamp/test-
   it.html~Test the indexer
19960331~http://mycompany.com/idxsamp/index.shtml~Test
   of auto-indexer
19960406~http://mycompany.com/idxsamp/a-filename.html~
   Yet another filename
19960406~http://mycompany.com/idxsamp/yet-another-
   filename.html~Yet another filename
```

```
19960406~http://mycompany.com/idxsamp/A-LIST-OF-THE-
    FILES-IN-THE-DIRECTORY.html~A list of the files
    in the directory
19960803~http://mycompany.com/forms/regist.html~
    Register Your Interest
19960826~http://mycompany.com/forms/regist2.html~
    Register Your Interest
19961106~http://mycompany.com/iref.html~No Document Title
19961106~http://mycompany.com/count/cnt1.shtml~Counter
    in Style 1
19961107~http://mycompany.com/count/cnt2.shtml~Counter
    in Style 2
19961108~http://mycompany.com/count/cnt3.shtml~Counter
    in Style 3
19961106~http://mycompany.com/count/cnt4.shtml~fake
    the count
19960902~http://mycompany.com/accesslog.html~No
    Document Title
```

The second piece of code is used to set the cookie (yes, we will be using cookies) and to process the user's request.

Displaying the Data

When the user comes in, we want to check to see if they have a cookie set. Now, as we are only setting one cookie, the cookie set for the site would be returned and processed as the cookie for which we were looking. If there are multiple cookies being set at a site, then the site could require that the cookie information be parsed for the proper cookie value for this procedure. For example, if there was a site cookie (on the root of the site, or even a higher level directory above the What's New page) that cookie value will also be returned as a valid cookie for the What's New page. In this instance we would have to parse the returned cookie information looking for the proper cookie-name for the page. (If you forgot all this, it was covered in the rules on cookies back in Chapter 3).

If we had multiple cookies at the site, we would have to extract the unique cookie pairs and check to see if the specific cookie had been set (see the getcookie1.tcl code in Chapter 3 on how that is accomplished).

Anyone Want a Cookie?

Way back in Chapter 3, we talked about maintaining the state of a transaction with a cookie. Here is a great example of doing just that. In this case, we want to be able to maintain the state of a visit across a session where the length of time between the transactions is actually the item being tracked.

We will be using a static Web page when the user first comes to the site. This Web page will load up an initial cookie. Because the cookie is loaded before we explain why, there is the possibility, if the user has set the browser to query on cookies, and the user indicates that they do not want the cookie when they initially come to the page, that the user may be required to come back in a second time, after ignoring the initial cookie.

To ensure that the user gets the greatest possible knowledge about the cookie, if there is no cookie sent, we will be displaying a special file before we dump the standard file out to the user. This special file explains the cookie that was placed, why it was placed and how it is used. It also details the information and format of the cookie.

Why do all this? Because we want you to know all this information before you place a cookie that has a long-term expiration date into a system. See, it's not nice to do something like that without telling the user. It may not be important if you are using this application on an Intranet; however, when you are placing data onto someone else's system, it is really considered good etiquette to tell them a bit about what your doing.

Once we have determined that we have a cookie, we can extract the data. If there is no cookie, follow the sidebar instructions; feed the cookie to the user and then dump the explanation file. After we have done that, we can dump the static data file to the visitor.

```
##
## standard CGI header output
## then set the new cookie value. Let's be
## politically correct and use the four digit date
## for the millennium concerned (it should be noted
## that the expiration of this cookie is 1999)
##
puts "Content-type: text/html\n\n"
set ocookie [clock format [clock seconds] -format %Y%m%d]
##
## Let's make sure we have a cookie - if
## so we can set the new cookie value and continue
##
if {[info exists env(HTTP_COOKIE) ] } {
  set icookie [lindex [split $env(HTTP_COOKIE) =] 1]
  puts "<head><META HTTP-EQUIV=\"Set-Cookie\" \
      content=\"newcookie=$ocookie; \
      expires=09-Nov-99 GMT\">"
} else {
##
## if not, then set the cookie,
## dump the explanation file and then drop them into
## the static procedure
##
  puts "<head><META HTTP-EQUIV=\"Set-Cookie\" \
      content=\"newcookie=$ocookie; \
      expires=09-Nov-99 GMT\">"
  puts "[exec cat /harcode-path/warn.txt]"
  static
}
##
## ho-hum, they were here already - drop them to the
## static page
##
if {[string match $icookie $ocookie] } {
  static
}
```

If we have extracted the cookie data, we will then process the cookie by searching through the data file our crontab created. We will be extracting all data into arrays. If the array doesn't exist, create it and load the data; if the array does exist, add the new data to the array.

```
set f1 [open /path-tothe/datefile.dat r]
while {[gets $f1 inlin] > 0} {
```

```
##
## does it match or is it newer than the last date visited?
##
   if {[lindex [split $inlin ~] 0] >= $icookie} {
##
## if so, see if we have started the array
##
    if {[info exists ostr([lindex [split $inlin ~] 0]) ] } {
##
## array exists, add the data to the existing array
##
        set ostr([lindex [split $inlin ~] 0]) "<dd> \
            <a href=\"[lindex [split $inlin ~] \
            1]\">[lindex [split $inlin ~] 2]</a> \
            $ostr([lindex [split $inlin ~] 0])"
    } else {
##
## array doesn't exist, create it.
##
        set ostr([lindex [split $inlin ~] 0]) "<dd>\
            <a href=\"[lindex [split $inlin ~] \
            1]\">[lindex [split $inlin ~] 2]</a>"
    }
  }
}
close $f1
```

Now that the array is filled, dump the data back to the user, but do it by newest item first (decreasing order, the reverse of the normal way that it would be returned). What we want to do here is generate a listing with the date (using a normalized format of MM/DD/YYYY) on one line and the links for the following date indented at one per line.

```
foreach indx [lsort -decreasing [array names ostr] ] {
  set odate [format %.2d/%.2d/%.4d \
      [string range $indx 4 5 ] \
      [string range $indx 6 7 ] \
      [string range $indx 0 3 ] ]
  puts "<dt>$odate [set ostr($indx)]"
}
```

Notice that we used the redirection of the [set ostr($indx)] to display the value of the array. The array had been filled with the HTML to display a string of "<dd>value" where the value was the HTML to display the hyperlink and the title.

That completes the *What's New* in Tcl. The complete code is shown in Listing 17.2. Figure 17.1 shows a sample *What's New* page.

Listing 17.2: getnew.tcl

```tcl
#!/usr/local/bin/tclsh
##
## getnew.tcl
##
## gets the cookie if it's not there dump a static
## What's New page
##
proc static { } {
  puts "[exec cat /hardcode-path/static.html]"
  exit
}
##
## put the standard header information
## Tcl7.5 note: we are using the clock function
##
puts "Content-type: text/html\n\n"
set ocookie [clock format [clock seconds] -format %Y%m%d]
##
if {[[info exists env(HTTP_COOKIE) ] ] } {
  set icookie [lindex [split $env(HTTP_COOKIE) =] 1]
  puts "<head><META HTTP-EQUIV=\"Set-Cookie\" \
    content=\"newcookie=$ocookie; expires=09-Nov-99 GMT\">"
} else {
  puts "<head><META HTTP-EQUIV=\"Set-Cookie\" \
    content=\"newcookie=$ocookie; expires=09-Nov-99 GMT\">"
  puts "[exec cat /hardcode-path/warn.txt]"
  static
}
if {[[string match $icookie $ocookie] ] } {
  static
}
puts "<title>What's new - listing</title>"
puts "<h1>What's new at the site - built on the fly</h1>"
puts "Unlike most <b>What's New</b> sites, this one \
    lists all links that have been updated since you \
    have last been here based on an identifier you \
    passed us when loading the page. As we set a new \
    identifier when this page was loaded, we suggest \
    that you might want to launch another browser as \
    the information on this page will be lost if you \
    exit and attempt to return to this page."
##
##
## Open the data file and build the list
## - display anything that is newer than the icookie
##
puts "<p><hr><H2>What's New</h2><dl>"
set f1 [open /home/wwinfo/test1.dat r]
while {[gets $f1 inlin] > 0} {
```

```
  if {[lindex [split $inlin ~] 0] >= $icookie} {
    if {[info exists ostr([lindex [split $inlin ~] 0]) ] } {
      set ostr([lindex [split $inlin ~] 0]) "<dd> \
          <a href=\"[lindex [split $inlin ~] 1]\">\
          [lindex [split $inlin ~] 2]</a> \
          $ostr([lindex [split $inlin ~] 0])"
    } else {
      set ostr([lindex [split $inlin ~] 0]) "<dd>\
          <a href=\"[lindex [split $inlin ~] 1]\">\
          [lindex [split $inlin ~] 2]</a>"
    }
  }
}
close $f1
foreach indx [lsort -decreasing [array names ostr] ] {
## use SCAN + FORMAT (not on CD this way - this
## is a better method)
  scan $indx %4d%2d%2d yr mo day
  set odate [format %.2d %.2d %.2d \
      $mo $day $yr]
  puts "<dt>$odate [set ostr($indx)]"
}
puts "</dl>"
##
## here you could do something like we did in the
## calendar and allow a page to be added, or even
## call the static page as well, after the changed
## listing. To call the static just uncomment the
## next two lines of code:
##
## puts "<p><hr><p>"
## static
##
exit
```

What's New, Perl Style

The Perl version of the Tcl code has been included in Listings 17.3 and 17.4. This particular code was written by Cameron Laird, who was acting as our technical reviewer throughout the development of the text.

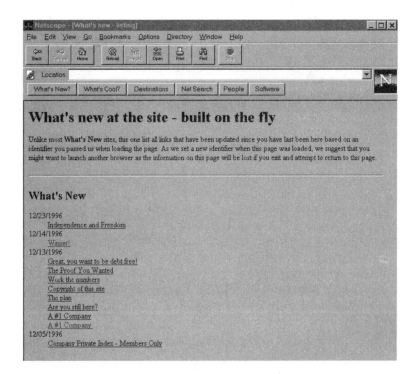

Figure 17.1: What's New!

Listing 17.3: agent-wn.pl

```perl
#!/usr/local/bin/perl
##
## agent-wn.pl
##
## This robot/agent is a recursive procedure that
## will traverse a given root creating a data file of
## all items in there with the last modified date and
## the name of the item (as a URL) as well as any
## "title" that would have been on the first 10 lines
## of the item
##
$fhandl = 'HANDLE';
open($fhandl, '>test2.dat');
bldit('/the/path/to/document-root',
      '/the/path/to/be/replaced/with/documenturl',
     'html',
     $fhandl,
     'http://www.myurl.com');
close $fhandl;
## Parameter    Value
##    0         Procedure name
```

```
##    1            The specified root
##    2            The DocumentRoot to be replaced by
##                     the URL
##    3            Valid extensions that follow "string
##                     match" criteria (glob) or regexp
##                     (as we use)
##    4            A file handle (the value given to the
##                     open file)
##    5            The URL to replace item 2
##
##
## NOTE: If you are going to index a public_html
## directory (the default for user directories) you
## may want to make sure that the regexp is a bit
## clearer, or the one below will list everything in
## the directory structure.
##
sub bldit
{
    use DirHandle;
    local($root, $rmrt, $sval, $fhandl, $url) = @_;
    if (-e $root."/.noindx") {
      return;
    }
      # Every bldit frame needs its own DirHandle.
    my $dirhandle = new DirHandle;
    opendir($dirhandle, $root);
    while ($fil = readdir($dirhandle)) {
        # Skip past ".", "..", ...
      if ($fil =~ /^\./) {
        next;
      }
      $fil = $root."/".$fil;
        # Recurse on directories found.
      if (-d $fil) {
        bldit($fil, $rmrt, $sval, $fhandl, $url);
      } else {
        if ($fil =~ /$sval/) {
          # - substitute the url for the root directory
          $ofil = $fil;
          $ofil =~ s/$rmrt/$url/;
          $dt = format_time($fil);
          find_title($fil);
          print $fhandl "$dt~$ofil~$ftit\n";
        }
      }
    }
    closedir $dirhandle;
}
sub find_title
{
```

```
    local($filename) = @_;
    $knt = 0;
    $ftit = "No Document Title";
    open(F1, $filename);
    while (($line = <F1>) && ($knt < 10)) {
      chop $line;
      $knt = $knt + 1;
      if ($line =~ /<title>.*<\/title>/i) {
        $ftit = $line;
        $ftit =~ s/<title>|<\/title>//ig;
        break;
      }
    }
    close F1;
    $ftit;
}
sub format_time()
{

    local($filename) = @_;

    ($def, $ino, $mode, $nlink, $uid, $gid, $rdev,
      $size, $atime, $mtime, $ctime, $blksize,
      $blocks) = stat($filename);
    ($sec, $min, $hour, $mday, $mon, $year, $wday,
      $yday, $isdst) =
                localtime($mtime);
##
## on the CD this is listed as the line below. That
## is a defect and will cause the system to use GMT
## not local time. Please make sure that you use the
## line above to get the local time for your system
##
##                gmtime($mtime);
##
    sprintf("19$year%02d%02d", $mon + 1, $mday);
}
```

Listing 17.4: getnew.pl

```
#!/usr/local/bin/perl
##
## getnew.pl
##
## gets the cookie if it's not there dump a static
## What's New page
##
##
## put the standard header information
```

```
##
print "Content-type: text/html\n\n";
$ocookie = format_time();
$icookie = process_head_header($ocookie);
##
if ($ocookie =~ $icookie) {
    static();
}
print "<title>What's new - listing</title>\n";
print "<h1>What's new at the site - built on the fly</h1>\n";
print "Unlike most <b>What's New</b> sites, this one \
    lists all links that have been updated since \
    your last visit here, based on an identifier you \
    passed us when loading the page. As we set a new \
    identifier when this page was loaded, we suggest \
    that you might want to launch another browser as \
    the information on this page will be lost if you \
    exit and attempt to return to this page.\n";
##
##
## Open the data file and build the list
## - display anything that is newer than the icookie
##
print "<p><hr><H2>What's New</h2><dl>\n";
open(F1, 'test1.dat');
while ($inlin = <F1>) {
    ($zeroth, $first, $second) = split(/~/, $inlin);
    if ($zeroth >= $icookie) {
        $body = "<dd>
          <a href = \"$first\">
          $second</a>";
        if (defined $ostr{$zeroth}) {
          $tail = "
            $ostr{$zeroth}";
        } else {
          $tail = "";
        }
        $ostr{$zeroth} = "$body$tail";
    }
}
close F1;

foreach $indx (reverse sort keys(%ostr)) {
    $odate = sprintf("%2d/%2d/%4d",
          substr($indx, 4, 2),
          substr($indx, 6, 2),
          substr($indx, 0, 4));
    print "<dt>$odate $ostr{$indx}\n";
}
print "</dl>\n";
##
```

```
## here you could do something like we did in the
## calendar and allow a page to be added, or even
## call the static page as well, after the changed
## listing. To call the static just uncomment the
## next two lines of code:
##
## print "<p><hr><p>\n";
## static();
##
exit;
sub format_time()
{
    ($sec, $min, $hour, $mday, $mon, $year, $wday,
      $yday, $isdst) =
                        localtime(time);
    sprintf("19$year%02d%02d", $mon + 1, $mday);
}
sub print_head_header()
{
    local($ocookie) = @_;

    print "<head><META HTTP-EQUIV=\"Set-Cookie\"
      content=\"newcookie=$ocookie;
        expires=09-Nov-99 GMT\">\n";
}

sub process_head_header()
{
    local($ocookie) = @_;
    &print_head_header($ocookie);
    if (exists $ENV{'HTTP_COOKIE'}) {
      ($ignored, $icookie, $ignored2) =
                split(/=/, $ENV{'HTTP_COOKIE'});
      return $icookie;
    } else {
      # print `cat /hardcode-path/warn.txt`;
      print "cat /hardcode-path/warn.txt\n";
      static();
    }
}
sub static()
{
    print "cat /hardcode-path/static.html\n";
    # print `cat /hardcode-path/static.html`;
    exit;
}
```

Summary

Since it really isn't practical to summarize the whole book here (as originally intended), here are few thoughts to walk away with.

As much as programmers like to make the art of programming into something akin to magic, it really isn't. CGI programming is an extension of the client-server model, and chances are that you already have created programs, or can modify the ones we created, to meet most of your needs. The best advice we can give as you continue to expand on your programming and take your CGIs on-line, is that it helps to share.

All the software in this book is on the CD and is also on the Prentice Hall Web site (www.prenhall.com/developers_resource_series). In addition, as we create new and useful tidbits, they will also be placed at this site or will be available at other locations on the Internet. See, the Net is about sharing what you learn, and that's when it's at its best. So, use the resources in Appendix B and become a resource yourself. Be creative, and remember to share.

We bid you peace.

APPENDIX A
QUICK REFERENCE

This appendix contains various tables that were used in the text. No, we weren't trying to increase the page count, we already exceeded that. These tables have been gathered together in one place since we really don't see a need for you to have to fold down pages and mark locations with yellow stickies. This is the information that we have in a small stack of papers that are constantly referenced when building CGIs or working with the HTTPd server.

In addition we included a description of the robots.txt file that you use to keep agents from accessing your site.

Tables Dealing With URLs and URIs

Table A.1: Rules used to define missing data from a URL in an HTTP protocol (see Table 2.1)

Missing items	Action
site	Use last site browser was at, same filepath and file
site and filepath	Use last site and filepath browser was at, look for the file at that location
site and file	Use last site browser was at, use the new filepath, and see the default file for the server (or, if not there and indexing is on, use the index capability)
filepath	Use the last site and look for the file in the root filepath for the site
file	Use the last site and filepath in the browser, look for the server's default file in that filepath (or, if not there and indexing is on, use the index capability)
filepath and file	Use the last site in the browser and look for the server's default file in the root directory for the site (or, if not there and indexing is on, use the index capability)
site filepath and file	Not permitted—one must be supplied

Table A.2: Protocols recognized by clients and servers (see Table 2.2)

http:	Hyper Text Transfer Protocol (the Web)
ftp:	File Transfer Protocol
mailto:	Standard Mail Network Protocol
file:	Open a local file
telnet:	Open a telnet session

Table A.3: URI GET request (see Table 2.3)

Protocol	Data
http	Domain (www.altavist.digital.com) Directory: cgibin Program: query Value-data pairs: pg=q what=web fmt=. q="Tcl CGI Development"

(See Chapter 3 for detailed descriptions on the POST and GET protocols of HTTP.)

Tables Dealing with Headers and Environment Variables

Table A.4: Cookie format (based on the specifications used by Netscape, see Table 3.1)

NAME=VALUE	**REQUIRED**: Here you establish your cookie name and it's value. There can be no use of the characters ";" "," or " " unless you use the URL encoding style and force them into hex notation (%[1..f][1..f]).
	Example: MYTRACKER=960825082334-pid13489
expires=DATE	**OPTIONAL**: You can set an expiry date for the cookie. The date format is defined in RFC's 882, 850, 1036 and 1123 (with the exception of requiring you to use GMT and using the "-" as the date separator) as: Weekday, DD-Mon-YYYY HH:MM:SS GMT If this optional attribute of the cookie is not specified when the cookie is set, then the cookie will have no persistence on the client side, and will expire when the client session is terminated. (Note: Not just the communications with your server, but when they shut down the browser)
	Example: expires=Saturday, 07-Dec-1996 12:00:00 GMT
domain=DOMAIN_NAME	In order for the browser to be able to associate a cookie with a location it creates an association between where it picked up the cookie and the domain it was at when the cookie was assigned. In order to return a cookie the browser will search this list of domains to which it has cookies to see if there is a cookie attached to the URL that it is about to go to.

The domain searching is done back to front.

If the URL was www.prenhall.com, the search would start with the fully qualified domain (in this example prenhall.com is the fully qualified domain). If there is no match on the qualified domain name, the search is dropped for that entry and the process moves to the next domain in the list. If a fully qualified domain is found, then the client goes through path matching to see if the cookie should be sent.

In searching for a qualified domain the client will use a rule set that states that a match is defined by at least two or three periods (".") within the qualified name. Qualified names in the "top seven" special domains ("EDU", "NET", "COM", "ORG", "MIL", "GOV" and "INT") require the two "."s all others require three periods in the qualified domain name.

Before you shout that the name prenhall.com only has one period, note that we are saying *qualified domain name*. In order to have a qualified domain name the system places a period at the end of the name. This makes the prenhall.com domain look like prenhall.com., which is now fully qualified, and has two periods.

The default value of the domain when the cookie is set is the host that is setting the cookie. This can create problems if you are using a virtual host. For instance, if you have a provider that is setting a cookie on all inbound queries. This could create a problem if you wish to override the cookie, as all queries have a cookie being set by the provider. Below there is an explanation on how you can delete a cookie that has been set from being sent anymore. (The Apache

Table A.4 (continued): Cookie format (based on the specifications used by Netscape)

	HTTPD server allows the server to set cookies for each person entering the site. These are written to the log file and can be used to track individuals. This could be considered intrusive and is one of the reasons I suggest setting the browser to tell you when someone has assigned a cookie to you).
path=PATH	The path is the location off the root (/) directory that you want to associate with a cookie.
	This allows you to send numerous cookies back to the client. In the example following this table there is a *shopping cart* method that allows you to store the entire cart in the users client using cookies.
	If a cookie passes domain matching, then the pathname component of the URL is compared with the path attribute. If there is a match, the cookie is considered valid and is transmitted in the header to the server.
	The path "/book" would match "/bookcgi" "/book/cgi/" and "/book/cgi-top.html". The most general path is the root (/). If there is no path specified the default path is the one used in the response from the server as to the path of the document that is being served.
Secure	A secure cookie is one that is only transmitted to a server that is running a secure communications channel. At this time that limits these cookies to only being sent over a channel using HTTPS (HTTP over the SSL security protocol). The default is to not specify a cookie as secure.

Header	Description
Content-type:	The only required header. This header is the mime-type declaration. In the data portion of this header a proper MIME type in the format of type/sub-type must be supplied. Example: text/html (Please see the chart in Appendix B for a full list of acceptable MIME types.)
Content-length:	This field is used to specify the length of the data being returned in bytes. If it is omitted the server supplies the response. The size must be specified in the number of bytes being returned. Example: 1024
Content-encoding:	While not used by everyone (since this information can be supplied by using the clients Mime types defaults) this is a way to specify the encoding method that was used to compress the file. There are two acceptable responses that can be passed to the client. These are: x-gzip (if the file was compressed with the GNU gzip compression method) and x-zip-compress (if the file was compressed with the standard unix compress command).
Expires:	Back when we talking about security and how caching could defeat your logging of information I kept a secret on how the problem of caching could be overcome. The CGI programmer can expire the documents that the clients are served. This allows a date and time (in GMT) to be inserted into the header information. This header information states that a document is no longer considered a valid response from the server. If the docu

Header	Description
	ment is cached and the client goes for the cached copy and sees the expired header it will go back and get a new copy from the original server. Example: Sunday 25-Sep-96 23:00 GMT
Location:	This is used to do a piece of magic called *Redirection*. In Chapter 7 there are examples of how redirection use can enhance a site (click on an advertisement banner. This banner calls a local program to register the click-through, and then redirects your click to a new location). Example: http://www.wwinfo.com/fifree/
Status:	Returns the status code for the page. Common status codes are 200 (success), 302 (redirect), 400 (bad request), 500 (server internal error) and the most common 404 (document not found). When a redirect is sent the headers used are generally Status 302 Location: http://site/path/file.

Table A.6: SSI commands and tags (see Table 3.5)

Command	Tag	Description
config	errmsg defines the message returned to the client in the case of an error while parsing. Errors, if they occur are logged in the HTTP Server's error log. Timefmt gives the server a new format to use when providing dates. In Unix it uses the same formatting values used in the strftime library call. Sizefmt is used much like timefmt, but in this case it is used to define the format of sizes of files. File size information can be returned as the number of bytes in the file (the bytes tag value) or using the tag value abbrev the file size will be returned as the number of kilobytes or megabytes.	config is used to define formats for display of both time and file sizes.
include	virtual allows the path given in the tag to be a *virtual* path to a document on the HTTP Server using the Document Root, or a defined Root on the server as the starting point. While the virtual tag allows you to include another .shtml (parsed) file, it will not allow you to access a CGI script in this manner. The file tag allows a path relative to the current directory. The limitations to this are that the uplevel format of "../" is not permitted in this path. Additionally an absolute path can not be used either. This format is best used when you want to include a file that	The include SSI command allows the insertion of text or another parsed document into a parsed document.

Table A.6 (continued): SSI commands and tags

Command	Tag	Description
	is in the current directory, or one that is under the current directory structure.	
echo	The tag var is used to echo the value of an environment variable (see the table below)	This command allows the value of one of the include variables to be inserted in the output. Dates and filesizes are output in the formats that were defined for them in the config command.
fsize	valid tags are the same as the include command.	This command prints the file size of the specified file. It will use the format as defined in the config command.
flastmod	valid tags are the same as the include command.	This is how you get the *date the file was last modified* in the footer of the displayed HTML (actually, some editors will save it there using macros, but in the case of using and SSI, this is how it's done. Once again, the format is defined using the config command.
exec	The value cmd can be used to pass a shell command to the HTTP Server to be parsed. Yes, this is a dangerous command as a SSI could be written to issue the command "rm -rf /*". The method of protecting yourself from this is	Permits the SSI to issue Unix shell command or run a CGI from a valid CGI virtual path.

Command	Tag	Description
	discussed in the chapter on system configuration and security in Section 3. The other possible value CGI was shown and discussed in the example that started this portion of the chapter. The path to the CGI is one of the virtual paths defined in the configuration files for the HTTP Server. Be aware that the server performs no error checking, so if you generated a binary dump or a gif file to the standard output it will make a lovely mess of the returned display.	

Table A.7: Accessible Variable's in SSIs (see Table 3.6)

Variable	Values
DOCUMENT_NAME	Filename of the document being accessed
DOCUMENT_URI	The virtual path to this document (note that the document URI doesn't include the document root information, so a document at /usr3/wwwspot/docs/thisdoc.shtml would be displayed as /docs/thisdoc.shtml if the document root was set as /usr3/wwwspot
DATE_LOCAL	The current date and local time zone. (a simple replacement for the datetime.tcl CGI) the format is subject to the format as defined in the config command
DATE_GMT	DATE_LOCAL in Greenwich mean time
LAST_MODIFIED	The last modification date of the current file in a format as defined by the config command (yes this does appear to duplicate the flastmod command)

Table A.8: Available Environment Variables to non-SSI on NCSA HTTPd 1.5 (see Table 3.7)

Variable	Description
SERVER_SOFTWARE	The name and version of the information server software answering the request (and running the gateway). This information shows up in the access_log file and has the format of: name/version (ex: HTTP/1.0)
SERVER_NAME	The server's hostname, DNS alias, or IP address
GATEWAY_INTERFACE	The revision of the CGI specification used on the server. Format: CGI/revision (ex: CGI/1.0)

Table A.9: Additional Environment Variables (see Table 3.8)

Variable	Description
SERVER_PROTOCOL	The name and revision of the information protocol this request came in with. The format of the environment variable is: protocol/revision
SERVER_PORT	The port number to which the request was sent (generally port 80)
REQUEST_METHOD	The method that the browser used to make the request (ex: "GET", "POST", etc.) This piece of information is also logged in the access_log.
PATH_INFO	The extra path information, as given by the client. To see how this can be used, look at some of the examples that follow.
PATH_TRANSLATED	The server provides a translated version of PATH_INFO. The PATH_INFO data is decoded and any virtual-to-physical mapping required will be done. The resultant output is stored in this variable.

Variable	Description
SCRIPT_NAME	A virtual path to the script being executed. NCSA says that it can be used for self-referencing URLs. I have yet to see a real good use for this, but I could be wrong
QUERY_STRING	The information which follows the ? in the URI that called the CGI. This is part of the GET processor. The query information has been discussed earlier in this chapter. Including why you may not want to use get requests (for security reasons).
REMOTE_HOST	The hostname making the request. If this is unset look to see if the value in REMOTE_ADDR has been set. *THIS IS NOT TO BE TRUSTED INFORMATION*
REMOTE_ADDR	The IP address of the remote host. *THIS IS NOT TO BE TRUSTED INFORMATION*
AUTH_TYPE	If the server supports user authentication, the value in this variable defines which protocol-specific authentication method is to be used to validate the user.
REMOTE_USER	If the server supports user authentication, a protected CGI will use this user name for authentication. *THIS IS NOT TO BE TRUSTED INFORMATION*
REMOTE_IDENT	If the HTTP server supports RFC 931 identification, then this variable will be set to the remote user name retrieved from the server. *THIS IS NOT TO BE TRUSTED INFORMATION (use it for logging only)*
CONTENT_TYPE	This defines the attached information when using the POST method.
CONTENT_LENGTH	The length of the content in stdin as determined by the client.

Image Map Definitions

Table A.10: Imagemap Map Region Definitions (see Table 13.2)

Region	Definition
rect	The most common of all region definitions. In this case, a rectangle area is selected by identifying two opposing corner points.
Point	A single selectable point within the image map
circ	A circle is defined by the center point of the circle and either a radius or a single point on the circle's edge (this depends on which "format" your server uses).
poly	A polygon allows you to define the points that make up a line that will enclose a defined area. Generally that includes a start point at least one mid point and an end point. The system will create a virtual line from that end point to the start point. Try not to make a straight line; they don't generally encircle areas.

Security with .htaccess

Table A.11: Directives within the .htaccess file (see Table 15.1)

Directive	Description
AuthUserFile	The location and name of the file where the password information will reside.
AuthGroupFile	The location and name of the file where the groups and group members are defined. Use /dev/null if there is no AuthGroupFile being used.
AuthName	When prompted for the password, this is the title of the prompt. It is also used to store the

Directive	Description
	password authorization so the user won't be prompted for the password if they return to this location in this session. Try to use something descriptive, yet not common.
AuthType	In most cases. this would be "Basic." Some browsers and servers will support other types of authorization. Options include; PEM, PGP, KerberosV4, KerberosV5, and Digest.
<Limit ...>	Starts the list of limitations. Limitations can be on "GET", "POST", and "PUT", either individually or as a group.
order deny,allow	This allows a directory to allow or disallow its access based on from where the person trying to gain access (the IP address or its associated domain name).
deny from	The domain name to be denied (keyword all).
allow from	The domain name to be allowed (keyword all).
require	Used to ensure that one of the three, if not all three, of these criteria are met prior to allowing access: Keywords: user (that the user's name is valid in the database), Group (only users of a certain group can access the database), valid-user (only a user with the proper user name password combination is allowed access).
satisfy	Allows the file to state that any match criteria is acceptable. Keywords: any/all (all is the default).
</Limit>	End of limitations.

Table A.12: Allow and deny (acceptable formats for location; see Table 15.2)

Item	Format
a domain name	.localdomain.com
a host name	badkid.localdomain.com (note that there is no preceeding ".")
a full IP address	192.168.1.100
a partial IP address	192.168.1. (note that it must end in a ".")
all	The keyword for every host in the world.

Server Configuration File Directives

Table A.13: Complete list of NCSA HTTPd 1.5 Server Directives (see Table 16.1)

Directive	Use	Description
ServerRoot	ServerRoot /path/tofiles/	Declares the path for the server's files. This allows all server configuration files and locations to be made relative to that root, rather than requiring an explicit and complete path name for each file or location. The helps the administrator perform server maintenance as it allows the server to be moved from one disk location to another (say you decide you need more space and need to move the server to a larger disk partition) without having to worry about changing a large number of path references.

Directive	Use	Description
AccessConfig	AccessConfig filename	Tells the location of the access configuration file (default: conf/ access.conf. The filename can be the complete path or a path relative to ServerRoot.
ResourceConfig	ResourceConfig filename	Tells the location of the resource configuration file (default: conf/ srm.conf). The filename can be a complete path or a path relative to ServerRoot.
TypesConfig	TypesConfig filename	Tells the location of the mime.types file. The filename can be a complete path or a relative path to ServerRoot.
KeepAlive	KeepAlive state	State can be either ON or OFF. KeepAlive allows the server to keep the connection between the server and the client open if the client understands KeepAlive. This permits requests for additional items that are embedded in the original request to be obtained over this stated connection. In this way, an HTML file that contained three images using KeepAlive would be able to serve the document and its images to the client in a single instance rather than having to go through the start-up time for each requested item.
MaxKeep-AliveRequests	MaxKeep-AliveRequests #	The maximum number of requests that the KeepAlive will service. Default is 5 and use of MaxKeep-AliveRequests 0 will allow it to stay open until KeepAliveTimeout has been reached.
KeepAlive-Timeout	KeepAlive-Timeout #	The number of seconds before the connection is timed out. Default is 10.

Directive	Use	Description
ErrorLog	ErrorLog filename	The name of the error log file. The default filename is logs/error_log and is a relative path from the ServerRoot. Setting ErrorLog /dev/null effectively turns off all error logging.
TransferLog	TransferLog filename	The name of the transfer or access log. Officially called the transfer log, this log file is also referred to as the access log, as the default filename for the log file is logs/access_log.
AgentLog	AgentLog filename	The name of the log that captures the agent information from the client. The default is logs/agent_log
RefererLog	RefererLog filename	The name of the log that captures the referrer information from the client. The default is logs/referrer_log.
RefererIgnore	RefererIgnore string	Many times there is a desire to ignore certain information from the referrer. That is especially true when you don't want to see all the information about pages on your system that reference other pages. In this instance, you can tell the server to ignore all headers that have in it the string you declare. You can declare as many strings as you want and they will not be logged.

Table A.15: Noteworthy Resource Directives (Without Indexing Directives; see Table 16.3)

Directive	Use	Description
AccessFile-Name	AccessFile-Name filename	For those of you who want to obscure the security a bit more, you can use this directive to set the access filename from .htaccess to another name, like .htacces2.
DirectoryIndex	DirectoryIndex filename	At the end of the Chapter 15 (and in Chapter 2) we talked about directory indexing and default file names. This is the value that you set to establish the default filenames to be sought. As of NCSA HTTPd 1.5 you have been allowed to use a list of filenames and it will return the leftmost one it finds.
AddType	AddType type/sub-type extension	Used to override the mime.types file's default configurations. In this case, a new type of file can be defined, along with the extension for that file. When a header is sent, it is sent with mime type information which allows it to be changed based on the file extension. For example, when we build the header and put out the type as Content-type: text/html\n\n we are doing the task normally done by the server when it sees the extension of the filename.
ErrorDocument	ErrorDocument type file	Can be used to override the system default documents based on error type.

Table A.16: Additional Environment Variables Used by ErrorDocument (see Table 16.4)

Variable	Description
REDIRECT_REQUEST	The request as originally sent exactly to the NCSA HTTPd server.
REDIRECT_URL	The requested URI that generated the error.
REDIRECT_STATUS	The status number and message that NCSA HTTPd would have sent to the client had it not been circumvented by the srm configuration.

Table A.17: NCSA HTTPd status codes (see Table 16.9)

Code	Meaning
302	REDIRECT
400	BAD_REQUEST
401	AUTH_REQUIRED
403	FORBIDDEN
404	NOT_FOUND
500	SERVER_ERROR
501	NOT_IMPLEMENTED

Directive	Use	Description
Directory	<Directory dir>	Where dir is the absolute pathname of the directory being defined/ protected.
	</Directory>	There is a closing directive to this </Directory> once completed. All the directives within this table can be used between the opening and closing of the Directory directive.
Options		See the detailed text in Chapter 16 and Table A.19 below.
AllowOverride	AllowOverride type	Where type is one of any of the following: *None:* No Access Configuration Files are permitted *All:* Access Configuration Files are unrestricted in this directory *Options:* Allows use of the options directive (see below) *FileInfo:* Allows use of the AddType and AddEncoding directives *AuthConfig:* Allows the use of the directives permitting authorization configuration (items in this table that begin with "Auth") *Limit:* Allows the use of the <limit> directive and all the subdirectives *Redirect:* Allows the use of the Redirect directive (Redirect is an srm.conf directive and allows for entire virtual directories to be created and then redirected at the server level to physical disk locations)
AuthName	AuthName nameval	The name of the secure area. I have heard this referred to as the domain (to be confused with DNS domains) and realm, as in the lands

Directive	Use	Description
		one has control over. I guess I find neither satisfactory. This is the name for the secure space you are defining.
AuthType	AuthType type	Currently the only valid type is basic.
AuthUserFile	AuthUserFile filename	The full absolute path to the user authorization file (created with the .htpasswd program) for the directory.
AuthGroupFile	AuthGroupFile filename	The full absolute path to the group filename for the directory.
Limit	\<limit\> \</limit\>	Used to enclose the limitation directives below.
order	order x	Where x is either:
		allow,deny
		deny,allow
		mutual-failure
		This specifies the way all limit directives are evaluated. It allows you to clearly state who is allowed, and anything not allowed is denied (first option). The reverse can also be stated (second option) and then a third option that says that anything not either explicitly allowed or denied is denied by default.
Deny	deny name	Used to deny access to a directory. The following forms are allowable:
		The keyword all
		The IP address or complete domain name
		A single host name or the single IP address of a host

Directive	Use	Description
		A partial IP address (10.1.10. would match all addresses in that class C domain). If the trailing dot is omitted and the address is 10.1.10 it would close off both the 10.1.10.* class C and the 10.1.10[0-9]. Class Cs - the dot is very important)
allow	allow name	Used to allow access to a directory. The same forms are supported for allow as for deny. In both directives, the default is keyword all.
Require	require entity [1-n]	Requires authentication for the entity where the entity is: user group valid-user Where user allows only named users, group only allows people within named groups (from the AuthGroupFile) and valid-user allows any user defined in the AuthUserFile.
Referer	referer URL	Where the URL is the a complete or partial URL/path of the documents that must be accessed prior to accessing the ones within this directory.
Satisfy	satisfy all|any	When require is used with allow, this directive makes it an or and and condition before access can be granted. The default is all the and condition. In this condition, both the allow and the require must be satisfied before access is permitted.
OnDeny	OnDeny URL	Where URL is the path to the redirect for access denied.

Table A.19: The Options Directive (see Table 16.6)

Subdirective	Description
None	All features for the directory are disabled.
All	All features for the directory are enabled
FollowSymLinks	If symbolic links are used within the directory, the server will follow them.
SymLinksIfOwnerMatch	A tad more restrictive, symbolic links will only be followed if the target file/directory is owned by the same UID as the link that was pointing to it.
ExecCGI	This is it! Once this command has been issued the directory is permitted to run CGI scripts.
Includes	Yet another one! This is required if Server Side Include files are permitted to be run from this directory.
Indexes	Allows the server to generate server side indexing in the directory.
IncludesNoExec	They can use Server Side Include directives with the exception of the exec directive from within this directory.

CLF and ELF Record Structure for Transaction Log

Table A.20: The Structure of the Transfer Record (see Table 16.8)

Record Item	Description
host	DNS resolved name or IP of the client
rfc931-info	Any information returned by identd from this client (default is a "-")
authuser	Set when user authorization has taken place (user has entered an authorized/protected directory on the server, the default is a "-")
date	The date in the format: [DD/Mon/YYYY: hh:mm:ss] (brackets included)
URI	The URI request sent to the server. (Security note: That means the entire URI request. In the case of a GET, as we discussed earlier, that includes all the information that was passed in with the GET request)
status	The status code for the completion of the server's action on the request (Table 16.9 contains status code values)
size	The number of bytes transferred (excluding some header information)
referrer	OPTIONAL: Requires ECLF. This file lists the name of the page the user was on prior to issuing the command. The value of having this data is to know how people move around the site. With authuser set, we could trace the way a user transverses the site which provides insight to site design and enhancements.
agent	OPTIONAL: Requires ECLF. This field will list the agent information about the visitor. In most cases, this isn't of extreme value as an associated record to this log. The exception is when a visit come from a search engine or a site indexer. In these instances, the value in this field can indicate that it was an autonomous agent or robot that was at the site.

Robots, Spiders, Wanderers...

In Chapter 17 it was stated that we would provide details on how to build an Agent that came and indexed your own site. There are other Agents (also known as Robots, Spiders, Wanderers . . .) that come to visit that aren't of your own device. These are things that come to a site that generally doesn't have a user viewing it. A good example of that is the Alta Vista agent, named scooter, discussed in Chapter 16 (when covering the transaction log file).

As of this writing, the site http://info.webcrawler.com/mak/projects/robots/active/html/index.html lists 119 of them (known) and a host of questionable ones.

There is a way to exclude these robots from your site. Most of these robots will follow the exclusion rules. The rules are maintained in a file called robots.txt, which is described here. By going to the specified URL you can obtain a list of all the robots and see which ones use the exclusion file, and how they use it.

The following text details the use of the exclusion file and it's formats and directives. The file consists of one or more records separated by one or more blank lines (terminated by CR,CR/NL, or NL). Each record contains lines of the form:

```
<field>:<optionalspace><value><optionalspace>
```

The field name is case insensitive. Comments can be included in file using # convention. A # character is used to indicate that the remainder of the line (from the # to the line termination) is discarded. If the # starts a line (white space excluded) the entire line is considered a comment and will be discarded. The record starts with one or more *user-agent* lines. That line would be followed by one or more *disallow* lines.

A User-agent is the name of the robot the record is describing access policy for. Multiple user-agent records can be combined to define the same exclusion policy for multiple agents. There must be a minimum of one user-agent record. A value of * indicates that this record is the default exclusion policy for all robots that have not had a match on any other policy record.

The value of a disallow field specifies a partial URL that is not to be visited. There must be one disallow record for any user-agent record. If the value in the record is null or empty, it means that all URLs are allowed.

This can be confusing as the rules for how to express the URL are not glob or regexp. Consider the following:

```
/temp.html
/temp/temp.html
```

Now, we want the robot to be able to get /temp.html but not /temp/temp.html . The following disallow *will not work:*

```
disallow: /temp
```

This disallow will disallow access to both files. In order to ensure that the first file is allowed and the second is disallowed, the rule has to be more specific. It should look like:

```
disallow: /temp/
```

This states that all the disallowed files are in the sub-directory /temp/*

Here are two examples of robot.txt files:

Example one: Don't go there (or a general denial file). No agents should go to /private/, /book/ and /giflib/

```
# robots.txt for http://www.myco.com/
User-agent: *
Disallow: /private/
Disallow: /book/
Disallow: /giflib/
```

Example two: We like the agent bookmaper enough to let it got to out private book area

```
# robots.txt for http://www.myco.com/
User-agent: *
Disallow: /private/
Disallow: /book/
Disallow: /giflib/
User-agent: bookmaper
Disallow: /private/
Disallow: /giflib/
```

APPENDIX B

REFERENCE MATERIAL

This is a reference appendix. That means that it will list books that the authors feel are good to have, mailing lists and news groups that meet certain needs, and then a handful of Web sites that are good on-line resources.

You may not know it, but you are a reference too. You have a piece of knowledge that no one else has, a piece to a puzzle that someone else is trying to solve. The Internet, and all of the best things about it, come from you sharing what you know, what you have learned, and what you have done. The resources below are all about that; the free sharing of information between people. We hope that you will use these resources, and over time, become one yourself. We look forward to seeing you on the Net.

Mailing Lists

Mailing lists permit people with common or shared interests an opportunity to share information about a specific topic area. The best on-line references to mailing lists are:

- http://www.liszt.com/
  The directory of e-mail discussion groups
- http://catalog.com/vivian/interest-group-search.html
  From the author of: *Internet Mailing Lists Navigator*–Vivian Neou, (Prentice-Hall 1995, ISBN 0-13-193988-2)
- http://tile.net/listserv/
  The reference to Internet discussion groups–a searchable list of mailing lists
- http://www.neosoft.com/internet/paml/
  A list of mailing lists available primarily through the Internet– compilation © 1995, 1996 by Stephanie da Silva

A quick search for Tcl based mailing lists at http://www.liszt.com/ showed over 20 lists on Tcl (three which the authors actually knew about). The best way to determine if a mailing list meets your needs is to subscribe to it for a while. See the type of information that flows, the signal to noise ratio (how much is really useful to you) and the quality of the respondents answers to the hard questions. See who the respondents are, and look them up in the search services. See who they are, how they get listed, what they have done.

Usenet Newsgroups

These are open discussion groups, sort of like a world wide bulletin board. They are hierarchical in nature. For instance, If I wanted to know about Perl I would look in the computers languages area (comp.lang) and sure enough I would find five newsgroups on Perl.

Here are some of the more common and useful newsgroups:

Tcl

- comp.lang.tcl
- comp.lang.tcl.announce

Perl

- comp.lang.perl
- comp.lang.perl.announce
- comp.lang.perl.misc
- comp.lank.perl.modules
- comp.lang.perl.tk

WWW

(Note: the values in [ ]s mean that all the newsgroups have the same beginning, only the last value is different)

- comp.infosystems.www.
- comp.infosystems.www.advocacy
- comp.infosystems.www.authoring.[cgi.images,html,misc]
  (Note: the cgi newsgroup is self moderated. Please read the Frequently asked Question (FAQ) before posting.)
- comp.infosystems.www.servers.[mac,misc,ms-windows,unix]
- comp.infosystems.browsers.[mac,misc,ms-windows,x]

Security

- comp.security
- comp.security.announce
- comp.security.misc
- comp.security.firewalls
- comp.security.unix
- comp.risks

Miscellaneous

Newsgroups that are useful but aren't a priority unless you are working in that area are:

- comp.protocols.*
  TCP-IP and other network protocols
- comp.dcom.*
  Data communications

- comp.os.*
  Various operating systems

A good place to look for newsgroups would be: http://www.cyber-fiber.com/news/index.html

The signal to noise ratio in Usenet newsgroups can vary based on how the particular newsgroup is operated. Some newsgroups have moderation (where one person approves all postings), some have self moderation (where you have to approve your own posting), some are digests (where a moderator puts together a bunch of postings and posts them all at once), and some are wide open.

The best thing you can do before you post to a newsgroup is to read the last few days or weeks worth of postings. Also use the search engines that maintain postings, like Deja News (http://www.dejanews.com/) and Alta Vista (http://www.altavista.digital.com/) to search old articles. Try to understand the flavor and activity of the members of the newsgroups. See the people that answer questions, versus the ones that flame. Notice who provides light, and who gives off heat. Read the FAQs that are posted regularly to most newsgroups. If you can't find them on the server, look at:

- ftp://rtfm.mit.edu/pub/usenet/news.answers/index or
- http://www.cis.ohio-state.edu/hypertext/faq/usenet/FAQ-List.html

It is considered bad form to post before looking at the FAQs. A great number of people have spent a great deal of time trying to make sure that the most common questions are answered already in the FAQ. It also can let you know if you are about to post a message to the wrong newsgroup, before you send it around the world.

Web Resources

The key problem with listing Web resources lies in the fact that we hope that you will be one. Every day there is someone coming onto the Net, putting up a page and creating yet another wonderful Web resource. In order to provide the latest information, we will keep a resources page listing at our Web site (www.prenhall.com/developers_resource_series). We also will include some of the top resources, today, in this appendix. The fact that we have listed them here doesn't exclude others from being as good. In fact, we have listed less than 20 percent of the bookmarks that we use from time to time.

Tcl

- http://www.sunlabs.com/research/tcl/
  The home of Tcl
- http://www.sco.com/Technology/tcl/Tcl.html
  Excellent Tcl resource
- http://www.elf.org/tcltk-man-html/contents.html
  The Tcl and Tk man pages in HTML format
- http://www.NeoSoft.com/tcl/
  The Contributed Source Archives
- ftp://ftp.neosoft.com/pub/tcl/
  Also the Contributed Source Archives

Perl

- http://www.perl.com/perl/index.html
  Tom Christiansen's Perl site
- ftp://ftp.digital.com/pub/plan/perl/CPAN/
  CPAN: Comprehensive Perl Archive Network
- ftp://uiarchive.cso.uiuc.edu/pub/lang/perl/CPAN/
  Another CPAN site
- http://www.perl.org/
  The Perl Institute
- http://w3.stonehenge.com/merlyn/
  Randal Schwartz's Site

CGI

(We assume you want locations besides ours. Here are some guys who we thank in the Acknowledgment portion of the Introduction)

- http://worldwidemart.com/scripts/
  Matt Write's Web site
- http://www.netexpress.net/~mkruse/www/scripts/index.html
  Matt Kruse's Web site

There is also the Web developers Virtual Library. (See General WWW Resources below.)

HTML

- http://www.w3.org/pub/WWW/MarkUp/Wilbur/
  HTML 3.2 Standards
- http://www.w3.org/hypertext/WWW/MarkUp/MarkUp.html
  HyperText Markup Language (HTML): Working and Background Materials
- http://kuhttp.cc.ukans.edu/lynx_help/HTML_quick.html
  HTML Quick Reference
- http://www.synapse.net/`woodall/html.htm
  The Compendium of HTML Elements
- http://www.ncsa.uiuc.edu/General/Internet/WWW/
  HTMLPrimer.html
  A Beginner's Guide to HTML

HTML Extensions and Special Features

- http://home.netscape.com/assist/net_sites/html_extensions.html
  Netscape extensions
- http://home.netscape.com/assist/net_sites/tables.html
  Tables Tutorial
- http://hoohoo.ncsa.uiuc.edu/docs/tutorials/includes.html
  NCSA Tutorials
- http://home.netscape.com/people/hagan/html/frames/
  Frames Tutorial (we didn't discuss them, but they are becoming more prevalent)
- http://www.netscape.com/newsref/std/cookie_spec.html
  Cookies

General WWW Resources and References

- http://www.stars.com/
  The Web Developer's Virtual Library (also at www.wdvl.com),
  this site covers just about everything from CGI and Java to
  images and HTML A must stop for those interested in Web
  development.
- http://www.w3.org/pub/WWW/
  The World Wide Web Consortium [W3C]
- http://sunsite.unc.edu/boutell/faq/www_faq.html
  Thomas Boutell's World Wide Web FAQ

Security

- http://ciac.llnl.gov/ciac/
  U.S. Department of Energy's Computer Incident Advisory
  Capability.
- ftp://info.cert.org/pub/cert_summaries/
  CERT Advisories
- http://www.cert.org/
  Computer Emergency Response Team, or just CERT, (the
  proper name is: CERT Coordination Center)
- http://www.greatcircle.com/
  Great Circle Associates, Inc.–Firewall information

Servers

- http://www.netscape.com/
  Netscape
- http://www.microsoft.com/
  Microsoft
- http://www.apache.org/
  Apache
- http://hoohoo.ncsa.uiuc.edu/
  NCSA (There are excellent tutorials here on many subjects, and
  information can be found to enhance Chapters 15 and 16.)

We can't express that there are search engines and directories (like http://www.yahoo.com/Computers_and_Internet/Internet/) that provide great places to start when looking for help and answers. Once again, we want to point you back to our site where we will try to keep a reference list updated for you.

Books

Why books? Because some people still don't take computers everywhere. So finally, for those of you who insist on purchasing books (and we thank you) here is a list of some of the ones that live on our bookshelves: Yes, there are no other CGI books listed, we think that this is the only one you will ever need.

TCP/IP and Networking

Internetworking with TCP/IP series
by Douglas Comer
Prentice Hall
Complete set listed below

TCP/IP Network Administration
by Craig Hunt
O'Reilly & Associates
ISBN: 0-93-717582-X

Internetworking With Tcp/Ip: Design, Implementation, and Internals
David L. Stevens and Douglas Comer
Volume 2; 2nd Edition
ISBN: 0-13-125527-4

Internetworking With Tcp/Ip: Client-Server Programming and Applications : Bsd Socket Version
David L. Stevens and Douglas Comer
Volume 3; 2nd Edition
ISBN: 0-13-260969-X

Internetworking With Tcp/Ip: Client-Server Programming and Applications: At & T Tli Version
David L. Stevens and Douglas Comer
Volume 3; At & T tli Edition
Prentice Hall
ISBN: 0-13-474230-3

Internetworking With Tcp/Ip: Principles, Protocols, and Architecture
Douglas Comer
Volume 1; 3rd Edition
ISBN: 0-13-216987-8

The Internet Book: Everything You Need to Know About Computer Networking and How the Internet Works
Douglas Comer
ISBN: 0-13-151565-9

Computer Networks and Internets
Douglas Comer
ISBN: 0-13-239070-1

Internet Services

Managing Internet Information Services
Cricket Liu, Jerry Peek, Russ Jones, Bryan Buus and Adrain Nye
O'Reilly & Associates
ISBN: 1-56-592062-7

The Web Server Handbook
Peter L. Palmer, Adam Schneider and Anne Chenette
Prentice Hall
ISBN: 0-13-239930-X

Security

Practical Unix & Internet Security
Simson Garfinkle and Gene Spafford
O'Reilly & Associates
ISBN: 1-56-592148-8

Firewalls and Internet Security: Repelling the Wily Hacker
Steven M. Bellovin and William Cheswick
Addison-Wesley Professional Computing
ISBN: 0-20-163357-4

Halting the Hacker: A Practical Guide to Computer Security
by Donald L. Pipkin
Prentice Hall
ISBN: 0-13-243718-X

Perl

Programming Perl
Randal L. Schwartz, Tom Christiansen, Stephen Potter and
Larry Wall
2nd Edition
O'Reilly & Associates
ISBN: 1-56-592149-6

Learning Perl
Randal L. Schwartz
O'Reilly & Associates
ISBN: 1-56-592042-2

*Software Engineering With Perl: Prototyping & Toolsmithing
for Better Software-Sooner*
Mark Pease and Carl Dichter
Prentice Hall
ISBN: 0-13-016965-X

Tcl

Tcl and the Tk Toolkit
John K. Ousterhout
Addison-Wesley Professional Computing
ISBN: 0-20-163337-X

Practical Programming in Tcl and Tk (Book and Disk)
Brent B. Welch
Prentice Hall
ISBN: 0-13-182007-9

Exploring Expect
Don Libes
O'Reilly & Associates
ISBN: 1-56-592090-2
(Expect is written in Tcl and you can use Tcl to extend it)

Other places to look on-line for references (the on-line booksellers):

- http://www.amazon.com
- http://www.virtualbooks.com
- http://www.opampbooks.com
- http://www.bookweb.org/bd-bin/list_bd (every bookseller on the net, it seems)

We, of course look forward to you visiting our Web site at:

www.prenhall.com/developers_resource_series

APPENDIX C

README FILE FROM THE CD

First a few author notes . . .

- The copyright is real. The ownership of the code isn't yours. You get to use it, play with it, modify it to meet your needs, but the **authors** are the owners.

- In the code on this CD there are comments as to what has to be changed or modified to operate the software on your system. In general, there are bogus paths to files that are used. These will have to be modified. There are also instances where bogus URLs are used. These too require that you modify the code.

- Copies of Tcl and Perl have been supplied in the /kore directory. Tcl 8.0 alpha has been supplied for those of you willing to experiment. However, there wasn't enough time to validate the software against the latest Tcl release. Similarly, much of the software was not optimized to operate in Perl 5.03. We suggest that you modify the software for optimization, or look at the Prentice-Hall Web site (www.prenhall.com/developers_resource_series) where the authors will be updating text, keeping porting notes, patches, and even a few new programs.

• In a perfect world all you would ever need would be on this CD. This is not a perfect world. We highly suggest that you use the Web site. We plan on making the latest information available there. Visit it.

Disk Structure

We had a whole CD to work with, so we figured, why compress? We didn't.

Every chapter in the book containing software has been given a directory in this CD. In addition the /kore directory contains Tcl and Perl distributions (/kore was used as some systems would do automate cleanup of any file named core.

Within each chapter directory there is a README file describing the contents. To use the software, go to the appropriate language directory and the software for that chapter will be there. In some cases, you may have to make minor modifications to the software to get it to run on your platform. If this is necessary, there will be comments within the code. For the core distribution installation, instructions have been included within each distribution. We have made distributions available in as many formats as possible.

Unless it states otherwise, the software on the CD was written by:

J.M. Ivler (Tcl)
or
Kamran Husain (Perl)

The CD would not have been possible without the expert help of Greg Horne. His advice, good cheer, and technical abilities made putting this together and generating the masters possible. Thank you Greg.

The Contents of the CD

/ch03: (cookies and also some SSIs)
    README
    /ch03/perl:
        getcook.pl
        getcook2.pl
        mkcook2.pl
        mkcookie.pl
    /ch03/tcl:
        getcookie.tcl
        getcookie1.tcl
        getmon.tcl
        getyr.tcl
        mkcookie.tcl
        mkcookie2.tcl

/ch04: (unescaping)
    README
    /ch04/perl:
        unencode.pl
    /ch04/tcl:
        unencode.tcl (From NCSA's FTP area)
    /ch04/uncgi: (From Steven Grimm <koreth@hyperion.com>)
        uncgi-1_8_tar.z
        uncgi18.zip

/ch05: (forms to email)
    README
    /ch05/perl:
        mailme.pl
    /ch05/tcl:
        email.tcl

/ch06: (counters)
    README
    /ch06/img:
        /ch06/img/img1:
            0.gif
            1.gif
            2.gif

/ch08: (randomness)
   README
   /ch08/perl:
         plopad.pl
   /ch08/samp-data:
         adfil.dat
         urlfil.dat
   /ch08/tcl:
         plopad.tcl

/ch09: (calendar)
   README
   /ch09/data:
         cal.dat
   /ch09/html:
         cal.html
   /ch09/perl:
         cal.pl
         xdocal.pl
   /ch09/tcl:
         cal.tcl

/ch10: (data file manipulation)
   README
   /ch10/html:
         data-delete.html
         data-entry.html
   /ch10/perl:
         docal.pl
         rical.pl
   /ch10/tcl:
         decal.tcl
         rical.tcl

/ch11: (SSI - Directory Lister)
   README
   ch11/perl:
         getidx.pl
   /ch11/tcl:
         getidx.tcl

/ch12: (On-line Downline)
   README

```
/ch12/perl:
        join.pl
        levget.pl
        levload.pl
        reqslot.pl
/ch12/tcl:
        join.tcl
        levget.tcl
        levload.tcl
        reqslot.tcl
```

```
/ch13: (Intranet - Office Directory)
    README
    /ch13/html:
            whitepgs.html
    /ch13/perl:
            padmin.pl
            pdisplay.pl
            pupdate.pl
    /ch13/tcl:
            getpg.tcl
            inout.tcl
            inupdt.tcl
```

```
/ch14: (Intranet - Systems Utilities - Disk Status)
    README
    /ch14/perl:
            append.pl
            disklog.pl
            diskstat.pl
    /ch14/tcl:
            diskstat.tcl
            getdata.tcl
```

```
/ch17: (What's New)
    README
    /ch17/perl:
            agent-wn.pl (From Cameron Laird)
```
*(Authors' note: There is a known defect in the code on the CD
that was fixed in the book and in the code on the web site:
The "gmtime" should say "localtime." The consequence is that
the times are off by however many hours there are between
your local time and Greenwich Mean Time. It doesn't "break"*

the code, but it is a defect that should be fixed if you use the version of the code on the CD.)

        getnew.pl (From Cameron Laird)

/ch17/tcl:

        agent-wn.tcl

        getnew.tcl

/kore: (the core Perl and Tcl distributions)

    README

    /kore/perl:

        perl5_002_tar.gz

        perl5_003_tar.gz

    /kore/tcl74:

        tcl7_4_tar.gz

        tcl7_4_tar.z

        tk4_0_tar.gz

        tk4_0_tar.z

    /kore/tcl75:

        tcl7_5p1_tar.gz

        tcl7_5p1_tar.z

        tk41p1.zip

        tk4_1p1_tar.gz

        tk4_1p1_tar.z

    /kore/tcl76:

        tcl76b1.zip

        tcl7_6b1_tar.gz

        tcl7_6b1_tar.z

        tk42b1.zip

        tk4_2b1_tar.gz

        tk4_2b1_tar.z

        win76.exe (Windows 95 executable)

    /kore/tcl80:

        tcl80a1.exe

        tcl80a1.zip

        tcl8_0a1_tar.gz

        tcl8_0a1_tar.z

        tk80a1.zip

        tk8_0a1_tar.gz

        tk8_0a1_tar.z

NOTE: Core distributions will become outdated. The /kore/tcl80 directory contains the next generation Tcl in alpha release (that was the state of the code when this text was released). Please see Appendix B in the text for the locations of the /kore/ releases. In addition the Web site for the book will contain a link to the latest stable version of the core distributions.

Special thanks from the authors to Greg Horne who was instrumental in the making of this CD. His patience in putting up with a moving target when we were to burn it, his technical expertise and advice on how to make it, and his skill in helping produce it were invaluable. Also, thanks go to Cameron Laird who was able to provide the Perl for Chapter 17 in time to include this last minute addition on the CD.

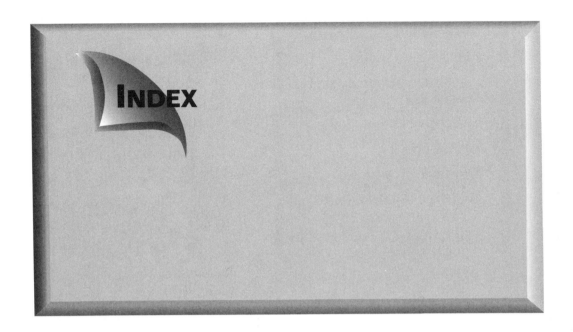

INDEX

S

8.   **LIMITED WARRANTY AND DISCLAIMER OF WARRANTY:** The Company warrants that the SOFTWARE, when properly used in accordance with the Documentation, will operate in substantial conformity with the description of the SOFTWARE set forth in the Documentation. The Company does not warrant that the SOFTWARE will meet your requirements or that the operation of the SOFTWARE will be uninterrupted or error-free. The Company warrants that the media on which the SOFTWARE is delivered shall be free from defects in materials and workmanship under normal use for a period of thirty (30) days from the date of your purchase. Your only remedy and the Company's only obligation under these limited warranties is, at the Company's option, return of the warranted item for a refund of any amounts paid by you or replacement of the item. Any replacement of SOFT-WARE or media under the warranties shall not extend the original warranty period. The limited warranty set forth above shall not apply to any SOFTWARE which the Company determines in good faith has been subject to misuse, neglect, improper installation, repair, alteration, or damage by you. EXCEPT FOR THE EXPRESSED WARRANTIES SET FORTH ABOVE, THE COMPANY DISCLAIMS ALL WARRANTIES, EXPRESS OR IMPLIED, INCLUDING WITHOUT LIMITATION, THE IMPLIED WARRANTIES OF MER-CHANTABILITY AND FITNESS FOR A PARTICULAR PURPOSE. EXCEPT FOR THE EXPRESS WARRANTY SET FORTH ABOVE, THE COMPANY DOES NOT WARRANT, GUARANTEE, OR MAKE ANY REPRESENTATION REGARDING THE USE OR THE RESULTS OF THE USE OF THE SOFTWARE IN TERMS OF ITS CORRECTNESS, ACCU-RACY, RELIABILITY, CURRENTNESS, OR OTHERWISE.

IN NO EVENT, SHALL THE COMPANY OR ITS EMPLOYEES, AGENTS, SUPPLIERS, OR CONTRACTORS BE LIABLE FOR ANY INCIDENTAL, INDIRECT, SPECIAL, OR CONSEQUENTIAL DAMAGES ARISING OUT OF OR IN CONNECTION WITH THE LICENSE GRANTED UNDER THIS AGREEMENT, OR FOR LOSS OF USE, LOSS OF DATA, LOSS OF INCOME OR PROFIT, OR OTHER LOSS-ES, SUSTAINED AS A RESULT OF INJURY TO ANY PERSON, OR LOSS OF OR DAMAGE TO PROPER-TY, OR CLAIMS OF THIRD PARTIES, EVEN IF THE COMPANY OR AN AUTHORIZED REPRESENTA-TIVE OF THE COMPANY HAS BEEN ADVISED OF THE POSSIBILITY OF SUCH DAMAGES. IN NO EVENT SHALL LIABILITY OF THE COMPANY FOR DAMAGES WITH RESPECT TO THE SOFTWARE EXCEED THE AMOUNTS ACTUALLY PAID BY YOU, IF ANY, FOR THE SOFTWARE.
SOME JURISDICTIONS DO NOT ALLOW THE LIMITATION OF IMPLIED WARRANTIES OR LIABILITY FOR INCIDENTAL, INDIRECT, SPECIAL, OR CONSEQUENTIAL DAMAGES, SO THE ABOVE LIMITATIONS MAY NOT ALWAYS APPLY. THE WARRANTIES IN THIS AGREEMENT GIVE YOU SPECIFIC LEGAL RIGHTS AND YOU MAY ALSO HAVE OTHER RIGHTS WHICH VARY IN ACCORDANCE WITH LOCAL LAW.

ACKNOWLEDGMENT
YOU ACKNOWLEDGE THAT YOU HAVE READ THIS AGREEMENT, UNDERSTAND IT, AND AGREE TO BE BOUND BY ITS TERMS AND CONDITIONS. YOU ALSO AGREE THAT THIS AGREEMENT IS THE COMPLETE AND EXCLUSIVE STATEMENT OF THE AGREEMENT BETWEEN YOU AND THE COMPANY AND SUPERSEDES ALL PROPOSALS OR PRIOR AGREEMENTS, ORAL, OR WRITTEN, AND ANY OTHER COMMUNICATIONS BETWEEN YOU AND THE COMPANY OR ANY REPRESENTATIVE OF THE COMPANY RELATING TO THE SUBJECT MATTER OF THIS AGREEMENT.

Should you have any questions concerning this Agreement or if you wish to contact the Company for any reason, please contact the publisher, in writing at the address below.

Robin Short
Prentice Hall PTR
One Lake Street
Upper Saddle River, New Jersey 07458